ECONNED

HOW UNENLIGHTENED SELF INTEREST UNDERMINED DEMOCRACY AND CORRUPTED CAPITALISM

YVES SMITH

palgrave
macmillan

To my mother

ECONNED

Copyright © Aurora Advisors Incorporated, 2010, 2011.
All rights reserved.

First published in hardcover in 2010 by PALGRAVE MACMILLAN® in the US—a
division of St. Martin's Press LLC, 175 Fifth Avenue, New York, NY 10010.

Where this book is distributed in the UK, Europe and the rest of the world, this is by
Palgrave Macmillan, a division of Macmillan Publishers Limited, registered in
England, company number 785998, of Houndmills, Basingstoke, Hampshire RG21
6XS.

Palgrave Macmillan is the global academic imprint of the above companies and has
companies and representatives throughout the world.

Palgrave® and Macmillan® are registered trademarks in the United States, the United
Kingdom, Europe and other countries.

ISBN: 978-0-230-11456-2

Library of Congress Cataloging-in-Publication Data

Smith, Yves.
   ECONned : how unenlightened self interest damaged democracy and corrupted
capitalism / Yves Smith.
      p.   cm.
   Includes bibliographical references and index.
   ISBN 0-230-62051-5 (alk. paper)
   (paperback ISBN 978-0-230-11456-2)
      1. United States—Economic conditions—21st century.   2. United States—
Economic policy.   3. Financial crises—United States—21st century.
4. Economics—United States—History.   5. Neoclassical school of economics.
6. Free enterprise—United States—History.   I. Title.
HC106.83.S65   2010
330.973—dc22

                                                                            2009039960

A catalogue record of the book is available from the British Library.

Design by Letra Libre

First PALGRAVE MACMILLAN paperback edition: October 2011

10 9 8 7 6 5 4 3 2 1

Printed in the United States of America.

CONTENTS

Acknowledgments   v

INTRODUCTION   1

CHAPTER 1
THE SORCERER'S APPRENTICES   8

CHAPTER 2
BLINDED BY SCIENCE   29

CHAPTER 3
FINANCIAL ECONOMICS, COURTESY P.T. BARNUM   66

CHAPTER 4
NEOCLASSICAL ECONOMICS: THE TRIUMPH OF SIMPLISTIC MATH
OVER MESSY FACTS   92

CHAPTER 5
HOW "FREE MARKETS" WAS SOLD   105

CHAPTER 6
HOW DEREGULATION LED TO PREDATION   127

CHAPTER 7
LOOTING 2.0   160

CHAPTER 8
THE WIZARD OF OZ   199

CHAPTER 9
THE HEART OF DARKNESS: THE SHADOW BANKING SYSTEM
SELF-DESTRUCTS   233

CHAPTER 10
PLUS ÇA CHANGE, PLUS C'EST LA MÊME CHOSE   270

AFTERWORD   306

Appendix I   309
Appendix II   316
Notes   320
Bibliography   355
Index   358

ACKNOWLEDGMENTS

One of the surprising and gratifying aspects of writing a blog is the way a community of like-minded readers develops and chats among themselves and with the authors. These conversations are extremely instructive, since those who comment often have relevant experience and insight and bring up issues and ideas that add considerable depth and color. They are also relentless in pointing out errors, omissions, sloppy thinking, and my personal *bête noire,* typos.

I was fortunate to have a number of blog readers of wide-ranging backgrounds offer to help with this work. Having so many smart, well-informed advisors who were not shy about their views was invaluable. Their generous contributions, ranging from ideas, expert perspectives, helpful criticism, editorial advice, and relentless attention to detail, made this a much better book than it would have been otherwise. Needless to say, any shortcomings are solely my responsibility.

Tom Ferguson and Doug Smith have read and patiently commented on numerous drafts from the proposal stage onward. Tom's "hawkeye" was immeasurably helpful in catching miscues, and he also supplied frequent and very useful suggestions for sources. Marshall Auerback gave extensive feedback and helped pare down some overlong chapters. Tom Adams provided a great deal of first-hand knowledge on collateralized debt obligations and helped develop the roadmap of some key crisis mechanisms.

Andrew Dittmer and Steve Waldman served as guardian drill sergeants on Chapter 2, putting me through what seemed to be a Sisyphean number of rewrites on a core argument. When my patience was starting to get frayed, Andrew produced a version of the chapter in teaching guide form, "Chapter 2 for sixth graders," which provided some badly needed comic relief and was quite popular among the book collaborators. Readers can see his hand in appendix II. He also gave extensive and extremely valuable edits on other chapters, particularly on how to make some of the financial concepts more accessible to laypeople and in pointing out how and where to strengthen the logic. I am profoundly indebted to both him and Steve.

Richard Smith and Andrew were in the trenches in the two weeks before the book was put to bed. Richard gave several close readings of the entire book, served as a sounding board on many aspects of the argument, did last-minute research, and cleared up many editorial details when deadlines loomed. This was an absolutely critical role and of enormous value.

Satyajit Das provided considerable input on the many sections that dealt with derivatives, financial models, and risk management and always responded quickly to requests for clarification on financial esoterica. Richard Kline provided historical perspective and some vivid images. Richard Alford, William Black, Paul Davidson, Tim Duy, James Galbraith, Steve Keen, Rob Johnson, Susan Lee, and Rob Parenteau all gave valuable suggestions on the economics arguments. Walt Pohl gave feedback on a key chapter. Two industry experts who asked to remain anonymous (you know who you are) commented extensively on the section on collateralized debt obligations. George Weinbaum provided advice and a great deal of reference material on accounting issues.

A team of talented and highly responsive researchers ran down a myriad of open issues and also performed analyses. Olivier Daviron, James Duesterberg, Ben Fisher, Megan Fries, Marc Kelechava, Doru Lung, Falk Mazelis, Rajiv Nunna, Iain Simpson, and Jason Windawi all made important contributions. Kristina Melomed did the heavy lifting of checking citations.

This book would not have been possible without the help of guest bloggers who contributed to Naked Capitalism while I was researching and writing, namely Ed Harrison, Leo Kolivakis, Rolfe Winkler, plus "George Washington," "Jesse," "Lune," and "Tyler Durden." Ed was exceptionally generous in providing insightful commentary while I was on "book leave."

Melissa Flashman of Trident Media approached me about the idea of doing a book and was an invaluable sounding board throughout. Her assistant, Adam Friedstein, took up the yeoman's job of whipping the bibliography into shape.

An editor's task is generally a thankless one. But without the support and ongoing feedback of Laurie Harting and her assistant, Laura Lancaster at Palgrave, I could have never got this book completed. I am very grateful to both of them. Laurie was a thorough and diligent editor, and Laura took on many crucial and time-consuming tasks that were key to meeting a tight schedule. Yasmin Mathew shepherded the manuscript through the production process. A seasoned and creative marketing team, namely, Lauren Dwyer, Michelle Fitzgerald, and Suzanne Fowler, were generous with their energy and experience.

INTRODUCTION

The great enemy of the truth is very often not the lie—deliberate, contrived, and dishonest—but the myth, persistent, persuasive, and unrealistic. Belief in myths allows the comfort of opinion without the discomfort of thought.

—John F. Kennedy

I n the early 1990s, one of my clients was the biggest securities firm no one had ever heard of. O'Connor & Associates was a proprietary derivatives trading business with over 750 employees. It was cutting edge on a number of fronts: an early entrant and then leader in equity and foreign exchange options, regularly accounting for 5% of New York Stock Exchange transaction volume in the course of hedging its options positions; a technology innovator, running the largest private Unix network in the world on sleek NeXT workstations; and an early adopter of a casual dress code when suits were still the norm in finance.

Based in Chicago, O'Connor had made a very good living doing statistical arbitrage, meaning it looked for often fleeting price disparities between what derivatives "ought" to be worth (the "theoretical price") and the prices on offer. But as these markets became more liquid, the profits on a typical transaction shrank, putting its entire business model into question. The firm decided to start pursuing trading with "customers," meaning end users like big corporations, pension funds, and substantial individuals.

The partner in charge of technology, Craig Heimark, a former index trader, noticed that some competitors like Morgan Stanley had found that their trading software was of little remaining value to them, and so were selling it to clients in an effort to make some extra money. Heimark felt this was not a good deal for the clients, since Morgan Stanley was not committed to providing upgrades and support for the programs. Heimark instead wanted to encourage O'Connor's clients to use the firm's own cutting-edge programs (with appropriate firewalls), an early version of what would now be called an application service provider. That way the clients would get upgrades automatically when O'Connor brought out new tools for its own use.

Even though this approach would create considerable loyalty and, with it, lucrative transactions, it would also make the clients feel more comfortable about using derivatives. Heimark and his fellow partners still had some doubts about this idea: "This stuff is really dangerous. They can blow themselves up with it." Indeed, their first client was interested precisely because it had just reported large foreign exchange losses on botched hedges. Giving a company like that more sophisticated tools without making sure it understood what it was doing would be like giving a bad driver a high performance car: the expected result would be a more spectacular wipeout.

O'Connor went to considerable lengths to ascertain whether its initial customers had a good enough understanding of their underlying business exposures to define their hedging needs well, and also made sure users invested in the needed training in derivatives. (O'Connor was recognized as a leader in teaching people how to trade options.)

That solicitous attitude was not limited to this project. I would regularly hear O'Connor partners inveigh against the markups their biggest competitor, Bankers Trust, would charge on their trades. One would think O'Connor would be delighted to have another firm set high prices, since that would give the Chicago firm the opportunity either to match them and earn similar egregious profits, or to undercut Bankers Trust and gain market share. But O'Connor as a firm was acutely aware that sharp practices could hurt everyone in the market by doing lasting damage to the image of derivatives: "They will burn customers. Those deals cannot work out with the edge [i.e., markup] they are putting on them."

Strange as it may seem now, that customer-oriented stance was not unheard of in finance. When a company or a salesman sets a price, that action means making a decision about the seller's interests versus the buyer's. An ambitious fee is obviously good for the vendor. But charging a lot on a regular basis will either encourage the customer to find cheaper options or, if he has limited alternatives, possibly damage his business. Smart reps will not kill the geese that lay the golden eggs. Many adopted the compromise that Goldman Sachs called "long-term greedy." Yes, a banker may take his client now and again, but an astute one will do it only when the client believes he is making money, or cannot easily tell he has been had.

O'Connor's user-friendly attitude soon became an anachronism. Big financial firms recognized that product complexity was their best friend, offering all sorts of hidden traps and snares by which they could take more money from unwitting clients. Big financial firms became increasingly inclined to prey on their customers and, ultimately, the societies in which they lived.

·   ·   ·   ·   ·

On one level, this book is about how largely unproved but widely accepted economic theories led to policies that produced the global financial crisis that began in 2007. On another level, it illustrates how ideologies establish and defend themselves even as evidence against them mounts.

Many of the analyses of the crisis have focused on description—how this disaster unfolded—or on lower-level mechanisms that played a meaningful role in its development. For instance, the media have given considerable play to the sourcing of subprime mortgages: the aggressive, often deceptive, actions of mortgage brokers; the hapless borrowers who signed up for more house than they could afford; the bad incentives that discouraged participants from looking too hard at the operations of the sausage factory of structured finance that turned loans of dubious quality into pristine AAA-rated instruments; the questionable conduct of rating agencies who were paid by the sponsors, who in turn needed high ratings to persuade buyers that this risky paper was a good investment. While this line of inquiry is instructive, it nevertheless misses the true drivers of this calamity.

George Santayana's maxim, "Those who cannot remember the past are condemned to repeat it," is invoked often precisely because it is so seldom heeded. A fragmented perspective on the past can be as dangerous as ignorance. If we understand the mechanisms behind the financial crisis only in an atomistic fashion, we will at best devise only partial remedies. Unless we examine the faulty logic that justified, nay endorsed, the practices that drove the financial system off the cliff, the odds are high that we will do it all over again, with only a few changes in the particulars. We need to look not just for symptoms but also underlying causes.

John Maynard Keynes, a seminal Cambridge University economist active during both World Wars, once noted:

> The ideas of economists and political philosophers, both when they are right and when they are wrong, are more powerful than is commonly understood. Indeed the world is ruled by little else. Practical men, who believe themselves to be exempt from any intellectual influences, are usually the slaves of some defunct economist.[1]

Accordingly, the causes of this financial crisis should not be sought merely among the actions of particular individuals and companies, but also among the ideas that made it possible. Most important were beliefs about markets and how they operate—in a phrase, economic theories. Anyone who has worked in markets, be it for art, bonds, corporate acquisitions, commodities, and, particularly, O'Connor's high-octane world of derivatives, knows they have a dark side. Heimark and his partners understood all too well that in markets power prevails and the trusting are often fleeced.

Yet modern economists have, by and large, succeeded in becoming oblivious to practically every imperfection marring supposedly "free" markets.

．　．　．　．　．

In 1776, Adam Smith published *The Wealth of Nations*. In it, he argued that the uncoordinated actions of large numbers of individuals, each acting out of self-interest, sometimes produced, as if by "an invisible hand," results that were beneficial to broader society. Smith also pointed out that self-interested actions frequently led to injustice or even ruin. He fiercely criticized both how employers colluded with each other to keep wages low, as well as the "savage injustice" that European mercantilist interests had "commit[ted] with impunity" in colonies in Asia and the Americas.

Smith's ideas were cherry-picked and turned into a simplistic ideology that now dominates university economics departments. This theory proclaims that the "invisible hand" ensures that economic self-interest will *always* lead to the best outcomes imaginable. It follows that any restrictions on the profit-seeking activities of individuals and corporations interfere with this invisible hand, and therefore are "inefficient" and nonsensical.

According to this line of thinking, individuals have perfect knowledge both of what they want and of everything happening in the world at large, and so they pass their lives making intelligent decisions. Prices may change in ways that appear random, but this randomness follows predictable, unchanging rules and is never violently chaotic. It is therefore possible for corporations to use clever techniques and systems to reduce or even eliminate the risks associated with their business. The result is a stable, productive economy that represents the apex of civilization.

This heartwarming picture airbrushes out nearly all of the real business world. Yet uncritical allegiance to these precepts over the last thirty years has produced a world in which corporations, especially in finance, are far less restricted in their pursuit of profit. We show in this book how this lawless environment has led the financial services industry to pursue its own *unenlightened* self-interest. The industry has become systematically predatory. Employees of industry firms have not confined their predation to outsiders; their efforts to loot their own firms nearly destroyed the industry and the entire global economy. Similarly destructive behavior by other players, often viewed through a distorted lens that saw all unconstrained commercial behavior as virtuous, added more fuel to the conflagration.

Some economists have opposed this prevailing ideology; indeed, comparatively new lines of inquiry focus explicitly on how economic actors can fool themselves or others into making poor, even destructive, choices.

But when the economics profession has used the megaphone of its authority to dominate discussions with policymakers and the public, it has spoken with one voice, and the message has been the one described here. We therefore confine our criticism to these particularly influential ideas.

Theories that fly in the face of reality often need to excise inconvenient phenomena, and mainstream economics is no exception. Idealizing the rational aspects of business decisions means refusing to notice behavior that is predatory, destructive, criminal, or simply stupid. Believing that risk is manageable through mechanical systems has required not just unrealistic assumptions but also willful blindness to clear signs of danger.

We offer here another point of view. This book lays bare both the actions leading to the credit crisis and the economic constructs that defended, facilitated, and even exacerbated this behavior. Our case makes clear that if our economic system is to harness the self-interest of individuals to achieve the general good, it must be supervised within a democratic society and responsive to criticism by outside voices of those who are unafraid to think independently.

. . . . .

In this book, I have sought to explain to the lay reader how the widespread adoption of largely unproven (or in some cases, disproven but nevertheless widely used) economic theories produced the financial crisis that began in 2007. Nearly all of their flaws have been described by economists and most are well known within the discipline. Yet these problems have been dismissed as inconsequential or merely inconvenient.

The most common retort is that economics "works," that it provides sound policy prescriptions. This book will demonstrate that this defense is patently untrue. Sweeping changes, backed only by the unsupported beliefs of the neoclassical loyalists, resulted in indifference to rising levels of indebtedness, greater and greater risk taking by financial intermediaries and consumers, and more and more frequent financial crises, finally culminating in the global debacle. With the financiers who caused the pile-up still in the driver's seat, along with most of the actors who designed the failed policies, an extensive, costly safety net has been deployed under the financial system, while no one has been forced to account for what happened.

We now have a financial system that is not only spectacularly predisposed to train wrecks, but will be very difficult to put on a sounder footing, absent a far more radical restructuring than anyone appears willing to undertake at this juncture. Few people in authority seem ready to accept that the seeming free lunch of burgeoning debt levels is over. Any move to healthier practices will result in more costly and less readily available credit.

We need to implement economic policies that treat finance as the handmaiden of commerce, not its master. This task is made even more difficult by the wealth and power that the banking interests now possess as a result of the radical "free markets" policy program. With the financial services industry and its lobbyists even more influential than before, thanks to even greater state support for their gambles, the stage has been set for continued plutocratic land grabs and economic crashes.

This book takes a critical look at the foundations of the ideology of "free markets" and then explores how this world view came to drive government action. It sets forth how the resulting macroeconomic policies led to the use of higher, ultimately unsustainable levels of borrowing in order to compensate for flagging growth in worker incomes. At the same time, deregulation led to structural changes in the financial services industry that not only made it less stable but also predatory, fixated on its own profits rather than on serving customers or the broader society.

As a result, this work takes a broad historical sweep. It first looks at how developments in economic thinking, primarily in the 1940s through the 1980s, translated into new policy initiatives from the 1970s onward that set the stage for the current crisis. In particular, chapter 2 reviews key methodological choices, made in the discipline of economics in the 1940s and 1950s, that over time redefined what it meant to be an economist, or at least a respectable mainstream member of the discipline. Chapter 3 discusses the development of financial economics, a separate subdiscipline that came to dominate how investments and risks are managed. It also shows how those same approaches depict financial markets as far less risky than they really are. Chapter 4 discusses the considerable shortcomings of the neoclassical paradigm, the wellspring of the "free markets" ideology.

Chapter 5 reviews how the distorted "free markets" popularization was marketed aggressively, and how it failed abysmally when implemented in Chile and Russia.

Chapter 6 describes how deregulation of financial services led to a rapid rise in predatory behavior. Chapter 7 sets forth how major capital markets players are now engaged in large-scale looting, in which an excessive short-term focus, aided by pliable accounting and lax regulation, leads them to value executive and staff bonuses over the health of the enterprise. Chapter 8 covers how the new "unfettered markets are always best" policies perversely resulted in both destabilizing global imbalances and an interventionist posture in the Federal Reserve under Alan Greenspan, which ran to the assistance of financial markets, encouraging more risk taking.

Chapter 9 discuses the growth of the shadow banking system, a cluster of largely unregulated financing activities, and how it imploded. Chapter 10 describes how current financial reform proposals are far too accommodating to the industry responsible for the global crisis, and sets forth a more tough-minded program.

The argument goes into a bit of technical detail at points in the interest of accuracy, but I hope I have broken the issues down sufficiently to make them informative and instructive to generalists. These sections are found mainly in chapter 2, which discusses the use of mathematics and models in economics, and in chapter 3, on financial economics.

We can no longer afford to genuflect before a failed orthodoxy. It falls to us to challenge the economics discipline's authority and demand ideas that tell us something about the real world. When we have found the courage to do so, we will also have a chance to frame practical, sane, and decent policies. I hope that this book will contribute to that effort.

CHAPTER 1

THE SORCERER'S APPRENTICES

History is the long and tragic story of the fact that privileged groups seldom give up their privileges voluntarily.

—Martin Luther King

I t was January 2007, and the Great Moderation was in full swing. Economic policy makers and central bankers were congratulating themselves for creating an over two-decade period of long economic expansions and relatively mild downturns. Crises, severe recessions, nay, anything other than largely steady growth, were a thing of the past, with any hiccups due to events like the September 11, 2001 attacks, which were clearly outside economists' control.

As this paean illustrates, the economics profession looked upon its handiwork with great satisfaction:

> . . . we are living through one of the great transformations of modern history. Almost unnoticed, most of the industrialised world, especially the Anglo-Saxon part of it, has enjoyed a period of unprecedented economic stability. . . . The wild fluctuations of employment, output, inflation and interest rates have been firmly damped. . . .
>
> Economists are debating the causes of the Great Moderation enthusiastically and, unusually, they are in broad agreement. Good policy has played a part: central banks have got much better at timing interest rate moves to smooth out the curves of economic progress. But the really important reason . . . is the liberation of markets and the opening-up of choice that lie at the root of the transformation. The deregulation of financial markets over the Anglo-Saxon world in the 1980s had a damping effect on the fluctuations of the business cycle. These

changes gave consumers a vast range of financial instruments (credit cards, home equity loans) that enabled them to match their spending with changes in their incomes over long periods. . . . The economies that took the most aggressive measures to free their markets reaped the biggest rewards.[1]

Yet the Great Moderation was, as bodybuilders describe steroid-abusers, a Cadillac body with a Chevy underneath. Its rate of expansion was lower than previous postwar growth phases. Inflation-adjusted worker wages had been stagnant. Dampened swings in the real economy were accompanied by more frequent and severe financial crises. The supposed better timing of central bank intervention merely led financial market participants to believe they could count on the authorities to watch their backs, encouraging more risk-taking. But perhaps the biggest danger was that blind faith in the virtues of markets converted regulators from watchdogs into enablers.

The very few economists who recognized that the vital signs were moving into danger zones and tried to alert officials were rebuffed. For instance, Yale's Robert Shiller (of *Irrational Exuberance* and S&P/Case-Shiller Index fame), recounted how, as a member of the economic advisory panel to the Federal Reserve Bank of New York, he had to soft-pedal his concerns about the developing real estate bubble:

> In my position on the panel, I felt the need to use restraint. While I warned about the bubbles I believed were developing in the stock and housing markets, I did so very gently, and felt vulnerable expressing such quirky views. Deviating too far from consensus leaves one feeling potentially ostracized from the group, with the risk that one may be terminated.[2]

Shiller gave more pointed warnings in 2005 to the Office of the Comptroller of the Currency and the Federal Deposit Insurance Corporation, both bank regulators, urging them to impose tougher mortgage lending standards. He was brushed off.

The Yale professor believed his views were rejected because they were based on the theories of behavioral economics, a new branch within economics that looks at how people behave when presented with various economic choices, a real-world perspective notably absent in orthodox theory. In his words, "Behavioral economists are still regarded as a fringe group by many mainstream economists."[3]

But Shiller's views conflicted with conventional thinking in a more profound way. Remember, the profession had succeeded, since the 1970s, in implementing policies that conformed with the view that unfettered markets were the royal road to prosperity. The touted Great Moderation was taken as a triumphal confirmation of the mainstream's collective wisdom. If this supposed success proved to be mere Potemkin prosperity, a facade masking an underlying deterioration, then it would call the credibility of much of the work in the discipline into question.

Shiller sounded alarms before the most toxic phase of mortgage lending started, in the second half of 2005, early enough to have contained the damage. Another warning was dismissed in August 2005, at the Federal Reserve's annual Jackson Hole conference, an end-of-summer gathering at the resort area in Wyoming for Fed officials and elite economists. It was the last of these forums chaired by Alan Greenspan. The participants were throwing verbal bouquets at the retiring Fed chief, with one notable exception.

The former chief economist at the International Monetary Fund (IMF) Raghuram Rajan presented a paper, "Has Financial Development Made the World Riskier?"[4] His conclusion was "yes." Rajan had set out to establish that the financial innovations during Greenspan's tenure had increased safety. But the further he dug, the more troubling evidence Rajan found of bad incentives encouraging undue risk taking. One was the burgeoning market in credit default swaps, a relatively new product that allowed investors to buy or sell insurance against the possibility that a borrower would go bust. The sellers were massively undercapitalized, which meant that the insurance might be worthless. The result was a financial system in danger of a meltdown due to widespread holdings of high-octane, high-risk product.

Rajan met withering criticism and was dismissed as a financial Luddite. Yet two years later, when the crisis he predicted began to unfold, Fed presidents began citing that very paper in their speeches.[5]

．　．　．　．　．

Not everyone was a true believer. Some could see the signs of the coming storm. For instance, Gillian Tett of the *Financial Times* was so alarmed by a flurry of e-mails from readers that she did something unorthodox. She wrote them up.

The troubling messages arrived in January 2007, the same month as the self-congratulatory assessment of the state of the global economy quoted at the start of the chapter. By contrast, Tett, a seasoned capital markets editor, had just published a story on a question that nagged at her: was growth in the murky, mushrooming world of structured finance distorting lending?

Structured finance was the latest flavor of "securitization," a technique of using loans as the foundation for investments (see "A Primer on Structured Finance," pages 12–13). This process, which started in the 1970s, meant that banks no longer held most loans to maturity. After it made loans, a bank often sold them to a packager, usually an investment bank, which performed its financial wizardry and offered the resulting particular pieces of the deal to eager buyers. This process is sometimes called the "originate and distribute" model.

A newly popular, complex structured finance product, collateralized debt obligations (CDOs), had grown explosively since 2004. The concern was that CDOs allowed borrowers to continue to get cheap funding even when central banks like the U.S. Federal Reserve were trying to choke it off.[6]

What caught Tett's attention was the tone of the e-mails she received in response to her structured credit musings. For instance:

> I have been working in the leveraged credit and distressed debt sector for 20 years . . . and I have never seen anything quite like what is currently going on. Market participants have lost all memory of what risk is and are behaving as if the so-called wall of liquidity will last indefinitely and that volatility is a thing of the past.
>
> I don't think there has ever been a time in history when such a large proportion of the riskiest credit assets have been owned by such financially weak institutions . . . with very limited capacity to withstand adverse credit events and market downturns. . . .
>
> The degree of leverage at work . . . is quite frankly frightening. . . . Very few hedge funds I talk to have got a prayer in the next downturn. Even more worryingly, most of them don't even expect one.[7]

And the leverage, which is the degree to which an investor or business uses borrowed money, was stunning. A hedge fund might borrow a dollar for every dollar invested, not terribly aggressive in that world.

But a fair portion of that hedge fund's money did not come directly from wealthy individuals and institutions like insurance companies, but via funds of funds, entities that invested in multiple hedge funds. The theory was that the fund of funds manager would make an expert assessment and select a good mix. But many of those fund of funds borrowed money, often three dollars for every one invested, to make their returns look better and compensate for the additional layer of fees.

Now suppose the underlying hedge fund invested in the riskiest layers of a structured credit deal, say a collateralized debt obligation that could be effectively geared nine times, meaning it behaved as if it had nine dollars of debt for every dollar of equity. As one of Tett's sources explained:

> Thus every €1m of CDO bonds [acquired] is effectively supported by less than €20,000 of end investors' capital—a 2% price decline in the CDO paper wipes out the capital supporting it.

A PRIMER ON STRUCTURED FINANCE

Once upon a time, investors had comparatively few moneymaking options: stocks, corporate and government bonds, and money market investments, like certificates of deposit.

Traditionally, if a large company wanted to borrow money for a long period of time, say ten years, it would sell bonds to investors. Bonds are a promise to pay interest, typically every six months, and to repay the amount borrowed (the "principal") on a specified date. Investors such as life insurance companies and pension funds liked bonds because it was clear how much money they would receive and when. These companies needed to be prepared to pay out money in the future (for instance, life insurance companies needed to make payments when there was a death), and often they could use statistics to get a fairly good idea of what their future obligations looked like. The predictability of bonds meant that these investors could use them to match their reliable cash flows with what they expected to have to pay out down the road.

In that simpler world, the big risks of owning bonds were credit risk (that borrowers would go belly-up and fail to make the expected payments) and interest rate risk (a bond with a coupon of 6% looks like a good deal when inflation is at 3%, but if inflation rises to 7%, investors will want a higher rate of interest to compensate for the faster erosion in the value of their money. That means bonds that don't pay a high enough interest rate will fall in price).

Both interest rate volatility and the fact that investment banks were interested in selling new financial products helped fuel the growth of structured finance. As oscillations in interest rates created serious risks for commercial banks, they became receptive to the idea of selling the mortgages and credit card loans they had originated to third parties, thereby reducing their exposure to interest rate swings.

However, what is appealing for the seller (or "issuer," which in this case is the commercial bank) isn't so hot for the buyer (the investor). Those old-fashioned bonds were predictable. Mortgage payments are much less so. Homeowners can decide to pay off their mortgages early, and the resulting uncertainty is called "prepayment risk." Some prepayment risks are fairly predictable, like those due to death and relocation. But prepayments also occur when homeowners refinance their mortgages due to a drop in interest rates. Not only are interest rate changes difficult to anticipate, but a security that pays off when interest rates fall is intrinsically unattractive to investors (bonds usually rise in price when interest rates decline, but here the borrowers, when they refinance, take your profit away from you).

Of course, on Wall Street, anything can be solved by price, so some investors would accept these unattractive features if these new mortgage-backed securities paid enough extra interest. But what broadened the market considerably for this sort of paper (a term used in finance for stocks, bonds, and other financial instruments) was tranching.

Rather than have all investors exposed to the vagaries of these payments, some could buy more tailored products that relied on the underlying loan payments, in this example, from mortgages. Rather than buy the right to get a simple pass-through of mortgage payments, an investor can choose among different classes of participation, say A, B, and C. Class A is promised a certain interest rate, lower than what the pool of mortgages is expected to pay. But the Class A investor gets first dibs. All the money coming in is first allotted to him, and only when he has gotten his cut does Class B get any money. Class B gets a higher interest rate for agreeing to stand behind Class A. Class C gets what's left. Most deals have more layers and much more complexity, but the general premise is the same.

From asset-backed securities like these, investment banks then constructed resecuritizations called collateralized debt obligations (CDOs). CDOs can contain a dog's breakfast of assets, including whole corporate or mortgage loans and equipment leases. But a big component of pools behind these instruments is typically pieces of other asset-backed deals, almost always the high-yielding layers (for instance, if there were Classes A through E, the CDOs would typically take the "mezzanine" C and D pieces). Because the mix of assets in each deal is different, each CDO had its own structure. That made the market murky and even harder for investors and regulators to understand.

Borrowing magnifies the impact of profit and loss: If you buy a house for $300,000, put up only 5% of the price and borrow the other 95% (20:1 leverage), then if the value of the house falls by more than just 5%, you lose your entire investment. But the seduction is that if the price increases a mere 5%, you double your money.

The razor-thin cushion against losses wasn't a risk just to the hedge funds, but also had wider ramifications for the credit markets. If the decay in CDO prices is big enough, the hedge and the fund of fund middlemen don't just deliver losses to their investors in their funds but can also partially default on the money borrowed, usually from one of the big investment banks active in that business, such as Goldman Sachs, Morgan Stanley, or the now defunct Bear Stearns. If the hedge funds were losing money on their CDOs due to a general worsening of conditions in that market, the investment banks would probably be taking losses directly on CDOs they held as trading inventory and speculative positions. And investment banks similarly funded those positions to a significant degree with borrowed funds.

It was a house of cards, a train wreck waiting to happen. The savvy players knew it was likely to end badly, yet with eager buyers and sellers, it seemed foolish to turn down the opportunity for profit.

And that was the right bet in January 2007. There was one last fat bonus year before the wheels really came off the financial system.

■ ■ ■ ■ ■

Tett had been early to recognize the dangers of structured finance, particularly its hottest offering in the new century, collateralized debt obligations, and had sounded warnings two years before.

In 2005, Michael Gibson, the head of trading risk analysis for the Federal Reserve, remarked that perhaps as many as 10% of CDO investors did not understand the risks of the product.[8] Other comments at that time suggested that some of the most sophisticated investors in this product were out of their depth. For instance, Cynthia McNulty of Integrated Systems stated: "There is such a buzz about credit derivative products now that there are hedge funds getting into it without the requisite abilities."[9]

Indeed, regulators had been scrambling to get a handle on the market. Because CDOs were not reported to any authority and trades were arranged privately between a host of product peddlers and buyers, even the estimates of market size varied widely, with Thomson Financial pegging the total sold in 2004 at $120 billion, while J.P. Morgan put it at $366 billion. To put that in perspective, the low estimate of $120 billion exceeded the value of all the corporate bonds sold in Europe that year.[10]

Shortly after the Gibson comment, Tett weighed in with an eerily prescient take on the promise and dangers of this rapidly growing type of investment. She acknowledged the benefits but then turned to the downside. CDOs had been so successful at pulling funds into the credit markets that they were lowering interest rates on bonds, which gave investors false comfort. As prevailing yields fall, prices of outstanding bonds rise, so investors in bonds show profits. Thus, the success of early investors encouraged others to join the party.

But a good thing could go too far. While the falling yields for existing CDOs were a vindication to those who owned them, given their complexity, they had to offer higher income than so-called plain vanilla products, such as straightforward corporate bonds that carried the same credit rating. To compensate, banks were turning to more aggressive structures, often using riskier assets, to generate the higher income that was so alluring to investors. In other words, even as far back as 2005, the market was getting a frothy feel.

And Tett also noted:

> Meanwhile, the fact that CDOs disperse credit among multiple investors means that, if a nasty accident did ever occur with CDOs, it could richochet [sic] through the financial system in unexpected ways.[11]

As we will discuss in detail later, that is precisely what came to pass.

．　．　．　．　．

The signs of trouble became more and more evident as 2007 progressed. A reader of the *Financial Times* would have seen not just Tett's warnings, but ample evidence of superheated activity in other markets, such as takeover lending. Even the *FT*'s measured chief economics editor, Martin Wolf, not the sort to make market calls, warned in March 2007 that equities globally were substantially overvalued by historical standards.[12]

Yet later that March, two months after Tett replayed market participants' alarms about leverage, the then president of the Federal Reserve Bank of New York, Timothy Geithner, gave a largely comforting speech on credit market innovation.

The New York Fed is not merely the biggest of the twelve regional Federal Reserve Banks, but, more importantly, it is responsible for implementing Federal Reserve policy through the trading desks of the New York Fed. By virtue of his location and role, the head of the New York Fed is in regular contact with

Wall Street and presumed to be particularly knowledgeable about market conditions. And by this point, the subprime cloud was large enough to have merited official comment. The message from Geithner: its impact did not appear to be significant.[13]

In his remarks, Geithner set forth the concerns about the plethora of new complex financial products, but also noted that financial alchemy offered considerable advantages: more credit, better pricing, more choice for investors, and better diversification of exposures. He asserted that the past three decades of experience with financial innovation were reassuring. The growing pains had been manageable.[14]

Yet this seemingly evenhanded description gave plenty of cause for pause. First, Geithner pointed out that banks, the credit-providers that are most closely regulated, held only 15% of the "nonfarm nonfinancial" debt outstanding (remember financial institutions lend to each other, so that is excluded when trying to measure debt that is important to the real economy). Thus, while the Fed has good information about what banks are doing, and can send in examiners when warranted, it had no idea what the biggest players in the credit markets, such as investment banks, hedge funds, sovereign wealth funds, and Tett's increasingly edgy European investors buying U.S. products, were really up to. Thus, Geithner was trying to assess the health of an elephant when he could scrutinize, at most, its leg.

So his argument boiled down to, "Our current structure and distribution of risks is outside the bounds of anything in financial history. We can conjure some arguments as to why this should be OK, and so far, it has been OK."

Second, Geithner claimed regulators were powerless:

> We cannot turn back the clock on innovation or reverse the increase in complexity around risk management. We do not have the capacity to monitor or control concentrations of leverage or risk outside the banking system. We cannot identify the likely sources of future stress to the system, and act preemptively to diffuse them.

Third, the Fed chief noted that companies weren't borrowing overmuch; in fact debt levels in the corporate sector were below recent norms. But that statement was misleading. Overall private sector borrowings had exploded, thanks to a debt-fueled consumer spending spree, and was over 180% of the Gross Domestic Product, markedly above the level at the onset of the Great Depression, 164%.[15]

How could the authorities ignore the dramatic growth in debt? Federal Reserve officials had fallen into classic bubble-era rationalizations. The Fed chairman, Ben Bernanke (who succeeded Greenspan in 2006), had dismissed concerns about rising consumer borrowings, noting that household assets were rising too.[16] But debt has to be serviced, which comes ultimately from income or the sale of property. With consumer savings rates approaching zero, the public was reaching the limits of how much debt it could support.[17]

In his speech, Geithner did warn that if things went badly, the outcome could be worse than in the stone ages of finance, when products were simple and markets less interconnected: "The probability of a major crisis seems likely to be lower, but the losses associated with such a crisis may be greater or harder to mitigate."

That statement is tame considering what actually came to pass.

· · · · ·

The initial eruption of the crisis, the failure of two Bear Stearns hedge funds in June 2007, seemed a mere intensification of subprime woes. Yet the vast majority of experts, including the Fed, expected the damage to be contained and less costly than the U.S. savings and loan crisis of the early 1990s.

But the outbreak turned virulent. The credit upheaval moved through four acute phases, each requiring increasingly extreme interventions. What seemed to be a peak event, "the mother of all bailouts," the rescue of Fannie Mae and Freddie Mac in early September 2008, merely set the stage for a broader unraveling, with the bankruptcy of Lehman Brothers, the sale of Merrill Lynch, and the unprecedented efforts to salvage the world's biggest insurer, American International Group, coming a mere week later. And that tidal wave was succeeded by a potentially even larger currency crisis. Banks in Europe, who had funded some of their balance sheets in dollars, were unable to renew these short-term loans as dollar interbank markets dried up. They tried borrowing in local currencies and exchanging them for dollars, effectively transferring the stress in the credit markets to the foreign exchange markets. The Federal Reserve provided dollar swap lines, which were foreign exchange facilities to other central banks, which in turn provided dollar-based loans to their home-country financial firms. These overseas central banks also provided emergency facilities of their own. It was effectively a global banking rescue.[18] Similarly, a run on emerging markets was stanched only by the U.S. offering unprecedented dollar swap lines to key countries and backing a new International Monetary Fund facility.

The extraordinary measures to stop the collapse, with facilities authorized to supply as much as $23.7 trillion in the United States,[19] failed to halt damage to the real economy. The wreckage continues. U.S. unemployment for August 2009 was nearly 10%, with higher levels expected.[20] U.S. household net worth fell

9% in the fourth quarter of 2008, the biggest decline in the more than fifty years of that data series.[21] Former titans of commerce like General Electric have had to persuade analysts that they are viable. Growing tent cites and shanty towns symbolize the American Dream gone sour. While the economy appears to be stabilizing, both the Great Depression and Japan's near depression saw a multi-month respite after the initial financial shock before the real economy decay resumed. Even if the worst is indeed past, with a large debt overhang and a financial system that seems better at generating state-backed profits for itself than serving the vital social function of providing credit, the foundations for a solid recovery are not in place.

The United States is not alone in reaping the bitter harvest of lax regulation and reckless lending. The UK, Spain, Ireland, the Baltic states, and Australia all have tolerated rapid credit growth; European financial firms are exposed to dodgy debt via purchasing securitized assets from other markets. And even though we escaped a collapse of the financial markets, we have already suffered the worst downturn since the Great Depression, and most expect a lackluster recovery.

Countries dependent on consumption by chronic debtors like the United States and UK are suffering as well. Trade has plunged, falling globally at 41% of the annualized rate from November 2008 to January 2009,[22] shuttering factories in China and driving millions of unemployed workers back to the countryside. The IMF forecasts that Japan will be worst hit, with its GDP expected to contract by 9% in 2009.[23] While trade volumes showed a modest recovery in early 2009, due to the effect of stimulus programs launched in major economies, those gains started to slip later in the year as some initiatives began to expire.[24]

And the prognosis is poor. Financial crises are deep and persistent. Economists Carmen Reinhart of the University of Maryland and Kenneth Rogoff of Harvard have created an extensive dataset of financial crises through history.[25] Unlike those of prototypical unhappy families, the miseries caused by differing crises are surprising similar. Output declines from peak to trough by an average of over 9%, and it takes three years from the nadir to return to normal levels. Unemployment peaks at 7% over pre-crisis levels, which for the United States would be nearly 12%. Housing takes five years to bottom. And the United States was in worse condition on some important metrics before the implosion started, and unlike its past peers, it cannot rely on global growth to help pull it out of its ditch.

■   ■   ■   ■   ■

Seldom have so many experts been proven so wrong. The minority that saw the danger signs—rapid growth in borrowing, the near-abandonment of due diligence standards for debt, strained valuations in many asset classes, accompanied by telltale "this time it's different" rationalizations—were ignored and marginalized. The theory, as we saw with Geithner's and Bernanke's speeches earlier, was that we lived in a Brave New World of modern finance, that deep markets, sophisticated instruments, and advanced technology allowed for risks to be sliced, diced, and better diversified, reducing the danger to individual players, and by extension, the financial system. But the existence of better brakes, instead of increasing safety, merely encouraged everyone to drive faster. And the brakes haven't performed too well either.

Remarkably, we've had a Katrina-like intensity of coverage of the economic crisis, with none of the corresponding outrage at the performance of the architects and FEMA equivalents. Yes, we've had plenty of attention and ire directed at various players who helped bring about this disaster: ratings agencies, mortgage brokers, hapless or greedy borrowers, overpaid bankers, inattentive regulators, even the unduly thrifty Chinese.

But unlike the Great Depression, we've operated in an economic system redesigned in accordance with the prevailing beliefs of mainstream economists, as confirmed by their willingness to take credit for it when the outcome appeared to be positive. And that Brave New World allowed the perpetrators to operate in ways that would have been considerably constrained under the prevailing rules of forty years ago.

Had any other profession presided over such a disaster, there would be public denunciations, Congressional inquiries, lawsuits. However, policy makers, save Alan Greenspan, have received remarkably little critical scrutiny. While the former Federal Reserve chairman may be a deserving target, he operated well within established orthodoxies. Indeed, major actors such as Ben Bernanke and Timothy Geithner still are in leadership positions, with their past conduct receiving remarkably little criticism despite their having helped design the policies that precipitated the meltdown.

Is it fair to attack the economics profession? To a large degree, yes. The specialty has done itself and the wider world considerable damage through its pursuit of a misguided, overly ambitious goal of putting itself on a scientific footing. But rather than produce greater understanding, the result is Potemkin science, all facade and no substance.

The advancement of knowledge in science results from an interaction of observation and abstraction. The purpose of theorizing is to generate testable and, best of all, falsifiable hypotheses.[26] But as we will see, economics became enamored of constructs utterly disconnected from reality. Economic theory is full of dubious assumptions and predictions that run afoul of real world behavior. And even the more empirically oriented economists use methods for analyzing data that are limited. The result is that they can and do produce misleading results. Some recognize the constraints of their methodologies and are duly cautious in their conclusions, but this is far from a common stance.

The dominant economic paradigm, neoclassical economics, became ascendant in part because it offered a theory of behavior that could be teased out in elegant formulations (the "free markets" construct is neoclassical economics light). Yet it rests on assumptions that are patently ridiculous: that individuals are rational and utility-maximizing (which has become such a slippery notion as to be meaningless), that buyers and sellers have perfect information, that there are no transaction costs, that capital flows freely. Another highly influential line of thinking, financial economics, looks at the behavior of financial markets and the relationship of variables used in them, including prices, interest rates, and ways to measure risk. It rests on a seemingly rigorous foundation and elaborate math, much like astrology. Even an outsider can readily discern how the reach of the discipline exceeds its grasp. Consider:

- Social sciences operate with **limited data.** Human beings are costly and difficult to study; information is often collected in specific settings, which means generalizations need to be made with great caution.
- Economics attempts to work around this difficulty in coming up with useful generalizations by **seeking a higher level of abstraction.** One route that has had a pervasive influence on the discipline is the use of arguments that resemble mathematical proofs, where assumptions are set forth, terms defined, and relationships stated via formulas.

   To make the formal statements work requires the use of assumptions that are often unproven or poorly supported. While this process allegedly makes the logic of a paper explicit, if the assumptions have only a tenuous connection to reality, reliance on these assumptions at best constitutes a sophisticated form of storytelling, at worst a garbage-in, garbage-out exercise.
- Even in those specialties where the data are cheap and comparatively plentiful, as in financial economics, the predominant theories, on which much trading market practice is based, **rest on assumptions made so that the math will be manageable.** Even though these constructs were found to have considerable shortcomings over forty years ago, they still serve as the bedrock of modern investment techniques and risk management.

   If these techniques were only slightly out of whack with how markets worked, the value of having a methodology and standards would indeed outweigh the dangers of oversimplification. Unfortunately, the foundations of financial economics—the capital assets pricing model and modern portfolio theory—greatly understate market and liquidity risk and also overstate the ability to reduce it via diversification.

• As a result, the analyses performed in economics **seldom make for convincing findings.** In the physical sciences, researchers devise experiments that can validate causal relationships. Except in behavioral economics (a new specialty that uses laboratory exercises to see how subjects react to specific choices, and whose findings contradict the assumptions of neoclassical economics), economists cannot readily test their theories (you can't, for instance, construct two identical economies to test the impact of different tax policies on income distribution and output). Thus economists frequently rely on correlation, which is a very weak form of proof, and problematic statistical procedures. As a result, on contentious issues, the press, public, and politicians will often be assaulted with persuasive-sounding studies that come to wildly different conclusions.

Compare real science with the wannabe science of economics. Materials perform in a predictable fashion. Engineers know how steel behaves in tension and compression at various temperatures. That information in turn enables them to model how buildings will respond to various stress scenarios with great confidence.

By contrast, people are erratic and inconsistent. Every social science save economics rests on the assumption of human irrationality. Behavioral economics experiments have found repeatedly that subjects will react differently to the same economic proposition depending on how it is presented. And it gets worse when we go beyond simple transactions to larger economic structures. Those systems are dynamic and evolving constantly. Behaviors that held true in the past may no longer be operative now. Yet remarkably, as we will discuss in the next chapter, a crucial assumption that undergirds much of the output of the profession is that economies and markets operate in a consistent and therefore predictable manner.

Even if a theory is flawed or incomplete, it is still possible for it to be useful in practice. For instance, even though Western medicine rejects the logic behind acupuncture, studies have found it effective in reducing inflammation and pain. However, key precepts of economics are often untested, or, when they can be validated, often garner (at best) inconclusive support.

But the widespread acceptance of the phony precepts of financial economics and neoclassical economics helped bring about the financial crisis by endorsing policies and practices that allowed financial firms to exploit customers, shareholders, and taxpayers on a scale heretofore seen only in banana republics.

. . . . .

Not only are many of the precepts and predictions of orthodox economics wildly at odds with reality, but even worse, their powerful influence on policy and the popular imagination means that they impose their goals on society as a whole. And to add insult to injury, it isn't uncommon for economists to bend the truth to defend pet ideologies.

Most citizens like to believe that the push and pull of political processes will filter out bad, extreme, and untested ideas. But economists have become the only social scientists with a seat at the policy table, and their expert status is above challenge. This is a peculiar, and not sufficiently recognized, aggrandizement of the economist's role at the expense of democratic processes or even input from other disciplines. That in and of itself distorts policy formation.

Economists have shaped the assumptions of what the goals of policy are, namely maximum growth consistent with moderate inflation and unemployment. And "growth" means rising output, most commonly measured by gross domestic product, or GDP, which measures all the goods and services produced in an economy in a given year.

GDP was never meant to serve as a proxy for social welfare. Indeed, the Nobel laureate who was one of its main creators, Simon Kuznets, warned, "The welfare of a nation can scarcely be inferred from a measurement of national income."[27] Yet it has become an article of faith, particularly among politicians, that growth in output is tantamount to improving standards of living.

Simple income or output measures mean that anything that leads to more spending looks like a boon, whether it really is or not. For instance, the Exxon Valdez oil spill, with its sizable remediation costs, litigation, and expenses incurred by the media in covering the disaster, boosted Alaska's GDP more than if the shipment had arrived in port safely.[28] Similarly, if someone were to discover a cheap cure for cancer, it would probably lower GDP due to the loss of income to doctors, hospitals, and drug companies. Another failing is that GDP fails to capture non-income based measures of progress, such as social stability. As Robert F. Kennedy said, "It measures everything, in short, except that which makes life worthwhile."[29]

In addition, many economists would support programs that led to higher GDP, and not trouble themselves too deeply if the result was that Bill Gates became richer and everyone else was less well off. While that example may seem extreme, rising income inequality has been rationalized as an inevitable and acceptable outcome of lower trade barriers and the application of technology that promotes overall growth. It is, of course, impossible to know whether other policy mixes might have produced the same or higher levels of overall growth, while simultaneously ensuring more equitable distributions of results.

But income inequality is of concern to non-economists, too. A study by public health experts in the United States and abroad that was, predictably, not well publicized in the United States itself, found that inhabitants of countries with *greater income inequality* show *lower life expectancy* on average even after adjusting for differences in income levels and diet. A *Financial Times* article summarized the findings:

> Yet, if you look for differences between countries, the relationship between income and health largely disintegrates. Rich Americans, for instance, are healthier on average than poor Americans, as measured by life expectancy. But, although the US is a much richer country than, say, Greece, Americans on average have a lower life expectancy than Greeks. More income, it seems, gives you a health advantage with respect to your fellow citizens, but not with respect to people living in other countries. . . .
>
> Once a floor standard of living is attained, people tend to be healthier when three conditions hold: they are valued and respected by others; they feel "in control" in their work and home lives; and they enjoy a dense network of social contacts. Economically unequal societies tend to do poorly in all three respects: they tend to be characterised by big status differences, by big differences in people's sense of control and by low levels of civic participation.[30]

More recent studies provide further confirmation.[31] Findings like this are stark reminders that framing policy choices solely in economic terms may miss vitally important considerations. After all, many people would trade off a longer, healthier life against more income, but economics refuses to consider this preference.

Admittedly, some influential economists, such as Nobel Prize winners Joseph Stiglitz of Columbia University and Amartya Sen of Harvard are looking at the limits of GDP and how to come up with better measures.[32] But the fact that most economists touted the Great Moderation as a pinnacle of success, solely because it delivered what appeared to be steadier and arguably higher growth, suggests the conventional view will be slow to change.

The power of economists in public life hasn't simply led to output-driven thinking driving policy formulation. It is starting to corrupt the discipline of economics itself.

Let's face it. Economists are seldom brought into lobbying efforts or legislative battles to opine which approach might be best. Most of the time, they are working on behalf of a particular interest group or politician. It's well-nigh impossible be an honest broker and an advocate, yet that is the position that some prominent economists endeavor to play. And the conflict shows.

Consider trade. The United States has long favored more open trade (although our agricultural subsidies show we often don't walk our talk). Yet more exposure to foreign competition often leads to unemployment via outsourcing, offshoring, and factory closures. Even if society overall is in theory better off, displaced individuals frequently are unable to find new jobs at their old pay level. Nevertheless, most economists see anti–free trade sentiment as a sign of economic illiteracy, and regularly produce statistics citing the remarkable gains in incomes due to trade.

Dani Rodrik, a development economist and economics professor at Harvard's John F. Kennedy School of Government, who is pro-trade, has nevertheless repeatedly taken on fellow trade economists for overstating their case. In a blog post, Rodrik mentions that a fellow economist claimed globalization was clearly beneficial. This colleague cited a speech by Bernanke which in turn quoted a paper by Bradford, Grieco, and Hufbauer. That paper contended that eliminating all barriers to trade would increase household incomes by $4,000 to $12,000, which is 3.4% to 10.1% of the U.S. GDP. The pro-globalization academic argued that critics needed to provide "actual evidence," as this paper had.

Rodrik is a believer in the value of trade, so note how he reacted:

> That is a whole chunk of change! . . . I do have a big quarrel with the kind of numbers presented. . . . They seem to me to be grossly inflated. . . .
>
> First a reality check. . . . There is no way of tweaking this formula [for calculating the gains of free trade] . . . that would get us a number anywhere near the Bradford et al. estimates. For example, using the generous numbers . . . the gains from moving to complete free trade are a meager 0.25% of GDP (compared to Bradford et al.'s lowest estimate of 3.4% of GDP).
>
> Now of course this is a back-of-the envelope calculation. . . . The most accomplished work along these lines takes place at the World Bank and at Purdue. A representative recent estimate comes in a paper by Anderson, Martin, and van der Mensbrugghe—hardly a bunch of rabid anti-globalizers. Their bottom line for the U.S.: full liberalization of global merchandise trade would eventually increase U.S. income by 0.1% by 2015 (see their Table 2). No, you did not read that wrong. The gain amounts to one-tenth of one percent of GDP![33]

Rodrik then goes on for another four paragraphs to describe in gory detail how Bradford, Grieco, and Hufbauer cooked their analysis to produce such great results. He concludes:

I don't really mean to pick on Bradford et al. (although as a particularly egregious example, their paper fully deserves it). . . .

What puzzles me is not that papers of this kind exist, but that there are so many professional economists who are willing to buy into them without the critical scrutiny we readily deploy when we confront globalization's critics. It should have taken Ben Bernanke no longer than a few minutes to see through Bradford et al. and to understand that it is a crude piece of advocacy rather than serious analysis. . . . Why are we so ready to lower our standards when we think it is in the service of a good cause?

Let's take a look at the implications of Rodrik's discussion:

- One of the most widely cited factoids in defense of free trade is rubbish.
- Analyses of the benefits of more open trade by the top experts in the field show improvements to be so modest as to be marginal, suggesting that other factors, like disruption to communities, might be worth trading off against them, or that we, like many of our mercantilist trade partners, can afford to play a pick-and-choose game with liberalization.
- Some of the people citing the trumped-up study knew or ought to have known it was crap, yet continue to cite it. At best, this is misguided paternalism.
- The type of analysis used in trade economics (as in other branches of economics) is sufficiently specialized that economists who work primarily in other areas cannot recognize shoddy or questionable work (the economist who brought up the paper initially and demanded that others disprove it was a macroeconomist, not a trade economist).
- The great unwashed masses cannot participate in these discussions. Were an autodidact to uncover the same type of flaws that Rodrik discussed, his opinion would be rejected due to his lack of credentials. A big chunk of policy development and vetting is in the hands of a mandarin class that often is uninterested in and unresponsive to the concerns of the public at large.

Consider the ramifications. The economic constructs that have had the greatest influence on financial markets regulation and practice are intrinsically flawed. Moreover, economists in public service roles, like Ben Bernanke, are so heavily invested in this paradigm that they either do not question dubious research that bolsters it, or worse, cynically tout the most impressive-sounding figures knowing they are bunk.

. . . . .

But how did these flawed theories do damage? Faulty financial technology not only understated risk, but its widespread adoption created a lingua franca of sorts, namely, approaches for measurement and modeling. Those standards facilitated trading and investment, since they gave investors benchmarks for how they "ought" to invest and think about pricing.

But these approaches were, and still are, as commonly accepted and as valid as the theory of the four humors (black bile, yellow bile, phlegm, and blood) that was the foundation of Western medical practice through the nineteenth century. The major financial intermediaries and regulators have also embraced these practices for risk management, favoring computational convenience over soundness.

Worse, while these techniques do appear to work on a day-to-day basis, they greatly understate the risk of catastrophic loss. Witness the fact that Long-Term Capital Management (LTCM), a hedge fund with two Nobel Prize winners, Myron Scholes of the Black-Scholes options pricing model and Robert Merton, an exemplar of modern financial wizardry, blew up and nearly took the financial system with it. A successor hedge fund started by Scholes and other LTCM principals suffered substantial losses through October 2008 and halted redemptions.[34] Other so-called quant funds using similar approaches showed equally disastrous results and many are in the process of winding down.

Another way in which bad theory caused harm was via deregulation of the financial sector. While more liberal rules eliminated secure, easy profits, such as fixed commissions on stock trades, they also weakened relationships and put financial firms on a transactional footing with many of their customers. While in the old days, brokers and intermediaries did best by being "long term greedy," in the new paradigm, there was far less reason to be protective of customers, and far more reason to extract as much as possible when it was there for the taking. Clients became stuffees for lucrative, complex products with hidden risks, like the CDOs that worried Tett.

Similarly, deregulation shifted activity away from bank balance sheets and onto trading markets via securitization of loans originated by banks. Over-the-counter trading has strong scale economies and network effects, but also requires large amounts of capital. The big broker-dealers moved from being private partnerships, very mindful of risk, to an "other people's money" format with public shareholders. The very biggest banks, who had long been jealous of investment bank pay and profits, eventually became successful players by dint of a decade plus of effort and selective acquisitions.

But the change in scale of operation and incentives led to large-scale looting, with firms running with too little equity and taking on undue risk to maximize short-term profits. So-called producers extracted far more than they were worth, given the risks being taken, and their outsize compensation moved the pay goalposts for all in the fold (recall that Merrill Lynch CEO John Thain's driver earned $230,000 in a year[35]). And pay is far and away the biggest expense at the firms, so systematic overpayment can and did leave them undercapitalized relative to the risks assumed. At Goldman, for instance, individual compensation across the firm averaged $630,000, totaling 44% of net revenues, and nearly twice net earnings.[36] And for 2009, the year after the *annus horribilis* of the worldwide implosion of the financial system, the firm is on track for a record bonus year, with average pay projected at $700,000 per employee.[37]

Taxpayers have learned, much to their chagrin, that the idea that Wall Street was a bastion of capitalism was nothing more than a well-run public relations scam. Precisely because the government is unwilling to declare these failed firms bankrupt, out of fear of causing runs, the public cannot use bankruptcy fraud (more formally known as fraudulent conveyance) to claw back overpayment. Instead, the gains went to a few individuals and the losses are being socialized.

Even worse, the Fed chairman and other senior policy makers appear unable to question a defective framework. It is as if they are unable to process what has happened since 2007. It isn't simply that they are trying to restore status quo ante; they seem to believe that the only possible operative paradigm *is* the status quo ante. The emergency measures were tantamount to patching up failing machinery with duct tape and baling wire. While the equipment is currently operational, it is far from its former level of performance. And with the underlying, flawed incentives and processes in place, it is only a matter of time before we have more dislocations.

Seeing the world as you'd like to see it may be comforting, but basing policies on what amount to romantic views comes with considerable risk. And in the case of the United States, it has resulted in substantial costs, with the accounts yet to be fully tallied.

. . . . .

Not only were the public and policymakers blinded by the trappings of science, but even worse, the leaders at the U.S. Treasury and Federal Reserve are still clinging desperately to a failed orthodoxy that in turn helped create and now serves to justify an overly powerful and self-interested financial services industry. The idea that markets are often a useful means to an end has been perverted into the notion that markets are ends in and of themselves, that their operations are by nature so virtuous that they must be left to their own devices. The banking industry and other business interests often explicitly or subtly invoke "free markets" to forestall interventions that might crimp their profits or executive pay packages. The economist and former central banker Willem Buiter calls the syndrome "cognitive regulatory capture,"[38] in which the minders have absorbed the world view of the industry they are supposed to be overseeing.

This peculiar codependent relationship means that instead of reform, we see more coddling, not just of the industry but even of the very individuals who drove the financial system off the cliff and are dragging the real economy with it. Until the powers-that-be recognize that the big banks gorged themselves on debt, and that the industry needs to shrink and be reconfigured so as to no longer pose a public menace, our best outcome is a Japan-style stagnation.

However, it may be too late. As the former International Monetary Fund chief economist Simon Johnson warns, the financial industry, much like oligarchs in developed countries in need of rescue, has a stranglehold on policy.[39] Instead of being leashed and collared, the big troubled players are receiving massive subsidies with few strings attached, disguised in programs too complicated for the layperson to puzzle through.

In other words, "free markets" ideology, with its libertarian idealism, has in fact produced Mussolini-style corporatism. And until we learn to call the resulting looting by its proper name, it is certain to continue.

CHAPTER 2

BLINDED BY SCIENCE

In theory, there is no difference between theory and practice. In practice there is.

—Yogi Berra[1]

In the first half of 2008, oil prices were on a tear. In early January, a survey had found that economic forecasters expected the price that year to average $78 a barrel, which was 20% below its then-current level, just shy of $100 a barrel.[2] But markets often humble those who try to read their mood. The price of the black commodity started on a relentless upward trajectory.

The rise was so rapid that seasoned investors, like hedge fund manager George Soros, and commodities experts, like strategist Mack Frankfurter, deemed the skyrocketing prices to be at least in part the result of speculation, not merely supply and demand.[3] Even old-guard oil traders, who would seem the least likely to say bad things about market practices, deemed the levitation to be in significant measure the result of an influx of financial buyers.[4] Oil industry executives and the Saudi government said that the prices did not reflect real economy forces. Jeroen van der Veer, chief executive of Royal Dutch Shell, remarked, "The fundamentals are no problem. They are the same as they were when oil was selling for $60 a barrel."[5] Some even went as far as to use the "B" word, as in "bubble." In fact, the increase in oil prices as of early June, with a high of $139.12 on the New York Mercantile Exchange, exceeded that of NASDAQ stocks through the peak of the dot-com frenzy.[6]

Yet economists were almost universally opposed to the idea that speculation was playing much of a role in the oil price spike. A *Wall Street Journal* survey found that 89%, as close as you ever come to unanimity in most polls, saw the increase in commodity prices, including oil, as the result of fundamental forces.[7] Nobel Prize winner Paul Krugman argued the case forcefully in a series of *The New York Times* op-eds and blog posts with titles like "The Oil Non-Bubble," "Fuel on the Hill," and "Speculative Nonsense, Once Again."[8]

Krugman's presence in this camp lent credibility to the "oil prices are warranted" view. The Princeton economist had been a Cassandra on the housing mania and had also correctly anticipated that the deregulation of energy prices in California could lead to manipulation. So Krugman, although sensitive to the notion that speculation can distort prices, nevertheless fell in with the argument that oil prices were the result of real-world buying and selling.

Yet that belief was spectacularly incorrect. Oil peaked at $147 a barrel in July and fell even more dramatically than it had risen. By October, prices had plunged to $64 a barrel. *Bloomberg* columnist Caroline Baum described the world as "drowning in oil."[9] A report by the Commodity Futures Trading Commission attributed the large swings in oil prices to speculation. CFTC commissioner Bart Chilton said earlier studies that found that the moves were the result of supply and demand relied on "deeply flawed data."[10]

Why were economists unable to read the information correctly, and so inclined to dismiss the views of experts and participants in the energy markets who were saying that prices were out of whack with what they saw on the ground?

The short answer, which we will discuss at much greater length in this chapter, is that they had undue faith in their models. Modeling has come to be a defining characteristic of modern economics. Practitioners will argue, correctly, that economic phenomena are so complex that some abstraction is necessary to come to grips with the underlying pattern.

Good models filter the "noise" out of a messy situation and distill the underlying dynamics to provide better insight. The implications of a mathematical model can be developed in a deliberate, explicit fashion, rather than left to intuition. Models force investigators to contend with loose ends and expose inconsistencies in their reasoning that need either to be resolved or diagnosed as inconsequential. They also make it easier for the researchers to communicate with each other.

Yet any model, be it a spreadsheet, a menu, a clay mockup, or a dressmaker's pattern, entails the loss of information. Economists admit this is a potential danger. But this inherent feature is precisely what makes laypeople and even some insiders uncomfortable, because *what was discarded to make the problem manageable may have been essential.*

Worse, someone who has become adept at using a particular framework is almost certain to be the last to see its shortcomings. A model-user is easily seduced and starts to see reality through his creation. Practitioners can become hostage to their constructs, exhibiting a peculiar sort of selective blindness—when they stop engaging critical thinking about one facet of a problem, it seems the ability to even identify that angle stagnates and perception fades. Cats form their visual synapses from the moment their eyes open, when they are two to three days old. If they do not get certain inputs at that early stage, the brain circuits never get made. A kitten who sees only horizontal lines at this age will bump into table legs the rest of its life. Models necessitate and reinforce this applied blindness.

That analogy may seem insulting. Scholars, including economists, manage to steer clear of such undignified behavior. But the refusal to see what is in front of them can at times be profound, as we saw in chapter 1, when Robert Shiller's and Raghuram Rajan's warnings were rejected with hostility, precisely because they ran afoul of the widely accepted view that whatever markets did was ever and always virtuous—a clear example of experimenter bias, of rejecting new data because they do not fit a preferred paradigm.

And it happened with oil prices as well. Krugman made two central arguments. First was that if the price for oil was too high for anything other than a short time, there would be excessive inventories. You can see a representation of that argument in the accompanying figure, which is a simple model. The intersection of the downward sloping demand line and the upward sloping supply line represents the price that would be set by market forces. The horizontal line drawn over the intersection point represents the "too high price" and the

Figure 2.1

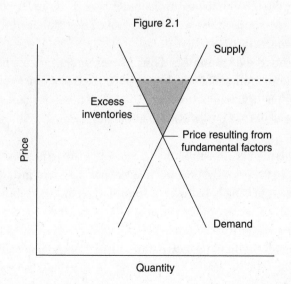

triangle underneath that line shows the oversupply. Yet because oil inventories were in line with normal levels, it followed, according to Krugman, that the price must be right.

Krugman's second argument had to do with futures trading. Futures are a long-established way for buyers and sellers of various products (and more recently, financial instruments) to hedge against the risk of price changes. Futures contracts are an obligation to buy or sell a specified amount of a particular item at a particular date. If a big food manufacturer wanted to protect itself against the possibility that wheat prices would rise and make its baked goods more expensive, it would buy futures contracts that corresponded to the dates and amounts of its expected purchases. Similarly, someone who wanted to protect himself against falling prices would sell futures contracts.

In early 2008, when commodities prices were soaring, some observers claimed that speculation in futures was playing a major role. For instance, investors were buying commodities futures, in many cases via commodities index funds, as a hedge against inflation. Krugman claimed that these futures were mere side gambling that did not have anything to do with the spot price, which is the price at which someone would buy or sell for immediate delivery. So all the investors who were using futures as a way to invest in commodities could not be affecting the crucial price, the spot price.

Krugman and his colleagues were wedded to the story embodied in the image, and dismissed counter-arguments as mere opinions of the economically illiterate. He and others refused to consider conflicting information. There was, in fact, plenty of inventory accumulation going on, in China: not in the form of oil, which is expensive and nasty to store, but in a product refined from it, diesel fuel. Moreover, the U.S. Strategic Petroleum Reserve, a stockpiler not included in the private inventories most economists looked at, had been increasing its inventories during this period.[11]

As important, these economists didn't bother understanding how oil was traded. They heard "futures" and assumed oil worked like other commodities markets, where physical transactions were based on the spot market price and the futures market served only for speculation and hedging.[12] But that was incorrect.

The spot oil market in the past had been subject to "squeezes" or trading strategies to goose the price.[13] As a result, many major exporters, including OPEC, moved away from pricing based on the spot market and used formula prices based on a weighted average of futures prices. Thus, contrary to what Krugman said, futures prices were not mere side bets, they were, according to the Oxford Institute for Energy Studies, "the heart of the current oil-pricing regime."[14]

An astute reader might point out that the problem wasn't Krugman's model, but how he applied it. But that assessment misses a much bigger issue. The high value that economics assigns to the notion of "rigor" blinds many of its members to the limitations of their methodologies.

In turn that produces a series of failings that we will discuss in this chapter:

- **Overconfidence.** Economists have undue faith in their theories and analyses.
- **Drunk under the street light syndrome.** This is based on the oft-told joke of the drunk who looks for his keys under the street light, where he can see better, rather than where he lost them. Economists restrict their inquiry to where the established, familiar methodologies function well, neglecting areas and information that are troublesome.
- **Biases.** The desire of economists to turn economics into a hard science has required that certain assumptions be made. But the outcomes depend on the hypotheses. To put it differently, the risk that the assumptions determined the results isn't treated as seriously as it should be. One reason this is a danger is that economics doesn't simply rest on the axioms one often hears mentioned, like "perfect competition," but also deeper assumptions that undergrid some approaches, yet are seldom subject to scrutiny. The result is that the professional ambitions of the discipline in fact produce significant biases and blind spots, the most serious being uncertainty and instability.
- **Inappropriately large political role.** Economists have come to hold a position that is dangerous in a democracy. Their use of science-like procedures gives them authority that is often unwarranted. Even though they like to cast themselves as benign umpires, they wield far more influence. Moreover, as individuals, they usually have a clear position on the right/left spectrum that is reflected in their recommendations. Power without accountability is a dangerous position for any group to hold in a democracy.

None of these issues is new. As we will see, they have been discussed by some members of the academy as well as those outside. These concerns have been brushed off, with the discipline claiming that its prescriptions are useful and beneficial. We will argue, here and in the balance of the book, that this is a self-serving and overly generous assessment. The methodologies that came into vogue not only promoted some schools of thought, namely financial economics and neoclassical economics, over others, but also effectively gave a free pass to some of their most dubious and damaging beliefs.

We'll look first at how the prevailing methodologies used in economics have changed, and then we'll look at the shortcomings of the most influential type of work, namely theoretical, and we'll then look at some of the particular approaches.

We spend some time on the 1940s and 1950s, although we also discuss more recent developments. The post–World War II period is when new ideas about how to practice economics developed, became institutionalized, and came to dominate mainstream economics. As readers will see in later chapters, they provided intellectual support for the policy thrust that led to widespread deregulation of financial services that began in the 1970s. Similarly, a new philosophy toward trade, how to foster growth, and interest rate policy took hold in the 1980s. The concepts and many of the major tools used in risk management today also date from the 1950s to the 1970s, and we will discuss those separately, in chapter 3.

Thus to trace the origins of the crisis, we need to look at the foundations of economics, both the practice of the discipline and the ideas that were tested and shown wanting in the financial collapse.

．　．　．　．　．

Once upon a time, economics was very different than it is today. Papers seventy years ago bear scant resemblance to those published in top venues now. The *American Economic Review* in the 1930s had only the occasional numerical table and eschewed equations; it is now chock full of them. Economics as practiced then was far more narrative and descriptive and made much greater use of thought experiments and analogies.

The impulse to make the discipline more scientific began in the later part of the nineteenth century, with the rise of neoclassical economics, which we will discuss in greater depth in chapter 4. Neoclassical economics, which focuses on how prices are set and incomes determined through the operation of markets, dominates modern microeconomics.

The key figures were Léon Walras, an economics professor who taught in Switzerland, who in parallel with William Jevons (a professor of logic, philosophy, and political economy) and Carl Menger (a professor of economic theory who had also taught law and finance), developed some fundamental concepts, such as marginal utility. Walras is also credited with the notion of equilibrium: he envisioned repeated auctions to find the price at which all goods would be sold yet no bidders left with unfilled orders, a process he called *tâtonnement* or "groping." We would now call that result "market clearing" and the magic price "the market clearing price."

Of the three, Walras was keenest about the use of mathematics. Ironically, that worked against his ideas being well received by his contemporaries, but has led his work to be held in high regard today. Walras's successor at the University of Lausanne was Vilfredo Pareto, whose first career had been as an engineer, and he brought an interest in equilibrium analysis with him.

Nevertheless, only a few scholars then took up the mathematical charge. Some of the highly regarded economists of the 1920s and 1930s, even ones who were unquestionably facile with mathematics and used it in their work, such as University of Chicago economist Frank Knight and John Maynard Keynes, the father of modern macroeconomics, were leery of undue reliance on it. They were concerned that it could be a Procrustean bed, forcing economists to discard aspects of behavior, in particular uncertainty, that were vital to understanding the underlying phenomena.

Ironically, the Great Depression was the best thing that ever happened to the discipline, although it certainly didn't look that way at the time. It laid waste to the reputations of the economists most closely associated with the "new era" thinking of the 1920s, most famously Yale's Irving Fisher, who had the great misfortune to declare that stock prices had reached "a permanently high plateau" mere days before the bubble burst. The conventional economics of the day, which was an earlier, less fully developed form of our modern neoclassical thought, then as now failed to anticipate an economic crisis and was silent as to what to do about it.

The rise in the political authority of economists can be traced to Keynes, in particular his thinking in response to the Depression. The British economist had established his reputation with his bestselling *The Economic Consequences of the Peace,* a scathing criticism of the Treaty of Versailles imposed on Germany at the end of World War I. Keynes had been involved in the negotiations as a member of the Treasury and had quit in disgust. Keynes correctly foresaw that the punitive agreement would only sow the seeds of future conflict and argued that clemency and policies to promote prosperity would do more to secure peace than retribution would.

But the big boost for the influence of the discipline came with the success of Keynesian policies in the Great Depression.

Keynes viewed its cause as a collapse in demand, more specifically private consumption, and urged governments to step into the breach with large-scale deficit spending. The United States followed this program in the Roosevelt administration, not out of an adherence to Keynes (Marriner Eccles, Federal Reserve chairman from 1934 to 1946, had independently come to similar conclusions, that government stimulus was the right remedy). And there was a more pragmatic reason for government to intervene: relief was a way to prevent social breakdown. One not well-understood fact is that the innovative big business of that era, a "multinational block" of large manufacturers and international banks, backed Roosevelt's program out of fear of growing violence and the rising power of radical unions.[15]

Keynes was vindicated after World War II when growth remained strong.[16] There was widespread fear that the economy would sink back into depression, due to the great increase in the workforce as soldiers returned home, at the same time as the stimulus of massive wartime deficit spending ended.

Despite the apparent success of Keynes's ideas, they were a fundamental threat to the orthodoxy. Classical economics saw the economy as self-righting, with its natural state as full employment. All you had to do was let price mechanisms work and all would be well.

By contrast, Keynes held the future was fundamentally uncertain, and there was no strong pricing mechanism or other equilibrating force in the economy that would lead the economy toward a full employment outcome. Even though he took issue only with some elements, the damage to the edifice was profound. First, it meant that market forces, left to their own devices, were not always the panacea that classical and neoclassical economists believed them to be. Second, something as ephemeral, elusive, and hard to pin down as savers' liquidity preferences, meaning their desire to hold cash or other very safe assets, rather than put their money in riskier investments, could wreak havoc. If a change in conditions, or simply a shift in psychology, spooked savers, and they decided to pull in their horns en masse, it could exert an enormous toll on the real economy. And why might they do that? Because the future is unknowable. Investors, businesses, and consumers could decide to sit pat and defer action until they thought they had a better grasp on a situation.

That is not to say that Keynes's line of thinking was fully fleshed out . Indeed, given that the Cambridge economist admitted to having rejected some of his earlier views in coming up with his General Theory ("I myself held with conviction for many years the theories I now attack"[17]), it would be reasonable to regard Keynes's new ideas with some skepticism. After all, he might change his mind again. Nevertheless, Keynes had identified fundamental flaws in the traditional construct, provided better alternatives, and, perhaps most important, was blazing a path toward integrating the operation of financial markets into mainstream thinking.

Needless to say, the efforts to stuff Keynes in a box began almost as soon as he published his 1936 *The General Theory of Employment, Interest, and Money.* Some of this was due to the reluctance or inability to accept the implications of his ideas; another impediment was his new insights as he formulated them were less amenable to being "mathed up" than neoclassical economics, with its fixation on equilibrium and view of price as the answer to all evils. As we will discuss, the efforts to "formalize" the orthodoxy already were underway and Keynes was fitted to its Procrustean bed.

Thus, the push to make economics more scientific wound up cherry-picking Keynes, even though the Cambridge economist's ideas were innovative. Not only was Keynes willing to recognize forces that could create instability, but as an investor himself, he was attuned to the role of uncertainty, meaning the unknowable, which by definition could not be measured. Thus Keynes's famed "animal spirits" was the acknowledgment that businessmen often leap into the void, moving forward when there is little rational basis for action.

But rather than embrace and expand upon Keynes's ideas, English economist John Hicks managed, mathematically, to turn Keynes's *General Theory* into a special case of classical economics, a move Keynes derided, and, many years later, Hicks himself renounced.[18] As Keynes's biographer Robert Skidelsky said, "Thus his theory was robbed of theoretical bite, while retaining its relevance for policy."[19]

The damage was done. The fact that humans have limited knowledge and little foresight had been airbrushed out of Keynes's construct.

· · · · ·

Let's start by discussing how methodology has come to shape the practice of economics and why that is problematic. It's important for laypeople to appreciate that the aim of economics, contrary to what they might believe, is not, say, "to find better ways to characterize the underlying phenomena." Economics is about what economists want it to be about. And the choice of which methods, or one might say tools, are acceptable has a considerable influence on what qualifies as suitable subject matter.

It is also important to recognize how textbooks and standards anchor a field of inquiry. For instance, dictionaries play an important role in stabilizing languages and setting standards for proper use.

Economics is hardly alone in having its focus influenced by its tools and research methods. For instance, biology has shifted its focus to be significantly "about" the analysis of genomes, even if the "so what's?" of some of the work may not be fully apparent. Similarly, Western medicine is largely "about" drugs and surgery. While it recognizes and diagnoses catastrophic illnesses and infectious diseases, where it decides to draw the line on whether a lesser complaint is a pathology often has to do with how amenable it is to treatment by the presently available techniques. For instance, depression is diagnosed with much greater frequency than in the past. Is the population really in that much worse shape? Possibly, yes, but that change seems to be the direct result of the development of new and less side effect–prone antidepressants. It appears that where doctors draw the line between health and illness has shifted as a result of the existence of improved treatments. Similarly, one of the reasons for the rising popularity of alternative medicine is its interest in, and claims of ability to treat, some conditions deemed to be subclinical by Western doctors.

None of this would matter much if economics were merely another social science. But the fact that the discipline has so much influence over policy means that how it conducts its affairs is of vital public interest.

The shift in attitude and practices that led to greater use of mathematics came in the decade right after World War II. Excitement over science and technology seemed part of the zeitgeist. New advances had played a major and highly visible part in military victory. And the development and growing use of computers made all sorts of new mathematical procedures possible, particularly in the field of statistics. Operations that had been impossibly cumbersome to perform manually were suddenly viable.

But America's vast productive capacity had also been vital to success. And America now faced a new opponent: the USSR, which had achieved the impressive feat of industrializing in the twentieth century. There was a nagging fear that an authoritarian regime could mobilize resources in a way that would be impossible in a democracy. So one could argue that economic productivity wasn't simply a matter of social welfare, but was also important to national security.

The effort to remake economics as a science and use mathematics-based exposition got a considerable push forward from Paul Samuelson, the first American Nobel Prize winner in economics. Samuelson was a towering figure in the discipline, and was unusually prolific, writing influential papers on a wide range of topics, including welfare economics, logic, international trade, and linear programming. He described himself as the last generalist in economics.[20]

Samuelson came of age when the economics discipline was swept up with an ambition to make greater use of mathematics. Ironically, although Samuelson is widely seen as a Keynesian, in fact his most influential work, as far as the profession is concerned, was Walras version 2.0.

Samuelson's doctoral dissertation was awarded a prize at Harvard and was published in 1947 as *Foundations of Economic Analysis*. This treatise set forth, in impressive mathematical detail, the early twentieth-century neoclassical canon. It set out to demonstrate that nearly all economic activity could be characterized as minimizing or maximizing in relationship to a constraint. And that in turn made it subject to formal development, that is, step-by-step mathematical-like proofs. Samuelson saw, as Friedrich Hayek later put it, "physics as the science for economics to imitate."[21]

The appeal of this approach was considerable. As Samuelson's fellow Nobel Prize winner Robert Lucas put it:

> He'll take these incomprehensible verbal debates that go on and on and never end and just end them; formulate the issue in such a way that the question is answerable, and then get the answer.[22]

But was this development as salutary as those within the discipline believe?

Any sort of focusing on one set of methodologies to the *exclusion* of others has considerable risks. Requiring fealty to that approach means *insisting* on not seeing those elements that the approach minimizes or excises.

And that is precisely what happened to Samuelson, and to the discipline, as it chose to go down the same path. He had steeped himself in neoclassical thinking in writing his dissertation. Samuelson admitted to instinctively rejecting Keynes's *General Theory,* even though he saw the performance of the U.S. economy in the Roosevelt years as incontestable proof that Keynes's conclusions were correct. Samuelson decided that the reason those policies succeeded was that wages and prices were rigid, meaning they did not fall enough.[23] Readers may recall from our discussion earlier that this is the story you would have to believe if you looked at the problem from a Walrasian, or neoclassical, perspective, that prices were too high.

But Keynes had explicitly rejected that line of thinking in his book and offered another explanation. Moreover, the evidence of the Depression was a glaring contraction. Prices had fallen sharply, and men, desperate for work, would accept almost any wage.[24]

Nevertheless, Samuelson's *Foundations* had a considerable impact on standards in the discipline, and Keynes's ideas did not fit that template very well, so they were shoehorned in.

Why would instability be so inconvenient to economic thought? Uncertainty and instability throw monkey wrenches into the step-by-step proofs that the discipline embraced. A system that exhibits unpredictable behavior, for instance, one that can undergo a phase change into a chaotic state, simply does not fit into the mathematical procedures that economists adopted.

Samuelson is widely seen as the father of Keynesianism in America, but it is key to understand that "Keynesianism" is not Keynes. Samuelson put a second important imprint on the discipline through his 1948 introductory economics textbook (*Economics: An Introductory Analysis*), which sold several million copies in sixteen editions, the latest in 1997, nearly fifty years after its initial release. And it was this work that defined what Keynes came to mean not just to students, but also, along with John Hicks's work, to most people in the profession.

How could that be? Keynes's work was hardly secret. Why would economists rely on an interpretation rather than the source? Even shortly after its release, *General Theory* developed a reputation of being difficult and, arguably, confusing (well, if you were steeped in neoclassical economics, that would certainly be the case). And it became perversely normal to go on about Keynes's *General Theory* without having read it. For instance, Robert Bryce, a student who had attended some of Keynes's lectures, wrote an essay on Keynes's ideas. That article, along with Bryce's participation in an informal group that met at Harvard, became the foundation for what most economists at Harvard in the late 1930s thought Keynes was about.[25]

But there was a second, powerful reason to change Keynes for American consumption. A Canadian student of Keynes, Lorie Tarshis, published an economics textbook in 1947, *The Elements of Economics*, which included his interpretation of Keynes. It also suggested that markets required government support to attain full employment.[26] It was engaging and well written, and sold well initially, but fell off quickly, the victim of an organized campaign by conservative groups to have the textbook removed.[27] The book, and by implication Keynes, was inaccurately charged with calling for government ownership of enterprise.

Any taint of Communist leanings would damage the career of a budding academic. So aside from his refusal to accept some fundamental elements of Keynes's construct, Samuelson had another reason to distance himself from the *General Theory.* Samuelson said he was well aware of the "virulence of the attack on Tarshis" and penned his text "carefully and lawyer like" to deflect similar attacks.[28] He also took care to present his opus as "neoclassical synthesis Keynesianism."[29] The fact that Samuelson presented Keynes primarily through equations also made him less subject to political attack.

But Samuelson and his fellow neoclassical synthesis Keynesians, like Nobel laureates Robert Solow and James Tobin, told a story about the operation of a modern economy that was fundamentally at odds with Keynes's precepts. Underneath the hood, Keynesianism was merely a branch of neoclassical thinking: while the economy could *in theory* work fine if left to its own devices, all sort of pesky real-world obstacles got in the way, like time lags and the ability of organizations to influence economic activity. Because pricing mechanisms didn't always work correctly, an economy could fail to achieve full employment. That meant having the government stimulate the economy was a valid remedy.

Keynes, by contrast, saw the economy as fundamentally at risk of instability not due to factors that undermined how prices allocated resources and guided behavior, but due to how investors behaved: they could simply change their minds about how they felt about taking risk. If they became cautious on a large scale, the economy would suffer, and if the change was dramatic enough, it would go into a self-reinforcing downward spiral.

So Samuelson's own antipathy to some of Keynes's core ideas, and his ability to steer clear of political landmines, meant "Keynes lite" developed a substantial following in the United States. But in the end, were we well served? Keynes was in the process of developing a new paradigm, more fitting to advanced economies confronting issues of trade, unemployment, and international funds flows. In fact, as we will show in later chapters, the shortcomings of the neoclassical view of these issues lay at the root of the crisis.

. . . . .

As a result of the impact of Samuelson's *Foundations,* and the general enthusiasm for more "rigor," one approach that gained in importance in the economics profession was the use of proof-like arguments, in which assumptions are set forth and implications developed from them, in a step-by-step process. That sort of work is generally described as "theoretical." Empirical work, by contrast, is statistical, taking a data set and teasing conclusions from it, typically using regression analysis. We'll focus here on theoretical work and return to empirical studies later.

In theory papers, since the findings follow from the axioms, the conclusions rest on the assumptions made. Donald (now Deidre) McCloskey of the University of Illinois argues in an only somewhat tongue-in-cheek paper that economists can produce whatever results they want in theoretical work by adeptly tweaking the assumptions:

> I am pleased to announce a theorem about theorems which describes tolerably well how half of economics has developed. It goes like this:
>
> ### The A-Prime/C-Prime Theorem
> For each and every set of assumptions A implying conclusion C, there exists an alternative set of alternative assumptions, A', arbitrarily close to A, such that A' implies an alternative conclusion, C', arbitrarily far from C.
>
> Take free trade. Suppose that the first set of assumptions, A, are competition, convexity, full employment, and so forth, which lead to the blackboard conclusion, C, that "the North American Free Trade Agreement is swell for the American economy." Imagine a paper published at time t drawing such a conclusion. . . . You know as well as I do what will happen before time $t + 1$: a paper will be published showing that, on the contrary, if the assumptions are jiggered a bit, to A', b introducing, say, a nonconvexity in the ith industry, then

the old conclusion falls, and C' is erected in its stead: "the North American Free Trade Agreement is rotten for the American economy." If you don't like nonconvexity (it covers a lot of ground), try transaction costs or macroeconomic considerations.[30]

Now this is said in good humor, but the implications are pretty serious. Even with the use of math, theoretical work is seldom tested, and is by nature difficult to prove or falsify conclusively, and you are left with a discipline that has managed to convince itself that telling stories in mathematical form rather than a purely verbal fashion somehow comes closer to establishing their validity.

In fact, accomplished mathematician, Nobel Prize winner, and former president of the American Economic Association Wassily Leontief resigned from Harvard shortly after receiving the prize in 1974 and stopped writing economics papers altogether in 1984 out of his frustration with data-devoid theorizing,[31] which by his tally accounted for more than half of the articles published in the *American Economic Review*.[32] He argued that those who were interested in how the economy really worked were marginalized. He called for a reassessment and reorientation of the research methodologies in economics.[33] Asked in the late 1990s if anything had changed, Leontief said, "No."

. . . . .

One way to assess mainstream economics is to look at the assumptions and ascertain whether they make sense. One of Samuelson's major assumptions that undergirds much of mainstream economics, and one that Keynes rejected, is ergodicity.

In simple terms, "ergodicity" means that no matter what happens in the world, everything will reach a point where things stop changing, which, in economics, is the prized equilibrium. It also means that a system acts consistently over time. For example, if someone is performing a statistical analysis, and if he runs tests over a long enough time frame, the data points obtained are a valid representation of how the process performs.[34] Um, but how does he know how long "long enough" is? And what if the system itself changes? Data from Victorian England would probably have limited application to the world of commerce today. In fact, in the hard sciences, it is difficult to prove that a system does exhibit ergodic behavior.

Now this hypothesis may sound innocuous (or more accurately, impenetrable), but it is a straitjacket. As analyst Greg Davidson and economics professor Paul Davidson of the University of Tennessee explain:

... the ergodic presumption permits physicists to predict that an unhindered pendulum will always come to the same long-run point of rest at the bottom no matter where in the swing we start from. In economics, the "ergodic" analogy of the swinging pendulum is that an unhindered economy will always come to the same position of rest (at full employment) no matter where in the business cycle the swing starts from.[35]

This is breathtaking. To make the preferred formal apparatus work, economists *assume* a Panglossian outcome, namely, that not only does the economic system tend to self-correct on an aggregate level and come to a stable outcome (remember, not all equilibria are stable), but the end result is the best possible place an economy can be—full employment! Yet England suffered from high unemployment from the end of World War I through the beginning of World War II. So a stable condition, which one would assume was an equilibrium of sorts, fell considerably short of full employment.

In case readers think I am making overmuch of this issue, Samuelson said that, if economists are to change economics from a historical exercise and bring it into the arena of science, they must apply the "ergodic hypothesis."[36] This assumption is fundamental to the scientific aspirations and branding of the discipline.

It is easy to find examples that contradict the ergodic hypothesis. One is the tragedy of the commons, where herders sharing a grazing area destroy it because each puts as many beasts as he can on the field. A real-world example is the overfishing of the Grand Banks, once one of the richest fishing grounds in the world. Cod, once abundant, collapsed in the mid-1990s, and other fish stocks have been depleted.

Similarly, anyone familiar with systems dynamics can tell you that premise may not operate. Activities can either be self-dampening (a negative feedback loop) or self-reinforcing (a positive feedback loop), where actions reinforce each other and the system spins out of control. A nuclear chain reaction, like the runaway at the reactor at Chernobyl, is an example of how a positive feedback loop operates.

Ignoring or downplaying positive feedback loops leads to serious problems when describing the economy in which we live. Financial markets, unlike goods markets, do not tend to equilibrium. Credit is a vital element in anything more advanced than a barter economy, yet it creates instability (we discuss how in chapter 8).

By focusing on equilibria to the exclusion of other considerations, economics effectively assumes that the financial system is stable, and that the only feedback loops are so-called negative feedback loops, where perturbations naturally dissipate.

This bias has serious implications for policy. Because stability is taken for granted, economists failed to consider that various measures might produce crises.

But businesses, increasingly effective in lobbying, have succeeded in arguing against restrictions on their actions as costly to them and therefore damaging.

At its best, this is a demand for greater efficiency. But any systems designer will tell you that highly efficient systems are often unstable and prone to breakdown. When something goes wrong, everything is so highly connected (the term of art is "tightly coupled") that problems propagate quickly though the system. There aren't enough firebreaks to halt its progress.

Biological systems, tuned over millennia for stability (the redundancy of two lungs and two kidneys, for instance, is inefficient but pro-survival), illustrate how tweaks in favor of efficiency reduce robustness. Consider racehorses: the catastrophic injuries suffered by Barbaro in the 2006 Preakness Stakes and Eight Belles in the 2008 Kentucky Derby are the tragic illustrations of a long-term trend of a rising level of breakdowns in so-called stakes races. The possible culprits? Putting the factors that maximize the commercial value of the horses foremost, and in particular, ensuring that the horses look pretty for yearling sales. The way to do that is to keep them inactive during their first year, when romping and roughhousing, once the normal course of affairs, would lead to sturdier bones but sometimes also mangled coats. Performance enhancing and inbreeding also play major roles.[37] Yet even after these high-profile deaths, industry practices remain unchanged.[38]

A more mundane example is the vogue among manufacturers to whittle down their supplier networks. The logic is that by concentrating his purchases among fewer parties, a buyer will have more power, allowing him to extract concessions on prices and other issues.

While these advantages are real, having fewer vendors puts the manufacturer at greater risk of an interruption in his parts deliveries, say if one of his vendors halts production due to a major accident.

The belief in equilibrium processes meant that policymakers assumed that stability was automatic, and so economic policies could (in fact should) encourage greater efficiency. But any systems engineer will tell you that stability is a first order design consideration and efficiency is second.

Thus the ergodicity idea, and more generally, the desire to make economics more scientific, led to policy prescriptions that favored efficiency at the expense of stability.

■　　■　　■　　■　　■

The ergodic assumption includes a second bit of sleight of hand. Samuelson said "ergodic hypothesis" was "a belief in a unique, long-run equilibrium independent of the initial conditions."[39] The "initial conditions" part may sound innocuous, but it isn't. The practical implication is that history does not matter. No matter what path an economy or a market has been on, it will "want" to wind up at the same stable position.

Despite Samuelson's claim, the hard sciences do not insist upon the ergodic hypothesis. One does not have to look very hard in disciplines like physics to show both that the ergodic assumption does not hold in some not-terribly-complex situations AND that it was still possible to have rigor of the prized mathematical sort in arriving at that conclusion.

In the late nineteenth century, one of the unsolved puzzles from Newtonian physics was how to describe, given their initial positions, mass, and velocity, vectors of three or more objects or "bodies," as in celestial bodies.[40] The force of gravity would lead the planets to fall into various orbits relative to each other, but what pattern would result? This question had been open for more than two hundred years, and was deemed so important and difficult than King Oscar II of Sweden offered a large prize for anyone who could solve it.

French mathematician Henri Poincaré proved a result in 1899 that while technically not a solution to the king's requirements, nevertheless was so striking in its implications as to be judged significant and won the prize. Poincaré found that even though the problem was deterministic and had only one correct solution, that solution was so sensitive to the initial conditions (location, masses, velocities) that they had to be specified to such a level of detail as to make the problem of three-body motion unpredictable in practice.

Thus, the state of the object at the starting point determines the path that it will follow. But if there are even very slight errors in those measurements of that original state (say an inch for the location of one of the planets), then the actual path of the object will diverge from the predicted path. Those deviations increase as time passes, so that the actual path may lose all resemblance to the predicted path. A Finnish mathematician named Karl Sundman came up with a further result in 1912 that solved the king's original problem in the form of an infinite series. However, the series converges so slowly as to be useless for practical purposes—in order to get an accurate estimate, you would have to sum an enormous number of terms.[41]

Poincaré was the first to discover the enigmatic phenomenon of sensitivity to initial conditions. Consider the implication: a system that does not seem monstrously complicated is for all practical purposes unpredictable. You only have three celestial bodies. The "rules" by which they operate are understood and can be set forth in mathematical form. Ah, but the paths of these celestial bodies are also interdependent; their gravitational fields act on each other.

Now how many times in commercial settings do you think situations like that might arise? Let's assume we actually do understand how the actors operate well enough to specify it with mathematical formulas that are highly accurate.

That is already a huge assumption, one clearly not observed in economics today. Even so, it is also likely in many, if not most, cases that their actions are not independent, but are influenced by the actions of others in the system, from overall consumption levels to the cost of various inputs to the moves of competitors.

In other words, unless you are focusing on comparatively simple, contained aspects of economic activity, any attempts to predict what will happen are likely to be subject to the same problem that Poincaré stumbled upon: even if you can describe the forces at work accurately, you cannot make useful predictions, at least not over anything other than very short time frames. Is it any wonder economists find it hard to make forecasts?

Now why would Samuelson set out quite deliberately and explicitly to limit economists to a methodology that would seem to be ill-suited to the nature of a great deal of economic activity? Samuelson's justification for his prescribed methods was to make economics more "scientific" and he appeared to be taking physics and pure mathematics as his template. Yet in physics, when models conflict with experimental results, the empirical findings take precedence. Although there may be practical and methodological obstacles, the aim of science is to find better ways to characterize real-world phenomena.

Yet Samuelson, and the majority of his colleagues, put aesthetics ahead of fidelity, and that choice has had profound implications, not just for the discipline, but the public at large.

· · · · ·

The scientific pretenses of economics got a considerable boost in 1953, with the publication of what is arguably the most influential work in the economics literature, a paper by Kenneth Arrow and Gérard Debreu (both later Nobel Prize winners), the so-called Arrow-Debreu theorem. Many see this proof as confirmation of Adam Smith's invisible hand. It demonstrates what Walras sought through his successive auction process of *tâtonnement,* that there is a set of prices at which all goods can be bought and sold at a particular point in time.[42] Recall that the shorthand for this outcome is that "markets clear," or that there is a "market clearing price," leaving no buyers with unfilled orders or vendors with unsold goods.

However, the conditions of the Arrow-Debreu theorem are highly restrictive. For instance, Arrow and Debreu assume perfectly competitive markets (all buyers and sellers have perfect information, no buyer or seller is big enough to influence prices), and separate markets for different locations (butter in Chicago is a different market than butter in Sydney). So far, this isn't all that unusual a set of requirements in econ-land.

But then we get to the doozies. The authors further assume forward markets (meaning you can not only buy butter now, but contract to buy or sell butter in Singapore for two and a half years from now) for *every commodity and every contingent market for every time period in all place*s, meaning till the end of time! In other words, you could hedge anything, such as the odds you will be ten minutes late to your 4:00 P.M. meeting three weeks from Tuesday. And everyone has perfect foreknowledge of all future periods. In other words, you know everything your unborn descendants six generations from now will be up to.

In other words, the model bears perilous little resemblance to any world of commerce we will ever see. What follows from Arrow-Debreu is *absolutely nothing*: Arrow-Debreu leaves you just as in the dark about whether markets clear in real life as you were before reading Arrow-Debreu.

And remember, this paper is celebrated as one of the crowning achievements of economics.

. . . . .

Economists have a ready answer for complaints about credulity-straining axioms. They tell the unbelievers that unrealistic assumptions are better than realistic ones. Part of "thinking like an economist," a phenomenon we will discuss later in the chapter, involved being exhorted to subscribe to this sort of thing.

This line of reasoning was the brainchild of Milton Friedman, a pioneering, Nobel Prize–winning monetary economist. He was the intellectual leader and public face of the Chicago school of economics, famed for advancing neoclassical economics, presented in popularized versions as "free markets." Friedman, like his peer Samuelson, played an important role in defining what constituted proper methodology. An oft-invoked section of an influential 1953 paper:

> Truly important and significant hypotheses will be found to have "assumptions" that are wildly inaccurate descriptive representations of reality, and in general, the more significant the theory, the more unrealistic the assumptions. . . . The reason is simple. A hypothesis is important if it "explains" much by little, that is, it abstracts the common and crucial elements from the mass of complex and detailed circumstances surrounding the phenomenon to be explained and permits valid predictions on the basis of them alone. To be important, therefore, a hypothesis must be deceptively false in its assumptions; it takes account of, and accounts for, none of the many other attendant circumstances, since its very success shows them to be irrelevant for the phenomenon to be explained.

To put the point less paradoxically, the relevant question to ask about the "assumptions" of a theory is not whether they are descriptively "realistic," for they never are, but whether they are sufficiently good approximations for the purpose at hand. And this question can be answered only by seeing whether the theory works, which means whether it yields sufficiently accurate predictions.[43]

Friedman's statement that "unrealistic assumptions" often prove the best is willfully false. In the absence of any evidence to the contrary, unrealistic assumptions are *worse* than realistic ones. An "unrealistic" assumption is one directly contradicted by present evidence. This amounts to a "get out of reality free" card.

The deceptive aspect of this argument is the slippery word "unrealistic." Now it is true that relaxing the known parameters of a situation can be very productive. In his paper, Friedman uses the example of how the "law" in physics that describes how bodies fall assumes a vacuum, which is an unrealistic assumption, at least on planet Earth. Similarly, a line in geometry has no thickness, again a condition never observed in real life.

But in this context, the vacuum is not an "unrealistic assumption" but an abstraction that *eliminates a known condition,* air resistance. It is not a feature grafted on to make a construct tidy, but the stripping away of an environmental element to see if getting rid of it exposes an underlying, durable pattern. This procedure is in keeping with how mathematics as a discipline evolved, through the successive whittling away of extraneous elements.

But in economics, core and oft-used assumptions necessary to make many theories work, such as "everyone has perfect information," are unrealistic not in the sense of stripping out real-world aspects that are noisy, but in *adding properties* that are not observed or even well-approximated in reality. Yet they are deemed valid and those who protest are referred to Friedman. Economists may argue that that isn't the case, that the "perfect information" assumption simply serves to eliminate the role of bad information in decisions. But the sort of all-encompassing knowledge often posited to make a model work goes well beyond that. Similarly, "rational" economic actors are super-beings with cognitive and computational capabilities beyond those of the best computers, capable of weighing all that perfect information

Friedman and his followers have a ready defense. The assumptions don't matter; all that counts is that the theory "works." Even though Samuelson wrote a harsh criticism of Friedman's "unrealistic" assumptions, both wanted economics to be "scientific." The sort of science they had in mind was what philosophers call "instrumentalist," which judges a theory by its predictive power alone.

This is Friedman's justification for odd-sounding axioms; you don't need to care how the black box works, so long as it does indeed tell you what will happen or makes other valid observations.

By the same logic, if one could prove that astrology gave good forecasts, instrumentalists would deem it to be valid. The fact that astrology relies on the peculiar procedure of studying planetary motion would be irrelevant.

But it is actually difficult to prove anything conclusively in economics. In fact, some fundamental constructs are taken on what amounts to faith. Consider the most basic image in economics: a chart with a downward sloping demand curve and the upward sloping supply curve, the same sort found in Krugman's diagram. Deidre McCloskey points out that the statistical attempts to prove the relationship have had mixed results. That is actually not surprising, since one can think of lower prices leading to more purchases (the obvious example of sales) but also higher prices leading to more demand. Price can be seen as a proxy for quality. A price that looks suspiciously low can produce a "something must be wrong with it" reaction. For instance, some luxury goods dealers, such as jewelers, have sometimes been able to move inventory that was not selling by increasing prices. Elevated prices may also elicit purchases when the customer expects them to rise even further. Recall that some people who bought houses near the bubble's peak felt they had to do so then or risk being priced out of the market. Some airline companies locked in the high oil prices of early 2008 fearing further price rises.

The theoretical proof is also more limited than the simplified picture suggests. Demand curves are *generally* downward sloping, but in particular cases or regions, per the examples above, they may not be. Yet how often do you see a caveat added to models that use a simple declining line to represent the demand functions? Not only is it absent from popular presentations, it is seldom found in policy papers or in blogs written by and for economists.

McCloskey argues that economists actually rely on introspection, thought experiments, case examples, and "the lore of the marketplace," to support the supply/demand model.[44]

Similarly, a prediction of a simple supply-demand model is that if you increase minimum wages, you will increase unemployment. It's the same picture we saw for the oil market, with different labels. In this case, the "excess inventory" would be people not able to find work.

Yet some empirical work by David Card, an economics professor at the University of California, Berkeley, and Alan Krueger, a professor of economics at Princeton, disputed the idea that increasing minimum wages lowers the number of jobs for the lowest-paid workers.[45] Needless to say, the studies got a great deal of attention, with the reactions often breaking along ideological lines.

One curious element of some of the responses was that they charged Card and Krueger with violating immutable laws of economics. For instance, Reed Garfield, the senior economist of the Joint Economic Committee, wrote:

> The results of the study were extraordinary. Card and Krueger seemed to have discovered a refutation of the law of demand. Economists were stunned. Because of these extraordinary results, they debated the results. Many economists argued that the differences . . . were more than simply differences of minimum wage rates. Other economists argued that the study design was flawed.[46]

Notice the assertion of the existence of "the law of demand," by which Garfield means "demand curves slope downwardly," when in fact no such "law" exists. And there are reasons the Card-Krueger findings could be plausible, the biggest being that the sort of places that hire low-wage labor may not be able to get by with fewer workers and still function.

In fact, all minimum wage studies that hazard a conclusion either way, that better pay reduces low-wage employment or it doesn't, wind up receiving considerable criticism. Some of it is fully warranted. The minimum wage debate illustrates the difficulty of proving theories decisively. That in turn raises considerable doubt about Friedman's "the proof is in the pudding" exhortations. If you can't establish whether or not a theory makes good predictions, you are left with Potemkin science.

Moreover, it isn't hard to come up with examples of models that had "unrealistic assumptions" that did cause problems when applied to real-world situations.

Let's consider the most important form of macroeconomic model, the Dynamic Stochastic General Equilibrium (DSGE) model. "Stochastic" means the model is not deterministic, that is, it uses probabilities to define ranges of outcomes, not single-point estimates. Every central bank worth its salt has its own DSGE model. DSGE models relate the behavior of the economy to that of individuals, but to make the math "tractable," introduce some extreme axioms. Everyone, like puppets in a totalitarian state, thinks alike and behaves the same. They also conveniently are eager to optimize, but the model does allow for the fact that that can't happen instantaneously.[47] Thus in this tidy world, the only departures from optimality, that ideal state prized by economists, is due to outside shocks, like major shifts in technology, the oil embargo of the 1970s, or 9/11.

This set of assumptions means that disturbances *cannot* come from within the system but always result from external forces.[48] Is it any wonder that central bankers dismissed imbalances in their own backyard?

Similarly, despite its peripheral relationship to any recognizable world of commerce, Arrow-Debreu is the justification for allowing any and every type of derivative market to be created. A model that was at most a demonstration of considerable mathematical prowess served as the rationale for a major policy thrust, namely, allowing the financial services industry to launch more and more complex products. If you read economists' remarks, you'll sometimes see support for allowing new types of derivatives as "completing markets" or "perfecting markets." That is a coded reference back to Arrow-Debreu as the basis for supporting this development.

Now, that is not to say that derivatives are always bad. Quite the reverse. Agricultural futures markets have been a great boon to farmers and food producers. Interest rate swaps allowed for banks in the high-inflation era of the early 1980s to offer floating rate mortgages with floors and ceilings on interest-rate moves. They protected the consumer from the floating rate shooting to the moon by correspondingly rewarding the bank (or more accurately, the party that provided the swaps) by allowing the floating rate to fall only so far.

But recall the extreme requirements of Arrow-Debreu. Everyone has perfect knowledge of the future till the end of time. The problem even in using derivatives simply for hedging is that we have no idea what will happen next. We have at best informed guesses. So an attempt to hedge, say by locking in oil prices at $140 a barrel on the fear that they are going to increase to $250 a barrel, can wind up being a bad trading bet.[49] So even simple derivatives can be used well or poorly.

And the problem with many of the additions to the universe of derivatives is that on balance they have been highly detrimental. We will discuss at considerably greater length in later chapters the damaging systemic effects of credit default swaps (which are actually not derivatives, but got the derivatives' free pass anyhow). Even their alleged advantages are dubious and come at considerable cost, namely, bad incentives and information loss.

But the proof comes in the aggregate pudding. Although financial services industry lobbyists tout the value of derivatives in laying off risk and in lowering the cost of fund-raising, their main use now is creating more leverage and fabricating risk. Derivatives expert Satyajit Das has said that the volume of derivatives trading is considerably in excess of the level of pure risk transfer and related liquidity-providing, meaning a substantial portion is purely speculative.[50] In other words, no one should be shocked that there is gambling in Casablanca.

· · · · ·

There is a subtler problem with arguments based on theoretical economic models. Despite their distaste for verbal reasoning and analogy, economists rely on precisely those forms of argument in policy making, by assuming that if their fantasy realms are a "good enough" approximation of actuality, surely then their implications can be applied as if they were true. The notion of what is a "good enough" resemblance is seldom tested. And the theoretical results that have addressed that question are generally ignored.

Already, in 1956, R. G. Lipsey and Kelvin Lancaster published "The General Theory of the Second Best," also known as the Lipsey-Lancaster theorem.[51]

Recall that the situations that economists stipulate in theoretical models are idealized, usually highly so. Consumers are rational and have access to perfect information. There are no transaction costs. Goods of a particular type are identical. Capital moves freely across borders. Using these assumptions, or similar ones, the model is then shown to produce a global optimum.[52] This highly abstract result is then used to argue for making the world correspond as closely to the model as possible, by lowering transaction costs (such as taxes and regulatory costs) and reducing barriers to movements of goods and capital.

But these changes will not produce the fantasy world of the model. Doing business always involves costs, such as negotiating, invoicing, and shipping. Capital never moves without restriction. Buyers and sellers are never all knowing, and products are differentiated. Despite the pretense of science, it is a logical error to *assume* that steps that realize any of the idealized assumptions individually move the system closer to an optimum state. The Lipsey-Lancaster theorem examines this thinking and proves it to be false.

The article shows, first in narrative form, then with the required formulas, that if all the conditions for the ideal state cannot be met, *trying to meet anything less than all of them will not necessarily produce an optimum*. Partial fulfillment of equilibrium conditions may be positively harmful, forcing the economy to a less desirable state than it was in before. Thus simple-minded attempts to make the world resemble hypothetical optimizing models could well make matters worse.

In general, outcomes at least as good as any "second-best" reality can result from a wide variety of different policy choices. So, while abusing rarified economic models to grope toward a unique hypothetical ideal can be harmful, many different messy policy choices can lead to improvements over any current, imperfect state. There is no one, true road to economic perfection. Trudging naively along the apparent path set forth by textbook utopians may lead followers badly astray, despite the compelling simplicity of the stories they tell.

Consider an example: one area where economists are in near universal agreement is that more open trade is ever and always a good thing; those who question this thesis are dismissed as Luddites. Since economists believe that open trade is better, it follows that they favor reducing tariffs and other barriers (note: they are willing to make some exceptions for developing economies).[53]

Yet in the early 1990s, concern in the United States rose as more and more manufacturing jobs went overseas. Indeed, the tendency has gone ever further, as entry-level jobs in some white-collar professions like the law have now gone abroad. Indeed, in software, some experts have worried that there are so few yeoman positions left in the United States that we will wind up ceding our expertise in computer programming to India due to the inability to train a new generation of professionals here.

How did economists react? The typical responses took two forms. One was that there would be job losses, but based on the model, the effect would not be significant. The other was that since the net effect would be positive, the winners could subsidize the losers. Since mechanisms to do so (more progressive taxes to fund job retraining, assistance to move to regions with better job prospects) have not been implemented on a meaningful scale, this is cold comfort to those who were on the wrong side of this deal. And as we will see, the naive stance of the United States in trade policy against countries, like China and Japan, that pursue mercantilist policies designed to maintain trade surpluses, led to persistent U.S. trade deficits. Those in turn led to excessive borrowing, one of the fundamental causes of the crisis.

The trade prescription illustrates how economists' claims of rigor break down. They spend considerable time and energy either developing rarified theories about how the economy operates or performing studies that are narrow or based on limited data.[54] The argument for deregulation, stripped to its core, was that the idealized, frictionless economy with all-knowing hyperrational consumers looked great on paper, and the more we could make the real world conform with that Platonic ideal, the better off we would be.

Yet Lipsey and Lancaster illustrate that in some situations, unilaterally opening trade not only can make the country worse off, but can leave the world as a whole worse off as production migrates inefficiently.

The Lipsey-Lancaster theorem is a wrecking ball as far as the usefulness of economic theory is concerned. It says that when the fantasy state is unattainable (and it always is), there are numerous policy combinations that can achieve a next best state. However, economics as currently practiced offers little insight into how to choose among these manifold real-world options.

· · · · ·

Notwithstanding these problems, as of the mid-1950s, the new practices were starting to be hard-coded into the economics discipline as preferred approaches. While most within the profession view that change as entirely salutary, that perception is hardly universal. For instance, a 1998 paper by the respected economic historian Mark Blaug called economics "an intellectual game played for its own sake." Blaug saw the use, or perhaps more accurately, the abuse, of mathematical procedures as a fundamental failing:

> Economists have gradually converted the subject into a sort of social mathematics in which analytical rigor as understood in math departments is everything and empirical relevance (as understood in physics departments) is nothing. If a topic cannot be tackled by formal modeling, it is simply consigned to the intellectual underworld. To pick up a copy of *American Economic Review* or *Economic Journal*, not to mention *Econometrica* or *Review of Economic Studies*, these days is to wonder whether one has landed on a strange planet in which tedium is the deliberate objective of professional publication. . . . The result of all this is that we now understand almost less of how actual markets work than did Adam Smith or even Leon Walras.[55]

Blaug also dismissed some of the defenses made by economists, namely, that the current work was more progressive. For instance, game theory, then a hot area, Blaug argued, yielded predictable outcomes only in one-off, cooperative settings, a trivial subset of the real world of commerce. Repeat contests yield infinite equilibria, a distasteful outcome to economists. Moreover, game theory focuses on optimal strategies, and does not consider what should be the focus of inquiry, namely what strategies people actually use.

Another line of criticism comes from a surprising source: E. Roy Weintraub, a professor of economics at Duke University and the author of *How Economics Became a Mathematical Science*. Despite his dim view of those who object to the rise of mathematical formalism in economics, he nevertheless points out that it falls short of the widely held "hard science" ideal:

> Science proceeds by a series of conjectures and refutations, by which bold hypotheses are ruthlessly subject to attempts at falsification. A real science holds all propositions and theories to be provisional, while serious scientists attempt to refute particular conjectures and theories. Science progresses by the weeding out of error and this self-correcting process is what is meant by scientific progress. . . .
>
> The falsification of economic theory by empirical/statistical evidence is virtually unknown to economists. . . . [If judged by the standards of a science like physics,] Twentieth-century economic thought is a mélange of prescientific musings about social problems wrapped in the language of science, without any real science in evidence, and writing histories of economics is akin to writing histories of phrenology.[56]

In addition, most sciences are open to new methods, albeit with some time needed to overcome professional resistance. Innovative approaches usually start as a fringe activity, viewed with suspicion until their proponents can present successes and win converts. By contrast, economists have shown a surprising lack of willingness to utilize new techniques. For instance, economists have for the most part refused to consider adding systems dynamics to their toolkit.

Systems dynamics was developed by Jay Forrester of MIT. It looks at how factors like feedback loops can affect the operation of complex processes. One of the strengths of this approach is that it can identify when even simple systems might exhibit non-linear behavior, which is tech-speak for "suddenly function abnormally or break down completely." And the virtue of systems dynamics identifies how that break in operation came about.

So why didn't economics embrace systems dynamics? The reasons appear to be aesthetic and ideological. Systems dynamics looks a lot like . . . engineering. It uses flow charts, rather than daunting physics-like formulas. It is employed in disciplines like computer systems architecture and urban planning, decidedly more downscale than the hard science positioning to which economics aspires.

Prejudice against systems dynamics was inevitable, but it was made more acute by the fact that economists perceived that the systems dynamics cohort was trying to encroach on their turf. One of the directors of the Club of Rome, an effort in the 1970s to look at what now would be called sustainability, asked Jay Forrester to get involved. One of the results was that Forrester tried to build a model that "interrelates population, capital investment, geographic space, natural resources, pollution, and food supply."[57] Forrester presented the findings of version 1.0 of this model in his book *World Dynamics* in 1971. An international team descended on MIT to assist Forrester in developing a more comprehensive model. The findings were summarized in the 1972 book *The Limits to Growth.*[58]

Forrester considered his findings realistic and middle of the road, but they were seen, particularly in America, as Malthusian:

> Growth is a temporary process. Physical growth of a person ceases with maturity. Growth of an explosion ends with destruction. Past civilizations have grown into overshoot and decline. In every growth situation, growth runs its course, be it in seconds or centuries.[59]

The Club of Rome went to some length to be cautious about its dour forecasts, but the media put a sensationalistic spin on them. The fact that a second, far more comprehensive set of models prepared by researchers at Case Western came up with more hopeful conclusions did not serve to dispel the association with gloom and doom findings. Nevertheless, at least among economists, there appeared to be more than a bit of guilt by association, with a process being seen as discredited when any approach to such an ambitious undertaking probably would have failed.

One has to wonder if systems dynamics was dismissed not simply for having come up short in a highly visible trial, but also by association with Forrester's antigrowth message. Expansion is the measure of success in capitalism and therefore in economics too; telling economists that they had the wrong goals could seem like a personal affront.

. . . . .

Economics has not been completely closed to new thought that threatens the orthodoxy. There are two tolerated heresies (heresies in the sense that their basic tenets contradict neoclassical economics): information asymmetry and behavioral economics, both of which have produced a clutch of Nobel Prizes. But neither school is (or could be) well integrated into the neoclassical paradigm that has dominated policymaking since the early 1980s.[60]

Information asymmetry looks at how differences in knowledge between buyer and seller affect behavior and outcomes, namely, the party with less understanding winds up getting the short end of the stick. Put another way, if you sneak a look at someone else's hand, then you'll probably win more than someone who doesn't peek. That's because you know your cards and their cards and they only know their own cards. Yet a central assumption in the neoclassical paradigm is that buyers and sellers have perfect information, so in their tidy world, the sort of problems that Nobelist George Akerlof, who wrote a seminal paper that is considered the start of this line of thinking,[61] and his coreligionists, including Nobel Prize winners Joseph Stiglitz and Michael Spence, worry about could never come to pass. Anyone who signed up for a subprime mortgage would probably beg to differ.

Behavioral economics grew out of the work of psychologists, in particular Stanford's Amos Tversky and Nobel laureate Daniel Kahneman, who looked at how the way people behaved differed from a key assumption of neoclassical economics, namely that consumers are rational. Amazingly enough, people in the real world are often stupid and do things that waste money. Behavioral economists have conducted experiments in laboratory settings that confirm that most people have cognitive biases that undermine their ability to function as logically and consistently as the neoclassical framework dictates.

An additional set of ideas, which are relevant to the crisis but narrower in their implications, is that of principal/agent theories. The neoclassical construct assumes that individuals enter into transactions directly, while there are many times when people hire someone to act on their behalf. To put the principal/agent problem in sixth-grade terms, if you give another kid your lunch and tell him to hold it for you, he might eat your chocolate bar and then tell you that someone stole it.

Some economists point to these emergent fields to defend the discipline's abject failure to foresee and prevent the crisis. The fault isn't in the methods of the discipline; we just happened to grab the wrong implements from our toolbox. For instance, University of California, Berkeley economics and political science professor Barry Eichengreen argued in *The National Interest* that the profession did have relevant frameworks, such as behavioral economics, principal-agent issues, and information asymmetry, that would have given better insight but failed to use them.[62] Dani Rodrik, an economics professor at Harvard's John F. Kennedy School of Government, made a similar defense:

> Why, for example, did China's decision to accumulate foreign reserves result in a mortgage lender in Ohio taking excessive risks? If your answer does not use elements from behavioral economics, agency theory, information economics, and international economics, among others, it is likely to remain seriously incomplete.
>
> The fault lies not with economics, but with economists. The problem is that economists (and those who listen to them) became over-confident in their preferred models of the moment: markets are efficient, financial innovation transfers risk to those best able to bear it, self-regulation works best, and government intervention is ineffective and harmful.
>
> They forgot that there were many other models that led in radically different directions.[63]

The Evergreen State College economics professor Peter Dorman argues that the defenses are a whitewash:

> There were important theoretical developments during the past 20 years that can be drawn on to understand what went wrong. . . . Nevertheless . . . economic theory, taken as a whole, is culpable. The core problem is that each theoretical departure, whether it is a knotty agency problem or a behavioral kink, is inserted into an otherwise pristine general equilibrium framework. The only way you can get an article published in a mainstream economics journal (and therefore reproduce the conditions of your existence as an academic economist) is to present your departure piecemeal, showing that it exerts its effects even in an otherwise pristine universe. . . . This is why the picture Eichengreen paints for us, in which multiple unorthodox insights come together and interact synergistically, is never seen in a peer-reviewed economics journal. As a result, even though every organ of 1960's-era orthodoxy is mortally wounded, the entire body strides vigorously forward. That is a prime reason why, despite the labors of so many clever and right-thinking economic theorists, we are in this mess.[64]

The problem is even deeper than Dorman suggests. Information asymmetry (the idea that one party to a transaction knows more than the other and will take advantage of it), principal-agent issues (that people you hire might take advantage of you), and behavioral economics aren't merely other tools; they represent direct contradictions to mainstream thought.[65] If people will be foolish, lazy, or cheat, the certainty, the scientific mantle is nothing but the emperor's new clothes. You can't have "rigor" and accommodate perspectives that contradict the core assumptions required to produce it. Economists have instead either fallen in with the orthodoxy or (unless they were a pioneer in one of the alternative schools of thought) have been marginalized.

It's bad enough when a patient who needed heart surgery instead learns he had his gallbladder mistakenly removed. It adds insult to injury for the doctor to say, "Yes, I do know how to put in a stent." There is no apology, and no collective effort to change procedures within the field to make sure this sort of monstrous error is less likely to happen again.

· · · · ·

Some economists will complain that this criticism is dated, that the profession in the last decade is engaged in more empirical work than in the past. That change resulted from a fair bit of self-recrimination among economists, as highlighted by a 1991 study commissioned by the American Economic Association (AEA), that found considerable dissatisfaction among professors, graduate students, and employers outside academia.[66] The AEA recommended that the discipline focus more on how to apply economics and stress more use of practical tools. Nevertheless, a 1996 *New Yorker* article by John Cassidy, "The Decline of Economics," and a raft of 1990s books with titles like *Against Economics, The Death of Economics,* and *The Crisis of Vision in Modern Economic Thought,* all highlighted unhappiness with the state of the discipline. But even though the Cassidy article stirred considerable discussion, many economists felt its charges were incorrect, that theoretical work had fallen in importance.[67]

But is that defense valid? It misses the heart of the objection, which is not primarily about theory versus empirical work, but *how the hard science aspirations of economics have distorted a social science.* Economists are so close to the problem that shifts that appear significant to them do not represent fundamental change.

Just because economists are now doing more studies that grapple with information does not mean that the discipline has changed in a meaningful way. First, as Dorman's walking corpse image suggests, the ideas that form the foundation of modern economics are intact, despite visible, abject failures. Mainstream theories influence how many economists filter and organize information. If data, like signs of a housing bubble, did not fit the prevailing paradigm, they were rejected or rationalized. And that is one of the dangers of a theory-fixated methodology where theory became an object in and of itself, a focus Leontief protested. He argued in the late 1990s, as he had before, that economists were weak in their understanding of the economy and that the proper use of theory was to organize facts.[68]

Indeed, appealing or impressive theories are often accepted without being validated. In 1971, highly respected economist, game theorist, and future Nobelist Thomas Schelling published an article, "Models of Segregation," which set forth the concept called the "tipping point." Schelling developed an elegant analysis using coins of two kinds placed on a game board to simulate mixed-race neighborhoods. He demonstrated that it would take only a small proportion who preferred living with people of the same race to lead to a series of moves that would produce racial segregation. Each set of departures would leave some of the people who remained uncomfortable with the new neighborhood mix, precipitating more departures.

Aside from being a clever and novel approach, Schelling's explanation may have become popular for darker reasons: after a period of protracted white flight from decaying inner cities, it suggested that most people weren't really all that prejudiced; it took only a few bigots to produce ghettos.

Although the theory seemed obviously true in 1971, more recent work by New York University professor of economics William Easterly has found that Schelling's predictions were for the most part not borne out. Easterly tabulated census tract data from 1970 to 2000 for metropolitan areas and found that whites had departed neighborhoods that were mainly white to a greater degree than they had mixed-race neighborhoods.[69] Easterly did stress that his findings were only a single check of the theory over a particular time frame. But his analysis still serves to illustrate how appealing stories are too often accepted as received wisdom.

A second reason to doubt the significance of the vogue for empirical work is that it has very serious limits, and as it is practiced now, is not doing as much to improve the understanding of the economy, despite protestations to the contrary. Henry Kaufman, the well-respected former chief economist at Salomon Brothers, expressed doubts that economics was tackling the big issues of the day:

> What is missing today is a comprehensive framework that pulls together financial-market behavior and economic behavior. The study of economics and finance has become highly specialized and compartmentalized . . . another reflection of the increasingly specialized demands of our complex civilization. Regrettably, today's economics and finance professions have produced no minds with the analytical reach of Adam Smith, John Maynard Keynes or Milton Friedman.[70]

Third, as we saw with the minimum-wage research, it is hard for economics researchers to reach definitive conclusions. Those on each side of that debate have pointed to significant shortcomings in the studies presented by the
opposing camp.

One major limiting factor in empirical research is the need to find not only
high-quality information, but information of a specific type. It must be "clean"
numerical information in sufficiently large quantities. Too few observations and
you can't say anything much, certainly not enough to publish. But restricting inquiry to where the information can be tackled statistically, as opposed to allowing the inclusion of qualitative factors, severely limits study. It's a classic example
of "drunk under the street light" behavior.

David Leonhardt, an economics journalist with *The New York Times*, in a
2008 article, "Making Economics Relevant Again," found that the resurgent popularity of the discipline did not necessarily mean a corresponding increasing in
insight. Pop econ translates into studies on inconsequential topics, like sports
gambling, speed dating, or violent movies, areas that New School economist
Robert Heilbroner had excluded from economic inquiry in the 1980s.[71]

The reason for the often trivial studies? As discussed in a conference at Stanford, it's hard to find the right sort of information for serious inquiries. As David
Starrett noted:

> . . . it's very costly to collect data and it is not as high a quality as you would
> like. In some sense, the technique has outrun the ability to test. That's a fair crit-
> icism but I am not sure what to do about it. . . . to do good experiments on
> human subjects is virtually impossible, compared to the physical sciences.[72]

Now consider what Starrett is saying: *the research methods are driving what
research is being done, not vice versa.* In other words, as we suggested earlier, the
topics that are being investigated are defined not by what is or could be important, but simply by the availability of data.

Does that sound like an exaggeration? In fact, the discipline's reluctance to
consider qualitative research or proxies where hard information does not exist
constrains it. For instance, it would be very useful from a policy standpoint to understand the role that deregulation played in the housing bubble. One proposal
called for looking at mortgage data to see if the origination channel had an impact on how lax the lending standards were: mortgage brokers, unlike banks, were
unregulated. If the mortgages that brokers wrote were dodgier than the ones provided by banks, that would suggest that lack of regulation made a difference.

However, the graduate students who wanted to pursue this topic ascertained
that the information they could obtain from existing databases was neither complete nor comprehensive.

Now there are other ways to come at this question. An investigator could use a combination of data analysis in those markets where good information was available, and supplement it with qualitative analysis (obtaining information on underwriting standards from lenders of various types, say by interviewing former managers or third-party servicers). In fact, the qualitative analysis would serve as a useful cross-check on the statistical work. But that isn't the style for doing this sort of research, so a paper of that sort would be deemed inadequate from an academic standpoint, no matter how useful it might be from a policy perspective.

. . . . .

Even when economists do find topics they can analyze empirically, there is reason to believe that statistical methods are often, perhaps even routinely, abused in an effort to find correlations that could be published.

One risk of any analysis of a particular set of data is "overfitting." This occurs when the investigator finds a pattern that holds up well on that particular sample but would not show up strongly or at all if the test were run again.

Of course, it is often expensive to repeat an experiment, and medicine and the physical sciences have come up with other ways to check and make sure the results of a statistical analysis are valid. One is replication, which calls for repeating the original experiment or taking separate samples under the same conditions. Another is cross-validation, where the researcher parses his original data into at least two subsets. He develops the model on the first group of information, the "training set," and then applies the model to the other sets to see how well it proves out on the validation sets.[73]

Economists look for results to be statistically significant, and the threshold is that the odds are less than 5% that the relationship is random. *But that standard is valid only if the statistician runs a single regression analysis.* What happens if he instead does twenty regressions, tweaking the variables? Well, just by chance, he should expect to get one result that passes muster. That isn't proper, but is in fact done all the time.[74]

Similarly, a study by Alan Gerber and Neil Malhotra looked at publication bias. It showed that studies that established a statistically significant relationship were more likely to be published, which sadly is no surprise (dog bites man, or the absence of a statistically noteworthy relationship, isn't sexy unless it disproves other studies). But Gerber's and Malhotra's paper does confirm the value of meeting that magic 5% cutoff. Perhaps even more important, it also showed a suspiciously large number of study results that barely made the cutoff point, again suggesting data mining, supposedly a no-no.[75]

Columbia University's Jon Elster argues:

> I suggest that a non-negligible part of empirical social science consists of *half-understood statistical theory applied to half-assimilated empirical material.*[76]
> [Emphasis original.]

·   ·   ·   ·   ·

Early in the days of the Nixon administration, the new head of the National Security Council, Henry Kissinger, asked the RAND Corporation to brief him on options for Vietnam. He was pleased that Daniel Ellsberg, who had spent considerable time in the country, was chosen to lead the project. During one of the sessions, Ellsberg felt compelled to give Kissinger some advice:

> You've been a consultant for a long time, and you've dealt a great deal with top secret information. But you are about to receive a whole slew of special clearances, maybe fifteen or twenty, that are higher than top secret. . . .
> First, you'll feel exhilarated by some of this new information. . . . you will forget there was ever a time that you didn't have it, and you'll be aware of the fact that you have it now and most others don't . . . and that all these *other* people are fools.
> Over a longer period of time . . . you'll eventually become aware of the limitations of this information. . . . In the meantime, it will become difficult for you to *learn* from anybody who doesn't have these clearances. Because you'll be thinking as you listen to him, "What would this man be telling me if he knew what I know?" And that mental exercise is so tortuous that . . . you'll give it up and just stop listening. . . .
> The danger is you'll become something like a moron. You'll become incapable of learning from most people in the world, no matter how much experience they may have in their particular areas that may be much greater than yours.[77]

Less than two years later, Kissinger, in a meeting with Ellsberg, dismissed the group resignation of a team of consultants in Cambodia in protest of the policy of escalation because "They never had the clearances."[78] Yet the consultants were right. That course of action proved to be a failure.

Many economists have fallen into the same trap as Kissinger: they assume that only they are qualified to opine about matters economic. That in turn produces two considerable biases. First, if an argument about economics comes from a noneconomist and does not happen to fall in line with orthodoxy, it must be wrong. It will be rejected even if it contains useful information. Second, the scientific mantle gives economists the trump card in policy discussions even though, as we have seen, those aspirations are not borne out in practice.

When an elite succeeds in monopolizing discussion on a given topic, an additional danger is that members of the privileged caste can become overconfident. The economics discipline has had, in fact, attacks of hubris.

For example, in the 1960s, a clutch of Keynesians believed they could "fine tune" the economy—Walter Heller, then the head of the Council of Economic Advisers, compared it to adjusting the settings on a radio. As we saw in chapter 1, many economists in the United States congratulated themselves for having brought about the so-called Great Moderation, and ignored signs of underlying decay: a near-zero savings rate, stagnant average worker wages, a yawning, persistent trade deficit, and corporations refusing to invest in growth (in a break with past patterns, corporations had become net savers in an expansion[79]). And the profession's defensive, circle-the-wagons stance toward its failure to anticipate and prevent the crisis suggests a widespread reluctance to admit error, a sign of pride taking precedence over personal and social responsibility.

Some of this disciplinary hubris comes from the adoption of mathematical procedures. Users wind up trusting the results because they follow from the axioms, irrespective of their initial understanding or whether the conclusions jibe with data. Recall Samuelson's need to make Keynes conform with Samuelson's own Walrasian framework, even though it meant rejecting central, well-known facts about the Depression.

Even when findings are empirical rather than theoretical, economists can give them more credence than they warrant. People tend to see figures as "hard" outputs: objective, reliable, repeatable, verifiable. But a good deal of economic data, such as unemployment, inflation, and GDP growth, are statistical approximations, rather than "hard" data points, like the boiling point of water at a specific air pressure. The high value that economics puts on mathematics makes the field vulnerable to losing sight of the limitation of the information and methodologies employed.

▪ ▪ ▪ ▪ ▪

As we noted earlier, economists make arguments that resemble mathematical proofs. That makes it easy for a reader to assume, or for an economist to imply to his political patrons, that the argument is true in some sort of eternal sense, without contingencies. This technique excludes the public from policy making, even though almost without exception, the matters on which economists opine are of vital public interest.

But recall that Lipsey-Lancaster showed that there is no simple "right" answer to most economic problems, and so the idealized world of theory cannot be projected onto real-world situations: assuming "closer to fantasy is better".

may be dangerously incorrect. In other words, *even within the framework of theoretical economics,* it does not follow that a clear "best" among these secondary optima can be selected by reference to the calculated ideal. That means the choice legitimately falls in the realm of the political.

For example, in dealing with trade questions, considerations that economists brush away as Luddite concerns are suddenly revealed by Lipsey-Lancaster to be valid. Criteria like loss of industries with important know-how, income disparity, and job losses can legitimately be used as criteria to weigh one secondary position against another.

Since in the real world there is no one obvious, "right" answer to economic policy questions, stakeholders do have a legitimate voice in economic policy. Consider the matrix below:

Figure 2.2

	General Knowledge	**Specialist Knowledge**
Public Concern	Hygiene, Rules of the Road	Economics
Private Concern	Gardening, Nutrition	Medicine, Plumbing

The upper right-hand quadrant is problematic in a democracy, and that is where economists have situated themselves. The seemingly scientific underpinnings of economics confer authority upon its members in policy discussions. Moreover, as we saw with Dani Rodrik's example in the first chapter, how these experts come up with their conclusions is often impenetrable, not only to the public at large, but even to economists in other fields who don't know the procedures and standards of other specialties, much as you would not expect a gastroenterologist to be able to assess the diagnosis of a cardiologist.

The irony is that many economists profess to be advocates of individual freedom, yet they simultaneously wield the authority of medieval prelates speaking Latin, making them the only authorities qualified to read sacred texts and divine the right course for their flock. It's a profoundly antidemocratic stance.

But a heretical thought: does economics in fact properly belong in that quadrant? Do economists really make better policy decisions than intelligent, well-informed outsiders?

The danger of letting any group lay a claim to that upper right quadrant is that it creates a cadre that asserts the authority to exercise power without checks from the public at large. And that is no abstract concern. Even in the one area where there is a case to be made for the Fed preserving its independence, namely, monetary policy, its input comes almost solely from financial and business interests, and an economics profession that has increasingly taken up their cause. Only someone of the stature of Nobel Prize winner Joseph Stiglitz could argue, as he does, that labor should have a voice in interest rate policy.

The Federal Reserve, largely in the hands of monetary economists, is currently being used as an off-budget funding vehicle by the U.S. Treasury to fund bank rescues. The Federal Reserve is being used to evade normal budgetary processes, in particular, congressional approval—an abuse of Constitutional procedures.[80]

And why is there little public hue and cry? Because this is a realm of expert knowledge (finance, in this case). Most citizens cannot see through the shell game, and so are blind to the dangers to democratic processes inherent in ceding authority to a policy elite.

. . . . .

Despite economists' attempts to position themselves as benign umpires, their role is inherently political. Economics was originally called "political economy," yet the scientific branding of economics serves to turn attention away from its intrinsically political role and uses. The public is rightly concerned when an eminent medical researcher is discovered to have drug industry ties. There is much less sensitivity to similar conflicts or ideological leanings among economists.

As we will discuss at length in later chapters, economists haven't simply been enlisted to make the case for various interest groups. On some vital issues, they have helped frame the debate so as to shift it away from broad social concerns to narrow output-driven considerations, which has a far more powerful and pernicious effect than mere advocacy. By what right do economists get to shape what optimal *social* results are? Yet the fact that no other social science has a seat at the policy table, while the laity can be dismissed as ignorant and emotional, means that the views of economists lack a meaningful counterweight.

As a result, economic ideas are the perfect Trojan horse for remaking the realm of commerce and, to some degree, society as a whole, along ideological lines. We'll show in subsequent chapters the cost of radicalism masquerading as science.

CHAPTER 3

FINANCIAL ECONOMICS, COURTESY P.T. BARNUM

In recent decades, a vast risk management and pricing system has evolved, combining the best insights of mathematicians and finance experts supported by major advances in computer and communications technology. A Nobel Prize was awarded for the discovery of the pricing model that underpins much of the advance in derivatives markets. This modern risk management paradigm held sway for decades. The whole intellectual edifice, however, collapsed.

—Alan Greenspan

Hedge funds come in many flavors. In this richly paid, secretive world, the quantitatively oriented practitioners constitute an elite group. Often headed by traders who made small fortunes for their Wall Street employers before going out on their own, these firms use complex mathematical models to spot mispricings or anomalous relationships they anticipate will revert to long-established norms. Many trade in high volumes to exploit fleeting opportunities and borrow heavily to amplify returns.

In early August 2007, which, by the standards of what was to come, was only a somewhat disruptive trading period, many quant funds hit an air pocket. Worse, as the price declines led to margin calls, some of the funds were forced to sell portions of their holdings. That intensified the dislocation, since these exits pushed prices lower, precipitating further margin calls and more forced sales. Goldman Sachs, widely respected for its hedge fund expertise, saw its GEO fund go from down a few percentage points for the year to minus 30% within a week. Its flagship Global Alpha fund plummeted to a 27% loss.[1]

Goldman's chief financial officer, David Viniar, tried to explain the mess: "We were seeing things that were 25-standard deviation moves, several days in a row."[2]

For those who have even a passing acquaintance with statistics, the statement was absurd, an admission the trading models were rubbish, although that presumably was not what Viniar meant to convey.

Here, "standard deviation" was to used express the odds that an event would occur. When you plot data visually, for many phenomena found in nature, the results will cluster around a particular level, such as 98.6 degrees Fahrenheit for human body temperature, and "tail" off from that. The more extreme an event is, the further away it is from the median of that cluster, and it can be calculated as a standard deviation. The larger the standard deviation, the more unusual the occurrence (assuming, of course, that the phenomenon does follow a normal, or bell curve–shaped, distribution of outcomes).

A mere ten standard deviation event is roughly as likely as having the same person win a million-to-one lottery three or four days in a row. A fifteen standard deviation event is so improbable that the universe isn't old enough to expect one to have happened yet. Multiply those two ridiculously small odds together and you have a single twenty-five standard deviation event. Yet the Goldman CFO claimed that an occurrence so improbable that there are no analogies in our reality happened multiple times on successive days!

Viniar was not alone in this line of argument, although he was a bit more extreme; other quant funds complained of fifteen plus standard deviation events.

The market tumult in October 2008 made August look placid. The Dow Jones Industrial Average had two days where the price moved more than 10%. Assuming the statistical approaches used in the vast majority of risk management models (a normal distribution or bell curve) and using their measure of daily changes from 1971 through 2008, the economists Paul De Grauwe, Leonardo Iania, and Pablo Rovira Kaltwasser calculated that moves like that could occur only every 73 to 603 *trillion billion* years. They noted dryly:

Since our universe, according to most physicists, exists a mere 20 billion years we, finance theorists, would have had to wait for another trillion universes before one such change could be observed. Yet it happened twice during the same month. A truly miraculous event.[3]

It's easy to underestimate the significance of these comments. As we will discuss in more detail, the tools used by even the most analytically sophisticated traders were widely known to underestimate the risk of extreme events, otherwise known as tail risk. They blew up in a completely expected way; one financial journalist said that "terabytes" had been written on this very subject.[4]

Yet the traders nevertheless came to see their world through their models, even though they were aware of their limitations. And in a spectacular show of cognitive dissonance, they described the failure *in terms of the model's metrics*, rather than being able to state the simple truth that events moved to a region where these abstractions break down, at considerable cost to them and other investors caught in the downdraft of their efforts to escape big losses before they got even worse.

Gross underestimation of tail risk isn't the only way widely used financial models fall short. Two other assumptions every bit as fundamental also understate risk. One is that the prices of various investments move in relationship to each other in a consistent manner. Another is that markets are ever and always there, and that an investor can buy, hedge, and sell whenever he wants to. As we will see, not only are these assumptions bogus, but like the faulty treatment of tail risk, *they lead investors and intermediaries to see markets as more predictable and much safer than they really are.*

What is even more disturbing is that these shortcomings were recognized early on. Yet rather than abandon flawed theories, academics, investors, and traders for the most part embraced them. One reason came straight out of Thomas Kuhn's *The Structure of Scientific Revolutions:* it was more comfortable to stick with what worked, even if it only seemed to work. Users may also have feared that any replacement for these "mathed-up" fables would be at best rules of thumb. Reverting to simpler, more approximate methods would frustrate the ambitions of economists and deprive financial professionals of tools and a mantle of science that enhanced the image of markets and their industry.

The second argument was that these models worked so well on a day-to-day basis that it made perfect sense to rely on them. By that logic, it is perfectly safe to build on flood plains, since most of the time there are no floods. The shortcoming is that when these approaches failed, they failed spectacularly. Any trader or serious investor is likely to be in the market long enough to suffer the consequences of placing too much faith in this faulty technology.

. . . . .

Strange as it may seem, it wasn't all that long ago that financial markets were seen as too disreputable to constitute a proper subject for formal study. In 1900, a PhD candidate in mathematics, Louis Bachelier, presented his dissertation, "*Théorie de la Spéculation*," on bond prices and options, and got a lukewarm reception. Henri Poincaré, one of the judges, conceded that the paper had some original elements, but dryly noted that the subject matter was "distant" from the typical (as in preferred) lines of inquiry. Bachelier received a mere "*mention honorable*," insufficient to secure an appointment at a well-regarded institution. He spent much of his career teaching high school and serving from time to time as a university lecturer, finally winning a chair nearly thirty years after receiving his doctorate.[5]

Yet Bachelier's line of thinking, rediscovered in the 1950s, is a cornerstone of modern finance. He had detected a similarity between how heat diffuses through materials and price movements. The novel element of his work was to view price changes in terms of probabilities and to put himself in the position of an investor trying to determine whether to buy or sell, as opposed to trying to discern patterns after the fact.

The speculator does not know what is going to happen next. Even if he has a point of view ("inflation is rising, therefore bond prices will fall"), that does not tell him what will occur when the next bit of news hits the markets. Perhaps a government announcement shows price pressures are easing, making other investors (possibly even our original trader) change their minds and buy bonds. And myriad other developments will impact their prices, such as government deficits and changes in political alignments that might affect government tax and spending policies.

Thus according to Bachelier and his successors, an investor, lacking a crystal ball, would have to assume that any security has equal odds of going up or down from its current level on its next trade. It would therefore look like the results of a fair game of chance, such as flipping a coin. The resulting possible outcomes from a large number of coin tosses converges to a pattern often found in nature, a bell curve, or normal distribution, or what quants and statisticians prefer to call a Gaussian distribution, after the esteemed mathematician Carl Gauss.

These distributions are the foundation of many of the models used in financial economics, both in the sense of the decision aids (computer-based programs and tools to help make specific investment choices) and in the more general sense we used the term in chapter 2, abstractions that describe meaningful behaviors in a messy-seeming underlying reality.

A PRIMER ON GAUSSIAN DISTRIBUTIONS

Large samples of frequency data, such as the frequency with which we encounter individuals of a particular height, often approximate normal, or Gaussian, distributions. If you plot the number of people of a certain height (X axis) versus their actual height (Y axis), you will get a shape something like a bell–this is the normal distribution, and this is why it's sometimes called the bell curve. It is a very pervasive pattern in the frequency of natural phenomena but not universal—there are other kinds of distributions.

The variance and the standard deviation are the two most widely used measures of how dispersed (spread out) the data are within a sample. They are simply two ways of expressing the same information about data dispersion, since one can be calculated from the other. The variance is calculated as the average squared deviation of each event from the mean. The variance is often calculated with a numerator of n–1 instead and is called "Bessel's correction" and in some ways it gives a better estimate of the variance. In a distribution with sample values of 1, 2, and 3, the mean is 2 and the variance is:

$$\frac{(1-2)^2 + (2-2)^2 + (3-2)^2}{3} = 0.667$$

A standard deviation is the square root of the variance and is often denoted σ, or sigma. One of the tidy features of a normal distribution is that if you know its average (technically, its mean) and standard deviation, you can determine the percentile rank of any datapoint in the sample. As illustrated below, in a normal distribution roughly 68% of the possible outcomes lie within one standard deviation away from the mean, while 95% lie within two standard deviations:

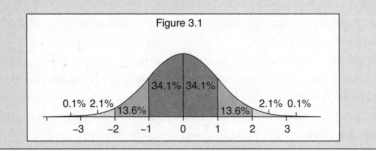

Figure 3.1

Bachelier's ideas remained fallow until they were discovered and put forward by Paul Samuelson in a thesis on options pricing, and developed further in the 1960s and 1970s by Samuelson and the University of Chicago's Eugene Fama. The result was the efficient markets hypothesis, or EMH. It is sometimes referred to as a "random walk" from the path securities prices take from their starting point, a term first coined in a different context by Karl Pearson, a seminal figure in the development of mathematical statistics,[6] and later popularized by economist Burton Malkiel.

The efficient markets school of thought holds that market prices reflect current information. The weak form of this theory is that past prices have no predictive power; you can't cut market data to devise a winning long-run strategy, which contradicts the beliefs of market technicians, who look to historical patterns for guidance. The semi-strong form holds that prices move quickly in an unbiased manner to incorporate new information, so investors cannot make money trading on news. The strong form states that prices incorporate all relevant information.[7]

This construct alone has had considerable impact, since the implication is that investors cannot consistently beat the market. That in turn led to the development of so-called passive investment strategies, in particular index funds. The premise is that it is better to minimize transaction costs and fees and buy the market (in some form) rather than pay extra for investment managers who in the long run cannot exceed the averages. Nevertheless, individuals and institutions spend considerable effort trying to do just that. Ironically, markets would not be efficient without parties searching for undervalued situations and bidding them up. In a sense, passive investors are free riding on the (presumably) fruitless effort of active players to achieve superior performance.

· · · · ·

A second cornerstone of financial economics came more than fifty years after Bachelier from an economics PhD named Harry Markowitz. A happenstance chat with a stock broker led Markowitz to choose the equity market as the topic for his thesis. The young University of Chicago economist had also just taken a course in operations research, in those days the hotbed of advanced statistical work.[8]

Markowitz puzzled over how investors behaved. One of the stock-picking bibles of the day recommended calculating possible values of a stock by discounting estimated future dividend streams and comparing them with the current price. To deal with the uncertainty over future outcomes, the author recommended coming up with different possible scenarios, weighing them by an assumed probability, and totaling the result.

But how would you apply that to a portfolio? If you really could pick a phenomenal stock, you'd hold only that. But real-world investors didn't do that, they held a variety of securities instead to protect against the possibility that things don't pan out. Markowitz concluded they were balancing risk against return, which led him back to his statistical training. Risk could be thought of as variability in returns. For instance, the stock price of a company with a very promising but unproven technology could move a great deal, making it highly risky, while a company with a much more predictable business, like a utility, would have a comparatively more stable price.

One of the notions in Markowitz's thesis was that of an efficient portfolio. For whatever level of risk an investor is willing to accept, there is a corresponding portfolio that will provide the maximum return attainable. The various possible combinations of stocks were idealized in Markowitz's original paper as a rough circle illustrating all possibilities, with the best tradeoff of risk and reward, the most risk-efficient, on the perimeter, or the "frontier."

Markowitz had created an elegant construct, but on limiting assumptions. Markowitz had assumed a normal distribution for stock market risk. In addition, creating efficient portfolios requires *accurate projections* of earnings, prices, and volatility for all stocks (and as real-world investors buy more than stocks alone, similar projections are needed for an even larger array of instruments).

Note that there is already some circularity in the logic. To create the prized "efficient portfolio" you need to know the future! But the reason for diversifying and creating a portfolio in the first place was to diversify risk because the investor does not know what will happen and thus is not willing to put all his money in one instrument. But if you did know future prices, you would simply buy the security that would go up the most over your chosen time horizon.

Moreover, for each stock, an investor also needs to ascertain how much its price moves in relationship to the universe of other stocks, or what its "covariance" or correlation is. For the New York Stock Exchange (NYSE) alone, that entails millions of calculations, since it requires running stock-to-stock correlations, which then need to be recomputed as prices move.[9]

Oh, and on top of that, an investor somehow has to be able to divine future correlations, not past ones. But if you already know what will happen, that should be trivial.

Milton Friedman, who was one of the thesis judges, argued that Markowitz could not receive his PhD because the paper was on mathematics, not economics. Apparently that was not a serious objection, because Markowitz was awarded his doctorate.

Markowitz's work was pioneering. One of Markowitz's algorithms was novel enough to warrant publication in a separate journal, and his *Journal of Finance* paper was on the leading edge of the model-building revolution. But its computational demands meant it was not usable in the field at the time, and it attracted only limited interest from economists.[10]

. . . . .

Serendipity helped lay the next foundation stone.

In 1960, an economics doctoral candidate, William Sharpe, visited Markowitz, who was working at RAND on research such as applied mathematics of linear programming. Sharpe, who had just joined RAND as a junior economist, had abandoned his thesis topic and was in need of a replacement.

Sharpe had done coursework in finance and came across the new theoretical work, including Markowitz's paper based on his dissertation. Even though Markowitz regarded his effort as complete, one issue had not been tidied up. Correlating securities information among all the possible stock pairs was a computational nightmare. If the returns could instead be tied against an "underlying factor," it would vastly reduce the number of calculations. Markowitz introduced Sharpe to this problem and served as an informal advisor.[11]

Sharpe made a number of simplifying assumptions. He posited the existence of the economist's favorite condition, an equilibrium, which we would now call a market clearing price, in this case for the entire market. He further assumed that all investors had the same estimates of variances, expected returns, and correlations with the as-yet-undiscovered underlying factor. That in turn implied everyone holds the same portfolio, which is the "market portfolio," the entire market itself.

Rather than correlating the volatility of each stock with every other stock, an investor could now simply determine its correlation with the market. Sharpe called that factor beta. High beta stocks (think novel, potential high-growth stocks) are more volatile than most equities, while safe, predictable ones are low beta and thus are more stable than the market as a whole.

With these changes, the efficient investment frontier was no longer the perimeter of an imagined lopsided circle, but a straight line, now stylized as the "risk/return tradeoff" that graces innumerable textbooks, with higher returns requiring higher levels of risk.

This construct is called the Capital Asset Pricing Model (CAPM), which soon became a popular method for assessing a wide range of investments, not just stocks. For instance, if Stodgy Co. is looking to invest in Sexy Startup, it

Figure 3.2

Risk/Return Tradeoff

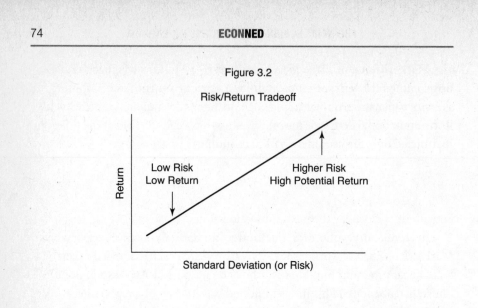

Standard Deviation (or Risk)

could apply CAPM to analyze the problem. The buyer would identify the cash flows that he thought the project would throw off, and then discount them back by the return required for companies like Sexy Startup.* If the discounted cash flows are higher than the purchase price, Stodgy Co. should proceed with the initiative.

Despite its conceptual advances, the CAPM did have a few loose ends. The biggest was that the concept of "the market" was ill defined. The definition in Sharpe's dissertation, the stock market and beta, the measure of volatility relative to broad indexes, is still widely used.

· · · · ·

A final breakthrough came years later, in the early 1970s.

While the edifice of financial economics was largely complete, an issue that had remained unsolved, at least to the satisfaction of academics, was the pricing of options. Options, along with futures, are important risk-management tools; the absence of a methodology was a nagging gap.

A future is a comparatively straightforward beast: it's the obligation to buy or sell a certain amount of a specified traded good, called the underlying, at a

---

* "Discounting" is a way to adjust for the fact that money received in the future is worth less than cash in the bank today. For instance, if a perfectly safe investment will pay 4% over a one-year time frame, an investor would need to receive $104 in one year for that to be equivalent to $100 today. "Discounting" takes those future cash flows and uses interest rate assumptions to reduce, or "discount" them to what they would be worth, in real terms, today.

certain date. Markets for agricultural futures appear to date as far back as ancient Babylon. The modern version includes not only markets on commodities, such as heating oil, frozen orange juice, and metals, but also financial futures, such as stock indexes and Treasury bonds.

Options, by contrast, are a *right but not an obligation* to buy or sell a certain amount of an asset at a specified price (the "strike price"). Like futures, options are time delimited. European-style options can be exercised only on their expiration date; American-style options can be cashed in any time prior to the expiration date.

Options and futures are derivatives, since their prices *derive* from the price of another asset.

Many economists had broken their pick on the problem of option pricing. The usual stumbling block was that the value seemed to depend on the price of the underlying at expiration. While assuming foreknowledge about prices was helpful in Sharpe's situation, it led to only trivial outcomes here.

Fischer Black made the first conceptual breakthrough. An applied mathematician who had dabbled in artificial intelligence, he came to be interested in businesses and investing through a stint at the consulting firm Arthur D. Little, then worked at the University of Chicago, and later, MIT.

Black decided to abandon the assumption of knowing the final price and developed some formulas, but the type of math involved was not his strong suit. Stymied, he put the work aside.

A weekly workshop at MIT, organized by Paul Samuelson, Franco Modigliani, and Paul Cootner, looked at new ideas in finance. Through it, in 1968, Black met a young Canadian economist, Myron Scholes, and they reopened the options pricing question.[12] Another young economist, an assistant to Samuelson with a keen interest in markets, Robert Merton, provided useful input.

The resulting formula identified key variables that affect what an option is worth: where the price of the asset is now compared to the strike price (where the price has to be for the bet to show a profit), how volatile the underlying asset tends to be, how much time before expiration, and prevailing returns on risk-free investments (buying options is more fraught than holding Treasuries, so the expected payoff needs at a bare minimum to exceed the returns of holding Treasuries over the same time period).[13] For instance, a call option is the right to buy an instrument at a specified price. It is "out of the money" if exercising that right is unprofitable right now (which in this case occurs if the instrument is at a lower price than the strike price in the option; you can't use the option to buy the instrument cheaply and sell it in the market at a higher price). That option is not going to be worth very much on the day before expiration if the underlying asset isn't very volatile. The investor would have to see an un-usually large price movement in his favor in a very short time for the option to pay off before it expires. However an option that is equally out of the money on an asset that shows large daily price movements with, say, two months to ex-piration will be worth considerably more, since the combination of time value and volatility means that an investor could see a payoff between now and the option expiration.[14]

Black and Scholes found it difficult to get the resulting paper published and it saw the light of day in 1973. A few years later, it was changing industry prac-tice. Since calculators were not permitted on the floor, and would have been too slow and cumbersome, traders took to using computers to generate cheat sheets, which the floor traders would carry, often rolled to display the prices most rel-evant to them that day. By 1975, Fisher Black had a tidy business selling monthly updates of theoretical prices of all U.S. exchange–traded options on loose sheets of paper, making them suitable for use in the pits.[15]

Options traders in the Chicago exchanges had used pricing methods, such as those of gambler and mathematician Ed Thorp, that had much in common with the approaches of Black and Scholes. Nevertheless, pricing started to align closely with the levels dictated by the new formula. However, Nassim Nicholas Taleb, himself an options trader, contends that these older methods made al-lowances for risks that the famous Black-Scholes model ignores.[16]

Despite the growing visibility and real-world impact of financial econom-ics, only a few mainstream academics like Samuelson had taken interest. In fact, for the most part, financial economics had always sat at business schools and had its own specialized publications, creating a physical and cultural gap.[17] The same impetus to move to science-like practices that influenced economics in the im-mediate post–World War II era also influenced business schools, which as of the early 1950s were an intellectual backwater. Financial economics was one of the focuses of this effort. While Carnegie Tech was at the vanguard, the two most sig-nificant hubs of activity were the University of Chicago, where Markowitz and Sharpe met, and MIT, where Samuelson, Black, Scholes, and many other schol-ars worked.[18] And it wasn't just pit traders who were interested in new theories; as early as 1959, major brokerage firms sponsored research (the aura of science gave further legitimacy to markets and smart investors are always looking for an edge).[19]

But even at schools with influential economics departments, financial econ-omists were a breed apart. Indeed, Larry Summers, who wrote a paper on the EMH,[20] described the difference between traditional economists and their fi-nancial markets cousins via "ketchup economics"[21]: both types are interested in price changes, but most economists would be concerned with fundamental factors that could determine ketchup prices, like tomato harvests, inflation, wage trends, and price competitiveness of ketchup substitutes. Financial economists would only look at prices in the ketchup market.

The narrow focus of financial economists, and in particular, their lack of interest in the institutional infrastructure within which markets sit, that is, the financial system, no doubt played a part in the failure of mainstream economics models to incorporate banking, credit, or the financial system as a whole, blinding them to the damage that errors in their theories could produce. If you see investments as a contained realm of self-interested, informed actors, the implication is that any bad ideas will be quickly weeded out and the fallout would be limited (one investor's loss would be another's gain). Even though some economists did recognize that markets as a whole could be overpriced (history was too full of examples of manias to rule that out), the idea that the new financial technology would become a powerful implement for blowing vast new bubbles was beyond anyone's ken.

• • • • •

By 1979, the main elements of modern finance theory were complete, although the efforts of sophisticated mathematicians pushed the margins out further, supplementing rather than transcending Black-Scholes and some of the other conceptual breakthroughs.[22] Newer theories built on the ideas or assumptions of the older ones.

Even more impressive was the way these ideas came to shape markets and investments. MIT professor Stephen Ross, himself responsible for important contributions to financial economics (the arbitrage pricing theory and the binomial options pricing model), wrote, "When judged by its ability to explain the empirical data, option-pricing theory is the most successful theory not only in finance, but in all of economics."[23]

Financial author and economist Peter Bernstein goes further:

> Despite its rigid assumptions about investor rationality and the role of information, the Efficient Markets Hypothesis remains the standard by which we judge market behavior and manager performance. Today, as in the past (and in some ways even more so than in the past) only a precious few investors have found strategies to beat the markets with any acceptable degree of consistency. . . . Markowitz's risk/return tradeoff is central to all investment choices. . . . The beta of the Capital Asset Pricing Model is no longer the single parameter of risk, but investors cannot afford to ignore the distinction between the expected return of an asset class and the risk in decisions to outperform the asset class . . . the Black-Scholes-Merton insights . . . have pervaded every market for every asset all around the world.[24]

Bernstein alludes to a very important change in the investment management industry. Historically, brokers and fiduciaries were judged informally, for instance, by whether they delivered decent returns (say, in excess of bond yields) and didn't lose money. Moreover, managers were not required to specialize. A manager who typically invested in U.S. stocks might buy a piece of a Canadian trust that owned drilling rights if he thought it fit his client's profile.

Now managers are expected to focus narrowly and their performance is measured against style benchmarks. A healthcare stock manager would be penalized for "style drift" were he to also buy shares in a defense technology company that seemed promising. Beating the benchmark is everything, even if it means losing money. For instance, if a farsighted equities manager had decided to sell everything and go into cash in fall 2007, he would be applauded by some clients but written off by the professional fund consultants who act as gatekeepers to big investors like endowments, pension funds, and insurance companies. The theory is that it is the client's (read: "the fund consultant's") job, not the fund manager's, to decide how much exposure to have to various strategies (stocks, bonds, cash, foreign stocks, foreign bonds, commodities, etc.), based on models that measure correlation among these various approaches.[25]

The beta and other measures of correlation to evaluate stocks, asset allocation models, index funds, and the valuation of mergers and venture capital investments all are based on the concepts developed in the 1950s through the 1970s. In addition, another important idea from that era, the Modigliani-Miller theory, held that a company's capital structure (that is, its ratio of debt to equity) and its dividend policy were irrelevant to its total value. That implied there was no particular reason for a company to take the extra effort to maintain the top credit rating, a triple A or AAA. In the early 1980s, thirty-two nonfinancial companies were in that exclusive group.[26] By 2009, there were only four.[27]

Regulators have also embraced these new techniques. One of the progeny of these new techniques is a widely used risk-management tool called Value at Risk, or VaR. VaR is a set of models that measures the likelihood of loss across a portfolio, even if that portfolio includes diverse assets and exposures. The beauty of it to non-math savvy decision makers like top management and regulators is that VaR provides a simple, single output, making it user friendly and keeping its complexity under the hood. This tool calculates the maximum dollar loss assuming a normal distribution to a specified probability over a specific time frame (generally not very long, since financial firms trade actively, so their portfolio composition changes). So if a large broker-dealer uses a 99% threshold, a weekly VaR of $15 million means that the odds are 99% you will not lose more than that amount (most big financial firms look at VaR at either the 95% or 99% certainty). The figures were wonderfully reassuring and made it easy to communicate with the not–statistically savvy. (We discuss VaR at greater length in chapter 7).

But the financial engineers had erected an edifice on quicksand. Nothing so complicated can be measured to that degree of precision. And the worst was that everyone was well aware of the problems, yet kept building.

▪ ▪ ▪ ▪ ▪

The troublemaker had surfaced in 1962, years before the publication of the Black-Scholes model, decades before the widespread adoption of Value at Risk.

Even by the standards of elite mathematicians, Benoit Mandelbrot was a wonder. Born in Poland, educated in France, Mandelbrot had an unusual intuitive capacity and could often immediately visualize complex mathematical problems. He invented an entire class of mathematics called fractal geometry. While earlier mathematicians such as Gottfried Leibniz, Bertrand Russell, and Mandelbrot's mentor, Paul Lévy, had made some important initial observations, the area that Mandelbrot later described as fractals was once regarded as a mere oddity. Over his career Mandelbrot took this construct much further, showing it to be far more significant than it had appeared to be.

Mandelbrot was an itinerant intellectual, working at Cal Tech, the University of Paris, the Institute for Advanced Study at Princeton, the University of Lille, and the IBM Research Center, in fields as diverse as aeronautics, statistical thermodynamics, computer science, income distribution, and mathematical linguistics. Unlike most scholars, who build within established paradigms, Mandelbrot was drawn to "the curious and bizarre."[28]

Mandelbrot had taken an interest in probability, both through his studies with Lévy, who had a family of probability distributions named after him, and his work in linguistics and economics.

And probability assumptions were central to the emerging field of financial economics. It was taken as a given that securities prices moved in a random fashion; that was the core of the EMH, and the later theories built on that. But what sort of randomness?

That question is not trivial. There are many types of randomness. All the models in the financial economics edifice assume a normal distribution. But not only is a normal distribution the most tractable form of randomness from a mathematical standpoint, it is also the least prone to wild extremes.

By contrast, there are types of random behavior that can be characterized mathematically, yet the resulting distributions *elude the explicit mathematical formulation that economists traditionally aim for.*

The Lévy distribution family is an in-between case. Lévy distributions have a property called "stability," which characterizes any distribution that will look roughly the same whether you take a thousand samples or a million.

Another property of Lévy distributions is "alpha." Alphas can range from zero to two. The lower the alpha, the wilder the distribution.

One limit case, when alpha is two, is the economists' best friend, the Gaussian distribution, which is familiar and easy to manipulate directly in formulas. But when alpha is any value less than two, the required mathematics becomes much more difficult, and the prospect of coming up with the sort of "proofs" that economists prefer becomes remote.[29]

However, these supposedly exotic distributions are for the most part deemed irrelevant to working statisticians. In classic drunk under the street light fashion, they stick to what is "tractable" or fits well with their tool kit, no matter how important the more difficult phenomena might prove to be. Yet again and again as we look at the crisis, we will see that the preference for computational convenience helped pave the road to disaster.

■   ·   ■   ·   ■

Probability is all about chance, and chance played a role in Mandelbrot turning his attention to financial markets. He had been invited to Harvard to give a talk and dropped in to visit the professor who invited him. He saw on the professor's blackboard a drawing that was identical to one Mandelbrot planned to use in his lecture. Surprised, Mandelbrot learned this was a plot of cotton prices. It also happened to fit the pattern of a joint distribution of two Lévy variables.

Mandelbrot got his hands on the cotton pricing data, which was the longest daily time series of trading prices extant, going back to the 1880s. He crunched the data on a daily, weekly, and monthly basis. All showed price movements far more dramatic than for a normal or even a log-normal distribution, far more consistent with the untamable Lévy distribution. Data on grain prices, railroad stocks, and interest rates showed the same tendencies.

■   ·   ■   ·   ■

Mandelbrot and his ideas began to circulate in the financial economics community. At first, the reception was positive. The European polymath became an informal thesis advisor to University of Chicago economist Eugene Fama, who had found that the prices of the members of the Dow Jones Industrial Average were indeed not "normal" but were what statisticians called "leptokurtic," with high peaks, meaning they had more observations close to the mean than in a normal distribution, but also much fatter tails.[30] In lay terms, that means day-to-day variability is low, but when unusual events occur, variability both is more extreme and occurs more often than would occur with a normal distribution. MIT's Paul Samuelson and other economists started looking into Lévy distributions and their implications.[31]

The problem with Mandelbrot's work, however, was it threatened the entire edifice of not simply financial economics, but also the broader efforts to use formulas to describe economic phenomena. Lévy distributions didn't merely have difficult math; that might have been an intriguing challenge. There wasn't even a way to calculate Lévy's "alpha" reliably, although Fama's efforts with market data did show that it was less than two, which confirmed the fear that the distributions were not normal.[32]

The backlash was predictable. MIT professor Paul Cootner, who later published a book of essays on the random-walk hypothesis, tore into Mandelbrot at a winter 1962 meeting of the Econometric Society:

> Mandelbrot, like Winston Churchill before him, promises us not utopia but blood, sweat, toil, and tears. If he is right, almost all of our statistical tools are obsolete. . . . Almost without exception, past econometric work is meaningless. Surely, before consigning centuries of work to the ash pile we should like to have some assurance that all our work is not truly useless. If we have permitted ourselves to be fooled this long into thinking the Gaussian assumption is valid, is it not possible that the [Lévy] revolution is similarly illusory? At any rate, it would seem desirable not only to have more precise and unambiguous evidence in favor of Mandelbrot's hypothesis as it stands, but also to have some tests with greater power against alternatives that are less destructive of what we know.[33]

But Churchill had been right. The British prime minister had advocated a difficult, perilous, and ultimately successful course of action, yet Cootner perversely invoked him to argue instead for a failed status quo. He wanted assurances that exploring new terrain would be successful, but that isn't the way a paradigm shift works. Indeed, Lévy distributions might not provide a comprehensive solution, but the point is to move toward better approximations, particularly when the existing ones have serious shortcomings.

Strip Cootner's objections to their core, and they resemble those of a Japanese bank officer, a client of the management consulting firm McKinsey & Company, when he was told of modern asset-liability techniques at a time when the

Japanese lagged badly behind the state of the art. He listened intently, then leaped up and stormed about the room, declaring:

> We are barbarians. We live in a little village. We are happy believing the world is flat. You tell us the world is round. We do not want to know!

To his credit, the Japanese executive, unlike the financial economics elite, did have the good sense to know his resistance was not in his best interest. Even a rigorous thinker like Fama decided to take comfort from the fact that longer stock-price time series looked closer to a normal distribution than the five-year data he had looked at initially.[34] While Fama's results showed that there were some limits to the effectiveness even of Lévy distributions in describing market behavior, they did little to revive enthusiasm for normal distributions among serious analysts of market statistics. Indeed, most experts have largely fallen in with Mandelbrot, recognizing that various sorts of alternate distributions are much better approximations than normal distributions to financial market trading data.

· · · · ·

Mandelbrot's findings were a fundamental blow to economic theory, and have been recently popularized by Nassim Nicholas Taleb, who describes the realm where normal distributions work as "Mediocristan" and the realm where wilder forms of randomness apply as "Extremistan" and shows how most social, economic, and market outcomes reside there.

Other elements of the financial economics superstructure started to look shaky. The CAPM essentially fell apart. One of the problems has been defining the "market" against which individual assets were valued. In principle, it should be much broader than the stock market, since investors buy more than stocks, and perhaps should include all investable assets.

Another fundamental proposition in CAPM was that that investors could borrow unlimited amounts at the risk-free rate. Even Sharpe himself acknowledged that making that assumption more realistic, namely, that real-world borrowers pay a premium to the U.S. Treasury, face credit constraints, and pay even higher premiums with more leverage, was fatal to his construct:

> The consequences of including such aspects of reality are likely to be disastrous in terms of the usefulness of the resulting theory. . . . The capital markets line no longer exists. . . . Moreover, there is no single optimal combination of risky securities; the preferred combination depends upon

the investors' preferences. . . . The demise of the capital markets line is followed immediately by that of the security market line. The theory is in a
shambles.[35]

At that time (1970) Sharpe nevertheless argued for continuing to use
CAPM, invoking Friedman's endorsement of unrealistic assumptions and the
belief that even a flawed theory was better than no theory.

But more work in the 1980s found continued shortcomings with CAPM
and the EMH. The final blow came in 1992, in an article by Sharpe's former student Eugene Fama and then University of Chicago professor Kenneth French,
colloquially called the "beta is dead" paper. The scholars looked at two anomalies that should not have persisted if CAPM was correct, namely, that stocks
with a low price-to-book value outperform, and stocks with a high price-to-
earnings ratio tend to lag. Fama and French found that these two factors explained most of the difference in the performance of individual stocks, hence
CAPM was moot.[36]

Not only have these constructs been demonstrated to have fatal theoretical
and empirical flaws, but many of their creators no longer defend them. Sharpe
in recent interviews points out that all pricing models rely on expectations, and
historical data cannot provide a reliable guide.[37] Markowitz has abandoned equilibrium models and is now experimenting with simulations to see what happens when market actors have rational and irrational preferences of various
sorts.[38]

And the loyalists have not helped their cause either. The Black-Scholes options pricing model is employed pervasively in hedging and risk management,
despite the widespread knowledge that it does not capture extreme events, the
sort that can wipe out portfolios and firms.

But as mentioned earlier, fat tails are far from the only problem with the
theories on which most financial models are based. That failing simply came to
light earliest and has received the most attention in the popular media. Two others, correlation risk, which vexed Sharpe's CAPM, and liquidity risk, are at least
as damaging. As with tail risk, commonly used models greatly understate these
additional risks, with the results that traders, investors, and firms routinely put
themselves in far more danger than they realize. Even worse, the beguiling, false
precision of the models makes investors believe that they do understand the
downside, when history, both of the crisis itself and revealing earlier episodes,
says otherwise.

Myron Scholes and Robert Merton, both of whom received Nobel prizes for
their work on the Black-Scholes pricing model, were the most celebrated of the

star-studded management team at hedge-fund Long-Term Capital Management (LTCM), which famously used state-of-the-art quant techniques. Scholes and Merton had advised John Meriwether at Salomon Brothers; Meriwether built a wildly profitable arbitrage group and decamped with key members of that team to start LTCM.[39] It blew up spectacularly in 1998 and nearly brought down the financial system with it.

The firm made two glaring errors. The first was not paying attention to liquidity risk, that is, the size of its positions relative to the markets it was in. In some cases, there was no way for them to exit (at least anything other than very gradually) without having a price impact. This was a disastrous mistake, almost embarrassingly fundamental. Graybeard traders unversed in modern techniques are very attentive to the size of their inventories relative to normal trading volumes. Yet the LTCM team, like the quants at the beginning of the chapter, came to see the world through their models, and the models assumed "continuous markets," meaning an exit would always be available, and did not treat overly large holdings as problematic.

One of the reasons for this bizarre blindness to the dangers of huge positions (LTCM came to hold 10% of the interest-rate swaps market,[40] an inconceivably hazardous choice for a firm using a lot of borrowed money) was faith in a bit of voodoo called dynamic hedging.

In dynamic hedging, your protection lies not in selling to limit losses if conditions worsen, but by using hedges. However, as Paul Samuelson, who remained somewhat skeptical of fancy financial technology despite his keen interest, said, "There is no such thing as a perfect hedge."[41] In dynamic hedging, the offsetting positions need to be adjusted, typically several times a day, precisely because they are not exact hedges.

The problem with this approach, like many of the nonperforming airbags that pervade the realm of finance, is that they often don't work, or even worse, backfire in difficult markets. The relationship between the price of the hedge and the underlying blows out in some unexpected way, so the trader needs to make a big adjustment precisely at the time when markets have gotten very thin, so making any trade, particularly a large one, will result in an even worse price.

The result is that the only way out for the trader is to sell, which is what his hedges were to help him avoid. And he may have no choice if he is getting margin calls.

LTCM's second big mistake was making the same bet, in trader-speak "short vol" or volatility, in a whole range of markets that were supposedly uncorrelated.[42] "Short vol" means the investor is gambling that when market prices become turbulent, they will revert and become a lot more placid than the consensus view among traders. But as anyone who tried shorting stocks in the dotcom era painfully remembers, what seems to be irrational behavior can become even more extreme before it reverses. But the giant hedge fund thought it had reduced its exposure to that danger by placing a lot of supposedly only slightly related wagers of that sort.

Yet in a crisis previously uncorrelated markets move together. Investors dump risky assets and flee for safety. So the protection supposedly offered by diversification proves illusory.

Two financial crises in close succession, a one-two punch to the markets, sent the once esteemed hedge fund over the brink. The Asian crisis of 1997 roiled financial markets around the world. The Russian default of 1998, a completely unexpected event, served as the second body blow, producing losses of an extent and magnitude not foreseen in LTCM's models. And since the giant fund worked with large amounts of borrowed money, over twenty-five times its equity,[43] it moved quickly toward collapse, saved only by a Federal Reserve–orchestrated rescue.[44]

Remarkably, the LTCM partners refused to believe that there was anything wrong with their approach, repeated the experiment, and got the same results. Scholes went on to found a second hedge fund, Platinum Grove, which lost 38% of its value and halted redemptions in 2008,[45] and has fired nearly two-thirds of its staff.[46] John Meriwether's new firm, JWM Partners, closed its main fund in the summer of 2009 after losing 44% of its value from September 2007 through February 2009.[47]

The collapse of multi-strategy hedge fund Amaranth in August and September of 2006 was almost a rerun of LTCM, albeit with far less collateral damage. Like LTCM, the fund was perceived to have considerable risk-management acumen, but post-mortems revealed it had failed to understand the dangers of correlation changes. Again like LTCM, Amaranth ignored liquidity risk and held nearly 10% of the contracts in natural gas futures, a breathtaking gamble. Any position that large, even in a very actively traded market, will prove very difficult to adjust quickly. It might pay off for a buy and hold investor to make such a bold wager, but a firm working with large amounts of borrowed money needs to be more fleet of foot. Adding insult to injury, when the fund was liquidated, the book was sold at what appeared to be a $1.4 billion discount to market prices (on top of roughly $4.4 billion of trading losses).[48] That illustrated the cost of ignoring liquidity risk. When the trading book had to be sold to satisfy creditors, the discount needed to unwind such a big position quickly was over a billion dollars below the "market" price, which is based on normal trading activity.

. . . . .

Even though most risk managers regard correlation risk as more troubling than fat tails, Wall Street denizens fell for another approach that minimized it, to their collective undoing. And this mishap, a major element in the current crisis, was a far more widespread error, involving every firm on Wall Street, major UK and European capital markets firms, and numerous credit market investors.

David Li, a quantitative analyst, had published a paper in 2000 in the *Journal of Fixed Income* with an elegant formula called the Gaussian copula function.[49] It was heralded as a major breakthrough and was implemented far more rapidly and broadly than the Black-Scholes option pricing model had been. The formula offered a seemingly better way to model correlation.

But the entire premise was a fraud. Any approach that tries to model correlation has to assume that the relationships will behave in a predictable way. It is one thing to use past patterns as a heuristic ("the dollar and gold tend to move in opposite directions") and be aware that that relationship is far from foolproof, and quite another to build elaborate pricing formulas and products on a rotten foundation. Yet the financial services industry did just that, even though Li himself cautioned against undue reliance on his new formula.

Li's model played a central role in the crisis. It appeared to offer a way to estimate the odds of default in very large groups of securities. This is a crucial input in assessing the riskiness of bonds that are based on pools of loans, such as mortgages and credit cards. And the trick with this model was that rather than relying on historical data, it used credit default swaps (CDS) to estimate the risk that borrowers will fail to pay. We'll discuss credit default swaps at greater length later. Suffice it to say that credit default swaps are contracts that allow investors to insure themselves against the risk that borrowers will miss payments or go bankrupt, leaving the lender with a loss.

The formula was wildly popular because it appeared to offer a way to price default risk in markets with little historical data, like subprime mortgages.[50] But the logic was hopelessly flawed. We already know that historical data are better than nothing, but not by much, in determining what the future might hold. Here we have a realm in which historical data are understood to be too limited to be reliable. So why should CDS prices be any better?

The enthusiasm, aside from the self-serving reason that it offered financiers a new way to make a buck, may have come from an incorrect analogy with prediction markets. Many believe that these markets are a superior means of aggregating and distilling information on relevant topics. But the problem is that this "information" is really opinion. If the opinion is informed, or the prediction markets are used as an alternative to polling, they can be very useful. But even in cases where they should be most reliable, they have on occasion failed spectacularly, as in the 2006 mid-term elections.[51]

But if prediction markets really were all that good at seeing the future, the horse with the best odds would always win the race. How often does that happen? Yet the halo around markets, and the opportunity to sell high-margin products, blinded users to these pesky issues.

Li's formula was used widely in estimating the risk of default on large pools of loans whose cash flows were structured various ways to make products look more appealing to investors, as we described in chapter 1. The key to making them work was that rating agencies graded the risk of the various instruments created from pools. And Li's model appeared to relieve the rating agency of the need to worry about all of the particular loans in the package. The magic correlation number solved that problem, or so it appeared.[52]

Yet this model repeated and amplified Sharpe's error. As Nassim Nicholas Taleb said, "Anything that relies on correlations is charlatanism."[53] Various experts, including Darrel Duffie, a Stanford professor and advisor to Moody's, one of the two most influential ratings agencies, warned that the copula formula was ill-suited for valuation and risk measurement.[54] Yet it became pervasive. It served as the basis for designing and pricing hundreds of billions of dollars of collateralized debt obligations (CDOs), particularly complex instruments that were often resecuritizations, tranched products made from tranches of (usually but not always) simpler deals. The burgeoning business of CDOs made from mortgages and their cousin, collateralized loan obligations made from so-called leveraged loans, which private equity firms used to fund takeovers, all rested on the flawed foundation of Li's equation.

The models started failing spectacularly in early 2008. Bloomberg reported that correlation-based trading models had gone "haywire" and were showing the odds of a default by an investment-grade company leading to a second default at greater than 100%, which was clearly impossible.[55] The sudden erratic behavior of a formula on which the pricing of many instruments had come to depend also pushed up corporate borrowing costs, even for the top-rated corporations, at a time when the Federal Reserve was cutting interest rates.[56] A story in the *Financial Times* nearly two months later said the distortions were likely to persist because a product that depended on the correlation models, synthetic CDOs, had "withered." With these instruments suddenly in disfavor, credit default swaps had become more volatile and more expensive. Via arbitrage, the dislocation in the credit default swaps market was putting pressure on borrowers who needed to raise money.[57]

And as we will see in later chapters, other distortions based on misguided faith in financial models played a central role in the crisis.

. . . . .

The focus on the large-scale losses that resulted from the misapplication of seemingly advanced risk management and pricing technologies may obscure a far more basic fact. It isn't simply that so-called financial innovations should be viewed with a great deal of skepticism. It is that the whole edifice of modern finance, even the mundane sort that retail investors use to manage their portfolios, is rotten.

First, the investment approaches that came out of financial economics *greatly understate the risk of markets.* As Benoit Mandelbrot discovered, and numerous analysts have since confirmed, specific markets show much greater price swings than the standard theories posit.

Now some quants will argue that they have fixes in the models for the fat tail shortcoming,[58] and also use other means, such as stress testing, to manage risk. But the problem is that these adjustments rely on observation of past events, and single high-risk events skew the entire sample.

Nassim Nicholas Taleb gathered price data on a very large set of market and economic variables and found that one single outlier would largely dictate how "fat tail" adjustments were set.[59] But how do you know if that one outlier will compare to the next one that arises? Similarly, consider how, in a different context, economists and laypeople are looking to the Great Depression for guidance to our present crisis. But relying on a single case example is frequently misleading.

Moreover, as we just discussed, the *models assume that relationships between different types of assets are stable.* Two mantras of investing for both professional and lay investors is to diversify holdings among a type of investment (that is, own a mix of stocks rather than a single stock) and to allocate asset among different types of assets (a.k.a. asset classes), for instance, domestic stocks, domestic bonds, cash, emerging markets, commodities, etc. And while this approach does reduce risk, the fact that the standard approaches treat the relationships of asset prices within and across markets as durable means that they encourage investors to treat diversification, whether done casually or in a more faux-rigorous fashion, as being more foolproof than it really is. The result is that investors are taking more risk than they realize.

Now it is easy to see intuitively why there is no reason to believe these relationships would be static and enduring. Rapidly growing companies mature, and as they solidify their position, their stock prices become less risky and should therefore vary less with the stock market as a whole. Currencies can also show changing fortunes. Switzerland has long been seen as a bastion of stability. But one of its biggest banks, UBS, like many of its peers, has taken significant losses on derivatives and real estate exposures, and, even worse, had very large dollar denominated debts. Even after the bailout of UBS, the size of those dollar exposures were large compared to the Swiss economy. When a country has a large external debt, it creates all sorts of financial instability. The issue of solvency (even for a supposedly rock-solid country like Switzerland) becomes a real concern. Anyone who tried to determine portfolio risk for the Swiss franc based on historical patterns would be sorely disappointed during the crisis.

Remember, the asset allocation notion comes from our old friend beta. You reduce risk of a particular security if you diversify well, but you are still left with the risk of that market. But the theory holds that you can further reduce risk without compromising returns to the same degree by holding asset classes that don't move together (or covary) strongly. But if these relationships indeed are not reliable, an investor might have chosen a mix of investments that appeared to buffer risk, but in fact failed to because the relationships morphed.

While that issue exists on a day-to-day basis, as we saw with the LTCM debacle, in a disrupted market it is extreme. Many financial assets that formerly traded somewhat independently move together. Investors dump risky positions and flee to what they perceive to be safe.

And that tendency, for seemingly unrelated markets to fall in tandem when the stress gets high enough, has been exacerbated by the theory-induced practice of diversifying across asset classes (or for the top-of-the-food-chain players, looking for anomalies across markets).

In brief, during the turbulent months of September and October 2008, there were many days when a particular investment, say gold, would take a dive, even though nothing particularly bad had happened in that market. Why? Hedge funds that had multi-market exposures were getting margin calls as stock and complex debt prices were falling. Sometimes they'd sell those instruments, forcing those markets down further. But in other situations, to avoid liquidating into a chaotic market, which would likely yield a worse price than if they held on, they'd dump a large position in a market that was (at least at that juncture) less impaired. We'll discuss this pattern, along with other forces that led to unrecognized connections between markets, at greater length in chapter 9, which covers the development and meltdown of the so-called shadow banking system.

Because financial theories treat markets as safer than they are (by understating their native risks and overestimating the protection that can be achieved), they unwittingly embolden investors to take on more risk. One way to do that is to choose more speculative or volatile holdings; another way is to take seemingly safe assets or strategies and borrow against them. Remarkably, the mainstream theories are almost cavalier about the risk of leverage and *encourage the use of debt.* Recall that CAPM and Black-Scholes both assume investors can borrow unlimited amounts of money at the risk-free rate (meaning at the same borrowing cost as the U.S. Treasury). Modern portfolio theory, which comes out of CAPM, clearly endorses borrowing[60] and does not imply any limits on leverage.

Combine these elements. Orthodox approaches considerably understate risk. They provide a technique to reduce that danger, namely diversification, that is far less reliable than it seems. Add to that an endorsement of borrowing, and you have a combustible mix. Leverage increases risk, yet the prevailing approaches treat borrowings as not merely benign, but the royal road to superior performance. So one source of peril is recast as a boon, and another is erroneously understated, and to large degree.

The prescriptions of financial economics are dangerous for another reason: they reinforce a well-documented human propensity toward overconfidence. Psychological and behavioral economics studies have found consistently that the vast majority of participants overrate their ability to predict future events. They also tend to treat information as more precise and reliable than it really is. And they fare poorly at estimating the odds of future events.

Moreover, overconfident people engage in riskier behavior. Companies with optimistic or overconfident executives borrow more heavily than most.[61] Entrepreneurs start new businesses not because they love gambling, but because they have an illusion of control and overestimate their understanding of the business terrain.[62]

The combination produced what verged on delusion among those who should have known better. Quant funds, even supposed best-of-breed ones at Goldman, suffered staggering losses. Investment banks, given free rein by regulators to choose their risk management processes, came to grief, either failing (Lehman), losing their independence (Bear Stearns, Merrill), or requiring government intervention (Morgan Stanley, Goldman). Supposedly sophisticated trading firms in the UK and Europe, such as the Royal Bank of Scotland, Lloyds, and UBS, have also been bailed out. And even those not receiving cash infusions have benefited from less obvious salvage operations, such as super-low interest rates and a raft of special borrowing facilities.

And this excessive risk taking was not always an "other people's money," "heads I win, tails you lose" syndrome. The LTCM principals had virtually all of their money in their fund,[63] as was the case with many of the quant hedge funds that started coming apart in late 2008.

But the models were so convenient, and worked so well on a day-to-day basis that everyone ignored the fact that using them was tantamount to building a castle on a flood plain.

Sharpe has been proven correct. Despite the central role played by these flawed constructs, they still remain the cornerstone of modern financial practice. People would rather have a bad model than no model at all. Or put more simply, delusions die hard.

CHAPTER 4

NEOCLASSICAL ECONOMICS

THE TRIUMPH OF
SIMPLISTIC MATH
OVER MESSY FACTS

Using models within economics or within any other social science is especially treacherous . . . The most we can expect from models is half-truths.
—David Colander, Middlebury College

A t first blush, the options pits of Chicago exemplify bare-knuckle capitalism. The spectacle of traders, almost without exception men, yelling, waving frantically, using hand signals to initiate and confirm transactions, is vivid yet weirdly anachronistic, undeniably physical in an era of impersonal electronic trading. Members push and elbow to gain advantage; fistfights are not uncommon. And the most successful traders claim the prized positions, on the higher tiers, where they can see across the press of bodies and have an advantage in calling out orders.

Yet these are exchanges, with rules on membership, reporting, trade settlement, so the seeming chaos takes place within a regimented framework. In addition, the social structure of the pits is far from a barely contained brawl. Participants have a strict code of acceptable and unacceptable behavior. Transgressors are frozen out, even though those measures can be costly to the enforcers. Actions to help the collective good are treated with respect. Smaller pits have more orderly price moves than bigger pits thanks to cooperation among members. Older traders help out youngsters, not out of an expectation of being paid back, but out of a belief that it is the right thing to do for the community; indeed, the recipients are sometimes instructed to help newbie traders when they can.[1]

So what would appear to be the epitome of individualistic market behavior in fact has a social structure, an unwritten code of conduct, and moral guidelines. As we will see, that runs counter to the predominant theory, namely that of neoclassical economics, of how markets operate.

.   .   .   .   .

Individuals transacting in markets is the core of the neoclassical school of economic thought. It succeeded the so-called classical school of economics set forth by Adam Smith and David Ricardo in the eighteenth and early nineteenth centuries, which stressed the self-corrective power of the "invisible hand" of day-to-day commerce.

The roots of neoclassical thinking date back to the 1800s, when philosopher Jeremy Bentham, famed for his extreme views (he advocated universal suffrage, animal rights, and health insurance), first came up with the notion of utility as a lens for viewing human activity. It amounted to a radical critique on behalf of a rising bourgeoisie against the strictures and social structures of tradition-bound England.

Bentham argued that people were essentially hedonistic, driven by pleasure and pain, operating out of self-interest. He dismissed community as a mere "fictitious body,"[2] no more than an aggregation of individuals. He believed the goal of policy was to produce the greatest happiness (which he also called the principle of utility[3]), which he took to mean to reduce individual suffering on as broad a scale as possible while also promoting collective satisfaction. Bentham sought to devise a "felicific calculus" to measure the impact of various actions.

Bentham's ideas, elaborated in greater detail later in the nineteenth century, dominated economics until the Great Depression and Keynes's new theories called them into question. But as we discussed in chapter 2, the neoclassical canon emerged largely intact and better formalized in the decade after World War II. Neoclassical economists have also added new constructs since that era, like the "rational expectations model," developed by John Muth in 1961, which gained a following from its use by the University of Chicago's later Nobel Prize winner Robert Lucas. "Rational expectations" means people act on their best guess of what will take place, that they use all available information, and do not make systematic errors, which is code for they are free of biases.[4]

. . / . . .

Neoclassical economics has been the dominant paradigm since the 1970s. Not only is it the core construct for microeconomics, but it also plays a significant role in macroeconomics, the study of the operation of the economies at an aggregate level.

One of the attractive features of neoclassical economics is, like financial economics, that it fit well with the post–World War II emphasis on theoretical frameworks and mathematical exposition. It rests on a small number of central assumptions:

- Individuals seek to maximize utility.
- People have rational preferences that are specific and can be related to a value.
- People operate independently of each other and make use of complete and pertinent information.

The common criticisms challenge the assumptions frontally, for instance, arguing that people are frequently irrational, swayed by emotion and group identification. The neoclassical construct also pares down commercial behavior to an absurd degree. Making some of its basic assumptions even slightly more valid leaves the theory in tatters. However, economists brush these objections off, citing the Friedman dictum that good theories often rest on counterfactual assumptions, and the real test is whether they "work."

But neoclassical economics does not work. In chapter 5, we'll turn to the real-world tests of neoclassical economics and show that they were abject failures. That chapter will also describe how ideas that came out of neoclassical economics, particularly the "free markets" concept, which is more a political position and differs from neoclassical economics in some key respects, were marketed aggressively to policy makers and the media. In this chapter, we look at some of the yawning problems with the theory qua theory.

. . . . .

One of the reasons for the acceptance of the neoclassical paradigm, or its dumbed-down version, "free markets," isn't simply that it hewed well with the preferred mode of academic work. It became popular because it makes a bold, superficially appealing claim: letting individuals pursue their own interests produces the greatest social welfare.

Of course, it's easy to think of counterexamples. For instance, rising rates of diabetes due to too little exercise and too many fats and sugars is hardly a good outcome. Our genetic makeup is designed to cope with scarce food supplies, not abundance, so we are predisposed to overeat. Another example is what Keynes called the paradox of thrift. While having individuals save would seem to be sensible and desirable, in fact too much prudence is damaging on a society-wide basis. In particular, it is most detrimental during downturns, when building up an even bigger buffer against adversity makes the contraction more severe by reducing demand and, with it, overall economic activity.[5]

But argument by anecdote doesn't cut it with the theorists, so let's turn to their edifice. Neoclassical economists build their construct from the ground up, starting with a very simplified model of a single consumer and how he trades off the purchase of two goods, say eggs and bread. That model seems to work nicely.

Now a market is not one individual; Robinson Crusoe does not make for much of an economy. *Yet when we go beyond a single individual, the model breaks down.* The assertion of the neoclassical adherents that more open markets provide better outcomes is unproven even on a theoretical level. You can see how the model fails in appendix I.

So how do the theorists finesse this problem? They build their models on a "representative agent," one person with static tastes who serves as a proxy for all. The assumptions needed to produce these results are even worse than the oft-cited horrors of Communist central planning: everyone consumes the same goods, rationed in the same proportion for both the rich and the poor. Gee, in the old Soviet Union, those at the top of the food chain got perks, like dachas and drivers.

While these assumptions are widely taught and treated as reasonable, the mathematical economists who found this fault line are not comfortable with it:

> Strong restrictions are necessary to justify the hypothesis that a market demand function is the same as a consumer demand line function. Only in special cases can an economy be expected to act as an "idealized consumer."[6]

Not surprisingly, other research has reached similar conclusions, that the "representative consumer" approach often produces results that differ markedly from models that take a bottoms-up approach and try to aggregate the actions of individuals.[7]

But these problems are airily dismissed. The essence of real-world consumer behavior—varied tastes, shifting buying patterns in response to changes in income and lifestyle changes such as aging or change in location—is cut off, Procrustes-style. Only one conclusion is acceptable: that a market economy produces maximum social welfare. Most people object to that sort of faux science of using theory to justify preordained conclusions and trying to persuade the young and impressionable when practiced by creationists. Yet the exact same logic by certain schools of economics elicits nary a protest.

Now, we dealt only with the demand side of the supply/demand story in microeconomics. The supply story has been equally shot full of holes (for example, a particularly devastating but nevertheless brushed-off critique comes from Piero Sraffa, a professor of political economy in Italy in the 1920s who was invited to Cambridge University by John Maynard Keynes when Sraffa's political views and friendships put him badly out of step with the fascists[8]). But the pictures look great, and the story, which is all it is, is terribly tidy.

In any other line of thinking save economics, the incumbents would recognize and acknowledge that the attempts to prove that a market economy produces maximum social welfare are not terribly impressive. The fact that they are discussed seriously at all does cast considerable doubt on the health of economic thinking.

· · · · ·

The inability to prove market behavior under anything other than absurdly restrictive assumptions is far from the only shortcoming of neoclassical theory. The assumption that usually elicits the strongest objections from laypeople is that of rationality. Every other social science rests on the view that humans are far from logical and are driven by a mix of logic, instinct, and impulse, yet economics makes a showcase of reason.[9]

Indeed, behavioral economists, who study behavior in laboratory settings, have found a myriad of cognitive biases. To name just a few:

- **Confirmation bias.** People tend to look for information that supports their views, rather than clinically trying to ascertain whether facts align with or dispute their initial hypothesis.
- **Conjunction fallacy.** People tend to make decisions based on storytelling rather than data. Tests have repeatedly found that most will judge a situation to be more probable if it is described in some detail, which makes it very vivid, even when a less detailed version of the same scenario is in fact more likely.
- **Overconfidence.** Humans overestimate the odds of success for their own activities.

- **Inconsistency.** How someone responds to the same economic proposition often depends on how it is described.

Moreover, rationality as defined by economists is of a highly demanding sort. People aren't simply expected to be logical and consistent; they are required to have access to complete information and act on it so as to maximize their utility, no matter how complicated the situation is.

In fact, human mental capacities simply aren't up to the task. Nobel Prize winner Herbert Simon argued that people and companies do not maximize, as the theorists hold, but instead "satisfice," that is, they look for outcomes that are good enough rather than optimal. One reason is the cost of gathering information. Consumers expend effort and energy on comparison shopping; business schools train students in the art of making decisions under uncertainty, recognizing the tradeoffs involved (not simply expense but time required, which can lead to missing an opportunity).

But Simon focused on a fundamental obstacle: the brain's limited processing capacity. Despite our fond wishes otherwise, we cannot handle much information. The brain works for the most part sequentially rather than in parallel. And what we can cope with is also very restricted, since data are held in short-term memory buffers. It also takes a comparatively long time (five seconds) to move material from short-term to long-term memory.[10]

Limited short-term memory means that humans can grasp at most seven variables when pondering a problem, and possibly as few as three.[11] Simon's investigation of decision processes also found that people find it hard to integrate new information into their existing knowledge, either overreacting to or ignoring it.[12]

Another gaping problem is that even if humans had the information-gathering resources and mental apparatus to be perfect, detached calculating machines, they can never obtain all the needed inputs. University of Chicago economist Frank Knight distinguished between risk (probabilities that can be estimated) and uncertainty, where the odds cannot be assessed:

> But Uncertainty must be taken in a sense radically distinct from the familiar notion of Risk. . . . It will appear that a measurable uncertainty, or "risk" proper, as we shall use the term, is so far different from an unmeasurable one that it is not in effect an uncertainty at all. We shall accordingly restrict the term "uncertainty" to cases of the non-quantitive [*sic*] type.[13]

These obvious facts, that there are both uncertainties that cannot be estimated, as well as "unknown unknowns" that intrude on the best-laid plans, are conveniently assumed away to make for a tidy theory.

. . . . .

Another part of the neoclassical construct that breaks down upon further in-spection is the concept of utility. Utility is generally described as a metric of rel-ative satisfaction, or a rank ordering of preferences. Recall Bentham's notion of seeking pleasure and avoiding pain. Utility, as originally conceived, is a hedo-nistic construct.

But economists have noticed that humans are sometimes altruistic, and have struggled to incorporate this into neoclassical theory. For instance, going to church cannot be explained by "the expected stream of 'benefits,'" so one fi-nesse was to posit "afterlife consumption."[14] Similar contortions justify saving rather than consuming (a "bequest motive"[15]) or generosity ("a taste for the perception of the welfare of others"[16]). Gifts are even more problematic. Neo-classical writers suggest that the present is not genuine (as in the donor wants to burnish his image) or that he derives pleasure from the enjoyment of the recipient.

Another vexing problem is when consumers spend money to improve their self-control. Diet support groups like Weight Watchers or clinics to help people quit smoking don't fit at all well with utility theory. Effectively, the individual has two sets of preferences that are in conflict (in these cases, pleasure now versus health later).[17] But the neoclassical model holds that economic actors have con-sistent and stable tastes.

The problem is that a theory that is twisted to justify any sort of behavior means it is no theory. Acting in your own interest is quite different than acting for others' benefit. A construct that justifies actions that can be diametrically opposed cannot give practical guidance. And remember, per the discussion of Milton Friedman's "get out of reality free" card of endorsing "unrealistic" as-sumptions, predictive power was one way that seemingly absurd assumptions might nevertheless pass muster. If the model yielded an accurate prognosis, it was treated as a black box, and therefore the axioms don't matter. But here we see a clear failure of the model, with people in fact behaving contrary to its pre-dictions. Instead of abandoning the framework and finding explanations that work better, all sorts of complicated rationalizations are invoked to disguise the fact that the emperor, or in this case, the model, is wearing no clothes.

. . . . .

The selfishness versus altruism problem shows up in another way: the implic-itly contradictory posture neoclassics take on transactions. You need trust for commerce to work, yet neoclassicals assume the converse, that everyone is out for number one. Nobel Prize winner Amartya Sen uses an anecdote to illustrate the problems of assuming actors act solely out of self-interest:

> Central to [the] problem is the assumption that when asked a question, the individual gives an answer which will maximize his personal gain. How good is this assumption? I doubt it is very good. "Where is the railway station?" he asks me. "There," I say, pointing to the post office, "and would you please post this letter for me on the way?" "Yes," he says, determined to open the envelope and check whether it contains something valuable.[18]

Sen's story illustrates that society rests on the assumption of a basic level of cooperation and trustworthiness, since the behavior he parodies, of extreme self interest, does not jibe with what most of us experience in our day-to-day lives. But neoclassical economics offers a polar view, that people are strictly self-motivated, and then assumes a simple solution, that they will nevertheless be bound by the agreements they enter into. You can see how this idea breaks down: if individuals aren't restrained by morality or the need to maintain appearances, why wouldn't they cheat on their promises?

Indeed there is ample evidence that people are often less than fully honest. For instance, one study taped students as they talked to a stranger for ten minutes. The students then were asked to review the tape and count the number of lies told. Sixty percent admitted to being untruthful, and tallied an average of 2.9 lies during the conversation.[19] And remember, the deception occurred even though there was nothing obvious to be gained. Patterns like this suggest that good conduct cannot be assumed.

Markets need ways to enforce that participants live up to their commitments. Neoclassical constructs ignore these issues and the related costs. When pressed, the backers of this world view offer cheery, simple-minded solutions that "the market" will drive out bad actors, that consumers will look for cues of who is honest and will deal only with those vendors. Another belief is that the courts system serves as a good remedy. We'll examine in later chapters how invalid those assumptions are in the realm of finance.

Now add to this set of problems another pitfall conveniently excluded from the neoclassical paradigm: that one side of the transaction, typically the seller, knows more than the other side. As we mentioned earlier, this problem is called "information asymmetry," and has generated a reasonably robust literature and a few Nobel prizes. But it isn't reflected anywhere in the neoclassical paradigm, since it contradicts one of the core requirements of the construct: perfect information (which means everyone is on the same footing). But there is a genre of papers, like the ones trying to explain why people go to church, that make an art form of trying to show that heretical ideas or inconvenient facts really can be reconciled with the construct.

When the seller knows more than the buyer (or vice versa), commerce in the neoclassical framework becomes costly. One option is dealing only with vendors a buyer has used before successfully. Even then, he runs the risk that the seller pulls a fast one now and again, taking advantage of him in ways he cannot readily detect.

If sellers cannot be presumed to be trustworthy (and the dictates of maximizing self-interest say they in fact won't be), consumers have to either spend money and effort to validate the quality of their purchase or accept the risk of being cheated.

Consider purchasing a computer in the neoclassical paradigm. The buyer has no way of being certain that the computer lives up to the vendor's promises. So the consumer will have to bring an expert to test the computer's functionality at the time of purchase (does it really have the memory and chip speed promised, for instance?). The seller will need to be paid in cash, otherwise the buyer could revoke payment.

And what happens if the computer fails in a few weeks? Assuming the vendor has not fled the jurisdiction, the only remedy is litigation, or an enforcer with brass knuckles.

But even that scenario is too simplistic. It assumes the buyer can evaluate the expert. But in fact, if you aren't a computer professional, you can't readily assess the competence of someone who has expertise you lack. And even if the person you hired is competent, he might arrange to get a kickback from the seller for endorsing shoddy goods. The same problem holds true in any area of specialized skills, such as accounting, the law, or finance. Many people judge service quality by bedside manner, which is not necessarily a good proxy for the quality of the substantive advice. And as we will see later, one of the factors that helped create the crisis was the willingness of investors to buy complicated financial products based on the recommendation of a salesman who did not have the buyers' best interests at heart.

An example of the dangers of the neoclassical model lies in the sad fate of Eben Byers, an athlete, industrialist, and man-about-town of the 1920s. After sustaining an arm injury that refused to heal, his doctor prescribed (and received a 17% rebate on) a patent medicine. Byers thought it did him a great deal of good and began taking the potion two to three times a day.

The drink, Radithor, was radium dissolved in water. Radioactive products were in fact touted as remedies, but most were too weak to do much harm. Unfortunately, the industry had become well enough established to have started to compete on product strength, and Byers got the real deal.[20]

Byers lost his teeth and most of the bone mass in his jaw, and before his death, developed abscesses on his brain and holes in his skull. But the maker of the toxic potion was never prosecuted, since selling radium drinks was not against the law.

By the time Byers had the vast misfortune to use Radithor, the risks of radium were coming to light, as factory workers who painted radium onto clocks and would use their lips to establish a point on their brushes were developing lip and mouth cancers. But the potion makers nevertheless continued to sell their tonics until Byers's death killed the industry.

While the example may seem extreme, the point is simple. Byers was a wealthy man; presumably his doctor was well regarded. Byers was unable to make an independent assessment of Radithor and paid for his trust with his life. And the sellers of the toxic product violated no law; in fact Byers got what he paid for, a radium drink. But the neoclassical paradigm simply assumes that honesty is not a problem (or that the market will weed out bad actors, despite also positing that individuals are out for number one), and that the court system is a sufficient remedy for violations of contracts or basic human decency.

· · · · ·

Another striking feature of neoclassical theory is that it insists that the only actors in markets are individuals. That flies in the face of modern life. The vast majority of goods and services that people in advanced economics buy are made and sold by companies, not solo craftsmen peddling their wares on pushcarts or over the Internet.

Larger forms of organization exist for a host of reasons. One is that it is costly to contract on a case-by-case basis to produce products; the savings of having employees typically outweighs the effort and uncertainty involved in rounding up resources as needed. Certain activities also exhibit economies of scale, network effects, or learning through repetition and routinization, all of which mean that larger entities can produce products more cheaply than individuals or small concerns. Indeed, most ventures are simply impossible for a solo entrepreneur to manage. You don't have one-person-operated airlines, steel mills, or oil rigs. Even a specialized, single-storefront retail business typically is beyond an individual's ability to operate. The neoclassical paradigm imposes a preindustrial construct, when, for instance, textiles were a cottage industry; our societies are well past that.

To put it another way: the neoclassical paradigm is that of pure competition,[21] where providers are mere price takers and cannot influence market dynamics. *But that is a profoundly unattractive business proposition.* Even if one were to wave a wand and reconfigure the modern economy along those lines, it would in short order coalesce into larger units as individuals did deals (either via alliances or merging operations) to gain the advantages of greater size, and sought to distinguish their offerings to give them pricing power. Differentiation doesn't necessarily mean having unique products, but can come through the service related to the products. For instance, convenience stores charge more for staples like milk by virtue of location (on highways where there are no alternatives nearby) or being open at 3:00 A.M.

Yet larger enterprises, or indeed anywhere group ties matter, are weirdly disturbing to neoclassical loyalists. One of the reasons they cling so fiercely to ideas like individuals as the locus of activity, along with rationality and welfare-maximizing results (despite the considerable distortions that result) is that they believe any other stance would support a restriction of personal rights.[22] (An aside: this view is counterfactual. Societies where social bonds have broken down and many individuals are isolated are in fact much more subject to totalitarianism and manipulation by propaganda.[23])

Neoclassics seek to eliminate power from the construct. As Nobel laureate George Stigler put it: "The essence of perfect competition is . . . the utter dispersion of power."[24]

But large-scale organizations inevitably involve concentrations of power. If Wal-Mart has wiped out many local retailers and you badly need a job, you have to accept Wal-Mart's terms. And while neoclassical theory acknowledges the existence of monopolies and oligopolies, they are treated as curiosities and put aside. Moreover, industry groups can achieve economic power via their access to and use of political influence, as anyone even dimly familiar with special interest group politics knows all too well. Wall Street is a prime example of political clout well in excess of votes.

But again, neoliberal thinkers see only the state as a threat to individual rights. They do not consider that businesses or other private groups can amass so much wealth that they can assume state functions or otherwise coerce individuals. They thus fail to consider that the government can play a useful role in restricting concentrations of power by private parties.

. . . . .

Let's turn to another reason the neoclassical paradigm is no more than a chalkboard construct. Even diehard libertarians admit the state performs some minimal necessary functions, namely, defense and the enforcement of contracts. Those require a military apparatus and a court system. Those in turn necessitate taxes, which also means government has to pay for the tax bureaucracy. So even a bare-minimum government has three budget items.[25]

There is no way to have a completely neutral tax system. Do you tax capital, income, or activities? In what proportion and at what rate? The mere introduction of taxes moves the toy economy away from the pure competitive state by creating distortions.

The inability to achieve the neoclassical ideal is more damaging to the theory than most imagine. The assumption underlying many policy measures is that the closer we can move to a "free market" paradigm, the better off everyone will be. Even if we set aside the discussion at the beginning of the chapter, that the proof that pure competitive markets maximize the collective good breaks down once you go beyond a single individual (and how can a single individual compete, anyhow?), there are other problems with this simple-minded prescription.[26]

That is not to say that economists are not well aware of these problems. After all, the requirements for perfect competition are daunting: even the biggest player can account for only a small portion of total industry sales; buyers need perfect knowledge of the products and the terms available from all vendors; sellers act independently (no price fixing or cartels); the items sold are divisible. It isn't hard to see that if even one of these conditions fails to hold, sellers can gain the upper hand.

But the fallback stance often adopted, sometimes in the literature and far more in public life, is that measures that bring the economy closer to this ideal are beneficial. But the emphasis of what sort of measures to favor has shifted over time.

Without invoking economic theory, the Progressive party, whose efforts were taken up by Theodore Roosevelt, curbed some monopolist wannabes via selective trust-busting (note that while Roosevelt famously pursued J.P. Morgan's railroad interests and J.D. Rockefeller's Standard Oil Company, he favored the "good trust" U.S. Steel, whose financier George Perkins backed TR's campaign). Mergers are still subject to antitrust review (the 1976 Hart-Scott-Rodino Act) to prevent excessive concentration (although enforcement varies over time). A good deal of consumer-protection law, ranging from truth-in-advertising laws to disclosure, tries to level the information imbalance between sellers and buyers.

Yet more recently, government intervention in markets, even when it was to address the sort of failings that the neoclassic would acknowledge, has been characterized as "interference." The virtues of the unattainable neoclassical paradigm have instead been conflated with the slippery, ill-defined idea of "free markets," where less government involvement is assumed to be preferable.

Recall our discussion of the Lipsey-Lancaster theorem from chapter 2. It argues that if any one requirement of perfect competition fails to be achieved, it no longer achieves optimality (so called "Pareto optimal," where the welfare of one individual cannot be bettered without imposing costs on someone else) on all fronts. Worse, the authors tell us, "the other Pareto conditions, although still attainable, are, in general, no longer desirable."[27]

To put it another way, incremental moves toward the abstract, unattainable ideal of perfect competition may not improve the collective good; indeed, they can make matters worse. And there are no simple rules for determining whether these changes will achieve progress or not.

If economists were as serious about rigor as they claim to be, Lipsey-Lancaster alone should have put a knife in the neoclassical paradigm as anything more than a teaching tool. Instead, we have a theory riddled with holes, mere scientism masquerading as science, driving policy for nearly three decades.

CHAPTER 5

HOW "FREE MARKETS" WAS SOLD

Regulatory policy is increasingly made with the participation of experts, especially academics. A regulated firm or industry should be prepared whenever possible to co-opt these experts. This is most effectively done by identifying the leading experts in each relevant field and hiring them as consultants or advisors, or giving them research grants or the like. This activity requires a modicum of finesse; it must not be too blatant, for the experts themselves must not recognize that they have lost their objectivity and freedom of action.

— *The Regulation Game*

The phrase "free markets" has come to have a peculiar, Pavlovian status in discourse in America, and to a lesser degree, in other advanced economies. Any right-thinking person is presumed to be a loyal supporter of "free markets;" conversely, an opponent must be anti-capitalist (horrors!), woefully ignorant, or operating from self-interest. Consider this laudatory passage from University of Chicago Business School professor Luigi Zingales's recent article, "Capitalism After the Crisis":

America's form of capitalism has long been distinct from those found elsewhere in the world—particularly because of its uniquely open and free market system.

> Capitalism calls not only for freedom of enterprise, but for rules and policies that allow for freedom of entry, that facilitate access to financial resources for newcomers, and that maintain a level playing field among competitors. The United States has generally come closest to this ideal combination—which is no small feat.[1]

Notice how Zingales identifies openness and fairness with his vision of a "free market" system. Indeed, for most economists, "free markets" means something like "market-based prices do a good job of resource allocation and are very useful, so we should rely on markets unless there is a good reason not to." Nevertheless, for the most part they also recognize a long list of situations in which unfettered commerce gives one party in a transaction considerable sway over the other or lets him impose costs on complete outsiders (pollution is a classic example), producing distortions. Thus intervention can improve outcomes by correcting for these failures.

But the sort of rules that Zingales argues are necessary, to limit power concentrations, directly contradict the sort of "free market" idea espoused by libertarians and staunch followers of Milton Friedman. They see government action of any sort beyond the bare minimum as "interference." That vision is in fact close to anarchy. Thus the same term, in the hands of different writers, stands for quite different things.

However, the zealotry of the "free market" fundamentalists means that people who use the same phrase to use something more moderate wind up seeming to endorse the more extreme version.

And this tactic has proven to be remarkably successful. The widespread acceptance and casual use of the expression "free markets" has become a form of Newspeak, distorting thinking and debate. The commonly held view in the United States that "free markets" are desirable creates a default position: that completely unrestricted commerce is preferable, and anyone who argues against it bears the burden of proof.

The generally approving way in which economists use "free markets" also means the discipline's trappings of rigor lend authority to this idea. Indeed, neoclassical economists, who dominate mainstream economics, are vocal supporters. Yet, as we explained in chapters 2 and 4, the discipline bases its claims to science on distinctly unscientific practices such as, one, a strong orientation toward theories that are seldom validated, and, two, narrow, self-justifying methodology in the place of open inquiry.

Many of the bedrock theories of economics inhabit a world that isn't simply unrealistic, but wildly different from any that humans will ever occupy. Nevertheless, many economists have embarked on a program to make the realm of commerce conform as closely as possible to their unattainable fantasy, even though this "closer is better" assumption is not only unproven, but can lead to detrimental policies.

The limited empiricism of economics allows for politicization of academic work in ways that would not be likely to occur among "real" scientists. One example of research serving as a Trojan horse for ideology occurred in a 2007 paper published in the *Journal of Economics and Sociology*. Titled "Is There a Free-Market Economist in the House? The Policy Views of American Economics Association Members," it surveyed members of the AEA, the most prestigious economics group in the United States, to learn where they stood on "free market" principles.

Despite the popular perception that economists support market-based activity, the poll found that in large percentages they reject its extreme form, the libertarian version of the "free market" construct. These "free market" advocates believe that there should be no restraints on agreements between consenting adults. They thus favor the legalization of illicit drugs and object to regulations of all sorts, including those to assure purity of food, water, and medicines. They also oppose tariffs, public education, gun controls, antitrust, and consumer protection laws. "Free market" boosters argue that such restrictions "contravene individual liberty."

The study found that only 8% of AEA members endorsed this position, and only 3% were strong supporters. That shouldn't be surprising; many other people, such as the economists surveyed, use the expression "free markets" to mean something much less radical.

But why was this paper odd? Social science research is supposed to be objective. For instance, if an anthropologist notices that members of a tribe go down daily to a river to wash, but then sees they miss a day, he records the change. He does not write "Bad dirty natives."

Yet that is precisely what the article did. It did not make an objective, fact based assessment, say comparing the support of economists for these ideas relative to the population at large, to other academics, or to self-identified conservatives. Instead, it set an arbitrary, subjective standard of near total agreement to its own definition of "free market" principles. The rationale:

> Many economists maintain that they are essentially free-market supporters. . . . In our way of thinking, being a free-market supporter is about favoring the *principles for social rules* that imply a free market. It is not an issue of the principles of economics. A "natural rights" libertarian who has

no economic understanding is nonetheless a supporter of free-market principles.[2] (Emphasis original.)

Bluntly, the paper measures economists' degree of adherence to a particular
ideology. Notice how the authors have to admit that their view on this matter is
strictly personal: "In our way of thinking," and that support for "free markets," as
they define it, is based on the view of a prototypical libertarian who has no knowledge of economics. In other words, the standard chosen *has nothing to do with
economics,* but is purely a political stance. Asserting that "free markets" means only
what the article says it means, in Red Queen fashion, is a tad presumptuous.

Nevertheless, that thrust would be valid if the study simply set out to identify what proportion of AEA members were libertarian true believers. Instead,
the article veers into advocacy, making both subtle and overt criticisms of the
economists who failed to salute the "free market" flag at every opportunity. For
instance, it chides the respondents for not taking positions that any "real free
market person would" and claims that "economists who study and judge FDA
regulation very clearly come out in favor of liberalization." That argument is
not even narrowly true. Some academic research has found that the FDA has
increased drug company sales because consumers view medication as safe. Similarly, the paper fails to mention that that studies that have been hostile to the
FDA's oversight in most cases have been funded by conservative think tanks that
openly oppose regulation of all sorts. Ironically, it is the medical industry itself
that has demonstrated how industry-funded research does indeed generate results that are favorable to its patrons.[3] Back to the article:

> We suspect that some economists are not quite honest with themselves. . . .
> They try to have it both ways, thinking of themselves as basically free-market
> supporters, but then neglecting the responsibility to research and think criti-
> cally about the contraventions of free-market principles that surround them.[4]

Can you see how extreme this view is? The survey itself establishes that fewer
than 3% of the economists who responded are strong backers of the way the
writers choose to use the term "free markets." Supporting market-based activity does not necessarily imply adherence to a particular *political* belief about
how markets should operate. Yet the paper argues that the first responsibility of
economists who support market-based activity, which is what "free markets"
meant to most of them, is instead to give high priority to advocating the radical version of markets *über alles* (that is the real message of the coded "neglecting the responsibility" clause). The article accuses survey participants who do
not hold extreme "free market" views of being intellectually dishonest. The sub-
text is that economists not only should subscribe to the policy stance the au-

thors extol, but also have a professional duty to infuse their work with an overtly political agenda.

At another point, the article argues that "economists who oppose freedom downplay that framework but *they never contest that analytic framework.*"[5] (Emphasis original.)

To call a belief system an analytic framework is also quite a stretch. As we discussed at length in chapter 2, economics strives to be rigorous and hence value free. Even the economists that the paper sets forth as setting the standard for "free market" support, such as Milton Friedman, did not consistently meet the litmus test proposed in this article. For instance, Friedman backed a negative income tax, which would redistribute income to the poor.

■ ■ ■ ■ ■

One of the fundamental problems with economics is that it is difficult to parse out political considerations from those that economists would like to see as "economic," which in this case means limited to technocratic concerns. However, that narrow a view is simply impossible. Economists love to twiddle with models to prove the existence of optima, but that begs the question of what is society trying to optimize? Most individuals have richer goals than simply making money and buying goodies. Yet the combination of the propensity of economists to focus on greater output as the main measure of success, plus their disproportionate influence in policy, means their world view has, over time, framed the objectives of collective action.

Certain subjects have fairly obvious implications for the public at large. For instance, some analysts have taken interest in the increasing concentration of income and wealth in the top 1% of people in the United States. This shift in distribution has been accompanied by over three decades of stagnant average worker wages and lower growth rates than in the earlier postwar period. Is this relationship causal, that is, did the policies and economic developments that led to the change in the sharing of gains also dampen overall growth, or are other factors to blame? If it turns out that having too much money and power at the very apex of the pyramid is indeed negative for growth rates, it would be a powerful argument for more progressive taxes.

While the arguments over this issue are heated, and tend to break along right/left lines, for the most part, the debate sticks to objective issues: how much has the concentration increased? How did it come about? Has this change had an impact on overall performance? In other words, even though the findings may have political implications, economists engaged in this debate are (for the most part) arguing over facts and how to interpret them.

By contrast, the "free market" advocates, as the paper above illustrated, start from an ideological premise and seek to trump objective analysis. In addition, they adopt an absolute, take-no-prisoners stance. In a pluralistic society, that sort of dogmatism is antidemocratic and authoritarian. To put it more simply, the "free market" camp fights hard and fights dirty.

That isn't to say that there should not be robust discussion about how to conduct commercial activity. Quite the reverse. The nature of enterprise itself evolves, with innovation, increased scale of activity, and global integration; social priorities change as well.

But in this complex and shifting mix of policy and activity, we find economists and the greater public increasingly mouthing the phrase "free markets," which one camp insists means only one thing: a hands-off posture toward enterprise that the overwhelming majority of economists in fact does not endorse. Yet the widespread use of this term, which most people (economists included) take to mean something less radical, is often depicted as endorsement of a more extreme position. How did this curious state of affairs come to pass?

■ ■ ■ ■ ■

Even though the "free markets" paradigm is often associated with neoclassical economics, in fact they differ in many respects. The key element they share is the view that independent individuals are the right, nay, only locus for viewing economic activity.

However, the commercial realm presents a very different picture. Once you get beyond dealing with solo service providers (say, cab drivers, baby sitters), most goods and services are provided by larger entities. Even doctors, lawyers, and accountants operating as sole practitioners usually have support staff. As we discussed in chapter 4, many activities are subject to economies of scale and other factors that favor larger forms of enterprise.

Consider also: the ideal, perfectly competitive world of neoclassical economics is a lousy setting for businessmen. With all goods the same and no one able to influence prices, profit opportunities are thin to nonexistent. Entrepreneurs seek to gain advantage by creating new products or by differentiating them in a host of ways. Thus it is the actions of private actors, looking to better themselves (as the theory says they will) that move the economy considerably away from the neoclassical fantasy.

In fact, the main reason that the vast majority of economists endorse various forms of intervention in commerce is that many areas of activity do have a propensity toward concentration. Fewer powerful players lead to less competitive pricing, a sub-optimal outcome. Thus most economists endorse measures that partially reverse imbalances between influential producers and comparatively weak buyers, such as antitrust, prohibitions on restraint of trade, truth in advertising, and disclosure.

Yet remarkably, the backers of the extreme "free market" views maintain that the *only* factor that leads the economy away from the neoclassical ideal of optimal efficiency (which, as we discussed in chapter 4, breaks down even on a theoretical level) is "coercion" and even more remarkably, that it comes only from the government. The idea that private actors will achieve commercial advantage that gives them economic power over others is airbrushed out.

Another inconvenient fact is that commerce now plays some of the "coercive" roles formerly assumed by the state. The New School's Robert Heilbroner explains:

> Despite the appearance under capitalism of these dual realms, the political and the economic, both realms carry on both functions, one openly, one covertly. The political realm openly conducts the business of politics. . . . But at the same time it provides absolutely essential support for the private sector. It carries on economic activities which, were they privatized, would result in losses. It builds roads, infrastructure, it does things essential for the country that cannot be undertaken in the economic sphere because, by the rules of the game, these don't make money.
>
> Now you take the economic part. The economic sphere takes on a very important political task, which it doesn't recognize as being political, namely, assuring the essential discipline that maintains the work process. In feudal times, there's branding and clipping and a bailiff with a whip. In capitalism, no one whips the man who doesn't show up for work. Nobody assures discipline in the sense the feudal lord does. The disciplinary function, and it is there, God knows—the function of getting people to do work they don't particularly like and do it regularly—is provided by *the system,* in the form of the need to gain income.[6]

In case you think Heilbroner exaggerates, many Americans are blissfully ignorant of the fact that some large enterprises once had their own armed forces. Police power and the ability to resort to violence is the most naked form of coercion; to pretend that the government ever and always has a monopoly on that role is naive. As University of Boston political scientist and economist Thomas Ferguson explains:

> American history is replete with examples of business groups and individual firms retaining vast armies of military and paramilitary forces for long periods of time. In the nineteenth century many railroads kept private armies. The Pennsylvania Coal and Iron Police ran their own *Obrigkeitsstaat* [authoritarian state] for decades. General Motors maintained the Black Legion; Ford

sported a veritable *Freikorps* recruited by the notorious Henry Bennett; and any number of detective agencies, goon squads, "special consultants," and wiretappers have also been active. . . . Force on such a scale potentially menaces competitors, buyers, and suppliers almost as much as it does workers.[7]

No wonder most economists support constraining the power of business when it threatens to become extreme or impinge on public welfare.

■ ■ ■ ■ ■

Unless you lived through it, it is difficult to appreciate how much popular attitudes about business have shifted in the last fifty years. In the 1960s, it would be unusual to think of markets as virtuous. Even the stock exchange had a whiff of disrepute. Bank trust managers allocated portfolios heavily toward bonds and viewed stocks as speculative.

The popular media reflected this orientation. In 1965, *The New York Times* had sixty-six articles that used the phrase "free market," only a bit more than half the number using the expression "free enterprise." By contrast, 1,131 stories mentioned "citizen" and 1,342, "consumer." By 2008, the usage of "free market" had risen nearly five-fold, to three hundred stories. "Free enterprise" fell by more than half, to forty-three. Remarkably, in a presidential election year, the number of articles mentioning "citizen" fell from 1965 levels to 964. Those mentioning "consumer" more than doubled to 3,203. Admittedly, this is one indicator, but a sampling of books and magazines from this period confirms this view, a shift in collective identity away from membership in communities and toward actors in markets.

Time magazine in March 1961 declared that as economics was becoming more scientific, controversies across party lines were waning.[8] Interestingly, this article cites two preeminent conservative economists, Milton Friedman and Arthur Burns, both endorsing federal aid to education, when the survey cited at the beginning of the chapter saw opposition to public education as one of the litmus tests of "free market" orthodoxy. *Time* did feature the occasional complaint from conservatives about government meddling, such as the Kennedy tax cut to stimulate the economy, or government involvement in collective bargaining,[9] but by today's standards, the objections are infrequent and temperate.

What ended this era of good feeling among economists? Political strife and economic stresses. Antiwar, anti-establishment protests created a siege mentality among conservatives and big businessmen. The success of the 1964 tax cut in pulling the economy out of a stubborn recession also ended an era of fiscal rectitude. Even though both Walter Heller, the head of the Council of Economic

Advisers under Kennedy, and Milton Friedman warned in 1966 that budget deficits would produce inflation, spending on the space program, Vietnam, and reducing poverty continued.[10] Accelerating inflation, a trade deficit, and serious decay in the gold coverage of the dollar led to the "Nixon Shock," the abandonment of the Bretton Woods system, which had had the dollar convertible into gold and foreign currencies set at fixed rates against the dollar.

The 1973 oil crisis produced stagflation in the United States and many other advanced economies. Keynesian economists had been the architects of economic policy during the 1960s, and the initial triumph of the successful 1964 tax cut seemed more than offset by the malaise of the early 1970s. The final nail in the Keynesians' coffin was the result of Paul Samuelson's and another Nobel laureate, Robert Solow's popularization of a historical relationship called the Philips curve, which showed a trade off between unemployment and inflation; that is, low unemployment will lead to high inflation, and vice versa (an aside: Keynes himself did not subscribe to this idea, and offered different remedies for inflation, depending on whether it resulted from commodity price increases or from wages growing faster than productivity gains).

When the 1970s stagflation started to take hold, Samuelson and Solow asserted that letting unemployment rise to roughly 5.5% would tame price increases. Yet between 1973 and 1974, prices rose 12% while unemployment increased from 5% to 9%.[11] Milton Friedman instead argued for a "non-accelerating rate of unemployment" and mustered data to demonstrate that there was no long-term relationship between inflation and unemployment. He claimed that the solution to inflation was to foster more competition and let market forces work. The Keynesians had no answer to Friedman's arguments.[12] Protracted poor economic performance put pressure on politicians. Friedman and his followers offered a fresh and appealing-sounding approach. But as we will see, this solution was badly oversold.

■   ■   ■   ■   ■

Two of the *idées fixes* of the "free markets" advocates is that regulation is ever and always bad and that government is incompetent. The reality is far more complex.

Regulation has in fact scored noteworthy successes. Most major cities have master plans and building codes to prevent shoddy, dangerous construction. Washington, D.C. is a planned city, with the design largely the work of Pierre-Charles L'Enfant in 1791. Large-scale modern telecommunications depends on regulations to set standards for equipment and transmission. If there were no restraints, entrepreneurs would set up independent competing networks, producing fragmentation. Who would use which spectrum, and for what purpose?

And with spectrum use a free for all, equipment makers would not see a large enough market to warrant investing in equipment. The most likely result would be micro-scale amateur broadcast/network operators with hobbyist tinkerers as users.

Iceland offers a classic example of how regulation produces better economic outcomes. Iceland has abundant marine resources, but fishermen were chronically struggling. Each could catch as much as he wanted to, with the result that all kept fishing to the point where it was unprofitable for everyone. Overfishing was damaging the resource and depressing prices. Merely setting an annual quota would be an incomplete solution. It would preserve the industry long term, but individuals would compete to the point of marginal profitability. They would work more hours, buy bigger boats or more sophisticated equipment to try to get a greater share of a fixed pie.[13]

Two years of bad hauls in the 1970s spurred the government to act. It privatized fishing interests. Overall limits were established, and fishermen were assigned quota based on their recent catch levels. *And those quotas were tradable.* Permits moved over time into the hands of the best fishermen. And because they represented a claim against a revenue source, banks would lend against them.

The fishing reforms helped Iceland go from one of the poorest countries in Europe to the richest by 2000.[14]

Note that while this clever solution relied on market mechanisms, it also required government intervention: limiting the total catch size (determined by marine biologists each year) and assigning property rights in what once had been a common resource. Those interventions (in fact, interventions of any kind) fly in the face of "free market" absolutism.

In fact, arm's length, anonymous trading, the sort that takes place in financial markets, depends on regulation. The U.S. stock market was seen as the epitome of financial markets until the reputation of Anglo-Saxon practices started taking a dive. As Amar Bhidé, a former Columbia Business School professor and Wall Street proprietary trader, wrote in the *Harvard Business Review* in 1994:

> Without a doubt, the U.S. stock markets are the envy of the world. In contrast to markets in countries such as Germany, Japan, and Switzerland, which are fragmented, illiquid, and vulnerable to manipulation, U.S. equity markets are widely respected as being the broadest, most active, and fairest anywhere.[15]

The United States tried unregulated securities markets and the result was periodic crashes, culminating in the spectacular 1929 meltdown, the aftermath of rampant speculation, manipulation, uncontrolled leverage, and insider dealing. The stock market reforms embodied in the Securities Act of 1933 and the Securities Exchange Act of 1934 took a new tack of protecting investors by limiting the ways insiders and market professionals could exploit them. The innovative regulations provided for extensive disclosure of companies' financial results, organization, and operations; sanctioned insider trading; and barred various types of market manipulation, such as front-running (buying or selling ahead of a customer order to get a better price), spreading rumors, and making material misleading (including incomplete) statements. As Bhidé's praise indicates, these reforms were salutary and durable.

The "government is always incompetent" theme is similarly disproven by the success of large-scale, extraordinarily complex initiatives carried out over long time frames, daunting undertakings for any enterprise: the Marshall Plan, the U.S. space program, rural electrification, the interstate highway system. While it falls largely outside the U.S. tradition,[16] other countries have done well with industrial policy. Japan's Ministry of International Trade and Industry (now the Ministry of Economy, Industry, and Trade) played a major role in the rise of the island nation from the "starving times" of the post–World War II era to industrial might in a mere thirty years (and without Marshall Plan funding to rebuild).[17] Even in its post-bubble lost decade, Japan continued to be an export powerhouse; it was its domestic economy that flagged.

But the true believers in "free markets" place no stock in understanding the limits as well as the merits of private versus public action. It's much easier to paint the world in black and white than to try to make sense of the gradients in between.

. . . . .

It would be hard to find a more loyal and tireless advocate of "free markets" than Milton Friedman and his colleagues at the Chicago School of economics. He was originally a supporter of Keynesian economics and benefited directly from New Deal–related work in 1935 when scholarly employment was hard to find, but changed his views based on his monetary reading of history, namely that the Great Depression was the result of a contraction in the money supply. That led him to believe that Keynesian remedies, of greatly increasing government spending to compensate for a collapse in private demand, were the wrong medicine.[18]

The Chicago School, where Friedman did his initial graduate work in economics and where he returned as a professor in 1946, became a bastion of conservative thinking. Friedman himself was energetic and uncompromising. He gained in stature as he correctly predicted the 1970s stagflation. Federal Reserve chairman Paul Volcker's monetarist experiment, of clamping down on money supply growth to break the back of inflation, also added to Friedman's reputation. While Friedman's monetarism has fallen into disuse (it proved impossible for modern central banks to control the money supply as Friedman believed they should[19]), his political views still hold considerable sway.

While his laissez faire stance was seen as extreme in the 1950s, his weekly columns in *Newsweek* (from 1966 to 1984) caught the popular imagination by branding lack of government involvement as "freedom" (by contrast, his son David called him a "libertarian anarchist"[20]). Conservatives, in retreat during the success of the post–World War II social welfare model, and even more defensive in the antiestablishment 1960s, embraced his views.

As the economic and political tide turned, Friedman gained a bigger audience. Despite the present-day anxiety about terrorism, the Soviet Union in its heyday posed a much greater threat (after all, they had plenty of nukes). America's confidence faltered due to Vietnam, the oil shock, stagflation, and the hostage crisis in Iran. Friedman's die hard libertarianism fit the Reaganite/Thatcherite hostility to big government and vigorous defense of capitalist values, and offered a simple, appealing antipode to the "Evil Empire" of Soviet planning and central control.

When presented at that level of abstraction, democracy versus authoritarianism, individual choice versus government fiat, it's hard to argue with Friedman. But this Manichaean view doesn't translate neatly into the real world. When democratic decisions conflicted with his radical view of economic freedom, Friedman and his followers showed a disturbing tendency to give the economic realm primacy. Economist Lawrence J. Miller noted that the backers of "free market" orthodoxy took more extreme positions than the theory itself suggested:

> They emphasize the usefulness and relevance of the neo-classical economic theory, equate the actual and the ideal market, see and apply economics in to every nook and cranny of life.[21]

·   ·   ·   ·

Chile has been widely, and falsely, cited as a successful "free markets" experiment. Even though Chilean dictator Augusto Pinochet's aggressive implementation of reforms that were devised by followers of the Chicago School of Economics led to speculation and looting followed by a bust, it was touted in the United States as a triumph. Friedman claimed in 1982 that Pinochet "has supported a fully free-market economy as a matter of principle. Chile is an economic miracle."[22] The State Department deemed Chile to be "a casebook study in sound economic management."[23]

Those assertions do not stand up to the most cursory examination. Even the temporary gains scored by Chile relied on heavy-handed government intervention.

It is particularly troubling that "free markets" boosters cite Chile as a showcase, not simply because the facts say otherwise but also because this bogus "miracle" required a brutal dictator. In other words, despite the fact that the "free markets" advocates claim to be tireless supporters of individual liberty, their actions show a disturbing willingness to compromise what they claim as their highest ideal.

In 1970, Chileans elected Salvador Allende, a socialist. The United States cut aid to Chile and pressured lenders such as the World Bank and the Inter-American Development Bank to follow suit. Allende used large-scale public sector employment to reduce joblessness, increased the nationalization of copper mines and banks (which were heavily foreign owned), and went further with land reforms initiated by his predecessor.[24] The United States helped organize right-wing opposition to Allende,[25] which culminated in a military coup in 1973 by Augusto Pinochet.

The "Chicago boys," a group of thirty Chileans who had become followers of Friedman as students at the University of Chicago, assumed control of most economic policy roles. In 1975, the finance minister announced the new program: opening of trade, deregulation, privatization, and deep cuts in public spending.[26]

The economy initially appeared to respond well to these changes as foreign money flowed in and inflation fell.[27] But this seeming prosperity was largely a speculative bubble and an export boom. The newly liberalized economy went heavily into debt, with the funds going mainly to real estate, business acquisitions, and consumer spending rather than productive investment.[28] Some state assets were sold at huge discounts to insiders. For instance, industrial combines, or *grupos*, acquired banks at a 40% discount to book value, and then used them to provide loans to the *grupos* to buy up manufacturers.[29]

In 1979, when the government set a currency peg too high, it set the stage for what Nobel Prize winner George Akerlof and Stanford's Paul Romer call "looting" (we discuss this syndrome in chapter 7). Entrepreneurs, rather than taking risk in the normal fashion, by gambling on success, instead engage in bankruptcy fraud. They borrow against their companies and find ways to siphon funds to themselves and affiliates, either by overpaying themselves, extracting too much in dividends, or moving funds to related parties.

The bubble worsened as banks gave low-interest-rate foreign currency loans, knowing full well the borrowers in their own industrial group would default

when the peso fell. But it permitted them to use the proceeds to seize more assets at preferential prices, thanks to artificially cheap borrowing and the eventual subsidy of default.[30]

And the export boom, the other engine of growth, was, contrary to stateside
propaganda, not the result of "free market" reforms either. The Pinochet regime
did not reverse the Allende land reforms and return farms to their former owners. Instead, it practiced what amounted to industrial policy and gave the farms
to middle-class entrepreneurs, who built fruit and wine businesses that became
successful exporters. The other major export was copper, which remained in
government hands.[31]

And even in this growth period, the gains were concentrated among the
wealthy. Unemployment rose to 16% and the distribution of income became
more regressive. The Catholic Church's soup kitchens became a vital stopgap.[32]

The bust came in late 1981. Banks, on the verge of collapse thanks to dodgy
loans, cut lending. GDP contracted sharply in 1982 and 1983. Manufacturing
output fell by 28% and unemployment rose to 20%.

The neoliberal regime suddenly resorted to Keynesian backpedaling to quell
violent protests. The state seized a majority of the banks and implemented
tougher banking laws.[33] Pinochet restored the minimum wage, the rights of
unions to bargain, and launched a program to create 500,000 jobs.[34]

In 1985, a new finance minister, Hernan Buchi Buc, started reprivatizing the
banks, reduced government spending, and further opened international trade.
However, some of the policy reversals of the downturn, such as more extensive
regulation and some labor safeguards, remained intact. Economic growth returned. Pinochet left power in 1990 and democratic rule returned. Nobel Prize
winner Joseph Stiglitz has deemed Chile's post-Pinochet performance as "the
success of combining market with appropriate regulation."[35] The finance minister from the first post-Pinochet government, Alejandro Foxley, claims:

> If you compare the performance of the economy in the best Pinochet years
> with the performance of the economy [during] democracy, I challenge you to
> find one single economic or social indicator in which democracy hasn't per-
> formed much better.[36]

Even so, the picture for Chile is far less rosy than reported in the United
States. Chile has one of the most unequal income distributions in the world,
with the top 10% getting over 50% of output. Wages for average workers have
fallen since the 1970s despite minimum wage increases. Chile's exports depend
heavily on copper (still controlled by the government) and natural resources
(wood, fisheries) that are being exploited in excess of sustainable rates. By contrast, manufacturing has dropped from 30% of GDP in the 1970s to 18%.[37]

The lesson of Chile is vivid failure of "free market" principles. Just as the extreme left policies of Allende did damage by producing a high level of inflation and weakening private sector incentives, the Pinochet era spurred a plutocratic seizure of privatized companies and a channeling of funds into areas that would produce quick speculative profits rather than a foundation for long-term growth.

And that's before we consider the social costs. Given a choice, most people would put civil liberties—freedom of speech, the right to vote and belong to political organizations, the right to due process with an independent judiciary—at a higher priority than economic prerogatives. Not being at risk of being seized in the middle of the night and sent to a gulag, or worse, is worth quite a lot to most people. Pinochet shuttered the congress, eliminated political parties, unions, and professional groups. He also implemented a curfew, with everyone required to stay at home after 8:00 P.M. Roughly 4,000 citizens were murdered, with more driven into exile. Methods of torture included gang rape, the pulling out of nails and teeth, and electrical shocks to the genitals.[38]

Yet Friedman and his followers put their vaunted "free markets" over personal liberty in claiming Pinochet as their own. As historian Eduardo Galeano described neoliberal reforms, "People went to prison so prices could be free."[39]

. . . . .

The next major "free markets" experiment did not fare much better, and its failure was far more obvious. After the USSR collapsed in 1991, a group of young economists who were Chicago School devotees pressed Russia's new president, Boris Yeltsin, to privatize state-run enterprises quickly.

The result was another plutocratic land grab. Former state assets were traded at bargain prices. Yukos, an oil company, sold for $100 million and was valued a year later at $3 billion.[40] Russia didn't even get an early boost from leverage and speculation as Chile did, but went straight into a prolonged slide. The ten years from 1989 saw its GDP fall by 50%. It did manage to double something—its inequality, as measured by its Gini coefficient, a widely used metric. Those in poverty, defined as having an income of under $4 per day, rose from 2 million to over 60 million by the mid-1990s. Russia defaulted on its debt in 1998, precipitating a second leg down in the so-called emerging markets crisis.[41] By contrast, China, which devised its own program of modernization, doubled its GDP during this period. Moreover, it can be argued that China started in a worse position: Russia was already industrialized, and had a base of scientific, mathematical, and engineering know-how. China, by contrast, was dominated by subsistence agriculture, with a proportionately much smaller technical elite.

The "free market" diehards argued that the reforms were not aggressive enough, but there is ample evidence to the contrary. The neoliberals simply assume away the need for social and institutional structures to support capitalism. Yet sociologists from Max Weber onward recognize that widely shared values like deferred gratification are key to the success of capitalism. Barrington Moore, in his 1966 *The Social Origins of Dictatorship and Democracy*, found that a bourgeois revolution was a key element in the transformation from a feudal society to a modern democracy. Skip that, he argued, and you wind up with an authoritarian regime. Despite Friedman's fantasy of isolated individuals contracting on an arm's-length basis, a combination of legal mechanisms and social constraints needs to be in place for transactional commerce to be viable. And Russia, which went from a feudal society to central planning, had none of them.

Consider this assessment of Russia's privatization by lawyers Bernard Black, Reinier Kraakman, and Anna Tarassova:

> First, rapid mass privatization of medium and large firms is likely to lead to massive self-dealing. . . . Russia accelerated the self-dealing process by selling control of many of its largest enterprises cheaply to crooks, who got the funds to buy the enterprises by skimming from the government, and transferred their skimming talents to the enterprises they acquired. Second, profit incentives to restructure privatized businesses and create new ones can be swamped by the burden on business imposed by a combination of (among other things) a punitive tax system, official corruption, organized crime, and an unfriendly bureaucracy.[42]

Language like "crooks" is seldom found in social sciences research, which illustrates how extreme the corruption in Russia was. And that is precisely what results from the implementation of naive economic models that throw out legal and regulatory constraints and cheerily assume people will acquit themselves well. And it wasn't just the locals, suddenly liberated from the Communist playbook, who behaved badly. Harvard professor Andrei Shleifer and his protégé Jonathan Hay, on contract from the U.S. government through Harvard to advise on the reforms, began investing in violation of their agreement. Harvard, Shleifer, and others consented to pay at least $31 million to resolve litigation filed by the U.S. government alleging breach of contract (including hiring and expense account abuses) and conspiracy to defraud.[43]

Joseph Stiglitz, in analyzing the failure of Russian reforms, makes a key observation that the "free markets" advocates are fixated on their particular approach, rather than the objectives of creating a healthy, dynamic economy:

> It is not just the creation of market economy that matters, but the improvement of living standards and the establishment of the foundations of sustainable, equitable, and democratic development.[44]

Stiglitz is being too charitable. It was, like Chile, a "(fantasized) ends justify the means" approach. Wayne Merry, the chief political analyst in the U.S. Embassy in Moscow during the beginning of the privatization, said:

> The US government chose the economic over the political. We choose the freeing of prices, privatization of industry, and the creation of a really unfettered, unregulated capitalism, and essentially hoped that the rule of law, civil society, and representative democracy would develop somehow automatically out of that.[45]

Weimar Germany illustrates vividly that economic dislocation can lead a democracy to turn to the security of authoritarianism. Why should a country that had never experienced self-rule suddenly have it spring forth full blown, like Athena from Zeus's forehead, especially when order had already broken down?

. . . . .

Even his critics would agree that Milton Friedman was a true believer in his political views, not motivated by the prospect of financial gain. That cannot be said of many of those who promoted his line of thinking.

Friedman advised Barry Goldwater's failed 1964 presidential bid, as did the conservative (and at the time very small) think tank, the American Enterprise Institute. The effort to roll back New Deal reforms, curtail unions, and trim government, except for defense, continued and gained more urgency with the "anti-establishment" shift in society in the later 1960s. Note in particular that the attack on unions falls outside the neoclassical construct, which is silent on both the concept of large-scale enterprise (save monopolies and oligopolies, which are treated as curiosities and largely ignored) and unions as a countervailing force.[46]

Two loose but ideologically aligned efforts strove mightily to pursue a number of big business objectives, including reducing regulation. Starting in the early 1970s, some far right wingers began systematically to market their ideas and discredit the Left. While politics is a realm of hard-fought ideas, the ambition of these extremist conservatives was to reframe popular opinion to conform to their line of thinking. To a remarkable degree, they succeeded.

For instance, wealthy conservative lawyer and later Supreme Court justice Lewis Powell wrote a memo to the U.S. Chamber of Commerce in 1971 that galvanized the right wing. He argued that corporations needed to launch a coordinated and sustained attack to discredit liberals. Among the key elements was the creation of a well-funded effort that looked like a "movement" to press its cause with the media. Generously financed "scholars, writers, and thinkers" would demand fair treatment and "equal time" as the wedge for forcing the press to treat them seriously. In turn, they would recast issues, with the aim of reshaping opinion from the elite to the mass level.[47]

Another blueprint came from former Nixon Treasury Secretary William E. Simon, in his 1978 book, *A Time for Truth*. Disillusioned conservative journalist David Brock describes its program:

> The ideology of Barry Goldwater and Phyllis Schlafly and William Buckley would now be dry cleaned for mass consumption, and along with it came a neolexicon—a language reinvented by conservative practitioners trained in the use of manipulative, often Orwellian, rhetoric. Agenda items like gutting Social Security, rolling back civil rights protection, and slashing taxes inequitably would be smoothed out with deceptive Madison-Avenue-type branding slogans of the type used to sell commercial products: "privatization," "the new federalism," the "flat tax" and so on . . . funds would go exclusively to right wing ideologues, with no capitulation to "soft-minded pleas for the support of 'dissent'" . . . ensuring conservatives would have the unwavering message discipline, ideological uniformity, and seeming unity of purpose that seemed to go missing in liberalism. The work would carry an air of academic independence and authority, but it would be subject to no peer review or conflict-of-interest safeguards.[48]

Another conservative dismayed by the tactics of the New Right similarly described the new corporate lobbying efforts of the 1970s as "militant."[49]

In economics, the spear carriers were the think tanks such as the American Enterprise Institute (AEI), the Heritage Foundation, the Hoover Institution, and the Cato Institute. For instance, the AEI funded a series of publications, studies, and has endowed faculty chairs; Heritage prepared a 3,000-page blueprint for the incoming Reagan administration and then, a year in, scored its progress (61% of 1,270 recommendations implemented).[50]

A not-well-recognized issue is that the think tanks moved into a vacuum created by the orientation of economics in the 1950s through the 1980s toward theoretical work. Papers in top academic journals were increasingly inaccessible to the laity. These institutes could thus pick those theories (or simply aspects of theories) that were congenial to their world view. They also provided highly paid employment to economists who did not have a future in academia. For instance, Arthur Laffer, a proponent of supply side economics, said, "I knew there was no way in God's earth I could make it in the profession. So I went other routes—the press, the political press, consulting."[51]

What is troubling about these organizations is that their role is seldom evident to the public. Media reports often fail to disclose the affiliation of a researcher with a think tank that has as its sole purpose the promotion of a particular set of policies and ideas. And even when they do, many readers fail to recognize that the economists in the employ of these advocacy groups are lobbyists. Most people have learned not to trust industry-funded drug research. Why should industry-funded economic research be any different?

But the influence goes beyond the official products of these organizations: they also finance studies and provide grants. And again, the medical industry has shown that funding has an impact on how sponsor-friendly the results tend to be. And it is not that the researchers are corrupt or venal. Humans are extremely suggestible. Social psychologist Robert Cialdini, in his classic book *Influence: The Psychology of Persuasion,* noted that a gift as minor as a can of soda increases receptivity to a salesman's pitch. That is why some companies prohibit employees from receiving gifts or entertainment of any kind from vendors, no matter how trivial, and why drug detail men, until a recent voluntary moratorium, made sure to leave goodies like pens, notepads, and samples when pitching their products to doctors. If mere trinkets lead to more sales, imagine what cold cash does.

. . . . .

A second corporate-sponsored effort focused directly on the issue of deregulation. The push came on the science and technology front, but the same logic was extended to other industries.

Historically, the U.S. policy in science was to support national needs. That shifted in the Carter administration as industry began clamoring for the need to relax antitrust and "onerous" regulations, and change tax and patent policies. Remarkably, these lobbyists managed to sell not only a problem that did not exist, but also a solution of dubious relevance.

Business performance was indeed flagging in the 1970s thanks to inflation, high commodity prices, and lackluster growth in the United States and in most advanced economies. But poor performance in technology was not the culprit. From 1967 to 1977, the U.S. balance of trade surplus in R&D-intensive manufactured goods had increased three-fold.[52] Moreover, the large companies spearheading the effort (the petroleum and chemical industries, IBM, the member firms of the Industrial Research Institute and the Business Roundtable) were not innovators.

By the middle of the decade, a large body of research on innovation found that small entrepreneurial companies were the locus of new practices. In fact, the more big firms an industry had, the less innovative it tended to be. Ironically, government intervention could promote new developments, for instance, by requiring cars to meet new standards (the changes needed to meet the new demands often spurred other advances). And while experts agreed that innovation and growth seemed to be linked, there was no consensus on how to foster it.[53]

Indeed, the boosters of a new hands-off posture toward business were never able to prove a decline in innovation, much less that regulation was responsible. In fact, the supposed problem was (in a remarkable bout of candor) frequently characterized as a "perceived lag."[54] However, the science advisor to the White House, Dr. Frank Press, was co-opted despite the lack of real evidence and backed the corporate agenda.[55]

The logic used here was repeated again and again in subsequent pushes for deregulation: the superior wisdom of the self-regulating market and how other approaches compromised freedom; the redefinition of progress from social and collective benefits to the process of "innovation," irrespective of whether the results actually were positive. Another disturbing thread in this new line of thinking was an assault on democracy as the enemy of efficiency, order, and rationality, and the invocation of the superior judgment of experts.

As these initial efforts bore fruit, the big businesses backing the deregulation effort became emboldened and made more demands. They began to characterize government action as "interference," implying businesses had an absolute right to unfettered operation, and argued for lowered expectations on behalf of the public.[56] If corporations did indeed become more prosperous thanks to newly-won freedom, it would have been reasonable for the gains to be shared, particularly since some of the changes sought (lowered pollution standards, less stringent product quality regulation) imposed costs on the public at large. But the corporations wanted to have their cake and eat it too: fewer restrictions on their activities, and less collective participation in the upside.

•　•　•　•　•

The third avenue for promoting and institutionalizing the "free market" ideology was inculcating judges. It was one of the most far-reaching actions the radical right wing could take. Precedents are powerful, and the bench turns over slowly. Success here would make the "free markets" revolution difficult to reverse.

While conservative scholars like Richard Posner and Richard Epstein at the University of Chicago trained some of the initial right-leaning jurists, attorney Henry Manne gave the effort far greater reach. Manne established his "law and economics" courses for judges, which grew into the Law and Economics Center, which in 1980 moved from the University of Miami to Emory in Atlanta and eventually to George Mason University.

Manne had gotten the backing of over 200 conservative sponsors, including some known for extreme right-wing views, such as the Adolph Coors Company, plus many of the large U.S. corporations that were also funding the dereg-ulation effort.

Manne is often depicted as an entrepreneur in the realm of ideas. He took note of the fact that, at the time, the University of Chicago had one of the few law schools that solicited funding from large corporations. Manne sought to create a new law school, not along conventional brick-and-mortar lines (his ef-forts here failed), but as a network. He set out to become a wholesaler, teaching law professors and judges.[57] However, although Manne presented his courses as teaching economics from a legal perspective, they had a strong ideological bias:

> The center is directed by Henry Manne, a corporate lawyer who has under-taken to demolish what he calls "the myth of corporate responsibility." "Every time I hear a businessman acknowledge public interest in what they do," Manne warns, "they invite political control over their activities." At Manne's center in Miami, interested judges learn how to write decisions against such outside political control couched in the new norms of market efficiency.[58]

Manne approached his effort not simply as education, but as a political movement. He would not accept law professors into his courses unless at least two came from a single school, so that they could support each other and push for others from the law and economics school of thought to be hired.[59]

The program expanded to include seminars for judges, training in legal is-sues for economists, and an economics institute for Congressional aides. A 1979 *Fortune* article on the program noted that the instructors "almost to a man" were from the "free market" school of economics.[60] Through 1980, 137 federal district and circuit court judges had finished the basic program and 56 had taken additional "advanced" one-week courses.[61]

It is hard to overstate the change this campaign produced, namely, a major shift in jurisprudence. As Steven Teles of the University of Maryland noted:

> In the beginning, the law and economics (with the partial exception of its ap-plication to antitrust) was so far out of the legal academic mainstream as to be reasonably characterized as "off the wall." . . . Moving law and economics' sta-tus from "off the wall" to "controversial but respectable" required a combina-tion of celebrity and organizational entrepreneurship. . . . Mannes' programs for federal judges helped erase law and economics' stigma, since if judges—the symbol of legal professional respectability—took the ideas seriously, they could not be crazy and irresponsible.[62]

Now why was the law and economics vantage seen as "off the wall"? Previ-ously, as noted above, economic thinking had been limited to antitrust, which inherently involves economic concepts (various ways to measure the power of companies in a market). So extending economic concepts further was at least novel, and novel could be tantamount to "off the wall" in some circles. But with hindsight, equally strong words like "radical," "activist," and "revolutionary" would apply.

Why? The law and economics promoters sought to colonize legal minds. And, to a large extent they succeeded. For centuries (literally), jurisprudence had been a multifaceted subject aimed at ordering human affairs. The law and economics advocates wanted none of that. They wanted their narrow construct to play as prominent a role as possible.

For instance, a notion that predates the legal practice is equity, that is, fairness. The law in its various forms including legislative, constitutional, private (i.e., contract), judicial, and administrative, is supposed to operate within broad, inherited concepts of equity. Another fundamental premise is the importance of "due process," meaning adherence to procedures set by the state. By contrast, the "free markets" ideology focuses on efficiency and seeks aggressively to minimize the role of government. The two sets of assumptions are diametrically opposed.

This push to remake the orientation of the law would not have succeeded to the degree it has absent other political shifts, namely, changes in regulatory policy and politics of the federal bench during the Reagan administration, wider acceptance of "free markets" ideas due to their promotion on other fronts, and shifts in the practice of corporate law. By the mid-1980s, top law schools felt it necessary to have a solid law and economics program. The endorsement of the leaders assured its spread to law programs generally.[63]

The widespread acceptance of the notion of "free markets" is not the result of an organic shift in social attitudes, but of a clever, persistent, well-funded marketing plan by business interests that had much to gain from its adoption. The tireless and often faceless promoters of this ideology would have us believe that government is the source of all evil, and that any act to cut it down is a form of patriotism and an obvious win for the collective good. Yet in Chile and Russia, we have seen the polar opposite: tearing down the state's restraints on commerce produced a scramble by the wealthy and the well-connected to seize what they could. The result was not trickle-down prosperity, but dislocation, instability, and a lower quality of life save for those at the very top. And in America's "free market" experiment, we have seen a slower but equally relentless devolution. The coming chapters will show that regulation-free markets lead to honesty-free markets which lead to quality-free markets which lead to market meltdown.

CHAPTER 6

HOW DEREGULATION LED TO PREDATION

In manufacturing, the market price is set by the smartest guy with the best, cheapest production process. In securities markets, the price is set by the dumbest guy with the most money to lose.

—William Heyman, former head of market regulation, SEC

In 1994 and 1995, Bankers Trust, a premier derivatives trading firm, was getting a lot of bad press. Federal Paper Board, Gibson Greetings, Air Products and Chemicals, and Proctor & Gamble had sued the bank, claiming that it had taken advantage of them on derivatives trades and that they should recover their losses.

On the surface, none seemed to have much of a case. The lawsuits looked like a desperate effort to welsh on bad bets. After all, these were large corporations with sophisticated treasury departments, particularly Proctor & Gamble, with globe-spanning operations, routinely dealing in foreign exchange and interest rate markets. How could a savvy multinational claim to have been duped? And as the details emerged, the companies had policies against undue risk taking in their treasury departments, and their staff had violated them.

The situations for all four plaintiffs were broadly similar: the members of their treasury departments had gotten used to dealing with fairly easy-to-understand ("plain vanilla") derivatives. The experience of the treasury departments with other professionals, like attorneys, accountants, and doctors, had habituated them to trust what they were told. Moreover, people assume that someone in an ongoing business relationship will not take advantage of them, or at least not very much.

Perhaps thinking that using more complex products was a sign of sophistication, Gibson and its brethren had become emboldened enough to venture into the world of custom derivatives (derivatives that were not standardized and in many cases unique), with the encouragement of Bankers Trust.

But using customized derivatives made customers dependent upon BT, who had the models for pricing the derivatives.[1] For these arcane, highly customized trades, there would be no way to get an independent price. They had to go to BT to find out whether they were making or losing money on their positions. In less complicated cases, it would have theoretically been possible for the companies to build their own models and calculate prices. But even then, some of the key inputs, like implied volatility (a measure of how much an instrument's price is expected to move up and down, usually during the next thirty days), would be well-nigh impossible for a nonmarket participant to guesstimate. The firms could have gotten other bids, but that might have annoyed Bankers Trust, and another bank might not have provided a very good price anyway.

But being dependent upon information and advice from another party is a vulnerable position, and BT took full advantage of this dependence. For instance, Gibson had made a trade that had worked out well. BT called and offered to close it out for a $260,000 profit. But that was a rip-off; the profit should have been at least $550,000, perhaps as much as $750,000. The fact that Gibson had closed out an initial, fairly simple trade for much less than it was worth told BT it had a sucker ready to be fleeced.[2]

Gibson lost out on its next trade, and then entered into increasingly complex and risky wagers to try to dig itself out of the resulting hole. On its last gamble, Gibson was down $17.5 million, and rolled the loss into a new swap that, depending on how events transpired, would have either reduced the deficit to $3 million or increased it to as much as $27.5 million. That gambit failed and left Gibson with a loss of $20.7 million. At this point, Gibson sued Bankers Trust. BT had made $13 million from Gibson's various swaps, and all Gibson had ever wanted was a cheap hedge for fixed-rate debt.[3]

Procter was clearly a more sophisticated player, but even it appeared to be losing its case until BT was forced to produce some damning tape recordings. A few of many damaging remarks:

"We set 'em up."

"They would never know. They would never be able to know how much money was taken out of that," says one salesman. In reply: "Never, no way, no way. . . . That's the beauty of Bankers Trust."

The objective was "to lure people into the calm and then just totally fuck 'em."[4]

Procter obtained recordings from eight BT clients and all of them contained similar evidence of a deliberate effort to exploit customers. Procter added RICO (Racketeer Influenced and Corrupt Organizations Act) charges to its suit, tripling the amount of the damages that would be awarded if Procter won the lawsuit.

BT settled the cases, and the claimants ended up clawing back a large percentage of the losses they had incurred. BT also paid a $10 million fine to federal securities regulators over the charge that it had deliberately misled Gibson on derivative prices.

Like many other institutions that became addicted to pushing the envelope, BT was unable to change its behavior. Bankers Trust was done in four years later by a second, unrelated scandal, this one criminal (failing to turn over abandoned property to the state of New York and other states), which led to a takeover by Deutsche Bank.[5]

・　・　・　・　・

The BT story is different in degree but not in kind from a lot of Wall Street behavior. The 1990s and 2000s saw a broad deterioration of conduct in the financial arena. Incidents include the Salomon Brothers Treasury bond fraud (which we discuss in chapter 7), the E. F. Hutton check-kiting scandal, and Citibank gaming a Eurobond order system.

With each scandal, the same drama played out: a flurry of press stories, once in a while some Congressional grandstanding, then back to business as usual. The Bankers Trust case and these other abuses raise a host of important and puzzling questions:

- Why did supposedly sophisticated players, like Procter & Gamble, buy risky products that they did not understand?
- Why did financial firms decide it made sense to hoodwink customers on a large-scale basis? Bankers Trust's actions look bizarre, beyond comprehension to a Main Street businessman. You don't prey on your customers, at least if you plan on ending up with something more enduring than a fly-by-night scam. How did Wall Street come to operate with vastly different rules?
- Why was it easy for financial firms to exploit their customers?

- Why did the people who were supposed to be neutral arbiters in financial markets (such as regulators and ratings agencies) for the most part fail to recognize and address these practices?

Answering these questions is key to getting to the bottom of this financial crisis:

The customers of financial firms not only did not expect those firms to take advantage of them in the course of ongoing business relationships, but they were also reassured by a steady chorus of voices that proclaimed that new and clever ways had been found to manage their risks. In other cases, the customers were themselves hoping to use exotic financial products either to evade regulation or to ramp up their profits. At the same time, many investors such as pension fund managers were not particularly concerned about engaging in risky behavior, as long as they had plentiful company. In fact, competitive pressures meant that from a career standpoint, it was much safer to go with the crowd than stand out and possibly show lower investment returns. As Keynes remarked,

> A sound banker, alas, is not one who foresees danger and avoids it, but one who, when he is ruined, is ruined in a conventional way along with his fellows, so that no one can really blame him.[6]

Financial firms were once contained within a regulated environment in which they were assured moderate but steady profits in exchange for services that contributed to the stability of the economy as a whole. Deregulation (and the failure of regulators to respond to the industry's attempts to escape restraints) changed everything, leading financial companies to become much more like the fiercely competitive firms idealized in neoclassical economics. With each company fighting for market share and profits, the aggressive impulses that had been checked by oversight and by quaint notions like propriety were now unleashed.

It was easy for predatory firms to take advantage of their customers thanks to the rapid growth of a "shadow banking system," involving, in particular, over-the-counter markets derivatives. The financial services industry developed a range of products and services that were both very difficult for their clients to understand and also substantially outside of the reach of regulation.

In order to be ready to take advantage of fleeting profit opportunities, large financial firms also became more decentralized. Consequently, if misbehavior did come to light, it was often difficult to prove that top management had been responsible.

Finally, the people who were supposed to oversee financial markets had either absorbed enough of the ideas of neoclassical economics and the world view of the financial services industry that they had no interest in intervening (regulators, some judges in key decisions), or else they had a vested interest in keeping the party going (ratings agencies, along with accommodating accountants and attorneys).

Manias typically depend on funding sources becoming cavalier about risk. Normally, enthusiasm over new technology stokes escalating momentum trading, rationalized with "this time it's different" theories. But this pattern was a departure. Here we had people who should have known better falling for technology of a different sort, instruments that enabled them to take very particular wagers. This wasn't the typical "get on the bandwagon or you'll lose out" dynamic. Instead, it involved naive parties taking on far more risk than they thought they were absorbing. The initially poor risk/reward tradeoff is worsened by being cheated badly on pricing. Overpaying can turn even a sound deal into a turkey, and many of these transactions were not sound to begin with.

The result, that the cunning swindled the chumps, was predictable to anyone who had studied the 1920s, or had experience in a real market. Yet it ran afoul of "free market" dogma, which assumes that buyers and sellers are equally well informed and can watch out for their own interests.

That rosy view fails to operate, not just in financial markets, but also in many walks of life. How can you be sure your doctor or your attorney is skilled? Unless you are in the same profession, you really do not know. You resort to proxies, like bedside manner, reputation, credentials. But they are not necessarily valid indicators.

In fact, as we will see here and in later chapters, deregulated markets showed abuses on a far more pervasive scale, and with much greater losses, than those with sound rules, even in the recent environment of lax enforcement.

■ · · · ■

Let's look at another example. This is 1994. You are a portfolio manager at a mutual fund. A salesman from Morgan Stanley calls and offers something that sounds really appealing, an AA-rated instrument that makes payments that are markedly higher than typical AA-rated paper. He tells you that there is one hitch: if the value of the Mexican peso falls more than 20%, then the payments you receive from the bond (the instrument) will start falling in proportion to further decreases in the price of the peso. You know Mexico is a little rocky, but 20% is a very big cushion, so you take the plunge.

Now how does this deal work? Most important, who is taking the risk of the first 20% loss? Mexican banks. The first deal was done by one of the largest, Banamex. Remember, since this deal is with a party that is making payments in pesos, but you only want to be paid in dollars, someone has to bear the risk of changes in the value of the peso. If the peso declines in value, then either the Mexican party (in this case a trust set up by Banamex) will have to pay you more (measured in pesos), or else you will get paid fewer dollars. In this case, the Mexican bank suffers if the peso devalues, *provided that the fall in the value of the peso is less than 20%*. From then on, you're on the hook for any additional losses.

The structure managed to create the seeming miracle of allowing Banamex to sell some bonds that had fallen in value while keeping the bonds with the bank from an accounting standpoint. The bank thus freed up cash but avoided reporting a loss. It achieved this magic via a "cost" that looked free, that of taking the first and large loss on a peso devaluation, which the rating agencies clearly regarded as a near certainty.

Banamex was responsible for taking the losses due to the first 20% of peso price declines. The ratings agencies clearly thought that the peso was likely to fall. The grade they gave to Mexican government debt, denominated in dollars, was BB, a junk bond rating, while its peso debt was rated AA-.[7] Yet bizarrely (or maybe predictably in light of what happened later with subprime ratings) *Standard & Poor's assigned the same rating to these new dollar-denominated bonds* as it had to Banamex before the deal, the same AA- it gave to Mexican government *peso* debt.

Why was this a danger sign? The rating was tantamount to saying that odds of the peso falling further than 20% were nil.

But when central banks lose the battle in holding currency pegs or bands, the falls can be catastrophic. For instance, when the United States went off the Bretton Woods system in 1971, which had required that the greenback be backed by gold, the dollar plunged 50% in short order in gold terms.

So you have circumvention of regulations ("regulatory arbitrage") and probable misrating in one lovely package making this deal viable. No wonder it was so profitable.

Morgan Stanley peddled over $1 billion of paper along these lines to big name investors like AllianceBernstein, Scudder, and Merrill Lynch Investment Managers. Other banks copied the structure.

Risks that may be tolerable on a limited scale become a different kettle of fish if they mushroom. Having a shot of Scotch is different than downing a fifth. The Mexican banks and U.S. mutual funds went on a bender. Mexican banks had already been seen as a solvency risk as of the early 1990s, before they went on this binge. Irresponsible domestic lending, turbocharged by money inflows from U.S. mutual funds that were linked to currency bets, only made a bad situation worse. These loans of "hot money" were convenient for the Mexican banks, but they could dry up quickly, and if they did, the Mexican banks would be in trouble.

Back to 1994. The deals continue as doubts about Mexico were intensifying. Dollar-based investors are withdrawing from the country, putting even more pressure on the peso, which is at the bottom of its managed band. Salesmen at Morgan Stanley are placing bets on whether the currency will collapse. The firm, worried that it will go bust if Mexico suspends convertibility of the peso into dollars, creates some peso convertibility bonds that pay a mere extra 50 basis points (0.50%) to get customers to absorb that risk. It targets the most clueless, who cheerfully buy the paper.[8]

The investment banks that were intermediating these dollar/peso bets could see a crash was imminent; the only question was how bad it would be. Yet in the late stages, Mexican banks were hoovering up a product peddled by Morgan Stanley called the Cetes swap, which was the derivative equivalent of borrowing in dollars to buy higher-yielding Mexican bonds. They were stepping in front of the steamroller, piling on bets that would create huge losses if the peso tanked at precisely the time when Morgan Stanley was desperately arranging hedges to protect itself against the very same possibility. The banks acted as if the 8% spread between the dollar-based interest rate it was paying to borrow and the peso-based interest rate it earned when it invested the proceeds was free money.

A general rule in finance: if it looks too good to be true, it is.

These wagers were not just wildly imprudent, but were also a regulatory end-run. The banks were already at their legal borrowing limits, but the Cetes swaps permitted them to evade these rules by entering into deals that were the economic equivalent but did not have to be disclosed to regulators or the public at large.[9] So banks that were already exposed to failure skirted restrictions, took on even more risk, and predictably went bust.

Morgan Stanley's analysts were touting the prospects for Mexico while others inside the firm were reducing their Mexico exposures.[10] In the dot-com era, 10 firms paid a total of nearly $1.5 billion in fines when the analysts pushed stocks that they said internally were rubbish. Would the firms' staff acting to reduce Mexico risk when they were still peddling to clients have been an SEC violation? No, because derivatives, unlike stocks, aren't regulated by the SEC.

Did Morgan Stanley and its cohort knowingly push the Mexican banks toward the brink? Ex-Morgan Stanley derivatives salesman Frank Partnoy, who helped to peddle the Mexican deals, suggests as much:

> At the time, many US bankers regarded the Mexican banks as cash piñatas and were eager to smash them open . . . if they were piñatas, they weren't even close to full yet. . . . Our plan was to fatten the banks some more. . . . An easier path to a Mexican bank's wallet was through its stomach.
>
> What would we feed the Mexican banks? Obviously, it should be high margin and high volume. We wanted to make as much money as we could. It should be addictive too, so the banks would gorge themselves. Once the banks were bloated and couldn't eat another bite, it would be easy to bat them down. Then, at the appropriate moment one little nudge would cause the entire obese Mexican banking system to topple like Humpty Dumpty.[11]

During the month before the Mexico implosion, one of Partnoy's colleagues gloated, "You have to be a criminal to be good at this business."[12]

In late December 1994, the Mexican government tried relieving pressure on the peso by widening its trading band with the dollar, a de facto 15% devaluation. Chaos ensued as everyone realized the game was over and raced for the exits. A mere three days later, the government capitulated and floated the currency. The peso fell 55% and later stabilized at an over 40% loss.

Ironically, the popularity of peso gambles was probably Morgan Stanley's salvation. So many investors held peso-linked dollar paper that no one looked particularly stupid for having gotten on the bandwagon. Moreover, the damage was so widespread that Uncle Sam rode in to the rescue. The United States provided a bailout in the form of a $50 billion emergency loan. Congress had voted down the rescue, but Treasury Secretary and friend of Wall Street Robert Rubin broke open a Treasury piggy bank (the Exchange Stabilization Fund, a Depression-era creation to support the dollar) for an unintended purpose, namely, assisting U.S. banks and investors by propping up the peso. Some argued at the time that it would have been better to structure a bailout of the Mexican economy rather than of U.S. investment banks and investors, but to little avail.

. . . . .

The Mexico saga is a microcosm of our current crisis. Deregulation unleashed openly predatory behavior, which became entrenched much earlier than most observers realize. The *nature* of malfeasance that occurred during the credit boom was no surprise; the only thing that was novel was its scale. That in turn was the product of continued ideology-driven liberalization.

But to most businessmen, predatory behavior looks incredibly short sighted and dangerous. Even if there is a fast buck to be made, it puts your entire franchise in jeopardy. How did Wall Street come to think this was a good gamble?

Ideology-driven deregulation (and the failure to regulate in response to evolving conditions) shifted the investment banking world from a model driven by relationships with corporate clients to one in which making profits on every transaction was paramount. One of the securities law reforms of the Great Depression was the Glass-Steagall Act, which separated commercial banks, which took deposits and made loans, from securities firms, also known as broker-dealers or their upscale variant, investment banks. The barrier between the two types of financial firms came under relentless attack from banks eager to earn rich investment banking profits starting in the 1980s, and after it was riddled with holes thanks to all the variances they had won, it was formally dismantled in 1999.

Another factor that altered securities firms' posture toward their clients was various regulatory changes within the industry, for the most part designed to make markets more liquid and reduce transaction costs to customers. While these moves were intended to help investors, over time they had perverse side effects. The new rules changed businesses in which it had been easy to earn steady profits in conservative ways into businesses scrambling for profits, and as a consequence the industry gradually changed from a relatively low-risk "fee-for-service" model to one where the big firms acted primarily as traders. As we saw with Bankers Trust, traders tend to see transactions as a zero-sum game, even if that party on the other side is nominally a customer.

Former Goldman Sachs managing director Nomi Prins agrees that competitive pressures turned banks into predators:

> To retain supremacy, banks had to prey upon their existing and emerging corporate clients to increase the banking business they were doing. That meant they had to aggressively and deliberately increase the number of M&A [mergers and acquisitions], debt, loan, stock, and IPO deals they did. It was more than a thirst for fees and profitability; it was a drive for survival and dominant market share in a limited banking space.[13]

The Glass-Steagall Act in 1933, more stringent limits on investing set by the SEC, the establishment of deposit insurance for commercial banks in 1934, and other regulatory provisions drafted in the wake of the Great Depression inaugurated an era of fairly calm banking that endured into the 1980s. The combination of good profits for simply complying with the rules and the threat of regulatory intervention meant that the industry as a whole steered clear of financial crises. Even though there started to be problems in the 1980s (the Latin American debt fiascos, the savings and loan crisis), U.S. banking did not suffer a true systemic crisis until 2007.

Even the securities industry, now seen as an extremely competitive field, was a comfortable business in the postwar period, dominated by the stock trading business. As Robert Newburger, who had been a member of the New York Stock Exchange since 1940, said of the industry in the 1950s and 1960s:

> You didn't have to be particularly good to be successful. You didn't have to be particularly bright. Young kids coming out of Harvard, Princeton, Yale, or wherever, their father would buy them a seat and they'd go on the [New York Stock Exchange] floor . . . in those days, with no brains and no creative thinking, the average income was $50,000 a year. I'm talking about what would now correspond to $500,000 a year. So when one of those young fellows would first come on the floor, all the clerks would gather around on the side and yell, "Too dumb to be a doctor or lawyer, his old man bought him a seat."[14]

Let's take a look at the system that operated in the United States during this period. Afterward, we'll discuss how it was successively dismantled.

The world of finance prior to the 1980s was fairly simple. Commercial banks (often called simply "banks") made loans and took deposits. They also raised a portion of their funding in the money markets.[15] So-called savings and loans (S&Ls) were similar, but specialized in mortgage lending.

The major investors were insurance companies (they have money to invest because they are paid premiums by policyholders and only later pay out on claims), pension funds, mutual funds, and affluent individuals.

Investment banks helped large corporations to raise equity (by managing stock offerings) and to borrow money (by managing bond offerings) by distributing newly-created securities to investors. This role was called "underwriting," and it involved having the company that was raising funds (the "issuer") sell its stocks or bonds to a syndicate of securities firms (the "underwriters") with the "lead manager" (often with "co-managers"—other investment banks—in a subordinate role) acting as the interface with the issuer, pricing the deal, selecting the syndicate, and coordinating its sales efforts. Thus the underwriters bought and then turned around and resold the paper at a higher price to investors. The lead manager was also responsible for doing due diligence on the issuer and helping prepare the relevant SEC filings. Historically, in the 1960s, the roles were distinct, with a cozy cartel of so-called "white shoe" firms, Morgan Stanley, Kuhn Loeb, Dillon Read, and First Boston, lead managing the deals and organizing syndicates, which actually sold the deal.

Institution	Traditional role	Prominent examples (1980)
Commercial banks	Take deposits, make loans to individuals and businesses	Citibank, Chase Manhattan, Bank of America
Investment banks (securities firms, broker-dealers)	Raise money for corporations and governments entities (underwrite stocks and bonds), trade securities or help others to trade (market making and brokerage), help carry out or prevent corporate takeovers (mergers & acquisitions)	Morgan Stanley, Goldman Sachs, First Boston (acquired by Credit Suisse), Salomon Brothers (now part of Citigroup)
Institutional investors	Manage money for individuals, corporations, endowments, foundations, and try to increase its value in a secure manner. Subject to regulatory oversight	Insurance companies, pension funds, mutual funds
Largely unregulated funds	Manage money for individuals, corporations, endowments, foundations and try to increase its value quickly. Typically charge performance fees based on profits to investors in addition to annual fees. Minimal oversight.	Very few then; hedge funds small; venture capital and LBO (later "private equity") funds grew rapidly later in the decade. Not yet seen as "institutional"

This process may sound risky, since there was always a chance that the investment bank would end up having to sell off the securities at a loss. In fact, the traditional procedure was anything but. The managers marketed the deal to investors, getting "circles" or indications of interest, and did not price the deal until it was effectively presold.

The underwriting process meant that investment bankers had strong relationships with the CEOs and CFOs of the corporations involved. Underwritings seemed mysterious, serious money was at stake, and the process was

time consuming, so the investment banking team got a lot of face time with
top executives.

Investment banks also carried out stock transactions for individuals or institutions that wanted to trade. The commissions that the bankers were paid on
the trades were fixed, and thus a highly dependable source of income.

Finally, investment banks also made some money by trading securities for
their own benefit, or from making markets (that is, acting as a middleman) in
securities that did not trade on exchanges, like municipal bonds. But prestige sat
with the investment banking side of the house. Some of it was economic: everyone understood a dollar of revenue from a fee business like underwriting was
more valuable than a dollar of revenues from trading because advising corporations did not require capital. But it was also a matter of class: to serve corporate clients, the bankers had to meet a minimum threshold of presentability,
which often meant degrees from elite schools that helped to justify the fees the
banks charged.

Credit was mainly provided to companies by commercial banks. Only very
large companies raised money directly from investors in the bond and commercial paper markets. The bond business was far smaller in terms of industry
profits than stock broking, and was also comparatively placid. Nearly all of the
buyers were large institutions (pension funds, insurance companies, bank trust
departments) that seldom traded.

· · · · ·

The growth of the mutual fund industry in the 1960s was the first factor that
shifted power and profits. Stocks had fixed commissions, and the brokers were
clearly coining money on their large trades, proportionately far less work than
a comparable volume of retail orders. First came volume discounts in 1968, then
a complete deregulation of commissions in 1975.

For securities firms, the timing could not have been worse. The prosperity
of the great bull market of the 1960s ended abruptly when the NYSE compos-
ite plunged 37% from May 14, 1969 to May 25, 1970. The volume of stock trades
evaporated at the same time that commissions were falling due to the new rules.
Many firms failed. The survivors looked to find new profit sources, increasing
competition within the industry.

The pursuit of new profit opportunities started the upscale firms, who had
once been models of probity, down a slippery slope of predatory behavior. In the
1970s, with stocks cheap, big cash-rich companies went hunting, and investment banks decided to get into the business of supplying the maps and ammo.

Canadian miner Inco set off a wave of transactions with its hostile tender offer for ESM, the world's biggest battery maker, in 1974. Hostile deals were hardly new, but what was novel was that Morgan Stanley, the blue chippiest investment bank of all, backed Inco.[16] It was suddenly legitimate for respectable firms to lead raids on big companies. Goldman was the lone holdout, specializing in takeover defense. But this seemingly high-minded posture was self-serving. Morgan Stanley's clients were skewed toward the very biggest companies who were more likely to be on the attack. Goldman, a comparative newcomer that had successfully moved up the industry pecking order, had proportionately fewer Fortune 100 clients and more in the next tier, and so Goldman's clients were more likely to be potential prey. Goldman did not want those clients defecting out of a fear that the firm might use its intimate knowledge of their affairs to tee up takeovers.[17]

The die was cast. Wall Street could no longer be relied upon to be loyal, not even to its very best meal tickets.

Meanwhile, the bond business, previously a sleepy backwater to equities, also saw profound shifts, due to the inflation of the 1970s. Inflation whacked bond prices, and investors, whose supposedly safe portfolios were now swimming in red ink, were confronted with a new demon: interest rate risk. The old practice of buying and holding for the long term went out the window. Investors now wanted to be able to trade quickly and in large volume with dealers who could provide information on where the market was going. Bonds are an over-the-counter market, so dealers trade in and out of their own inventory. In any such trading market, size is an important consideration. The bigger your clientele, and the bigger your market share with them, the better your ability to buy and sell. The better a view any dealer has of the entire market, the better it can set prices. Clients prefer to deal with a firm that can handle sizeable orders and that is perceived to have a better perspective of what is going on in the market. Most business pitches to corporate and institutional accounts make an art form of creatively cutting statistics so that the bank in question can claim it is a leading player in the relevant market.

For all of these reasons, it was critical in the bond business to become large. Size was helpful in equities (stocks), albeit to a lesser degree, since stocks, unlike bonds, trade on centralized exchanges like the New York Stock Exchange, lowering the need for raw trading muscle. The term "bulge bracket" referred to the companies that had made it into the prestigious group of top underwriters. By 1975, institutional equity leader Goldman Sachs, bond powerhouse Salomon Brothers, and retail kingpin Merrill Lynch had joined this prized "bulge bracket," at the expense of the fading white shoe firms Kuhn Loeb and Dillon Read.[18]

All securities firms felt the loss of safe revenues. An industry that was full of small players changed radically from the 1960s to the 1980s and became more and more concentrated. The main source of profit shifted away from low-risk stock commissions to much higher risk activity, as brokerage commissions fell as a percentage of industry revenues from 53.8% in 1972 to 17.3% in 1991.[19]

Another often overlooked regulatory change had wide-ranging impact: Rule 415. This SEC provision, implemented in the early 1980s, allowed companies to use a new process for selling stocks and bonds. Back then, as now, if corporations made a stock offering, the price their stock fetched reflected on how the company was perceived. The elaborate traditional underwriting procedure was therefore very helpful for companies, since it made sure that there would be no surprises when new shares of their stock came on the market.

But bonds were a different matter. Issuers weren't particularly concerned if a bond deal went off badly, since each bond was unique, and one deal floundering did not have any implications for future debt sales. Companies simply wanted the highest price they could get for their bonds, since that meant cheap funding for them. And if the managers (the investment banks) set too high a price and took a loss when they resold them, well, that was their problem.

Bankers Trust in particular pushed for Rule 415, which meant that the company wanting to sell securities no longer had to specify an underwriter to the SEC. Instead, the company could file a "shelf registration" with the SEC, indicating that it might want to sell certain securities. Then the company would be allowed to sell them later when the mood struck ("off the shelf"). The new rule meant that companies, after filing a shelf registration, could call up several Wall Street firms and ask them to bid competitively for the bond offering, sometimes over the course of as little as 15 minutes. At the time, the investment banks were private and had much less capital than today, so the profit potential was skimpy and the risk of not being able to resell the bonds at a profit became much larger than before the rule change (and bond underwritings had not been a great business to begin with). But no investment bank worth its salt would refuse to bid, since the firm might lose access to future, vastly more attractive equities and merger and acquisition mandates.

BT's gambit had worked. Big corporations started to adopt an open-door posture, which helped big commercial banks, who had been aspiring for years to eat at the investment banking table.

This change drove another, even bigger wedge in the relationship between big companies and investment banks. Investment banks no longer spent the same amount of time together with company executives while preparing a stock or bond offering. The stock underwriting process stayed more or less intact, but even there large public companies moved to a more transactional footing, increasingly staging so-called "beauty contests" to determine who would manage their next stock offering.

Meanwhile, the role of commercial banks was also being eroded. Money market funds, created in the 1970s, competed for bank deposits. In the postwar system, smaller companies with lower credit ratings had depended upon the banks for funding. But in the 1980s, the investment bank Drexel helped the junk bond market to balloon into an alternative funding source for these companies. Junk bonds were a means by which investors would loan money directly to the companies by buying bonds, and often junk bonds made it possible for the companies to borrow more than the commercial banks would have allowed.

The end of restrictions on interstate banking meant local banks faced more competition from big regional players across a broad range of services. In the 1990s, U.S. commercial banks also had to contend with the more aggressive competition from European banks, who were intensifying their efforts to win business from U.S. customers. Unlike American banks, they were "universal banks" back at home, participating both in investment and commercial banking. Many of them enjoyed low-cost funding, and their sheer size was also an advantage in some activities.[20] Banks found their earnings under attack, with their best customers of various types cherry-picked by new entrants, and the surviving banks competing with each other ever more aggressively.

Thus a new competitive dynamic was in place for both investment banks and commercial banks. Deregulation and changes in banks' competitive environment not only forced consolidation, but also led to a pursuit of greater scale of operations. Among the larger investment banks, the change was dramatic. Underwriting, the ability to buy and resell high-quality new stock and bond issues, had once been the key to success. By the 1980s, the critical capabilities had become trading and institutional distribution.

Why was bigger better? First, size was particularly important in trading, as described above in the case of bonds. Over-the-counter bond markets showed the value of scale strongly in the 1980s, with Salomon Brothers becoming dominant. Trading prowess became a factor even in equities, which traded on exchanges. Block trades represented 60% of New York Stock Exchange volume in 1984.[21]

Second, the industry required a high level of minimum infrastructure and staffing. Firms needed to be in the major financial centers around the world, with large-scale computer operations for position and risk management and order processing. Firms made significant, ongoing investments in proprietary analytics. Investment banks increasingly needed to maintain costly infrastructure and staff levels, with the minimum level needed to compete growing all the time. The more volume you could pump through your platform, the better your bottom line.

These pressures drove firms to become larger, not just in terms of their operations, but also their balance sheets. That meant they needed more and more capital. And that drove the change that led to the biggest and most detrimental change to the industry, as far as society is concerned, namely the abandonment of the partnership form of organization.

Until 1970, the NYSE required that all member firms be partnerships, believing that the partnership form produced more financially responsible behavior than the corporate form, which limited liability to the owners.

Events have proven this old-fashioned view to be correct. The partnership model made sense for a host of reasons. First, partnerships do not have easy exit options for their owners; it is difficult to sell one's shares to third-party investors. Most often, the retiring partners were bought out, usually over time, by younger people in the firm who took over the business. That meant both seniors and juniors who aspired to become partners focused on the long-term health of the business.

Second, partnerships carry unlimited liability. Suppose your head salesman creates a completely fictitious company and sells $1 billion worth of shares in it, pretending your firm is behind it. Guess what, the wronged investors won't simply be trying to recover their losses from your business. If they win in court, they can go after you and your partners' private wealth.

That suited the NYSE, since it meant that firms would make more conservative decisions, particularly when dealing with investors.

Third, it was unseemly to have a firm's revenues and costs on view. Given that salaries and bonuses were far and away the biggest expense, it would not be hard for customers of a public company to come up with a good approximation of what professionals were paid. That concern has been borne out in the current crisis. One of the reasons for the widespread unhappiness about the bailouts is that public companies have to disclose what top officers are paid, and the public can also calculate how much the average employee makes. In the old days, when propriety mattered, most members of the securities industry did not want their clients to have even a rough idea of how much they earned. There was no point in risking the question, "Where are the customers' yachts?"

No one questioned the partnership approach until it came under strain. The first sea change resulted from the surge in stock orders that occurred during the 1960s bull market. The unprecedented level of transactions left the securities firms struggling to keep up, given that order processing was then done by hand and securities had to be physically delivered after a trade. Many not-as-well-managed firms failed or were picked up by their peers, often out of charity.

It was hard for owners of these partnerships to deal with this level of downside. If your partnership failed, you didn't have much of a prayer of making good the losses. Mortgaging your house will only take you so far. The industry was Darwinian and ultimately too Darwinian for the incumbents' taste.

It suddenly became respectable to seek "permanent capital," otherwise known as "other people's money," in order to buffer these risks. Donaldson, Lufkin & Jenrette, a retail brokerage firm, went public in 1970 over the NYSE's objections.[22] Merrill Lynch and other firms that had been most affected by the crisis followed shortly. The big institutional firms looked down on this practice until pressures resulting from their growth led them to relent. By 1987, all the major investment banks had either gone public, or had been acquired by a public firm. The only exception was Goldman, which went public in 1999.[23]

This change to outside funds largely replacing partnership capital turned out not simply to be a response to the scale necessary in sales and trading, but, in a self-reinforcing cycle, led to even more emphasis on those activities. Prestige once sat with the investment banking side of the house, partly because everyone understood a dollar of revenue from a fee business like mergers and acquisitions was more valuable than a dollar of revenue from trading because the former did not require capital. But outside funding was cheaper than partnership equity, and that meant that activities like sales and trading that required a lot of capital now looked more attractive.

As fixed income became more and more mathematically driven, and the creation of derivatives-based products amped up complexity by an order of magnitude or two, over time sales and trading operations started hiring far more highly educated people in many roles. They might not pass the country club test, but their resumes were nevertheless impressive. Power shifted to where the revenues were biggest, and that was increasingly on the trading side of the house.

Trading kept increasing in importance during this period, and the change had wider ramifications. Underwriting and other fee businesses are service businesses. You want your client to believe you have done a good job so that he will come back to you. Reputations and perceptions matter. The job description of a trader, by contrast, is to make as much as he can, whether in an impersonal market, or against the firm's customers. Investment bankers performing services for clients have reasons to try to establish a strong image for professionalism (even if some of that might be smoke and mirrors). But to put it bluntly, the constraint on salesmen and traders is simply to steer clear of scandals and regulatory violations.

Ironically, this set of developments worked to the advantage of traditional commercial bank aspirants to the investment banking crown. Commercial banks had tried, with an impressive lack of success, to compete in the unregulated areas of investment banking, most notably mergers and acquisitions. Although Citibank had created a new, important product (interest rate swaps), investment banks in the 1980s viewed the idea that commercial banks could ever be a competitive threat as ridiculous. Their cultures were polar opposites. Power in a commercial bank resided in the size of the operation that a manager oversaw; in an investment bank, it was strictly bottom line. Commercial banks promoted staff largely based on time in grade, while investment banks would exploit their money makers, moving the best ones up quickly.

Traditional banks were factories, processing huge volumes of transactions. They broke down tasks, routinizing them, limiting the discretion of frontline employees. Investment banks were freewheeling and adaptive, and the less-well-run ones could have disarray unthinkable in most other forms of enterprise. The effects of this form of organization will be seen in greater detail in the chapter on looting. For instance, Lehman Brothers, after the death of patriarch Bobby Lehman, fell into warring fiefdoms. It was not uncommon for several partners to pitch for the business of a large client independently, with no coordination, each as much in competition with his nominal partners as with other firms.

Never underestimate a determined competitor, particularly one that has more firepower than you do. The growing importance of over-the-counter market making, an unregulated area, played into the banks' big strength, the fact that they had access to so much capital. And they did have some expertise in trading from their own foreign exchange, Treasuries, and money markets operations. The rising importance of derivatives, another unregulated activity, was also a fortunate accident of timing. While derivatives weren't traditional investment banking, commercial banks could get in on the ground floor and use this sexy, high-margin product to fight their way up the industry food chain.

The commercial banks were themselves struggling to survive in their own highly competitive environment. To preserve profits, they adopted new business models, taking on more risk and using less equity to compete, as best they could, with the new entrants.[24] The biggest change was their expansion into activities that were largely unregulated, or what later came to be described as the shadow banking system.

So going public, and the shift in profit opportunities and influence to sales and trading, meant investment banks had less reason to restrain their predatory impulses. Meanwhile, the very large commercial banks were under similar competitive pressures, and over time their capital markets businesses became largely indistinguishable from those of investment banks.

By the time Glass-Steagall, the law separating commercial and investment banking, was revoked in 1999, most in the industry regarded it as a nonevent.

Banks had already gotten so many regulatory variances that the barrier between the two businesses was shot full of holes, with commercial banks already having large market shares in many capital markets activities.

Developments in London ran in parallel. After the "Big Bang," a radical deregulation of the financial markets in 1986, the local incumbent partnerships were supplanted, after some initial misfires, by large American players. Europeans who wanted to play (Credit Suisse, Deutsche Bank, UBS, ING) mostly merged with, or bought, American firms, or else hired key American talent. The French, as always, took a slightly different path.

By the mid-1990s, investment banking of a distinctly American flavor was by far the predominant style in the world's two largest financial centers.

. . . . .

Deregulation fed into the deterioration of standards by weakening external checks. And cheap capital and deregulation also fuelled the growth of over-the-counter markets, in particular negotiated, customized, or unique products, where customers would have difficulty evaluating the quality of prices they were being offered or the true risks they took on.

When most people who are not in the finance industry think of markets, the stock market is often their model. But U.S. equity markets are strictly regulated, with a host of rules about order placement, settlement and payment, lending, and use of securities held in custody.

To understand the broader impact of the deregulation of the 1980s and 1990s, let's step back and look at the safeguards set forth in SEC rules. They fall into three categories:

- Ongoing disclosure of important information about the issuer, including financial condition, officers, large shareholders, material contracts. This includes criminal penalties for making false or misleading statements or important omissions.
- Criminal penalties for insider trading.
- Prohibition of practices used to manipulate prices, such as front running (buying or selling in advance of customer orders), making misleading statements, creating the impression of active trading. Equity exchanges must register with the SEC and assist in enforcing member compliance with the regulations.

Most of the so-called innovation took place in the realm of over-the-counter derivatives. Securities are regulated by the SEC, while the Commodity Futures

Trading Commission (CFTC) has broad authority over futures and options. While the sweeping language of the 1974 Commodity Futures Trading Act gave the CFTC authority over "all services, rights, and interests in which contracts for future delivery are presently or in the future dealt in," the so-called Treasury amendment carved out foreign exchange, government securities, and other types of financial instruments. This exemption allowed for the explosive growth of over-the-counter derivatives.

"Over-the-counter" (OTC) instruments are not traded on exchanges where all orders go to one place. Each dealer makes a market, which means he is a mini-exchange. The dealer provides bid and offer prices depending on his inventory, how much capital the firm gives the trader, and his view of the market. Nevertheless, in liquid over-the-counter markets like major currencies (dollar versus yen), U.S. Treasuries, and simple interest rate swaps, there are enough dealers to keep pricing tight—plus most big companies subscribe to data services that give them a good enough sense of where the market is to limit how much they can be exploited by a market maker.

But in smaller or less liquid OTC markets, the fact that OTC products are unregulated makes a huge difference. Abuses in the Wild West of derivatives and over-the-counter markets, the purview of consenting adults, rarely come to light. The lack of the higher standards governing the SEC's terrain is keenly felt.

In the brawl of these OTC markets, no niceties apply. For instance, famed options trader Andy Krieger, who made seemingly inconceivable profits for his various employers, would use his counterparties' efforts to manipulate currency prices against them. If he wanted to sell, say, the French franc (this was in the days before the euro), he would enter a large buy order instead. Traders would rush to acquire the French franc ahead of his trade, pushing the price up. Krieger would then sell his intended order into their now-higher bid.[25] This was the simplest, crudest approach he would employ; most of his tricks to misdirect other traders were more complex, across multiple markets (cash, forwards, options).

But what made Krieger's market jujitsu work in this example was that the traders Krieger fooled assumed he was engaging in front running, that is, placing his orders ahead of a customer trade. That's forbidden in SEC land but perfectly kosher in unregulated markets.

Consider another dubious practice I witnessed first hand. Cash and near forwards in the big currencies (dollar, pound, yen, euro) in London are among the most liquid markets in the world, and therefore in theory less subject to bad behavior. The biggest foreign exchange dealer in London, the treasury department of a very large bank, had a saleswoman whose profits were vastly in excess of anyone else's. Her secret?

Some big companies had global currency netting programs. That meant that they had internal software that allowed them to cancel out offsetting transactions (say a sale of yen in one office against a purchase in another). They would then, once a month, go to the bank and trade whatever exposure was left over. The agreement with the bank specified that the orders, often pretty large, would be executed on a particular day between 10:00 A.M. and 11:00 A.M.

The saleswoman would put the trades through at 10:10 A.M., which meant that she sold or bought all of the currencies then and she knew what the prices had been. But that was not necessarily the price she reported to the customer. The system allowed her to record a price to the customer that was different than what the trade had executed at. She would then watch all the markets for the next 50 minutes. If the price got worse from the customer's standpoint, she would enter that price as the price to the customer. She would pocket the difference between the two prices as a profit for her bank, often producing sizeable markups on the trades.

Grounds for litigation? Probably yes, since the trade was in fact not executed at the price indicated; you'd have to read the contract to see if her actions were indeed a violation of the terms. Provable? Not unless you did an audit of all the trades in that hour. The clever choice of waiting out the first ten minutes meant that over time, not all the prices she reported to her customers would be the worst of the hour, only most of them, making a challenge unlikely.

Allocating someone the worst trade in a time period is a no-no under SEC rules; in fact, the SEC has gone to some lengths to specify the permitted timing of order execution to prevent this very sort of thing.

The point is a simple one. Even in the most liquid OTC markets, where it is in theory easiest for customers to take care of themselves, either by getting information services to get real time (but indicative) quotes or getting simultaneous bids, dealers could and did find ways to take advantage of their trust. And if it happens there, imagine how easy it is to pull fast ones with more complicated products where prices are less visible.

Sadly, this was not the view of Alan Greenspan, who argued:

> In the case of the institutional off-exchange derivatives markets, it seems abundantly clear that private market regulation is quite effectively and efficiently achieving what have been identified as the public policy objectives of government regulation. I am aware of no evidence that the prices of OTC contracts have been manipulated. Participants in these markets have been savvy enough to limit their activity to contracts that are very difficult to manipulate.[26]

Greenspan was hardly alone in his dogmatic belief in the wisdom of leaving "free markets" to their own devices. He had the backing of the "law and economics" stalwarts we described in chapter 5. As Judge Frank Easterbrook and Daniel Fischel, then University of Chicago Law School dean, asserted in 1991: "[A] law against fraud is not an essential or even necessarily important ingredient of securities markets."[27]

Easterbrook went as far as blocking a plaintiff from presenting a case that argued that an auditor had assisted in a fraud. The judge claimed it would be "irrational" for the accountant to behave that way, given his interest in preserving his reputation.[28] Hmm, might it not be a viable business strategy to establish a reputation for playing fast and loose? There is probably a lot of demand for very accommodating accountants.

It should come as no surprise that Fischel acted as an expert witness on behalf of Charles Keating of Lincoln Savings, and Enron's Kenneth Lay and Jeffrey Skilling. All were convicted of fraud.

But how could Greenspan have any basis for his assertion, that he was "aware of no evidence" that anything was amiss? That was a curious turn of phrase, and for good reason.

The Fed regulates banks, and also supervises government bond dealers. In theory, it could have used the latter role to make broad inquiries into the health of the major investment banks, but chose not to.

Although some like J.P. Morgan and Citigroup, and the U.S. subsidiaries of foreign banks like UBS, were pushing the envelope, the Fed dealt with only a limited number of participants in OTC derivatives and the products created from them. Even for "plain vanilla" products like interest rate swaps, and traditional OTC markets like Treasury and corporate bonds, Greenspan's cheery views were contradicted by attempts to game markets in various ways. The chicanery of the female foreign exchange dealer, while troubling, was chump change; a Treasury short squeeze in 1986 was not.

Moreover, his belief that most participants were sticking to the simple stuff was sheer fantasy. The fact that the products were unregulated meant the central bank would learn only what the commercial banks that also happened to be big dealers in these OTC markets chose to reveal. Is it any surprise that they told him there was no gambling in Casablanca?

In fact, Greenspan's statement demonstrated either stunning ignorance or brazen misrepresentation. In 1995, Brandon Becker and Jennifer Yoon of the SEC published an article that listed derivative losses by the company suffering the loss, derivative classification, and amount of damage in 1994.[29] Note that the compilation was based merely on reports in the popular press and thus was only a subset of the universe. That list ran to over 100 names. To give a sense of the range of players, here are the ones with names beginning with S:

Salomon Brothers
Sandusky County, Ohio
Seamen's Bank for Savings
Sears, Roebuck
Shanghai International Securities
Showa Shell Seikyu
Silverado Banking Savings & Loan
SinarMas (Indonesia)
Soros Fund Management
Southwestern Federal Credit Union
Southwestern Life
St. Lucie County, Florida
St. Petersburg, Florida

One factor that made these products popular was that they allowed investors to evade rules and hopefully boost performance beyond what they could do within their strategy or regulatory confines. Derivatives allowed supposedly dollar-based investors to take currency punts. The Banamex example cited earlier is a case where dollar investors were making bets on the peso. In another example, Credit Suisse issued a one-year AAA-rated note with redemption based on the proxy basket Thailand was using to manage its currency. A proxy basket is a portfolio of securities designed so that its price movements closely track a particular index or currency, in this case the baht. The note looked like a safe dollar investment, but was a bet on the baht.[30]

Derivatives could also lever returns for an investor who was not permitted to borrow money to invest or use options or futures. He instead could buy an instrument that amounted to the same thing and no one would be the wiser. And then of course you also have the investors who did not understand what they were buying, who heard a salesman's verbal description and couldn't, or chose not to, puzzle out the formula that described how the instrument really worked. For instance, consider this piece of artwork:

Maximum of $[0:NP \times [7 \times [(LIBOR^2 \times 1/LIBOR)-(LIBOR^4 \times LIBOR^{-3})]]$
$\times$ days in the month/360]
Where
NP = $600 million
LIBOR = 6 month dollar LIBOR rates

The beauty of this formula is that no matter what values were plugged in, the value was always zero. The client was paying $4 million a month for three years for the privilege of having an utterly worthless contract.[31]

So the opaque, deregulated markets were an ideal setting for chicanery. Some firms encouraged aggressive behavior. The Morgan Stanley derivatives salesman Partnoy, again:

> I began to crave the sensation of ripping someone's face off. At First Boston, I had never ripped a client's face off, and I certainly had not blown up anyone. Now as I watched Morgan Stanley's derivatives salesmen in action, I began to like the idea. Scarecrow [a manager] and others encouraged me.
>
> Morgan Stanley carefully cultivated the urge to blast a client to smithereens. It was no surprise I had caught the fever so soon. Everyone had caught it, particularly the most senior managing directors. My bosses were avid skeet shooters. . . . When they screamed "Pull!" they imagined a client flying through the air.
>
> Ten years ago, Morgan Stanley had decided to change its philosophy and the newly aggressive firm was the investment banking star of the 1990s. . . . This kind of aggressive fervor was new to me. . . . Morgan Stanley was a savage cult. I marveled at how quickly the firm had taken on such a fierce creed.[32]

Although Morgan Stanley begged to differ with Partnoy's account, he claims his former colleagues complained that he had omitted the most nefarious stories, and "barely scratched the surface."[33]

But Greenspan refused to believe that such behavior could ever occur. Brooksley Born, then the new head of the CFTC, was invited to lunch with the Maestro in 1996. The subject of fraud arose. Greenspan maintained no rules were needed. A customer would realize he had been treated badly and would find a new broker. Born was incredulous, having spent the better part of a decade dealing with the aftermath of Nelson Bunker Hunt's efforts to corner the silver market, which included a large network of coconspirators. Greenspan refused to be swayed, and cut off the discussion: "Well, Brooksley, I guess you and I will never agree about fraud."[34]

Born should not have been surprised. Greenspan's views were shared by the Clinton administration, particularly Treasury Secretary Robert Rubin and Deputy Secretary Larry Summers. A series of actions made it clear that the industry would be left to its own devices.

A few examples:

At the beginning of 1994, fund managers almost collectively were convinced interest rates would stay low, and many used derivatives to increase leverage or camouflage their wagers to that effect. When the Fed raised interest rates in February, the aggregate losses were $1.5 trillion, the biggest wipeout since the 1929 crash. But despite the hue and cry that ensued, SEC chief Arthur Levitt worked closely with industry lobbyist Mark Brickell to beat back new legislation. Indeed, the result was that Wall Street wound up better protected from liability and with greater leeway to manage its own affairs.[35]

Even worse was a BT development that seemed a mere footnote and came years after the settlements. Guillaume Fonkenell, who had priced one of the Procter & Gamble trades, had instructed the back office to make two separate changes to the volatility, which increased his take at the expense of the salesman. He was also charged with hiding the risks of two trades with Indonesian firms that led them to lose $100 million. Fooling with the accounting once a trade is entered, save to rectify an error, is falsifying books and records, a serious no-no. Remarkably, the Fed lost its case before an administrative law judge, who bought the dubious argument that marking to market involved "a number of judgment calls," when in this case there were readily available benchmarks.[36] This decision gave traders and managers carte blanche to use volatility, an input into pricing derivatives, to cook the books.

The Supreme Court, via a 1994 decision, reduced investor protection. In a stunning show of illogic, the court ruled in *Central Bank of Denver v. First Interstate Bank of Denver*[37] that plaintiffs could not sue advisors like investment bankers, accountants, and lawyers for aiding and abetting securities fraud. A suit against them could only proceed if the defendant was charged with primary liability, meaning the damaged party was his client. This was a radical decision, reversing sixty years of court and administrative rulings.[38] Thus, for instance, if an accountant signed off on fraudulent financial statements that an investor relied upon, the investor could no longer pursue the accountant to recover any losses that resulted from the unraveling of the fraud. Yet in criminal law, an accessory, like the car driver in a bank robbery, is subject to prosecution along with the gunmen who took the cash.

In 1997, Brooksley Born, the head of the CFTC, undeterred by her lunch with Greenspan, started looking into regulating derivatives and invited comments on particular types, including credit default swaps (CDS), a new, rapidly growing product.[39] In fact, CDS are not derivatives in the traditional sense, since their price is not based on, or "derived" from, something else. For true derivatives, like oil futures or stock options, the price relates to that of something that has a current, "cash market" price. For instance, there is a spot market for oil and current trading prices for particular stocks and equity indices.

CDS are unregulated insurance agreements.[40] One party, the "protection buyer," contracts with the insurer, called in finance-speak the "protection seller," to guarantee against the risk of default of a specified amount of exposure (say $100 million dollars) for a certain time period (three and five years are most common) for a particular company (say British Petroleum) or an index.

Even though calling CDS derivatives was debatable, that stance meant they were unregulated. And when Born threatened to change that treatment, the backlash was swift and hard. On multiple occasions, Greenspan, Treasury Secretary Rubin, Deputy Secretary Summers, and SEC chairman Levitt pressed her to back down. When she persisted, Greenspan, Rubin, and Levitt end-ran her in June 1998, going to Congress to bar her from acting until "more senior regulators" came up with a fix.[41] The fall 1998 implosion of the hedge fund Long Term Capital Management, widely seen as barely averted systemic crisis, vindicated her concerns. Here a firm composed of the very best and brightest, Nobel Prize winners and the very best traders and quants, had been unable to handle the risks of the new complex OTC markets. Yet, incredibly, Congress gave the CTFC a stunning rebuke, blocking the commission's regulatory authority for six months. Born resigned shortly thereafter.

Taking no chances, in November 1999, the "senior regulators" urged Congress to wrest all regulatory authority for derivatives from the CFTC. Arthur Levitt shepherded the Commodity Futures Modernization Act through Congress in 2000. It exempted OTC derivatives from regulation and went to some length to highlight that energy derivatives were included. Mark Brickell, the lobbyist representing the International Swaps and Derivatives Association, drafted important sections of the bill.[42]

■ ■ ■ ■ ■

We have seen how regulators and courts were either unable or unwilling to impede predatory behavior. What about the ratings agencies? Did they identify dodgy securities so that investors would be able to steer clear?

Unfortunately, just as in the Banamex case, investors frequently placed mistaken faith in rating-agency grades of complex instruments. Dubious rating played a central role in the peso crisis and our latter-day mess. Grades come from "nationally recognized statistical rating organizations," a designation conferred by the SEC. While the ratings agencies have a hundred-year history, their importance increased greatly in the 1970s as ratings were officially made a consideration for a host of investors. For instance, many institutions are prohibited from owning much of anything in the way of below-investment-grade securities, meaning those that scored lower than BBB or Bbb. Some bond funds commit to keeping their average ratings above a certain level. Bank capital use ratings, with higher-rated paper needing less capital held against it. Even the Fed uses ratings to determine how much of a haircut to take to paper pledged as collateral for loans, for example at its discount window and its recently created facilities.

Amazingly, despite their central role, ratings agencies cannot be sued for erroneous scores. Courts have upheld the rating agencies' argument that their marks are merely opinions of the credit strength of an issuer and thus subject to First Amendment protection.[43]

The ratings agencies have come under well-deserved fire for their lapses and complicity with issuers in peddling complex paper. Even though investors depend on the agencies' scores, the ratings are in fact paid for by the issuer, and structured securities pay better than simpler paper. The complexity of the deals meant the agencies may not have fully understood the transactions, particularly since staff who developed expertise would depart for better-paying jobs at investment banks or fund managers. And the fact that the organizations seeking the ratings were prospective employers of the individuals involved made pushback even less likely.

But at a higher level, the ratings had already been compromised. The very fact that ratings are enshrined in regulations means that a particular rating is presumed to be equivalent across products. An AA should mean the same level of risk whether the bond issuer was a corporation, a municipality, a sovereign state, or a structured vehicle (the ratings agencies have tried to claim otherwise as they have come under attack, but a reading of their past pronouncements shows otherwise[44]).

In fact, structured products like those using residential mortgages had important *inherent* differences from corporate bonds that made them riskier and therefore made their ratings misleading. For structured credits, the risks are biased to the downside. Moreover, highly structured paper like tranches in collateralized debt obligations is subject to catastrophic falls in cash flows when certain levels of default are reached, which lead to dramatic downgrades. In the world of corporate bonds, a ratings decline of more than a couple of grades is a rare event absent massive fraud. Yet in the credit bust, rating downgrades of twelve, and even as much as eighteen grades, were fairly common on subprime-related paper. It became a joke that a fund manager could go to lunch owning AAA-rated paper and come back and find it lowered to CCC, which is not merely junk, but speculative.

While rating agencies have received a great deal of well-deserved criticism for acting as enablers of the crisis, dubious treatment of off-balance-sheet vehicles also played a role. We will discuss those accounting issues in chapter 7.

■ ■ ■ ■ ■

Many factors impede misbehavior coming to light and being punished. If victims are professionals who have a fiduciary duty to their clients, exposing their incompetence would open themselves up to claims. So some wronged parties can have more to lose from revealing their errors of judgment than to gain in restitution, which invariably discourages legal activity. Moreover, as we have seen, some legislation and court decisions have raised the bar for private redress.

Finally, even in cases where regulators can do something, enforcement has become a rare event, limited to high-profile cases like the $65 billion Bernie Madoff Ponzi scheme (and even then only after the horse had left the barn and was in the next county).

It took not the SEC but New York State attorney general Eliot Spitzer to ferret out widespread fraud in the dot-com era, namely, brokerage firms touting stocks they knew to be junk, eventually extracting a $1.5 billion settlement from twelve firms. Similarly in 2008, it was states, not the SEC, who took the first action on the auction rate securities scandal, when retail investors were told these instruments were safe and liquid, only to find they could not access their funds when dealers quit supporting the market.

The "free markets" advocates have created a hall of mirrors. Milton Friedman believed that the courts were an important mechanism, if not the key mechanism, for preserving property rights and keeping markets fair. Yet the Department of Justice and the SEC effectively stopped going after complex cases, sticking to easy-to-prove cases with high media potential. State attorneys general have upon occasion moved to fill the gap, but they are not ideally situated to pursue high finance. That leaves private suits of the sort Friedman would endorse as the sole policing mechanism. Yet powerful interests and the very ideology Friedman backed succeeded in gutting this channel.

Now the only defense a hapless investor might have is looking for "reputable" firms. But if standards have decayed across the board due to the lack of legal and regulatory costs of bad behavior, why should any firm care much about its reputation?

What we can observe is therefore a very small fraction of underlying activity. But even with our current, fragmentary knowledge, it is clear that predatory tendencies of the intermediaries only grew and helped precipitate the crisis.

We will focus on the credit crisis and skip over well-covered abuses, such as the Wall Street equity analysts pushing dot-com stocks they knew to be dreadful, Enron, and the 2002 accounting scandals.

Let's review some elements that were critical both in the Mexican banking crisis of 1994 and now:

Use of derivatives to evade regulations, leading banks to be undercapitalized. In Mexico, the banks used derivatives to increase their economic exposures, which was tantamount to increasing the size of their balance sheet, when they were at the limits of what their equity levels would permit and should not have expanded any further. This contributes directly to systemic instability. Thinly capitalized banks are more prone to failure.

One very large example: AIG wrote over $300 billion of credit default swaps for European banks. Its financial statement for 2007 said they had written the CDS, "for the purpose of providing them with regulatory capital relief rather than risk mitigation in exchange for a minimum guarantee fee."[45]

AIG's role in providing what turned out to be fictive capital to European banks was a major reason the United States rode in to rescue the giant insurer. As of June 2009, the total size of the bailout was $180 billion.[46]

Investors taking on risks they did not understand and would never have knowingly accepted. This has been endemic, as insufficiently skilled investors too often relied on glib salesmen's descriptions and ratings. They lacked the skill to make an independent assessment. The biggest chumps seem to be government bodies and foreigners. For instance, Lehman and other major banks sold collateralized debt obligations (CDOs) to retail customers. Readers may recall that CDOs are highly structured paper, often a resecuritization (tranches of other structured deals often went into CDOs, which themselves were tranched into risk classes). They were designed so that the highest quality layers fetched AAA ratings. We discuss CDOs in more detail in chapter 9.

It was clear most buyers relied on the rating. The deals were very complex, containing pieces from many other deals, each of which needed to be assessed to come up with the likely cash flows that were the raw material for the deal, and then used to determine how those flows were distributed among the tranches. It could take a skilled person using specialized software a full weekend to evaluate a single deal. Yet the buyers included town councils and fire brigade boards in Australia (one reported losing 80% of its investment)[47] and Narvik, a Norwegian village 140 miles north of the Arctic Circle.[48]

The German Landesbanken, famous for their haplessness, took an estimated €300–500 billion worth of now-troubled U.S. assets, between purchases and guarantees to U.S. bank off-balance-sheet vehicles such as conduits (bank-like vehicles that funded consumer receivables, such as auto loans, credit card receivables, and student loans) and their more exotic cousins, structured investment vehicles, or SIVs.[49]

And it wasn't just subprime or structured credits that produced large losses. Jefferson County, Alabama, entered into a series of complex interest-rate swaps to lower the cost of a $3.2 billion financing for its sewer authority.

If the municipality declares bankruptcy, it will have the dubious honor of being the largest of its type, beating 1990s derivatives victim Orange County.[50] In Italy, 600 local bodies ranging from Milan to Polino (home to 290 people) entered into over 1,000 derivatives contracts on €35.5 billion of debt. Unrealized losses at the end of 2008 were €1.93 billion. Giorgio Questa, a former investment banker, now finance professor, stated the obvious: "It makes no sense for local governments to dabble in derivatives. At best they get ripped off."[51]

Related to the point above, but distinct, is **investors as bagholders, meaning a dumping ground for intermediaries' risks.** Recall that in the later stages of the Mexico mess, Morgan Stanley wasn't simply arranging trades to collect fees on those deals. It also teed up some swaps specifically to shift onto customers a risk that it wanted out of, namely, that of Mexico suspending convertibility of the peso.

Another class of cases was synthetic CDOs, which were used by investment banks and hedge funds to lay off the risk of credit default swaps. Recall that a credit default swap is effectively an insurance policy: the protection writer receives payments, based on the riskiness of the guarantee, then has to pay out if the entity it has insured defaults or goes bankrupt.

While AIG took this risk, most financial intermediaries did not. They would hedge it by entering into an offsetting contract, getting someone else to insure their insurance. While their guarantor often turned out to be AIG, the giant insurance company stopped writing many types of credit default swaps in 2006. Banks and traders needed new parties to eat their risks. A popular way was to bundle them into complex products and dump them on to clueless investors.

A regular CDO takes real assets, like mortgages, corporate loans, or pieces of other securitized deals, such as mortgage securitizations or securitizations of loans used to fund corporate buyouts. But in these cases, the underlying assets are loans of various sorts, which pay interest and principal. In a synthetic CDO, the cash flows come from the "premium" payments on various credit default swaps. This means investors in these CDOs will have to make payments if the defaults on the CDS guarantees exceed certain trigger levels. The bottom, equity layer takes the first losses. Then when it is exhausted, the next layer, the "mezz" or BBB layers, must make payments if defaults rise higher.

A common type of synthetic CDO held credit default swaps written on, or "referencing," corporate debt. These CDOs allowed large investment banks to offset the risk of credit default swap "guarantees" they wrote in the course of their regular business. Think of it as a form of reinsurance. Variants of this product were sold far and wide, including to Belgian banks, bush towns in Australia, retail investors in Singapore, and U.S. municipalities. These investors were unknowingly guaranteeing in aggregate trillions of dollars in U.S. debt. Estimates on how much they will have to pay out range from the tens to hundreds of billions of dollars.[52]

Often, buyers were treated as stuffees. Highly complicated paper was being sold to people clearly incapable of evaluating it.

An example: a synthetic CDO blew up on five Wisconsin school districts, causing losses of $150 million. It was bad enough that they were told by the broker that the investments were extremely safe, that the CDS were on high quality corporations, and the default trigger was almost certain never to be reached: "There would have to be 15 Enrons before you would be impacted"; "On the investment side, we're sticking to AA/AAA." The schools repeatedly asked whether the CDOs were exposed to subprime debt and were told no.[53] And had they understood the deal, there was not much additional return for taking on the extra exposure. The districts had $35 million to invest. Had they put this money into Treasuries, they would have made $1.5 million a year, while this deal, if everything worked out, would yield them $1.8 million a year. Oh, but we forget, a key difference was that this transaction also netted the brokerage firm $1.2 million in fees.[54]

In fact, the CDO contained credit default swaps that were written on risky credits, including home equity loans, subprime mortgages, and credit card receivables. Even worse, the districts, based on the broker's advice, borrowed $165 million on top of the $35 million that was their own money. When they took losses of $150 million on the $200 million they had invested, that meant they lost all of their own money and were faced with the prospect of paying $115 million to the lender.[55]

Derivatives expert Satyajit Das sums up the pattern here:

> Dealers began seeking new ways to improve profitability and started marketing structured products directly to retail customers, the widows and orphans of legend. . . . Structured product marketers set out into the suburbs and strip malls. The logic was compelling—you had less sophisticated clients, the margins would be richer. In short, you could rip them off blind.[56]

The investment banks were finally **hoist on their own petard.** Investment banks operate tactically, taking advantage of often-fleeting opportunities. Former Columbia business school professor Amar Bhidé called it "hustle as strategy." Morgan Stanley, when it embarked on its Mexican adventures, assumed it could operate as a pure middleman, simply arranging trades and taking big fees. It didn't envision that it would wind up getting in so deep that it would be exposed to the inevitable peso meltdown.

Yet short-term thinking has become endemic in the public company, "other-people's-money" model. For instance, Christopher Ricciardi, who headed Merrill Lynch's collateralized debt obligations group from 2003 to early 2006, built a business that produced an estimated $400 million in underwriting profits in 2005. But Ricciardi had become leery of the increased riskiness of the product and waning investor appetite. He had merely budgeted no growth for his highly profitable unit for 2006, and then, allegedly because he did not get a hoped-for promotion, left for a boutique firm. However, Ricciardi, who had been a pioneer in the late 1990s wave of CDO issuance, had managed the neat trick back then of leaving his employer right before the market fell apart.

Merrill, determined to show it was still a contender in this high-profit business, pushed ahead aggressively even as the market was clearly cooling. Ricciardi's successor charged ahead, issuing $44 billion, a more than three-fold increase from the 2005 level.[57] But as Ricciardi had foreseen, investor interest was flagging. Merrill wound up with more and more unsold paper on its balance sheet.

J.P. Morgan estimated that Merrill and other major CDO vendors like Citigroup, UBS, and Deutsche Bank wound up keeping roughly two-thirds of the top-rated tranches of the 2006 and 2007 deals, which accounted for the bulk of the value of a transaction, typically 65% to 80%.[58] To be conservative, two-thirds times 70% is roughly 50%, a simply massive retention. It would have been unheard of in the days of partnerships for an investment bank to hang on to an unsold underwriting (it would be seen as a horrid mistake, not to be repeated).

But the new world of other people's money produced a cavalier attitude toward risk. As we will discuss in chapter 7, accounting foibles meant traders could bring future earnings from these holdings back to the present and have their bonus payout based on years of future, unearned profits. The incentives were terrible and the banks paid out rich compensation on positions that in the end delivered enormous losses.

For instance, Merrill, which had held onto CDOs and other subprime paper, bet on the positions recovering in value. But when they continued to deteriorate, Merrill was forced to unload them. It sold one block of $30.6 billion of CDO paper for $6.7 billion, an eye-popping near–80% loss.

But even that summary overstates the sales price. The buyer, a hedge fund called Lone Star, paid only 5.5 cents on the dollar in cash; the rest of the payment was financed via a loan from Merrill. That loan was secured by the paper, which means if the value of the CDOs sold fell further, Lone Star could simply refuse to repay the loan and return the CDOs to Merrill. Thus Merrill would still take any further losses above the 5.5% payment that Lone Star[59] had already made. Market participants say it is a virtual certainty that the CDOs are worthless, meaning Merrill will suffer a 94.5% loss.

The Securities Industry and Financial Markets Association pegged global CDO issuance for cash flow and hybrid CDOs, at $411 billion in 2006 and $340 billion in 2007.[60] Of that total the type that has blown up most spectacularly, so-called ABS CDOs (for asset-backed securities) constituted 50% to 60%.[61] Recall the J.P. Morgan estimate, that the industry retained 50% of the value of those deals. Experts say that that even the "super senior" or the very top tranches of one type, mezzanine CDOs, which has riskier assets, are worthless. The somewhat less risky AAA tranches of "high grade" CDOs are worth 15 to 20 cents on the dollar as of this writing. Let's charitably assume an average across all types of 15 cents on the dollar. *That means the banks in aggregate have sustained $160 billion to $190 billion of losses on this product alone.* Their write-offs are short of this level, meaning unless current market prices are far too conservative, more losses are inevitable. And remember, end buyers and guarantors via credit default swaps written on CDOs also took huge losses.

. . . . .

It may seem incredible that the cunning of the big financial firms has redounded so severely against them. But neoclassical economics offers a ready explanation. Recall that in the theory, the locus of all economic behavior lies in the decisions of self-interested individuals, and larger groups like corporations are an afterthought.

In an aggressive profit-seeking setting, is it then any surprise that employees of the major financial firms turned their predatory instincts against their own companies? If the staff had found a way to line their own pockets at the expense of investors, then why would they stop even if maximizing their bottom line damaged the enterprise? After all, to Jeremy Bentham, groups were mere "fictitious bodies" and should not constrain a man's pursuit of pleasure. We'll see what happened when this reasoning was taken to its logical conclusion in the next chapter.

CHAPTER 7

LOOTING 2.0

Do not let someone making an "incentive" bonus manage a nuclear plant—or your financial risks. Odds are he would cut every corner on safety to show "profits" while claiming to be "conservative." Bonuses do not accommodate the hidden risks of blow-ups. It is the asymmetry of the bonus system that got us here.

—Nassim Nicholas Taleb

Joseph Jett is a rogue trader who maybe wasn't.

In 1991, Jett, a Harvard MBA, joined Kidder Peabody, a white shoe investment bank that had been acquired by General Electric. No one seemed bothered by his underwhelming record as a mortgage bond trader: Jett had been fired by each of his previous employers, Morgan Stanley and First Boston.[1]

Jett was deployed to trade long maturity U.S. Treasury bonds called STRIPS. A U.S. Treasury bond pays interest every six months until redemption, at which point the principal invested is also repaid. STRIPS decompose the Treasury bond into its constituents: a principal repayment and interest payments. With STRIPS, each of these future payments becomes a separate, tradeable instrument. The Federal Reserve facilitated this activity by allowing dealers to present bonds to be decomposed and recombine the pieces back into bonds.[2]

By investment banking standards, trading STRIPS was mundane work. It was a very liquid market with limited profit potential. Initially, Jett seemed to be

floundering. But suddenly his performance turned around. In 1992, Jett contributed $32 million of profits, far more than anyone at the firm had ever made
in that product. In 1993, he was promoted to be the head government bond
trader, and his personal bottom line grew to $151 million. His bonus that year
was $9.3 million. Jett's immediate boss, Edward Cerullo, benefited from Jett's
performance, earning more than $20 million that year.[3]

Early on, this pattern should have raised red flags: a mediocre trader suddenly turning in spectacular results, and in a market unlikely to yield outsized
profits. Anyone with an operating brain cell should have realized, pronto, that
something was amiss. The government bond markets are far too efficient for
there to be opportunities to reap enormous returns. Jett was either taking massive risk (which he wasn't; his positions were matched) or something didn't add
up. Even if Jett had discovered some sort of market anomaly, opportunities like
that are fleeting. It would have been miraculous for it to persist as long as a
month, let alone more than two years.

The alarms finally went off in 1994, when Jett showed $66 million of prof-
its in the first two months of 1994. Cerullo found that Jett had booked $40 bil-
lion in forward reconstitutions, meaning Jett would take interest and principal
components of bonds and reassemble them at a specific future date. In some
cases, the amounts he had entered for particular bonds was greater than the
total issue size, clearly an impossibility.[4]

This strategy was the sole source of Jett's spectacular returns, and it was
bogus. The accounting system erroneously showed that this activity was profitable at the time the trade was entered, meaning in advance of when the bond
components were scheduled to be recombined. Yet profit, if any, would occur
only in the future and depended on interest rate movements between when the
trade was entered into and when the reconstitution occurred. At the time Jett put
these forward trades on, there was no profit and no assurance there would be any
down the road. But the system made it look as if all these transactions were winners. However, these phantom profits would slowly erode in the accounting system as a transaction booked, say, six months out moved closer to the present
day. Jett had to keep entering larger and larger future trades to keep his appearances of profit going.[5]

Kidder recorded a $350 million "loss" reversing out Jett-related accounting
errors, some of which were recorded profits that never existed ($210 million of
paper profits[6] plus real losses Jett had incurred that the phony accounting had
masked).[7] Jack Welch, GE's CEO, was furious. Kidder's assets were quickly sold
to Paine Webber, ending the existence of the 130-year-old firm.

But how culpable was Jett? It isn't clear whether Jett understood that he was
taking advantage of a bookkeeping flaw. To this day, he maintains his profits

were real, a convenient position if you want to escape a sanction for fraud. His strategy, if you can call it that, was in full view to anyone who bothered to look; he made no attempt to devise trades or accounting entries that might hide his ploy and cooperated when the auditors started probing. He also recorded his transactions in large red ledgers that sat on his desk, which anyone could have inspected. He kept all of his bonus money at Kidder, which the firm promptly froze when things got ugly. Someone who knew he was up to no good would presumably have taken steps to make it much more difficult for his employer to seize his funds.[8]

Jett was partly vindicated. After an investigation, the U.S. Attorney's office decided not to press charges. The National Association of Securities Dealers (NASD) rebuffed Kidder's claim that Jett had perpetrated a fraud.[9] The SEC did not find Jett guilty of securities fraud, charging him instead with a record-keeping violation, which resulted in fines of $200,000 and disgorgement of $8.2 million.

Cerullo, Jett's boss, and his predecessor, Melvin Mullin, settled SEC charges of failure to supervise Jett. Cerullo was banned from the industry for a year and paid a $50,000 fine; Mullin was suspended for three months and paid $25,000.[10]

Jett wrote in his book, *Black and White on Wall Street,* that his money-losing trades were ordered by Cerullo, part of a plan to manipulate Kidder's balance sheet, and that the phony trades were to hide assets and make it look as if the securities operation was in compliance with GE's limits on it. While this claim strains credulity, it is also beyond belief that Cerullo, who must have seen daily position reports, failed to notice the enormous size of Jett's book until early 1994.

·   ·   ·   ·   ·

While *l'affaire Jett* may seem to be ancient history, its outlines have much in common with the looting that played a central role in the financial crisis:

- Traders taking advantage, either knowingly or innocently, of flawed accounting, metrics that understated risk, and inadequate risk controls.
- Immediate management, which benefited from the phony profits, not probing too deeply or perhaps even being complicit, since they were along for the ride.
- Top management being too removed to appreciate what was going on.[11]
- Managers immediately involved, and ultimately top officers, being paid based on phony profits, and keeping most of them even when the supposed earnings were revealed to be a chimera.

What differentiates Jett's actions from what occurred in the run-up to the crisis is a matter of degree rather than kind. When individuals who run a business care only about paying themselves as much as possible, and not about the health of the enterprise, they can quickly drive a venture into the ground. And remarkably, that occurred on a widespread basis.

Illusory profits are central to this phenomenon. Had Jett's losses been reported on a timely basis, he wouldn't simply have gotten no bonus; he would have been fired yet again. Even his salary during 1993 and 1994 was an overpayment. Cerullo gave up only $50,000 of his $20 million of 1993 earnings, a large proportion of which was presumably due to Jett's results. And even though Welch ultimately suffered a black eye, GE reported higher profits than it would have otherwise in 1993, while the Jett shenanigans were on, boosting GE's stock price.

Mind you, we are not talking only about rogue traders. Indeed, the details that come to light through those cases illustrate broader, more pervasive patterns in the securities industry. Jérôme Kerviel, whose trades in 2007 and 2008 ultimately cost his employer, Société Générale, €4.9 billion, or $7.6 billion, claims, like Jett, that management was well aware of what he was doing.[12] And that in turn raises a deeper set of issues: that employees and negligent or complicit managers are so eager to line their wallets that they will put their firms at risk. Worse, that relentless, blinkered focus on individual and small business unit profit has evolved in such a way as to destabilize markets.

In the years before the crisis, many advocates of the Brave New World of finance, with its sophisticated products and newfangled ways to slice and dice risk, argued that it lowered the cost of capital and would produce higher economic growth and more stability. Even though some, like Timothy Geithner, did offer the occasional reservation,[13] the measures taken in the 1990s and early this century show an abundant faith in the views of "free markets" advocates.

For instance, one remarkable move by the Federal Reserve in 1996 was to use the banks' own "verifiable internal risk measures" as the basis for capital requirements for trading businesses, officially putting the foxes in charge of the henhouse.[14] Greenspan's rationale:

> Our soundness standards should be no more or no less stringent than those the market place would impose. If banks were unregulated, they would take on any amount of risk they wished, and the market would price their capital and debt accordingly. Ideally, banks should also face regulatory responses to their portfolio risks that simulate market signals. And these signals should be just as tough, but no tougher than market signals in an unregulated world. Perfection would occur if bankers had a genuinely difficult choice deciding if they really wanted their institutions to remain insured or become unregulated.[15]

You can drive a truck through the flaws in the logic. First, it assumes "the market" is able to judge the risks of a bank trading multiple, complex over-the-counter products. While securities laws require public companies to make accurate and timely disclosure of their financial health, business strategies, and material developments, businesses simply cannot afford to put competitively sensitive information in the public arena, no matter how valuable it would be to shareholders.

What is the most competitively sensitive information a trading firm has? Its positions, meaning the various securities it owns and the exposures it has. What would "the market" need to know to assess the riskiness of a trading firm? Those very same positions. Even if people outside the bank had the expertise and information to evaluate a bank's holdings, they could never be told enough to make that assessment. That is why that job falls to regulators, because "the market" cannot provide adequate checks.

Second, Greenspan assumed that bank management would act prudently and preserve the health of the organization. We've seen how disastrously wrong that assumption was. But why?

The big mistake was in believing the interest of the key staff was to create a strong, healthy, long-lived enterprise. Instead, flawed management structures and systems, bad incentives, and questionable accounting worked together to produce widespread looting. Looting, as described by Nobel Prize winners George Akerlof and Paul Romer, occurs when *businesses have incentives to go broke at society's expense.*

The Akerlof and Romer paper, published in 1993, depicted this activity as criminal:

> . . . an economic underground can come to life if firms have an incentive to go broke for profit at society's expense (to loot) instead of to go for broke (to gamble on success). Bankruptcy for profit will occur if poor accounting, lax regulation, or low penalties for abuse give owners an incentive to pay themselves more than their firms are worth and then default on their debt obligations. Bankruptcy for profit occurs most commonly when a government guarantees a firm's debt obligations. The most obvious such guarantee is deposit insurance, but governments also implicitly or explicitly guarantee the policies of insurance companies, the pension obligations of private firms, virtually all the obligations of large banks, student loans, mortgage finance of subsidized housing, and the general obligations of large or influential firms. . . .
>
> Because net worth is typically a small fraction of total assets for the insured institutions, . . . bankruptcy for profit can easily become a more attractive strategy for the owners than maximizing true economic values. If so, *the normal economics of maximizing economic value is replaced by the topsy-turvy economics of maximizing current extractable value,* which tends to drive the

firm's economic net worth deeply negative. Once owners have decided that they can extract more from a firm by maximizing their present take, any action that allows them to extract more currently will be attractive—even if it causes a large reduction in the true economic net worth of the firm). . . .

The looters in the sector covered by the government guarantees will make trades with unaffiliated firms outside this sector, causing them to produce in a way that helps maximize the looters' current extractions with no regard for future losses.[16] (Emphasis added.)

Akerlof and Romer built their theory around a set of examples, such as Chile in the early years of the Pinochet regime, which we discussed in chapter 5, and the U.S. savings and loan (S&L) crisis. One key feature of the S&L debacle that seems to have been airbrushed out of the collective memory is that most of the losses incurred were not the result of thrifts being stuck with low rate mortgages in a higher interest rate environment and suffering losses as a result. That was the problem of the early 1980s. The S&Ls that toughed it out in most cases survived.

But the measures implemented to assist deeply underwater S&Ls (in the very high interest rate environment of 1980–1982) were exploited by outsiders to the industry, who acquired thrifts on extremely favorable terms. Many of them, like Charles Keating, had been previously charged with fraud or had criminal records. The resulting cohort of high-flying thrifts showed high profits and growth rates and were widely praised as proof that deregulation worked, until they crashed. It is easy to look like a winner if you cook the books. Over 1,000 executives at savings and loans were convicted of fraud, and the largest failures almost without exception involved control fraud, meaning the CEO was driving the criminal activity.[17]

Remarkably, mainstream economists refuse to consider the role of deception and sharp practices in commerce. "The market" is assumed to be able to ferret out bad apples. The victims of Bernie Madoff and R. Allen Sanford's scams, which include former Wall Street executives, no doubt take great comfort from the fact that economic theory says Madoff-type con artists will quickly be discovered, making supervision unnecessary. Indeed, law and economic school thinkers who have come to wield considerable influence over corporate governance theory, such as Judge Frank Easterbrook and Daniel Fischel, argue that the fact that investors are willing to buy equities shows that "the market" provides sufficient discipline.[18]

The economic profession, for the most part, has been unwilling to consider the studies of criminologists, who sit within the legal discipline.[19] The exception, scholars like Akerlof and other economists who focus on information asymmetry, have been given the backhanded complement of having their ideas feted yet relegated to a box outside the mainstream paradigm that dominates policy and academia.[20]

Now it may seem extreme to compare the behavior of leading financial firms to that of convicted criminals like Charles Keating. Yet the conduct is remarkably similar, including, as both Keating and later Enron did, building considerable political influence to win favorable regulatory and accounting treatment. In the case of Enron, Frank Partnoy, Morgan Stanley derivatives saleman turned law professor, has said,

> Enron, arguably, was following the letter of the law, in nearly all of its dealings, including nearly all its off balance sheet partnerships and its now infamous Special Purpose Entities.[21]

In fact, Partnoy contends, Enron's demise has been widely misunderstood. It was a handsomely profitable derivatives trader, albeit of the Bankers Trust take-no-prisoners school. But its lenders and investors had thought it was something quite different, and when they realized the risks it was actually running, they went into run-on-the-bank mode, fatal to any highly geared enterprise.

The point is not to suggest Enron was upstanding—far from it. Rather, per Akerlof and Romer's looting construct, malleable accounting allows for a company's behavior to be tarted up in a very misleading way, for its exposures to be masked and its profits exaggerated. When compensation based on phony paper profits rather than true economic profits happens on a comparatively small scale, like Jett, you merely have embarrassing pilfering.[22] On a large scale, it sucks money out of companies, either bankrupting them directly, or leaving them dangerously undercapitalized, almost assuring that a seemingly robust enterprise will quickly morph into smoldering wreckage when the environment becomes difficult. And on a large-enough scale, it drains entire economies, as Chile, Russia, and our own experience attest.

The worst is that we now have looting version 2.0, far more pernicious and difficult to extirpate than the initial release. In the original Akerlof and Romer construct, the behavior was clearly criminal and easy to identify *in retrospect*. But while it was in progress, the CEOs perpetrating control fraud created effective smoke screens by subverting controls and enlisting law and accounting firms, normally the protectors of the public interest, as allies. And recall from our discussion in chapter 6 that in 1994, the Supreme Court ruled that lawyers and accountants could not be sued for aiding and abetting securities fraud, so the barriers to this activity are lower than before.

In the financial services industry version of looting, we instead have firms where operational authority is decentralized, vested in senior business managers, or "producers." Because of industry evolution and perceived competitive pressures, these producers, as a result of formal incentives plus values held widely within the industry, focused solely on capturing the maximum amount possible in the current bonus period. The formal and informal rewards system thus tallies exactly with the topsy-turvy scheme of "*maximizing current extractable value.*"

In the past this behavior was positive, indeed highly productive, as long as it was contained and channeled via tough-minded oversight, meaning top management who could properly supervise the business. The main mechanisms are management reporting systems, risk management, and personal understanding of and involvement in day-to-day operations, plus external checks, such as regulations and criminal penalties. For a host of reasons, the balance of power has shifted entirely toward the forces that encourage looting. And because the damage that results cannot clearly be pinned on the top brass (like Cerullo, they have thin but plausible deniability), it is difficult to ascertain from the outside whether the executives merely unwittingly enabled this process or were active perpetrators.

Notice this excessive extraction that led to business failure took place even though these firms had high levels of employee stock ownership. At Bear Stearns, members of the firm owned roughly one-third of the shares.[23] At Lehman, they held nearly 30%, and the average managing director's stake was worth two times his annual earnings.[24] Economic theory says that share ownership by employees and managers should lead them to produce the best long-term results for the enterprise. Yet those assumptions were shown to be as flawed on Wall Street as they were with Enron, where 62% of the 401(k) assets were invested in Enron stock, and senior management also had significant share ownership.[25]

Just as we have seen in corporate America, using equity to align the interests of managers and shareholders has produced the converse of what the theorists expected, a pathological fixation on short-term results. On Wall Street, where the business model and rewards systems already emphasized the quick kill, widespread employee ownership was an ineffective counter at best and more likely served to reinforce the fixation on current performance, irrespective of the true cost of achieving it.

The very worst feature of looting version 2.0 is that it has created doomsday machines. In the old construct, the CEO fraudsters would drain a business, let it fail, and move on. The fact of bankruptcy assured that the trail of wreckage would catch up with them sooner or later. But here, the firms, due to their perceived systemic importance, are not being permitted to fail. So there are no post-mortems, in particular criminal investigations to determine to what extent fraud—as opposed to mere greed and rampant stupidity—led to what would otherwise have been their end.

Instead, rescues via subsidized mergers (Merrill and Bear) or bailouts (equity injections, a myriad of Fed "support the markets" facilities, plus super-low interest rates; abroad, salvage operations for banks ranging from Royal Bank of Scotland to UBS) throw a veil over what really happened. The acronym for the Troubled Asset Relief Program (TARP), the $700 billion bank rescue package, has proven peculiarly fitting. And in the one major bankruptcy, Lehman, no criminal or regulatory investigations are being made. The administrators of the bankruptcy, whose sole duty is to extract maximum value for the creditors from the remains, have been shunning information requests from parties with a stake in the outcome.[26] The liquidators clearly have no interest in opening up questions of fraud, which would further complicate their task.

Enron failed as its funding sources realized the level of gambles it was taking. They had been unknowingly subsidizing the derivatives bank, which had also made an art form of pushing the envelope on accounting, manipulating unregulated markets, and extracting huge returns from less sophisticated customers and counterparties.

The financial services industry, not just an isolated firm or two, but every one of the major capital markets players, has demonstrated itself to be either incompetent at managing risk or cavalier to the point of recklessness, which, in highly geared firms, guarantees eventual collapse. These firms make too many big wagers too often for the odds not to catch up with them. Moreover, as we will show, they have almost certainly misled the public or at best deluded themselves as badly as Jett appears to have done.

Yet now these reckless behaviors can, nay will, continue on an even greater scale. The interventions of 2007 and 2008 to prop up a wide range of firms and markets is a massive extension of formal safety nets, which will now be ex post facto formalized to a degree through financial stability regimes.[27] And the demands made by the authorities in return for this support are few and far between, woefully inadequate relative to the ample evidence of widespread failure to manage.

So it is vital to understand how this sorry state of affairs came about if we are to have any hope of remedying it. Otherwise, the members of the large capital markets firms will keep draining their enterprises and the rest of society along with them.

. . . . .

Back in the early 1990s, I saw a presentation by Sallie Krawcheck, then an equity analyst covering the securities industry and a rising star at Sanford Bernstein, in which she remarked, "it's better to be an investment bank employee than shareholder." While that statement was obvious to anyone who knew the business, it was also a warning of things to come.

Though investment banks have merged into or become banks, they were the model for commercial bank aspirants, both in the United States and abroad, who sought to play in the lucrative capital markets businesses. The management style and culture for today's major capital markets players evolved from the investment bank playbook. We will focus on the areas and activities where the big profit potential and operational risks lie, which is in the over-the-counter trading businesses, such as fixed income and OTC derivatives like credit default swaps, plus origination and product development related to these areas.

One of the salient characteristics of capital markets businesses is the amount of discretion given of necessity to non-managerial employees, meaning traders, salesmen, investment bankers, analysts. In pretty much any other large-scale business, decisions that have a meaningful bottom-line impact (pricing, new sales campaigns, investment decisions) are deliberate affairs, ultimately decided at a reasonably senior level. By contrast, these firms, because they live in a transaction flow that presents often-fleeting profit opportunities, delegate substantial authority. Most businesses are on an agricultural model, seeking to build repeatable, sustainable revenues. While some businesses housed in financial services firms are like that (funds management, where the income comes from low-risk fees on the amount of assets managed), many are on a hunter-gatherer model of being adaptive, reactive, and opportunistic (even though these hunter-gatherers have high-tech support beyond the comprehension of the stone knives and bear skins set).

Readers often bristle at this characterization, seeing it as a form of Wall Street exceptionalism. But we are not talking about the real-world impact of these decisions, we are talking about *their significance to the organization.* While an emergency room doctor clearly makes choices of great importance and often functions under acute time pressure, if he gets something wrong, while the results are catastrophic and people may die, his mistakes do not threaten the survival of his hospital. By contrast, a fairly junior trader, Nick Leeson, single-handedly blew up Barings, a 200-year-old merchant bank (the UK analogue to investment banks).

Other trading businesses and deal-oriented firms give decisions with considerable bottom-line impact to non-managerial staff. But the peculiar characteristic of big capital markets firms is that they still have a good deal of dispersed, delegated, profit-impacting authority in a wide range of businesses. By contrast, other powerful trading firms, such as Cargill, have a narrower span of businesses, which makes it easier for the top brass to supervise the enterprise.

Now let us consider a second set of issues: many of these businesses require considerable expertise. You aren't going to ask someone to trade a demanding market[28] or sell complex derivatives or negotiate the fine points of a merger who has never done it before. The industry is fond of that overused word "talent," which is, not surprisingly, a misnomer. You wouldn't ask an electrician to do the work of a plumber. Neither has "talent" per se, but each has specialized skills. And the skills of investment banking "talent" are well-nigh impossible to acquire except by working in the industry. That is one reason why it took commercial banks more than a decade of determined effort to make meaningful inroads.

Combine this with a third characteristic: many key activities, as we discussed in the last chapter, show increasing returns to scale, meaning that bigger players, provided they don't screw it up, can achieve a higher level of profit. Over-the-counter market making has strong network effects, plus many of the businesses have synergies among them (simple examples: if you trade foreign exchange derivatives, it behooves you to also trade in the cash market; firms looking to buy companies will often prefer a merger advisor who can provide financing). These all lead to advantages of greater scale and, in quite a few cases, scope.

On paper, capital markets enterprises look like a great opportunity. The firms that are at the nexus of global money flows participate in a very high level of transactions. Enough of them are in complex products or not deeply liquid markets so as to allow firms to find ways to uncover and in many cases create and seize profit opportunities. New, typically sophisticated products often provide particularly juicy returns to the intermediary. And in theory, clever, adaptive, narrowly skilled staff can stay enough ahead of the game so that the amount captured off this huge transaction flow is handsome.

Once again, however, the real world deviates in important respects from the fantasy. Why? *This business model is also a managerial nightmare.* We have a paradox: "success" and profitability in the investment banking context entails giving broad discretion to individuals with highly specialized know-how. But the businesses have outgrown the ability to monitor and manage these specialists effectively. The high frequency, meaningful stakes, and large absolute number of decisions made at the operational level, the geographic span of these firms, and the often imperfectly understood interconnections among business risks make effective supervision well-nigh impossible.

Some of the key tools to attempt to contain these risks are faulty. Complex products are often priced or hedged using mathematical models. That means they also help measure profit and loss and, as a result, help determine bonuses. Yet this process is fraught with problems. The models may have flaws or rely on inputs from staff who can use them to burnish results. While banks in theory have checks in place, in practice, a lot of errors and distortions slip through.

That means these blowups were not unpredictable. In fact, they were very likely given the high leverage, which makes business fragile, combined with weak regulatory checks, the inherent difficulty of supervision, competitive reasons to pursue leadership positions in various niches aggressively, plus hiring and pay practices and cultural norms that rewarded short-term focus, "creativity" that sometimes included bending already malleable rules, and aggression.

· · · · ·

Why have these firms become particularly hard to manage well? As we saw in chapter 6, the evolution of the industry in the 1980s and 1990s greatly increased the size, complexity, and risk assumption of these enterprises. As firms got larger and changed from partnerships to corporations, the management approaches did not keep pace, and in some key respects, actually got worse.

The fate of Salomon CEO John Gutfreund illustrates how these factors started to shift. Gutfreund had been a legend in his day, at the helm of Salomon during its rise to a leading, some might even argue dominant, position in the investment banking industry as of the mid-1980s. Commodities giant Phibro had acquired Salomon in 1981; Gutfreund achieved the impressive feat of engineering a coup and coming out on top.

In old securities-firm style, Gutfreund, himself a former bond trader, kept his desk on Salomon's cavernous trading floor, which he prowled during the day. He had an uncanny ability to read the room and would show up behind traders just as they were getting themselves in serious trouble. The firm was a barely contained brawl, with a swaggering, macho culture, taking huge market risks. And the firm pushed aggressively ahead into new territory, pioneering and dominating the market for mortgage-backed securities. This wasn't how the rest of Wall Street had worked. As firms like Morgan Stanley saw Salomon eating their lunch, earning more in profits than the rest of its competitors combined, they scrambled to respond to or copy the Salomon playbook.[29]

Bonds had become the front line of the application of serious analytical horsepower to trading and risk management, and Salomon had long been in the thick of it. The trend had started in the late 1960s, as rising inflation produced price volatility for bonds. Sidney Homer, who established the firm's bond analytics group, took the innovative step of buying a computer and hiring a mathematician, Marty Liebowitz, to calculate bond prices faster than the traditional route of looking them up in a very large book.[30] The trend accelerated

with the growth of mortgage-backed securities, which had a nasty new complicated feature, prepayment risk. But everything in the land of finance can be
solved by price. Offer an investor a premium return to something plain vanilla,
and you'll have takers.

Bond houses historically had sought to make their money as middlemen,
focusing on buying and selling on behalf of customers. That inevitably entailed
taking position, meaning inventory, risk. Although so-called "order flow" trading seeks to profit from the spread between bid and offer prices, the trader also
shades his prices and manages his inventory in the light of what he sees happening in the market, lightening up if he sees signs that prices will fall, going
long, say, to get in front of a rally based on good news.[31]

In 1977, John Meriwether, later of Long-Term Capital Management fame
(or infamy), set up a spread trading unit, the Domestic Bond Arbitrage desk.[32]
The group would speculate with house money, a principal trading group, and
not make prices to customers. Meriwether had a strong quantitative bent and as
his gambles paid off, he was made partner in 1980. He recognized something
that everyone heretofore had missed: trading could be approached in a far more
rigorous fashion. In 1983, he started hiring financial economists, many of them
with MIT affiliations.[33] They went churning through data looking for past relationships and tried to divine future patterns. They also hunted for inefficien-
cies for the traders to exploit.

As the group started minting money, Meriwether's reach expanded. The
Bond Arbitrage Group traded corporate bonds, Japanese warrants, Eurobonds,
and junk bonds, creating frictions with the traders who worked in the same
markets trading customer order flow.

Gutfreund was no longer in control. Although called the King of Wall Street
in those days as Salomon moved from strength to strength, Gutfreund had only
a dim notion of what the Bond Arbitrage Group or even the mortgage backed
traders were really up to. The complexity and mathematical intensiveness of
these profit machines were beyond his ken.[34] Even worse, he failed to install
proper controls on other rapidly growing areas, such as derivatives and mortgage trading. Salomon showed huge losses when mistakes surfaced.[35]

But like Cerullo, Gutfreund prospered even though he was not (*could* not)
be overseeing the firm adequately. He took home $3.1 million in 1986,[36] a
princely sum in those days, and he and his wife became fixtures on the New
York charity circuit, breaking into the A-list with a stylish but nevertheless nou-
veau riche display that in earlier eras would have been deemed unseemly.

The success of the Bond Arbitrage Group was Gutfreund's undoing. He
had secretly agreed to pay the unit 15% of its profit in bonuses.[37] It had become a de facto firm within a firm, always a bad arrangement. Mike Milken at

Drexel Burnham Lambert and the notorious Financial Products Group at AIG, a comparatively small group that ran the credit default swaps business, had similar deals. Both units proved to be the death of their parents.

The smallest bonus in the Bond Arbitrage Group in 1990 was $3 million; the top was $23 million to Lawrence Hilibrand, which made the front page of the *Wall Street Journal.*[38] The news produced outrage in the firm, with the angriest being Paul Mozer, who had been in the unit until 1988 and had been asked by Meriwether to leave to head government bond trading. He had not been included in the secret pact.

As seasoned Wall Street wags put it, "It isn't about the money, it's about the money." In the testosterone-charged culture of Wall Street, particularly its trading rooms, pay often ceases to become a means to an end but is an end itself. In many cases, it isn't greed in the way most people think about it. The object is not to acquire more stuff or get a name on a building, but *to win.* You can skip Thorstein Veblen's conspicuous consumption to prove that you are successful; as John Kenneth Galbraith pointed out, consuming is work. Pay becomes a very direct reflection of worth, the quick and easily verifiable way to sort out who is the real alpha dog among all the pretenders.

Joe Cassano, who headed AIG's Financial Products Group when it wrote the credit default swaps that drove it, and the markets, into free fall, was a domineering, capricious bully, a caricature of a controlling boss. Even though he had earned, or more accurately, extracted, $280 million, it did not translate into a flashy lifestyle. Indeed, Cassano stuck with a down-market car and clothes and lived at the office.[39] Similarly, Jérôme Kerviel seemed hungry to prove his worth as a trader, not to acquire better toys.[40]

Back to Salomon and Mozer. The bond trader, who made only one-fifth of what Hilibrand received, did not simply go ballistic, he also became obsessed. And worse, Gutfreund stoked the seething jealousies within the firm, saying that the Arbitrage Group's pay was a template for the firm, that pay would be linked far more closely with individual production.[41]

Even though Salomon had been a public company since its takeover by Phibro, this move was an explicit repudiation of the partnership pay model. Before this, it had been widely accepted in the industry that compensation was first a function of firm profits and second of individual performance. If there was no money in the till, the partners were not going to drain the firm to reward a stellar performer. As a senior Goldman staffer once remarked to me, "Better to be a C performer in an A year than an A performer in a C year."

In the new "every man for himself" model set forth by Gutfreund, Mozer set out to make $23 million.[42] But as we learned with Jett, Treasury bonds are not the most fertile grounds for money-spinning, at least via legitimate routes.

Mozer and other government bond dealers routinely traded an arbitrage that involved Treasury bonds traded on a "when issued" basis. The Treasury would announce its funding calendar, and traders would start making a market prior to when the bonds would actually be auctioned. The arb play involved shorting the "when issued" bonds. A short seller eventually had to buy the instrument to close out his position, so he was committed to making a purchase at some point.

Mozer decided to squeeze the dealers doing this trade, but to do that, he needed to control the Treasury auction in the maturity he targeted—the two-year note. Primary Treasury dealers like Salomon submit bids at Treasury auctions, both for themselves and for customers.

Mozer first tried bidding for 100% of the offered amount for Salomon. A Treasury deputy secretary called and politely but firmly reminded him that the government had a gentlemen's agreement that a buyer is restricted to a maximum bid of 35% of the total offered at any auction. The government, after all, wants to raise money on good terms, not enrich dealers, particularly ones engaging in anticompetitive practices. Remarkably, Mozer not only got abusive with the official, but became openly defiant, next submitting a bid for 240% of the auction. That led to another unproductive call from the Treasury to Mozer, plus a request to the Fed, which runs the auctions on behalf of the Treasury, to lower the bid to 35%. Mozer tried yet again with a 300% bid, the Fed haircut it again, and the Treasury made the 35% informal understanding into an official limit.[43] Mozer went on a rampage, submitting multiple 35% bids, making abusive calls to the Treasury, and trying to get media support.

The officialdom of the firm took notice, and the second most senior officer, Tom Strauss, ordered Mozer to apologize and take some time off.

But Mozer was not deterred. A few months later, he not only submitted 35% bids in Salomon's name, but also submitted bids on behalf of unwitting customers and created phony customer trades after the fact to cover his tracks.[44] He was clumsy about it. The Treasury got wind of what he was up to, conducted an investigation, and sent a letter to one of the clients that Mozer had falsely said was bidding, with a copy to Mozer.

When a firm crosses a regulator, the right response is to quickly roll over and show your belly: a massive display of contrition and swift punishment, at minimum a suspension, of the perp. That did not happen. Mozer showed the letter to Meriwether, his boss, who showed it to Strauss. They agreed it was very serious, "career threatening."

They were right, but the career it ended was Gutfreund's. He was out of town; the matter was left until his return. Mozer, still in place, submitted yet another phony bid at the next auction. When Gutfreund got word, he agreed the matter was serious, and the top brass debated whom to notify (the Treasury or the Fed). There was no discussion of reining in Mozer, much less punishing him.[45] The phony bids continued. Some hedge funds heard of Mozer's ploy and started placing similar buy orders (except theirs were legitimate).[46]

Gutfreund waited more than a month to leash and collar Mozer. His profits during this period were substantial, and Gutfreund thought he could hang on to Mozer's ill-gotten gains. When the Salomon chief finally sat down with the Treasury, he argued that the firm's conduct had been proper, even though the squeeze had become visible and costly to competitors. The Treasury was not satisfied. An investigation ensued and the results did not support Gutfreund's claims. When the Federal Reserve, the regulator in this matter, found out via reading the story in the press, the end came quickly. Gutfreund, Strauss, Meriwether, and the firm's general counsel resigned in a matter of days.[47]

. . . . .

Gutfreund's brazen defense of a persistent and profitable regulatory violation is not as rare as one might think; what made the bond squeeze unusual was the speed and vehemence of the reaction.

Anyone who remembers dot-com-era initial public offerings will recall that one of their salient characteristics was spectacular first-day gains. The old IPO rule that the lead manager tried to set the price so as to achieve a meaningful but not egregious first-day rise, say of 15% (enough to make these deals attractive to investors without shortchanging the individuals selling the shares too much), went out the window.[48] Offering date appreciation of 100%, 200%, or more, became surprisingly routine.

And there was good reason. CS First Boston (CSFB), which under technology star Frank Quattrone had become a leader in this business, was not content to take one of the richest margins in the business. The normal "gross spread," or difference between the offering price and the discount at which the underwriters bought the stock from selling shareholders in an IPO, was 7%. CS First Boston wanted, and got, considerably more.

Customers who were allotted stock by CS First Boston and guaranteed obscene profits via the unduly low offering price were not simply expected but actually told to kick a high percentage of the profit back, typically 25%, by paying super-high "voluntary" commissions on other stock trades.

The CEO, Alan Wheat, simply brushed off the regulatory investigations into the IPO quid pro quo. He had no intention of sacrificing Quattrone. CSFB's written response to the National Association of Securities Dealers was stunning. CSFB not only admitted to the arrangement, but tried to justify it, contending the practice was far from unheard of.[49] Credit Suisse, which owned CSFB, was not happy with Wheat's intransigence. Wheat was fired, and the new CEO John Mack negotiated Quattrone's departure.[50]

·   ·   ·   ·   ·

What is striking about these cases is that both CEOs chose to back employees who were breaking rules in a particularly flagrant way. They risked their careers and lost because they wanted to keep the profits these managers generated.

A reader might argue that Wheat and Gutfreund were simply lousy leaders. But that's a simplistic view. They were both celebrated for many years. Their cases illustrate a fundamental problem: that *it is all too easy for the top level of the firm to become hostage to the needs and demands of profit centers.* And as the Mozer case illustrates, a profit center can be as small as a trader plus his trading assistants.

Strange as it may seem, the closest analogy to the problems faced by investment banks are in the military, and the military has many more routes for controlling staff. The trend in modern warfare has been to drive decision-making authority down into the ranks, because more mobile and powerful apparatus (missiles, tanks, fighter planes) and better communications allow for considerable firepower to be deployed opportunistically. The Germans had started moving this way well before World War II, and it paid off handsomely. In World War II, there is compelling evidence that the German army units were more effective in combat compared to all other armies, and that was because they had pushed decision-making authority down the command chain.[51]

But despite the high stakes, the military has greater control over its troops. First, you cannot just up and quit. That difference isn't trivial. When key producers, or even sometimes staff, in rapidly growing new businesses leave, it takes time to fill the hole. Because the role requires particular know-how (and in certain cases, established relationships), unless the boss worked in that same business, he can't do what managers in other lines of work do: pinch hit until the replacement arrives.

That means compensation is a competitive weapon. A firm that consistently outpays other players can cherry-pick people from other firms, grabbing the best franchises. And if one house takes enough key players from another, the victim can slide into serious decline. The industry neuroticism about league tables and competitive standing is not completely unfounded. But the effect of this pattern is to justify higher levels of pay, again favoring short-term considerations over the long-term viability of the business.[52]

That gives the producers leverage over the top brass due to a second difference from the armed forces: in the military, no one has unique or hard-to-replace competencies. Yes, fighter pilots and senior officers may be very highly trained. But while a colonel could often step into another colonel's slot (albeit with some awkwardness as he assesses his direct reports), a managing director from one area at a capital markets firm can almost never occupy a peer's shoes. The military does not want to be vulnerable to the problem that investment banks face. A particular commander or unit may become invaluable by virtue of holding a crucial strategic location. But no one wants to be in the position that England was in during 1940 and 1941, of having its fate hinge on a very small group of people with unique skills, in this case, pilots of the Royal Air Force.

But that kind of dependence is endemic on Wall Street. Although far from the sole factor, one element in Lehman's undoing was the loss of key senior people with deep experience, in this case, a self-inflicted wound.

Lehman, one of the smallest of the major players, had chosen to concentrate its chips, meaning its staff and balance sheet, on some key businesses, and one was real estate. The head of that business, Mike Gelband, warned in 2006 that the markets were weakening and wanted the firm to rethink its strategy. CEO Dick Fuld, constitutionally aggressive, highly competitive, and committed to growth, took Gelband's caution as proof that he was risk averse, which Fuld saw as a fatal flaw. Gelband was ousted, and a series of non-experts tried to fill the gap. Some at the firm saw Gelband's exodus as the first indicator of the crisis at the firm.[53]

Second, the military controls its troops by, from a cultural and practical standpoint, insisting on compliance. Soldiers can be sent to the brig. By contrast, the worst outcome on Wall Street is to be fired, and the financial services industry is full of people who have failed upward, or at least sideways. And rather than obedience, the financial services industry often rewards rule bending and loophole seeking. Skills honed on clients are hard to dial down within the firm.

That isn't to say that there aren't plenty of careerists, in the bad sense, in the upper ranks of the armed services. The expression "not on my watch" comes from the Navy and contrary to popular use in America, can mean "I don't care about the consequences as long as I don't get the blame." The cynical use of that expression is the functional equivalent of the Wall Street "IBG-YBG": "I'll be gone, you'll be gone." While top military officers generally lack the polished sociopathy too often found in finance, ticket punching and the single-minded pursuit of personal advancement are far from unusual.

The point here, however, is more basic: the top brass in the military can and does contain the risk taking of the field and unit commanders by not giving anyone enough "commit authority" to jeopardize the entire fleet or theater of battle. Capital markets firms play much closer to the margin of safety as far as "money colonel" discretion is concerned.

Third, the modern military can control its troops through strong surveillance apparatuses. Satellite technology and advanced communications gives it an unprecedented ability to view combat operations in real time. By contrast, while financial firms have breathtakingly fast data capture, in that transactions are tabulated and combined into profit and loss statements and higher level reports, and the data pushed through various risk management tools, in fact, the computational prowess leads to overconfidence of the understanding of risk. Moreover, firms have overinvested in risk technology (the mathematical tools) while they for the most part treat decision processes and organizational issues as afterthoughts.

Large capital markets firms have two major command system problems. The first is the speed, volume, and decentralization of decisions, which is compounded by the fact that in many cases, making those decisions well requires narrow expertise. In combination, these decision-making issues make effective supervision very hard to achieve. The second problem is that industry evolution has increased the already high focus on short-term profits. And just as one man's terrorist is another's freedom fighter, what looks like dubious behavior on the outside is often celebrated and rewarded internally. So not only has power shifted toward the producers, but to compound the problem, it is a viable, often winning, strategy for them to operate as buccaneers.

■   ■   ■   ■   ■

Capital markets firms think they have an answer for the clear and ever present danger that employees can crater the enterprise. It's called risk management. Most of the concerns about staff and producer discretion vanish if you can determine how much damage they might do in a worst-case scenario and set limits so that you can survive if those events do pass. Thus you as senior management set boundaries (most important, restrictions on how much trouble the traders can get into) and, *voilà,* problem solved.

The wee complication with this notion is that every major capital markets player used the most modern risk management techniques and they still blew themselves up.[54] So what is wrong with this picture?

First, the risk management approaches are based on the use of financial models. Those models embody all the failings we reviewed in chapter 3, namely

- Underestimation of "tail" risk, that is, the odds of Seriously Bad Things happening.

- The dangerous assumption that correlations between different types of exposures and asset types are stable (as in the past is a reasonable proxy for the future as far as the interrelationship of prices is concerned).
- The dangerous assumption that markets are continuous (finance-speak for you can always and ever sell what you want in large volumes). Although not technically as accurate, another way of putting it is that markets are always liquid.

Second, the regulators and virtually all major capital markets firms have weak risk management discipline.[55] Even if they could assess the dangers accurately, risk managers typically have insufficient authority to rein in producers.

· · · · ·

Effective risk management took a giant leap backward with the creation of a widely used risk management tool, Value at Risk, or VaR.

VaR was born as a result of a demand made in the 1980s by the chairman of J.P. Morgan, David Weatherstone. Weatherstone, who had come up through the ranks in then typical J.P. Morgan style, was troubled that he did not have a good grip on the hazards the bank faced. Ironically, the chairman was considered an expert on risk, having headed the currency trading operations. But he wanted a way to compare and aggregate risks across businesses: how did the exposures across the bond business add up? Treasuries were less treacherous than emerging markets notes, but by how much? And how do you look at downside across business? Was the risk of the bond business simply an addition to that of, say, his old foreign exchange business, or did the risks offset each other to a degree? If the risks partially cancelled each other out, the bank could hold less equity, the reserve against losses. "Less equity" against known exposures translates into being able to take large positions against the same, existing capital base, with the potential to achieve a bigger market position and earn more profit.[56]

The team dedicated to satisfying Weatherstone's request decided the objective was to come up with a single figure that captured all the risks in a simple statistical fashion: what was the risk that the bank would lose a certain amount of money, specified to a threshold level of probability, in, say, the next 24 hours? The model output would say something like: "We have 95% odds of losing no more than $300 million dollars in the next 24 hours."

It took seven years of refinements to reach that goal, which should have been seen as a warning that it might not be such a good idea.

Mind you, there is nothing wrong with analyzing data to understand complex phenomena. That process has tremendous value in distilling which current industry practices might be valid and thus might be worth taking further, and which are mere urban legend.

But the danger of VaR was that the whole premise was flawed. Using a single metric to sum up the behavior of complex phenomena is a dangerously misleading proposition. It gives the users the illusion that they have an accurate grasp of the situation. As we learned with a comparatively simple risk problem, subprime mortgages, past performance, which had initially shown low levels of defaults, can't be assumed to be a valid predictor of the future.

Looking at numbers only without considering *how the markets themselves might be changing* is dangerous. But the scientism of quantitative analysis is powerful and often successfully silences those who ask, "But what about X new phenomenon?" In this case, the degree of abstraction required to produce the VaR computation inevitably required discarding important information about the behavior of the system.

The output formulation was designed around statistical convention, that of probability distributions. But *the part of the distribution that the analysis cut off is the very part that will kill a leveraged firm.* It was almost as if the team that produced VaR had drawn a map that simply marked the edge of the world with the legend "Beyond here lie dragons," when the treasure seekers will inevitably venture into those uncharted waters.

And the problem is that the conventional 95% or 99% cutoff used for daily VaR computations is not very high. A 99% probability of seeing a daily move below a certain level means you can expect one day out of every hundred, or 2.5 business days a year, to see a swing greater than that.[57] And the model is silent on how bad the losses would be then.

Yet users developed great confidence in VaR models because they were good at predicting day-to-day risk, exactly the ones that a bank does not need to worry about. This is classic drunk under the street light behavior, drawing conclusions based on where the information is plentiful rather than where the answer to your question lies.

While Weatherstone lectured against over-reliance on models, those outside his immediate circle did not heed his warnings.[58] Despite its fundamental failings, VaR has become the lingua franca of risk management. It enables managers and regulators who are often not quantitatively very savvy to labor under the delusion that they have a handle on an organization's exposures. VaR was particularly appealing to bank supervisors since it allowed them a simple way to make comparisons across institutions.

VaR was codified into practice by its widespread adoption by national bank regulators, and in particular, its inclusion in the Bank for International Settlement's so-called Basel II standards, which were implemented in 2004. Traditional banks, which included all the substantial capital markets players outside the United States, therefore had to use VaR—whether they liked it or not. But the Basel requirements which have been implemented in the European Union also led traders to devote a good deal of effort to finding ways to game the new system. That is, they came up with strategies that would be deemed less risky under VaR but might actually be more dangerous and potentially profitable in practice.

Defenders of VaR and improved versions of it will argue that they now have methods for estimating what might happen in that nasty dragon-inhabited region. Statisticians will also correctly claim that most firms don't rely solely on VaR but use other tools too, such as stress tests and Monte Carlo simulation. Yet all these approaches send broadly similar signals. The Bank for International Settlements noted that until mid-2006, the ratio of VaR to equity for banks declined, which said they were in a strong financial position even as their trading books got larger.[59] If other metrics had been an adequate cross-check, this would not have occurred.

But the idea that these other approaches do much to solve the underlying failing is sheer fantasy. As Nassim Nicholas Taleb has pointed out, even when quants do try to look at extreme events in any market, they are still looking through the rearview mirror and they have by definition very few data points in that region. In fact, for some markets, one observation will account for 80%, even 90%, of the "weight" in the estimation of the magnitude of the tail risk.[60] If you have seen one or two unusual events, you do not know if they are once-every-seven-years storms or once-every-ten-thousand-years storms.

Taleb puts the "fat tail" problem faced by banks in what he calls the fourth quadrant, where extreme events are hard to assess and the decision about how much to hazard involves multiple tradeoffs. Taleb argues that using statistics on fourth quadrant situations is dangerous. They cannot yield reliable results.[61]

But even that storm analogy is flawed, because it presupposes that market behavior is stable and durable. Taleb is talking about assessing the shortcomings of statistical models to define the odds of an extreme move within a single market. But recall how these models operate. They have a procedure for summing the risks across markets, and it is not a simple additive process. The models look for the degree to which risks offset each other. For instance, oil prices and the dollar tend to move in opposite directions, so if a firm was exposed to both, those positions would partially cancel each other out.

The models assume that the relationships between instruments and markets, called "correlation" or "covariance," is consistent, when in fact those relationships break down when markets are under stress. As the Nobel Prize winners Myron Scholes and Robert Merton found during the slow-motion collapse of the famed hedge fund Long-Term Capital Management, in a crisis all correlations move to one. In quant-speak, that means previously uncorrelated or weakly correlated assets move together, as in down. Investors dump risky assets and positions. And a synched downdraft means that trading liquidity, the ability to enter and exit positions, particularly large ones, is impaired. The "continuous markets" assumption on which risk management and hedging models are based is no longer valid.

In addition, not only do the correlations behave differently in upset markets than in calm ones, but the models do not do a good job of dealing with how the different variables interact. The formulas treat each input as if it were independent. But volatility and correlation vary with each other, something the models do not handle gracefully. Quants try to approximate this behavior by "shocking" the model, which is a fancy way of saying they make some extreme assumptions and see what happens. But those guesses by nature are somewhat arbitrary. Most risk managers will concede that this approach is only partially effective in representing what might happen.

In fact, changes in the financial services industry have increased the breadth and intensity of "tail" events and the correlation among markets in stress events.

Historically, most investors stuck with what they knew, which was usually their home market. Some investors might put money in foreign stock or bond funds. That was about as exotic as it got for the vast majority of investors. Swashbuckling cross-market quests for value were limited to hedge funds like Soros Fund Management's Quantum fund and Julian Robertson's Tiger fund.

But now, hedge funds have proliferated, with many pursuing "global macro," the new millennium brand for Soros-type international treasure hunts, or "multi-strategy," which basically means the managers can do more or less as they please. The investment bank's own proprietary trading desks are tantamount to hedge funds. And the vast majority of these traders borrow against their positions.

Cross-market players increase correlation among seemingly distinct types of assets, catastrophically so in a crisis. When prices fall sharply, levered investors like a hedge fund will be hit by a margin call, which occurs when an investor borrows against an instrument on margin, say $50 against a $100 investment. If the value of that investment falls below $50, he is required to put up more collateral, usually cash, to secure the loan. Otherwise the position is sold out.

But if the investor has other options, and thinks (or hopes) the price will come back up, the last thing he wants to exit is one of his most distressed holdings, which in this case would show a 50% loss. Instead, he will sell something that has a gain or at least a much smaller loss, which will often be in a market that is weathering the upheaval comparatively well. Suddenly a seemingly unrelated market is seeing large sale orders. If the resulting price declines trigger margin calls there, the slide in that market can gain momentum. So multi-market strategies served to broaden the types of investments engulfed by the crisis.

Another cross-market transmission mechanism was the yen carry trade. "Carry" is shorthand for "cost of carry," meaning the cost of holding a position. If you own a bond and the interest you earn on it is less than your cost of funding, the carry is positive. If you borrow to buy a non-income paying investment, the cost of carry is negative (you are making interest payments to finance the position and not earning any offsetting income).

For the last few years, "carry trade" has referred almost exclusively to borrowing in yen to invest outside Japan. Investments in most other countries offer higher returns than the super-low interest rates in deflation-plagued Japan. Far and away the biggest players are Japanese retail investors, mainly housewives. Like U.S. day traders, they are aggressive and confident speculators, and control enough in the way of financial assets so as to dominate the activities of foreign institutional investors who are also playing the carry trade.[62]

The danger of the yen carry trade is when the yen rises. If you borrowed in yen to invest outside Japan, that also implied you sold yen, since you would need to convert those yen into, say, Brazilian reals. The problem is you eventually need to pay off that yen liability, which means you have to buy yen in the future. If the yen appreciates, it makes the repayment more costly. This is a dangerous game, because the savings on the cheap borrowing can easily be wiped out by currency losses.

When markets were orderly, the Japanese traders saw a rise in the yen as an opportunity, since a higher yen meant they could acquire even more in foreign currency terms. So in finance-speak, they sold into yen rallies, which kept the currency weak, and no doubt made the carry trade particularly enticing to foreigners (if the Japanese retail buyers will stanch any price appreciation, which is the big risk in this arrangement, it makes it even more appealing).

But as the market perturbations became more severe, the kimono traders started to pull back. And as the yen rose, the hedge funds and other foreign investors quickly closed out yen borrowings, which meant they were buying yen. They would also dump positions that had been funded in yen. For instance, on February 27, 2007, the yen rose between 2% and 3%, triggering a nearly 10% drop in Chinese stock markets.[63] As the upheaval intensified, the yen would spike up on acute stress days, indicting that yen borrowers were unwinding their positions. They were selling non-yen holdings in a broad range of markets, again spreading the impact of the crisis far and wide.

We'll discuss the pernicious effect of yet another cross-market transmission mechanism that played a direct role in the crisis, repo finance, in chapter 9.

An additional development not adequately factored into models is that so-called innovations that are touted as providing liquidity to markets, meaning they increase the volume of trading and reduce bid-asked spreads, making it faster and easier to enter and exit, actually drain liquidity in times of crisis. Again, these will make stress events more extreme than in the past and make any historical models unreliable.

For instance, the first acute wave of the credit crisis, which took place in August and September of 2007, was more intense than it would have been thanks to credit default swaps, widely touted by dealers as promoting liquidity. In reality, they drained liquidity at the worst possible moment, adding fuel to the fire in the chaotic markets. It was an ongoing, but generally unrecognized, factor throughout the credit crisis.

CDS almost certainly exacerbated stress in the early stages of the crunch. Some astute players, such as the hedge fund Paulson & Co. and Goldman Sachs, were short subprime risk, meaning they were betting subprime would decline.[64] The prevailing practice was to short via CDS, and both presumably went this route.

In the subprime CDS market, you had more money wagering on the short side than parties that actually owned the instruments. That is true for the entire CDS market, that you have far more money betting on price declines than hedging risk. In stocks, this practice is called naked shorting and gets quite a lot of bad press, even though the level of short interest in stocks is trivial compared to that of CDS.

When an entity that has CDS referencing it goes into default, its CDS spreads rise sharply. In the industry, this move is called "jump to default." Anyone who has written a CDS contract suddenly has to post more collateral to show he can still make good on the insurance, since the odds of having to pay out have now become 100%; the only uncertainty is how much the actual amount will be.

But where do you get this extra collateral from? If you are an efficient, modern financial player, you don't have collateral sitting around doing nothing. You are probably very fully invested. You don't have a lot of free cash. That means you probably need to sell something to raise the dough. Thus CDS collateral postings act as an accelerant in the event of a large default. The supposed insurance makes matters worse, just as portfolio insurance did in the 1987 stock market crash.[65]

The other route for raising money on short notice is to borrow on credit lines with banks. That means additional stress in the interbank market.

The pressure from the CDS market was acute in the wake of the Lehman collapse, in which total payout was roughly $400 billion.[66] To give a sense of how large that is, the entire subprime mortgage market was $1.2 trillion.[67] Most observers looked at the orderly settlement of the Lehman CDS as a sign that fears about CDS were exaggerated. But they missed a key point: the settlement was weeks after the real stress event, which was the default, which triggered the need to give counterparties hard money proof that investors could make good on their promises. The outsiders were looking at the wrong indicator of how well or badly the process worked.

As one seasoned CDS trader put it:

> It's not that people can't fund, it is that people have *got to fund* these CDS positions. These banks don't have access to sufficient liquidity internally to fund, so they hit the London markets. . . . The Fed and the other central banks must start to deal with the huge overhang of currently hidden funding needs from the CDS and other derivatives.[68] (Emphasis original.)

This sort of liquidity pressure from CDS was a new feature in this crisis, and would not be captured in historical data.

In fact, the impact of CDS collateral postings *may mean that any big company with a lot of CDS outstanding is too big to fail quickly.*[69] Why were Chrysler and GM able to declare bankruptcy, despite large CDS outstanding written on them? The big stress event for them was in 2005, when auto paper started getting serious downgrades from rating agencies. Their CDS had required more and more collateral over the years, but for the most part, the increase was orderly.

So which firms are prone to the sort of rapid failures that can trigger a CDS shock? Big trading firms. They live on credit, and Lehman and Bear illustrated that if counterparties start to get cold feet and refuse to lend to them, a firm can go quickly into a death spiral. So credit default swaps reinforce the "too big to fail" problem posed by large banks.

Put simply, the risk models fail abysmally at doing their most important job: helping give accurate readings of the odds of catastrophic failure. And recent developments in finance assure that any attempts to "fix" the models by looking backward, at even recent history, will underestimate the dangers, because the linkages among markets are increasing, raising the severity of crises.

∎   ∎   ∎   ∎   ∎

Not only are financial risk models flawed, but the inadequate risk management procedures at most firms make a bad situation worse. The unwarranted faith in models means that senior officers and regulators act as if risk supervision can be treated like other management tasks: that generalists can do an adequate job of supervising through information reports. This leads them to continue to have top executives who are non-experts make decisions in areas that require knowledge of specific domains. As a consequence, they are often unduly influenced by politics and profits. It is the Gutfreund problem, with better trappings, of senior management who simply cannot fully grasp the complexity of the business dynamics. The use of fancy math and models camouflages the fact that the emperors have no clothes.

Put more bluntly, risk management is the most important responsibility of top management, and it is not treated that way. When David Weatherstone, who was considered knowledgeable about risks, realized he did not understand them, he set about to do what most top executives do: assume that he can fix things through better data and procedures.

But the conundrum is that *managers like Weatherstone are part of the problem.* Banks now have a variety of risk management tools and experts, but they have not recognized that risk management is a core competence, and that that in turn means they need people with very different skills sufficiently well represented in the top ranks, not a mere chief risk officer position. That in turn means thinking very differently about career paths. But that will never happen in the "money colonel" model of Wall Street. Producers are producers, overhead is overhead is overhead, and ne'er the twain shall meet.

Capital markets firms have made a half-hearted stab at a second approach to the problem, that of sticking with generalists at the top level and having expert staff act as a check. The German military pioneered this model. Colonel types could commit resources, but they still needed to run what they planned to do by staff. Those minders were not very senior; indeed, they were frequently lower in rank. But they had the overview that a battle commander might miss: forces needed, logistics, operations, intelligence.[70] The staff did not get any glory, but they were nevertheless committed to the control of the enterprise and its survival.[71]

The capital markets players use a badly watered down version of the German staff model of control. Richard Bookstaber, who was head of risk management at a major investment bank and author of *A Demon of Our Own Design*, depicted conversations with senior risk officers like him about pre-crisis questions over collateralized debt obligations that later turned toxic:

Session 1

Me: "Hey, guys, . . . our CDO-related inventory has been growing . . . we had just a few billion, and then it went up to $20 billion, and now nearly $40 billion. That seems worrisome to me."

Them: "Maybe that's because you aren't sitting here on the desk watching these things all day. . . . Look, you can't make money in this business without ending up holding some inventory from time to time. At least if you can, be sure to let us know how. And in this case a lot of this inventory is rated AAA. You wouldn't have a problem if we had a bunch of AAA corporate bonds, would you? I mean, that stuff is a better bet than our company is." . . .

Session 4

Me: "I'm sorry to bother you again. But, maybe we have been focusing on the wrong thing here . . . not if these are really AAA or not; our concern is not just with defaults. . . . The issue is whether these could trade substantially lower for any reason. . . . The instruments in our inventory are not very liquid. . . . So what if someone suddenly is forced to liquidate . . . it wouldn't take much of a price drop to hit us hard. When you have $40 billion of this stuff, a ten percent drop will lead to a mark to market loss that will wipe out all the profits you guys have made over the last few years."

Them: "Good to see you are cranking out the scenarios. But if we worried about every little "what if" that you can cook up, we wouldn't be doing anything. We are risk takers. That's how we make money. So if you want us to stop making money—or if you have a better idea on how to do it without taking risk—then let us know. Otherwise, do you mind if we get back to work here?"[72]

This dialogue illustrates that the traders have the advantage when risk managers try to rein them in. The fight is on their terrain. They know their markets better than the risk police ever can.

But there are much deeper problems with risk management as commonly practiced. The junior risk managers will earn more if they can apply their analytical skills on the product side. Anyone who is thinking about making that change is unlikely to ruffle the feathers of the producers. In addition, risk managers are bound to sound some false alarms. If they escalate every one, they wind up looking like nervous Nellies and lose credibility. And if they win and have exposures cut back on what turns out to be a nonevent, the traders will be sure to broadcast how much they "lost," as in failed to make, thanks to the interference.[73]

That narrow view illustrates a deeper problem: risk management is a form of insurance. Effective insurance *is* costly. You expect to miss a few calls, quite a few. But the noise back from the "money colonels" and the perceived importance

of maximizing current extractable value means that the expense of taking protective measures is deeply resented. The predictable result was that the banks
wound up being underinsured.

In fact, the obvious failings of risk management reveal an ugly truth: it is an
exercise in form over substance. If a firm was serious about this sort of thing, it
would not structure a supposedly crucial activity in such a way that guarantees
that it is politically weak and easily subverted. Risk management is often an exercise in providing cover for managers and directors, and thus serves as another
tool to hide looting.

That means it isn't surprising that Bookstaber alleges that many chief risk
officers make a full-time hobby of looking occupied, by running an organization
(many bodies are devoted to this futile task), preserving their standing in the
top brass by getting included in the right meetings, and reading voluminous reports. He argues that "the risk manager can end up looking really, really busy
while not actually doing his job."[74]

If firms had understood and accepted that their financial models had limited value, recognized their knowledge was imperfect, and proceeded cautiously,
the industry would have been much better off. But in the short-term focus of
Wall Street, a player that is careful about risk can be bested by cowboys. All the
incentives are for a race to the bottom.

·   ·   ·   ·   ·

A client, during a discussion of valuation issues, pointed to a chair in the conference room. "What do you think that chair costs? I can make it cost whatever
I want."

That may be news to people who have the good fortune not to deal much
with accounting issues, but it will not be a surprise to anyone who owns a business or has a managerial role in a large company. Accounting is very malleable
and can be used to make a company look healthier than it really is.

The financial services industry is hardly alone in winning and exploiting
favorable accounting treatment. But what makes it so dangerous is that these
firms are highly leveraged. Before the crisis broke, for every $100 of assets, U.S.
investment banks and Continental banks each on average had roughly $96.50
dollars of debt and $3.50 dollars of equity.[75] So if that $100 of assets were really
worth only $96, the bank is toast. Such a high level of gearing leaves perilous
little room for error.

Dubious accounting allowed banks to show more profit in the boom times
while endangering the health of the organizations. And to put none too fine a
point on it, some of the revenue accounting was suspect. Capital markets firms

pay a very high percentage of net revenues (revenues after interest expenses and trading losses) out as compensation, typically 40% to 50%.[76]

This is looting 2.0: firms over-levering themselves to extract excessive payment. The big difference from the classic looting pattern is that the distributions were widely shared within the organization, as opposed to the historical paradigm of funneling the cash to the CEO and close co-conspirators. And the worst is that the firms themselves, including the top brass that ought to have known better, like Joe Jett's bosses, believed the phony profits were real and paid themselves based on them. Moreover, outside investors, as with Enron, assumed that these enterprises were healthier than they really were and subsidized them by allowing them to finance on better terms than their true risks warranted. These entities appear to have, and may indeed have, positive net worth, but are more fragile than they appear and are vulnerable to shocks.

It is difficult to assess the economic impact of these questionable practices without doing forensic accounting, which would require access to banks' books. However, there is enough evidence of chicanery to indicate that this was a large-scale problem. Given how thinly the major financial firms were capitalized, it would not take much of this sort of thing for it to have played a driving role in their undoing.

In fact, the odds are high that Lehman engaged in fraudulent accounting. A survey of eleven research notes published by firms like Goldman Sachs, Sanford Bernstein, Fox-Pitt, Oppenheimer, and Merrill in the weeks prior to Lehman's demise, when it teetered on the verge of bankruptcy, shows that not one even considered the possibility that Lehman's net worth was negative. Remember, not only are these experts paid to evaluate the prospects of these firms, but they also have direct access to management and ask questions about the financial statements.[77] Some skeptical observers assumed Lehman would show perhaps $10 billion in negative net worth[78] on a roughly $640 billion balance sheet that showed $26 billion of equity on its last quarterly statement as of the end of May[79] (the bankruptcy was September 15, 2008). That means that the worst downside generally contemplated was a decay of roughly $36 billion (a change of plus $26 billion to minus $10 billion). No one dreamed that the firm had an even more massive hole in its balance sheet.

Yet the losses to creditors in the bankruptcy are not $10 billion, but $130 billion and counting, which meant the change in condition from its last financial statement was a stunning $156 billion.[80] One has to assume that the Treasury did not think the balance sheet shortfall was that large, otherwise it would not have allowed the firm to fail.

The bankruptcy consultant overseeing the messy global bankruptcy has tried to attribute the stunning losses to the disorderly collapse. But the black hole is simply too large for that explanation to be sufficient. Lehman's accounting was already coming under harsh scrutiny prior to the implosion. For instance, Lehman had large stakes in two end-of-cycle real estate investments, Archstone and SunCal, that looked certain to come a cropper. Although the exposures had been written down, critics still saw the valuations as far too rich. Similarly, in an effort to satisfy the experts, Lehman started making disclosures that only seemed to confirm doubts. For instance, in its March 31, 2008, report, it added a footnote disclosing its CDO exposures. The write-downs taken were a mere $200 million on $6.5 billion. That total included $1.6 billion of below investment grade tranches, sure to be badly impaired, making the low haircut a red flag.[81]

The general point is that the financial statements of complex financial firms are close to impenetrable, which often makes it hard even for experts to assess the true performance of these enterprises. With Lehman, verifiable valuations were suspect, calling the reports as a whole into question. If you are going to burnish your results, common sense says not to do it in an obvious way.

Indeed, as we will see, there are plenty of ways to goose the numbers, and ample evidence that these practices were widespread. Lehman was different in degree only, not in kind.

We will review the major types of questionable accounting:

- **Use of off-balance-sheet treatment** when the arrangement was neither arm's length nor non recourse. That meant some exposures were treated as if they posed no risk, when from a practical standpoint, they still did. This enabled banks to become even more leveraged in an economic sense than those worrisome capital ratios show.
- **Inflated valuations of positions.** Financial firms are required to use "mark-to-market" accounting for exposures held as trading positions, which means they should adjust their value to reflect current market prices. But some assets do not trade much, which gives banks latitude with what prices they assign to them, and that can be abused to inflate profits and make equity capital look higher than it is, overstating the firm's financial strength. Unwarranted high prices means that the banks are not only showing higher net worth than they really have, but are also understating losses, which makes profits look higher than they really are and thus allows for compensation to be paid on overstated results.
- **De facto upfront recognition of profit.** This will probably come as the biggest surprise to those outside the industry. The firms' internal reporting systems would reward measures to reduce capital used in

the operations. Some approaches that were used widely effectively brought expected but not yet earned revenues into the current year. Even worse, these future profits were included in profit and loss calculations for bonus purposes. And many of these trades blew up, meaning the profits were every bit as phony as the ones recorded by Joe Jett.

Let's illustrate how some of the tricks worked in practice.

Use of off-balance-sheet treatment. Unfortunately, Enron did not bring an end to "special purpose vehicles," the entities with names like Jedi and Raptor the derivatives bank used. The special purpose entities (SPEs) were types of off-balance-sheet vehicles, legal entities separate from the parent. They held particular assets and borrowed in their own name, with the sponsor usually holding some equity and receiving fees from managing its affairs. The theory is that if an off-balance-sheet entity craters, the sponsor's only exposure is the amount invested in the equity, since the borrowings were nonrecourse, meaning not guaranteed by the sponsor. Thus the debt and related assets do not have to be shown on the sponsor's financial statements.

A crucial quality of a QSPE (qualified special purpose entity) was that it was supposed to be a passive vehicle, but as we will discuss in chapter 9, that was often not the case, with parent companies coming to the rescue of their wayward offspring. That in turn implies these off-balance-sheet vehicles should have been consolidated, which meant their parents would have been required to have more equity capital. Again, we see the classic looting pattern: taking measures that boost reported profits at the expense of the health of the firm.

Off-balance-sheet exposures can be difficult to detect. For instance, when Lehman was trying to deleverage in mid-2008, it supposedly sold over $5 billion of rather fragrant assets to a hedge fund. But it turns out that hedge fund had Lehman as a major investor, it was operated by managers newly departed from Lehman, and it was located in Lehman office space. The deal came to light via a leak from a former Lehman executive[82] and likely would never have been detected otherwise. Lehman predictably insisted the relationship was kosher, a proper off-balance-sheet arrangement. Yet the accounting standards themselves (FAS 57) state that related party transactions "cannot be presumed to be carried out on an arm's length basis."[83]

Inflated valuations of positions. Many people assume that the vast majority of instruments owned by financial institutions can be priced readily. That is not true in many sectors of the market that are traded over the counter, particularly for complex credit instruments that were at the heart of the crisis (or perhaps more accurately, there are bids on the assets, but they are divergent enough to allow for cherry-picking). That in turn means dealers have incentives to show them at flattering prices on their books, both to avoid showing losses or to post exaggerated gains. Those moves do not simply make the balance sheet look better, but also have a profit impact. Avoiding recording losses or showing trading gains means higher revenues, which means higher bonuses. As Peter Solomon, former vice chairman of Lehman who now runs a boutique firm, put it:

> Everyone has an incentive in the short run to put the best face [on valuations]. Their compensation is totally based on it. In securities that don't have ready markets, particularly when the markets are troubled, it makes one totally suspicious.[84]

Traders have been known to work with investors, who trade securities among themselves at elevated prices. After the markets became disrupted, investors claimed that traders were marking positions based on their "offer" prices rather than where the market really was.[85] In particular, when investment banks and banks were stuck holding large inventories of takeover-related loans that they had bundled into collateralized loan obligations, hedge funds found that banks were refusing to give them prices, which the hedge funds needed for their own valuations for investors. The funds speculated that they were carrying them at full prices on their books and trying to avoid a write-down.[86] And some banks were clumsy. UBS, for instance, was found to be valuing subprime mortgages held on its books at prices higher than it was giving to customers who were looking to value similar paper.[87]

Some of the games traders play to avoid write-downs would be impossible for an outsider to detect. For instance, one ploy to avoid taking losses was to sell positions to a hedge fund, with an agreement that permits the buyer to sell the securities back after a specified period.[88]

These games are old hat to anyone familiar with market operations; one of the key jobs of management is to make sure traders are providing reliable marks. But as the Cerullo example illustrates, managers profit if they believe (or desperately hope) the strategy is sustainable, or the position will work out in the end. And in the stressed markets of the last two years, there has been good reason to think management is in cahoots. When banks mark down positions and show losses, it doesn't simply hurt their stock price, but it also leads to ratings downgrades. That in turn can put the capital market player on a slippery slope to a Bear Stearns finale of a run on the business. Downgrades make borrowing more costly, creating more earnings pressure. Repeated downgrades are blood in the water. Competitors start looking for signs of desperation. If they start to be reluctant to trade with the wounded firm and extend counterparty credit, the end comes swiftly. Bear was sold within two weeks of the first rumors that some European banks had stopped trading with it.[89]

But suspicious position marks, particularly ones where management must have been aware of the practice, are by nature hard to detect from the outside. One exception occurred in the course of the sale of Merrill Lynch to Bank of America. Bank of America marked down a single position, one on a "high vol 4 index," which led to a billion dollar swing, from a $100 million gain to a $900 million loss.[90] Readers may recall from chapter 6 that one of the unfortunate regulatory developments since the early 1990s permits dealers to use pretty much whatever volatility assumptions they want to in marking derivatives exposures, *even when market prices contradict these assumptions.* Despite the exotic sounding name, this was a very liquid index.[91] To put it bluntly, if massive mismarks were taking place on an exposure that could be easily priced (but where a misvaluation would not be counted as an SEC violation), imagine what went on with highly customized, one-off instruments like CDO tranches where there was no ready market price.

The accounting authorities went down the path of making financial firms disclose how much they were holding in the way of hard-to-value assets. The Financial Accounting Standards Board implemented a new rule, FAS 157, that set forth a three-class system for measuring "fair value" assets and liabilities, meaning ones that had to be carried at market prices, such as trading positions.

- Level 1 are assets that can be priced in active market, just like exchange-traded stocks.
- Level 2 applies to positions where there is no quoted price, but where prices can be extrapolated using "observable inputs." A corporate bond that didn't trade often could be valued that way, since dealers (in the old days) used credit rating, maturity, and coupon along with other considerations to interpolate a price based on how more actively traded bonds were priced. This is sometimes called "mark to model," but the key bit to keep in mind is all the factors involved in the estimate are verifiable.
- Level 3 assets are based on "unobservable inputs." This method of valuation is often called "mark to make believe."[92]

Although this move was no doubt intended to clarify how many assets might be the financial industry version of vaporware, some cute uses surfaced early. Wells Fargo chose to adopt the standard early. It reported Level 3 net gains of $1.21 billion, equivalent to 35% of pretax earnings, for the quarter ended June 30, 2008.[93] Another rule, FAS 159, told the firms they had to put assets in the lowest category possible. No calling assets Level 3 and marking them as you saw fit (in theory) if you could value them by other means.[94] But that is particularly hard to police on unaudited quarterly statements. However, experts estimated implementing this change could force $100 billion in write-downs.[95]

Even at that stage, Level 3 assets exceed net worth at every major investment bank save Merrill, and even there they were significant. At Morgan Stanley, they were 255% of equity, at Goldman, 184%, at Lehman, 160%, at Bear, 156%, and Merrill, 70%. At the larger and much more diverse Citigroup, they were a surprising 106% of equity.[96]

After the Bear meltdown (March 15, 2008), the SEC effectively gutted the Level 3 rules, barely three months after it became a FASB requirement.[97] And the signs continued of banks making clever use of it. For instance, for the first quarter of 2008, right after the regulatory relief came, Goldman increased its assets in the Level 3 category by 39%, and Morgan Stanley, by 45%. One analyst deemed the rises a "disaster waiting to happen."[98] In the third quarter of 2008, the biggest financial firms increased their Level 3 assets again by over 15%, to a total of $610 billion. While some of this move may have been due to difficult market conditions (that is, some assets that were formerly traded could now not readily be priced), observers at the time expected many of these assets newly classified as Level 3 to be written down later, meaning this rule change was abused.[99]

De facto upfront recognition of profits. This is the least well-known financial services industry dubious practice, and the one that strains credulity most. If you owned a commercial building, had an unbreakable lease to Uncle Sam, and also bought a contract from a AAA-rated insurer to protect you against increases in your operating costs, no one would consider it reasonable to take the future income, deduct the costs of the insurance policy, discount it back to the present day, and record all the income now. Yet banks did something very much like that on a large scale basis, and paid bonuses on those future earnings.

And as any sensible person might expect, things did not work out as planned and many of these phony future profits, just like Joe Jett's, will not come to pass. But unlike Jett, none of the recipients of bonuses related to this practice have been forced to disgorge them.

A common form of this practice occurs with a "negative basis trade." Negative basis trades can be executed when the cost of hedging a bond via credit default swap or another form of insurance is lower than the market yield on the same instrument. For instance, if you can purchase a bond at an interest rate of 400 basis points (4%) and buy a credit default swap of the same maturity referencing the company that issues that bond for 375 basis points (3.75%), the investor has 25 basis points (0.25%) of income. It is supposedly risk free, since any losses on the bond will be offset by gains on the guarantee.

This approach was extraordinarily popular with European banks, partly due to their regulatory capital rules.[100] Both the earlier Bank for International Settlements standard, Basel I, and the new Basel II standard called for banks to hold more equity against risky positions, but the more elaborate Basel II rules led to widespread gaming. The other factor that made negative basis trades possible was that the large European banks could borrow very cheaply.

Let's look at an example.[101] EuroBank buys a super senior CDO, rated Aaa/AAA. It has a floating rate coupon set at one month Libor (an interbank borrowing rate set daily in London) plus 50 basis points (0.50%). At its peak, EuroBank could fund this purchase by borrowing at Libor minus 20 basis points (–0.20%), so its "spread," or gross income, is 70 basis points (0.70%), which may not sound like much but is actually very good value for high-quality paper. But at this juncture this calculation doesn't capture all the costs. Since EuroBank does not have an infinite ability to borrow, it must also hold some much more costly equity against this position too, which makes the trade look less appealing.

Then the fancy footwork starts. EuroBank buys protection on the bond via a credit default swap from an AAA counterparty. It pays 20 basis points (0.20%), so its remaining spread is 50 basis points (0.50%). Acquiring this guarantee has two perverse effects. One is that, because the paper is rated AAA, the Basel II rules, which European bank regulators followed, let banks decide how much capital to hold. Not only did EuroBank decide to hold a small amount before this procedure, but then it further decided that the CDS hedge meant it had no risk and therefore no equity cushion was needed. [102]

But it gets even better. Assume the bond has a seven-year average life.[103] What would the internal profit and loss statement show? It would not simply count the 50 basis points as income this year. *It would show a profit equivalent to taking the earnings from years two through seven and discounting them back to the current year.*

How could this be? Remember that the revenues at a financial firm are not created equal. Revenues that come from activities that do not use capital are more valuable than ones that require large buffers against possible losses. Banks have tried to apply some discipline to the process of weighing the risks of various types of income based on how much capital they require to support them.

A granddaddy of this approach was a system developed at Bankers Trust starting in the late 1970s called RAROC, for Risk Adjusted Return on Capital. The Basel II rules that most foreign bank regulators observe and the philosophically similar approach employed by the Federal Reserve embody notions like those found in RAROC.

Most financial firms try to allow for the riskiness of income in internal measurements of business performance (banks have management information systems, including the ones used for calculating profit and losses for the purpose of determining bonuses, and these are separate from the reports used for financial accounting purposes, which have to comply with accounting standards and regulatory requirements). One widely used approach draws on so-called Economic Value Added models, which are supposed to align internal metrics better with what would help share price performance.

But why would these reports show that a hedge with an AAA counterparty of an AAA position would accelerate future income? While that was the economic effect, the mechanism by which it occurred looked different. Remember that magical original term, "risk adjusted return on capital." If you lower capital, the return on capital improves greatly. These systems are designed to reward measures that lower capital requirements. Hedging the AAA position with a guarantee from an AAA (supposedly impeccable) counterparty freed up the capital formerly needed to support it, at least according to these metrics.[104] An immediate profit was credited to the desk that put on the guarantee.

Now consider how this looks to traders, who focus strictly on their own bottom lines. This is free money, thousand dollar bills lying on the sidewalk. Many of these transactions are incredibly simple to arrange and require little to no monitoring once booked. The not-trivial danger, that the party that provided the insurance might not be good for it ("counterparty risk," the possibility that the other side of the deal might fail to perform), is treated as the bank's problem, not the trader's. The fact that there is no charge for the cost of equity also means the people on these desks will face far fewer risk management limits than for other types of business. In other words, they can enter into transactions like this in extraordinarily large volumes.[105]

This procedure did not apply simply to collateralized debt obligations, but also to what one market participant called "the whole gamut of acronyms,"[106] including collateralized loan obligations, and a less common type of collateralized debt obligation called TruPS CDOs made from pools of subordinated debt by small banks.

For U.S. investment banks, which set the norms for bonuses, average compensation is over 40% of revenues, and the capital markets operations at big commercial banks adopted similar policies. Since these trades looked unusually profitable and low risk, the share to traders, and to the managers above them, probably totaled at least that much.

In no other line of work is it deemed reasonable to pay staff for earnings that are expected to come years in the future. Is it any wonder that banks wound up holding boatloads of the paper used to achieve this wondrous result?

In fact, one bank, UBS, was so intoxicated with this idea that it went around purchasing other banks' AAA-rated CDOs.[107] Many of the other European banks were aggressive buyers of this paper, suggesting that they were using similar strategies.

American investment banks also wound up with large collateralized debt and collateralized loan obligation holdings when the credit party stopped, primarily because it seemed very attractive to gin up these deals (the profits on the underwritings were very rich) even if demand was flagging. Merrill increasingly kept unsold "super senior" CDOs on its balance sheet, believing it was not at risk of loss.[108] In the old days, a hung new issue was considered a disaster, since it meant you had overpriced it and would eat a loss. The solution would have been to lower the price of that tranche, which would increase the interest rate. The lower the interest on the super senior layer, the less appealing the deal was for investors, but the more the bankers could rip out of the deal in the form of structuring fees. Merrill took the view that it would eventually unload the stuff, that the interest covered its cost of funding, and was remarkably unconcerned with its burgeoning inventory. The result from the investment bank's perspective was a short-term profit and a near-certain back-end loss, but that route increased the payout to the bankers and traders.

． ． ． ． ．

Readers would no doubt prefer a more satisfying tale where the bad guys fit more familiar stereotypes: black hats and handlebar mustaches, or the modern version, Gordon Gekko-like swaggering Masters of the Universe who broadcast their belief that greed is good. And a minor genre of crisis narratives has emerged to feed the desire to pin the crisis on easily identifiable villains, in particular the CEOs of some of the firms that failed.

But in this version, the process of *maximizing current extractable value* was for the most part not in the hands of colorful characters, but a legion of more mundane perpetrators adept in the nitty-gritty of transaction structures and accounting considerations that allowed them to shift risk onto less-well-informed parties, which at times included their own employers. This happened all up and down the food chain, from hapless borrowers signing mortgages they did not understand, to former Goldman Sachs co-head, treasury secretary, and Citigroup chairman Robert Rubin admitting he didn't know what "liquidity puts"[109] were until they forced the bank to fund $25 billion of CDOs just as the market was imploding.[110]

Although shifting risk on a transactional level has become a highly developed art form, the main purveyors were hoist on their own petard, failing to grasp how these exposures created much greater danger on an aggregate level than they bothered to consider. And now that they operate under a large and generous government safety net, there is no reason for them not to do it all over again, on an even grander scale.

CHAPTER 8

THE WIZARD OF OZ

Giving liquidity to bankers is like giving a barrel of beer to a drunk. You know exactly what is going to happen. You just don't know which wall he is going to choose.

—Nick Sibley, former Managing Director, Jardine Fleming

Manias and financial crises are inextricably entwined with commerce. Neo-Sumerian kings of Ur, in what is now southern Iraq, opted for a free enterprise model during the Middle Bronze age and allowed merchants to operate alongside a "palace sector." Because the state, unlike some of its neighbors, could not finance large-scale trade ventures, merchants stepped into the breach in the first known example of privatization.[1] Before 1800 B.C., Ur's commercial law was well developed, with clearly defined property rights, particularly those of creditors, who could force borrowers to sell themselves and their families into slavery. The rulers tacitly supported indebtedness, since it spurred its subjects to higher levels of effort and output.[2]

Excavations in Ur found records of the earliest known financial center, with depositaries, short- and long-term interest-paying loans, usury laws (and ways around them, given the high level of mathematical sophistication, and comparative government cluelessness), a liquid market for promissory notes, merchant accounts (a precursor to our credit cards), a bond market, and syndicates of what amounted to limited partners backing maritime expeditions. Even small investors could participate in these consortia, making them analogous to mutual funds.[3]

Prices of pools backing copper ventures rose rapidly. Participants spent their expected gains before they received them.[4] The financiers, who gained control of the copper trade, were able to redistribute wealth, undermining the king's authority. In 1788 B.C., the king voided all loans, producing the first financial crash. The record shows an abrupt end to financial dealings (and to Ur's standing as a trade center), and a proliferation of lawsuits.[5] Capital fled to Larsa, a neighboring city, and economic weakness paved the way for conquest by the Amorites of Babylon under Hammurabi.[6]

. . . . .

While Tolstoy argued that unhappy families were each unhappy in their own way, manias and debt crises seem remarkably similar across time. The run-up to the Great Crash of 1788 B.C. shows striking parallels to the period preceding the global financial crisis that started in 2007: a proliferation of ways to borrow; the use of sophisticated techniques to evade regulations and achieve premium returns; the ability to spend paper (or in Ur, clay) profits.

But it is important to notice the differences as well. The reason that the financial reforms of the Great Depression proved effective and durable was that the Pecora Commission, a Senate Banking Committee investigation led by chief counsel Ferdinand Pecora, delved into the details of the abuses and provided the perspective needed for sound reforms.

Many experts and commentators have started to reexamine the pre-crisis economic tea leaves to divine causes. Unfortunately, in typical "drunk looking under the street light" fashion, the focus, in many cases, has been to try to explain the crisis in terms of well-recognized phenomena, such as deregulation and so-called global imbalances.

These factors, while important, are only partial explanations. Just as drought conditions increase the odds of raging brush fires, so too did policies that were overly accommodative to banking interests increase the likelihood of a systemic crisis. But what set off the fire? Was it something likely and hard to prevent, like a bolt of lightning? Or was it something more pernicious, like arson?

One of the distinctive elements of the period preceding the crisis was the so-called wall of liquidity phenomenon. For those outside the financial markets, it is hard to convey a sense of how extreme and unusual this was. While bubbles are common, this syndrome was a considerable deviation from the normal pattern.

Rising asset prices can fuel reckless lending. As prices of investments rise, their owners can borrow more against them. When their values shoot up, the typical dynamic is that lenders are first skeptical, but then are swept up in the frenzy.[7] A particular asset or market is usually the epicenter of the mania, but if it is big enough, it can spill into related markets. For instance, in the Japanese bubble era, real estate was the focus, with banks lending aggressively against property in major cities.[8] At its peak, the land under the emperor's palace in Tokyo was worth more than the state of California.[9] Companies would borrow against their real estate to buy Japanese stocks or make investments abroad, driving asset prices up in other markets because they looked relatively cheap.

However, speculation can take hold without the banking system being exposed in a serious way. For instance, the U.S. dot-com bubble, despite its impressive amplitude, was not driven by borrowing. Even at the peak for tech stocks, margin lending was not a significant percentage of total market capitalization.

In the 2004–2007 period, a different dynamic was in place. It was exceptionally cheap to borrow, no matter for what purpose. A broad swathe of investments sprinted to record levels on the rising tide of liquidity. It was a global credit mania.

But how did this come to pass? In the past, demand for the loans always came from the asset buyers. But the novel feature of this episode was that *loans themselves were the "product" at the heart of the bubble.* It was credit itself that was bid to insanely high levels. And recall that high prices for bonds mean low interest rates for borrowers.

This time, the investors, primarily investment banks and hedge funds, had an insatiable appetite for particular, new types of credit market instruments. Demand really did generate its own supply. Recall that bright young things in the Internet mania obligingly came up with companies like Pets.com and Boo.com that had no prospect of ever turning a profit, but were nevertheless briefly prized because they suited buyer appetites. In this iteration, the credit mania led downstream channels to gin up loans that were every bit as destined to fail as late-stage dot-com ventures. Moreover, most of the buyers of these instruments did not care about fundamentals, that is, whether the loan would be any good, but saw them only as useful components in seemingly attractive trading strategies. And the ones who did take note of their prospects were usually betting that they would fail.

Many commentaries on the crisis have treated the housing bubble as a distinct phenomenon, a morality tale with either greedy borrowers or predatory lenders as the main villains. But that focus ignores the fact that a host of credit instruments, from credit card receivables to commercial real estate to takeover loans, featured the same kind of reckless lending and are on a path to showing unprecedented losses. These train wrecks were not separate developments. They were the inevitable result of a voracious hunger for credit "product."

Any attempt to explain the crisis that does not come to grips with the wall of liquidity phenomenon is incomplete. This chapter will describe the environmental conditions that make it possible and chapter 9 will discuss the strategies that produced the "wall of liquidity."

. . . . .

In a nutshell, the generals, in this case central bankers and policy makers, were still fighting the last war, which was inflation, the demon of the 1970s. As long as inflation remained tame, pro-growth measures got a green light. And as we saw in chapter 5, business interests had pushed the notion that deregulation and "free markets" would spur innovation and thus produce greater output.

But these changes, in particular the liberalization of international trade and capital flows, and the growth of "market-based credit" at the expense of traditional banking, changed the structure of the economy in ways that economists did not fully appreciate.

Perhaps most important: since mainstream economic dogma held that markets were self-correcting, it meant that the orthodoxy gave the result of liberalization a free pass, no matter how problematic that outcome might be. Nary a thought was given to the possibility, foreseen in the Lipsey-Lancaster theorem, that efforts to move toward an unattainable ideal could make matters worse. Instead, anything that resulted from market activity was assumed to be beneficial, or at least benign.

Banks are regulated for a very good reason. Credit is essential to commerce, and having financial intermediaries collapse, particularly on a widespread basis, is disruptive. But deregulation meant that all sorts of banking activities took place in new, unsupervised channels. These measures weakened the foundations of the system by enabling previously unattainable levels of borrowing. The evidence of rising, ultimately destabilizing debt levels was in full view, but ignored or rationalized.

As we will discuss in chapter 9, financial deregulation spawned a shadow banking system, an unregulated sector that came to rival the traditional banking system in size. Contrary to the confidence of the "free markets" faithful, it, like credit extension in general, is predisposed to boom-bust cycles. The absence of measures to contain risk taking and force participants to hold cushions against losses made this sector fragile and prone to breakdown.

The part that most observers and regulators missed is that the bubble in credit products was as acute as the Japanese or dot-com episodes. The reason the extraordinary increase in expected (and in some cases, realized) profits has not been widely recognized is that it did not show up in a form visible and easily understood by nonparticipants. This mania lacked simple compelling anecdotes and images, like the classic moon shot chart showing a parabolic price rise, say of Cisco's stock or of the Nikkei from 1980 to 1989.

The outsized profits were not the result of *particular securities* showing spectacular gains, which is the shape of traditional bubbles. Instead, techniques that came out of financial economics allowed for risks to appear to be reduced and spectacular leverage to be applied. The frenzy was the result of the fact that borrowings amplify returns. An investment or trading strategy that yields 1% is unappealing to most investors. But if you can borrow, say, twenty or forty times against it, with few offsetting costs, the expected returns escalate by almost the same amount. And that was the hidden mania, that credit, which historically had been a decidedly unsexy arena, suddenly through new hedging and borrowing techniques became compelling, so seductive that vast new amounts of money flowed to these markets, with the new demand producing further gains.

The result was more and more debt being piled on top of teeny slivers of equity, the very phenomenon that Gillian Tett's worried sources warned of back in chapter 1. With such a small cushion, and with so many actors making highly levered bets, the whole system was vulnerable not just to shock, but to mere miscalculations.

This unprecedented level of system-wide risk taking turned what might have been a minor bush fire into a firestorm. And unlike the Long Term Capital Management crisis of 1998, when the world's biggest hedge fund imploded and nearly took the financial system down along with it, considerable damage was done not just by players who read things incorrectly and wounded themselves, but by the most successful actors.

·　·　·　·　·

Orthodox economics is peculiarly silent on the subject of banking and finance. Neoclassical models do not even assume the existence of money; they simply postulate a barter system. Macroeconomics, the study of the operation of the economy as a whole, has a similar blind spot here. As Rob Parenteau, research associate with the Levy Economics Institute at Bard College, noted:

> General equilibrium theory, the intellectual pinnacle of the profession, has no room for money. Real business cycle theory has no room for finance—negative shocks to productivity, virtually from out of the blue, are the stated source of recessions. The Taylor rule, which ostensibly guides central bank policy rate setting, has an interest rate but no room for either money or finance, unless it is packed away in the error terms of the canonical equations. Recently, the Henry Kaufman Professor of Financial Institutions at Columbia University

and his co-authors concluded the US housing bubble had little effect on consumer spending patterns. Huh?[10]

Yet credit is the lifeblood of a modern economy. Credit brings with it its own peril, namely, financial instability. That comes to pass in two ways.

The first is simply that banks are in the business of borrowing money from people and lending it to other people, who might not give it back. Banks hold deposits and pay interest on them. Depositors have the right to demand their funds at any time, but through experience, banks know that only a small percent of the funds they hold in trust will be withdrawn on any given day, and even that might be matched or exceeded by new inflows. Thus banks, to earn additional profit, lend out a portion of their deposits, typically $9 of every $10, at a higher interest rate than they pay to their depositors.[11]

Now banks allow for dud borrowers; the interest they charge is in part to compensate for defaults. But almost predictably, some banks miscalculate and incur large enough losses to put deposits at risk. Even if the bank turns out to be solvent (that is, its loans are worth at least as much as its deposits), its customers may not know that for certain. They hear of trouble and start to pull their funds out. That in turn produces what is called a bank run, or liquidity crisis. Even if a bank has a sound book of loans, it only has $1 on hand for every $10 of deposits; it can't convert those loans back into cash on short notice. If enough customers want their money back, the bank cannot perform and must turn them away.

This failure has ripple effects. Those customers who were denied access to their funds no doubt need them, perhaps in just a day or two, say to meet payroll, buy supplies, pay for existing orders, or make payments on debt. Thus they cannot meet those commitments, and that can lead others, who counted on those payments, to come up short.

If enough customers of the bank that got in trouble are believed to be in difficulty themselves, customers of other banks may worry that their institution is sitting on now-bad loans. So they will go and reclaim their deposits, precipitating more bank runs and failures.

Bank runs are not limited to traditional banks. Recall the Reserve Fund, a U.S. money market fund that suffered $785 million of losses when Lehman collapsed in September 2008. It "broke the buck," meaning it failed to maintain a $1 per share net asset value. Customers redeemed over 60% of the fund's assets in two days.[12] Representative Paul Kanjorski of Pennsylvania said that the chairman of the Federal Reserve told Congress later that week that money market funds had suffered massive withdrawals, $550 billion in a period of hours.[13] Even though money market funds are better able than banks to turn their investments into cash, a sudden panic leads to massive selling with insufficient buyers, producing losses due to a supply-demand imbalance.

A second source of instability is the interaction between lending and asset prices. While banks make some loans based on the borrower's overall income, many are also secured by specific types of property, such as real estate, equipment, automobiles. If their prices rise, both the bank and the borrower think they are wealthier. The seemingly better-protected bank is willing to lend the apparently more-prosperous debtor more money. Conversely, if asset prices fall, the bank will get nervous about its loan. If it can, it will charge the borrower a higher rate of interest. And the fact that it may now face losses on this loan and others like it will make the bank chary about extending new credit. Customers may be forced to sell assets to pay the bank, further depressing prices. Thus falling asset prices and credit contractions reinforce each other, leading to a downward spiral.

These two issues may seem trivial and well-known, but they create financial instability. It is essential to note that the second phenomenon, the feedback loop between collateralized lending and assets prices, contradicts standard economic models. Economics posits the existence of equilibria, and, lacking a model for financial systems, often projects the behavior of goods markets onto financial activity. In the world of products, higher prices generally reduce demand. Yet in the realm of finance, higher asset prices lead to more credit extension, which fuels more asset purchases. The financial system is predisposed toward credit expansion, followed by distress and a cycle of credit contraction. There is no propensity toward equilibrium.

Other factors feed the predisposition to cycles of credit expansion and contraction. First, as Hyman Minsky, an economist at Washington University, observed, periods of stability actually produce instability. Economic growth and low defaults lead to greater confidence and, with it, lax lending.

In early stages of the economic cycle, thanks to fresh memories of tough times and defaults, lenders are stringent. Most borrowers can pay interest and repay the loan balance (principal) when it comes due. But even in those times, some debtors are what Minsky calls "speculative units" who cannot repay principal. They need to borrow again when their current loan matures, which makes them hostage to market conditions when they need to roll their obligation. Minsky created a third category, "Ponzi units," which can't even cover the interest, but keep things going by selling assets and/or borrowing more and using the proceeds to pay the initial lender. Minsky's observation:

> Over a protracted period of good times, capitalist economies tend to move to a financial structure in which there is a large weight of units engaged in speculative and Ponzi finance.

What happens? As growth continues, central banks become more concerned about inflation and start to tighten monetary policy, meaning that

> . . . speculative units will become Ponzi units and the net worth of previously Ponzi units will quickly evaporate. Consequently units with cash flow shortfalls will be forced to try to make positions by selling out positions. That is likely to lead to a collapse of asset values.[14]

Ouch.

Second, measures to backstop the financial system and prevent bank runs (through deposit guarantees and the central bank role of "lender of last resort") are not "get out of jail free" cards as far as overall risk is concerned; they merely shift it from banks to society at large.

One of the unintended consequences of these safety nets is moral hazard. If someone is guaranteed not to suffer the consequences of his bad actions, he will tend to go and misbehave. In banking, moral hazard results when devices to prevent bank failures encourage banks to take greater risks. Similarly, there is no reason for protected depositors to seek out safe financial firms; they make their choice based on the deposit rate or other attributes. That reduces market discipline on banks.

The third factor: oft-repeated experiments in behavioral economics have found that laboratory versions of markets produce bubbles. Neoclassical adherents objected that this result was due to the absence of short selling (being able to bet on price declines) and margin lending (borrowing against the asset). However, adding those features to later experiments made the bubble larger.[15] All of these factors suggest that asset prices can readily rise to overvalued levels, and the interaction with credit extension turbocharges that dynamic.

Yet the U.S. Federal Reserve, tasked with maintaining the soundness of the banking system, viewed the world through a radically different lens until the crisis wake-up call. It did not give much credence to the idea that the financial system, left to its own devices, is prone to breakdown. The Treasury Department, which through its Office of the Comptroller of the Currency regulates nationally chartered banks, held similar views to the Fed.

Indeed, the most important models used by central banks to manage the economy, Dynamic Stochastic General Equilibrium (DSGE) models, treat the financial system as an afterthought. As Wolfgang Münchau, a columnist for the *Financial Times*, noted:

> This model [DSGE] has significant policy implications. One of them is that central banks can safely ignore . . . asset prices and deal only with the economic consequences of an asset price bust. . . . There is now a lively debate—to put it

mildly—about whether an economic model in denial of a financial market can still be useful in the 21st century.[16]

The adherence to economic *idées fixes*—that markets are self-correcting and "efficient," meaning, among other things, that they send valid signals about economic fundamentals—produced a series of policy measures that led to increasing levels of debt, increasing instability, and a run on an unregulated banking sector that had come to rival the size of the official one.

■　■　■　■　■

The United States and key bits of the rest of the world have gone on a borrowing spree since the early 1990s. Private sector debt rose from a level of roughly 100% of GDP through most of the 1980s to 125% in the early 1990s, a level it more or less maintained for that decade. In 1999, it took off in a near parabolic fashion, to reach its crisis level of over 175% of GDP, higher than at the onset of the Great Depression. And most of this debt was consumer debt, mortgages in particular.

But how did this explosion in debt come to pass? A number of factors contributed. The first was policies that permitted (one might say encouraged)

Figure 8.1

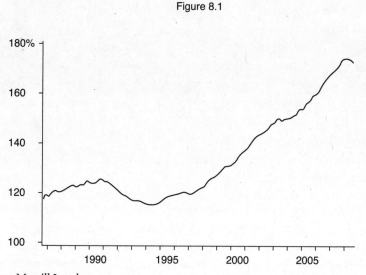

Source: Merrill Lynch

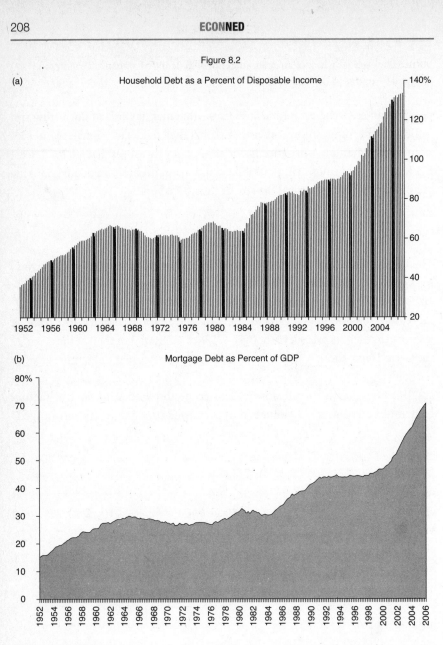

Figure 8.2

(a) Household Debt as a Percent of Disposable Income

(b) Mortgage Debt as Percent of GDP

Source: Federal Reserve

unprecedented buying of U.S. assets, mainly debt products, by large exporters such as China and Japan. When the United States runs sustained trade deficits, countries that run the corresponding trade surpluses will invest in dollar assets (more on that shortly). This pattern started to take hold in the 1980s and became institutionalized through the "strong dollar" policy of the Robert Rubin/Larry

Summers Treasury departments. That in turn allowed mercantilist trade partners, such as China and later the other Asian "tigers," to peg their currencies at artificially low rates without protest from the United States.[17] Over time, the U.S. savings rate dropped, reaching zero, even negative levels in the 2005–2007 period, as U.S. households borrowed to fund spending.

Borrowing per se is not a bad thing as long as it is either short term or to fund productive investments. But higher indebtedness by households in advanced economies does not lead to faster expansion; in fact, some studies have concluded it is associated with lower per capita GDP growth.[18] And in the countries that went on a debt binge, the borrowing was primarily for housing, not for productive investments that could generate income to help pay off the loans.

A second factor in the explosion of debt was the so-called "Greenspan put," the habit of the Federal Reserve under Alan Greenspan to break glass and lower interest rates at the slightest sign of trouble in the financial system, without being equally quick to choke off credit or otherwise intervene when markets got frothy. That served to protect investors and financial institutions, encouraging both to take more risk.

Third, the authorities noticed, indeed applauded, the growth of what then president of the Federal Reserve Bank of New York Timothy Geithner, among others, called the development of a system of "market-based credit." That is, a large and growing part of lending depended not on banks, but on placing credit instruments of various sorts with investors, a process called "securitization." Sometimes this was done directly, with borrowers, generally large corporations, selling securities directly to investors. However, most of the growth took place via securitization, in which loans of various sorts, such as mortgages, auto loans, buyout debt, student loans, and credit card receivables, were assembled into pools, packaged into securities, and then resold to buyers like pension funds, insurance companies, and even banks. (We discuss this phenomenon in chapter 9.)

However, the authorities neglected to consider the corollary of this pattern: just as traditional banks are subject to runs, so too were the participants in this "shadow banking system." But unlike banks, the authorities had only a sketchy picture of what these new funding sources were up to, and had no ready way to rescue them when they got themselves and the economy in trouble.

. . . . .

One view of how the United States and its bubble *confrères,* like the UK, Spain, Ireland, Australia, and the Baltics, got into this mess fingers an excess of global savings, particularly in China and Japan, as the culprit. By way of explanation, imbalances in trade (more accurately, the current account, but nearly all of that is trade) have to be matched by the capital account, inflows or outflows of funds in the form of investments of various types. Thus countries like China and Japan that run trade surpluses must invest the "proceeds" in foreign assets, such as bonds, real estate, stocks, or other holdings. The portion of these foreign investments held by the monetary authorities in the form of foreign bond and currency deposits is called "foreign exchange reserves."

In the "which came first, the chicken or egg" question of what drove trade imbalances, the "savings glut" version of the story holds that the level of savings in Japan and China was too high compared to their opportunities for investment at home. In other words, they should have been consuming more and saving less.

That reading ignores the fact that Japan and China, along with many of our trading partners, were pursuing mercantilist trading policies. Big trade surpluses mean a country will have a high savings rate and "underconsumption," relative to domestic output. China pegged its currency against the dollar at a level widely seen as too cheap, a de facto massive export subsidy; Japan in its post-bubble years also pursued economic policies (to try to revive its economy) that wound up keeping the yen low. The United States chose to tolerate these practices until they became problematic, but by then they were so ingrained as to be well-nigh impossible to unwind.

If you look through the other end of the lens, the issue is one of U.S. overconsumption (or alternatively, underproduction) and inadequate savings, leading to a yawning trade deficit that the trade calculus demanded be met by savings somewhere else in the world.

This "savings glut" version of this story, although it has the convenient effect of getting U.S. policymakers off the hook, does not hold up to close scrutiny.[19] Moreover, it takes two to tango, and the "savings glut" would have been impossible absent U.S. cooperation. A reading of history shows the "savings glut" version conveniently omits how the United States tolerated (one might say encouraged) this pattern. And it also ignores the fact that credit growth was well out of proportion to what can be explained even by the massive growth of foreign exchange reserves in China: the result of their "funding" our considerable trade deficit with them. In other words, the "global imbalances" were a culprit, but far from the sole perp.

· · · · ·

The inflation of the 1970s, plus the success of the pro-business push, led to a fundamental shift in policies. One of the big factors that made the stagflation price rises self-reinforcing was that workers had meaningful bargaining power. Wages and price increases thus kept leapfrogging each other.

Prior to the 1980s, U.S. policy was mindful of average worker wages and trade deficits. But starting in 1979, the character of U.S. business cycles changed. Large trade deficits, debt increases in excess of income growth, asset price increases, and a failure of workers to capture the benefits of productivity growth became the norm. As Thomas Palley, former chief economist of the U.S.-China Economic and Security Review Commission, explained:

> The new cycle rests on financial booms and cheap imports. Financial booms provide collateral that supports debt-financed spending. Borrowing is also supported by an easing of credit standards and new financial products that increase leverage and widen the range of assets that can be borrowed against. Cheap imports ameliorate the effects of wage stagnation.[20]

Before, U.S. policymakers saw trade deficits as a cause for alarm, a sign that U.S. demand was being dissipated abroad rather than supporting at-home production and employment. But the new world view was that any trade imbalance was the result of market forces, and hence virtuous. Moreover, given that keeping inflation at bay was now a high priority, the Fed saw competition from foreign workers as a way to keep U.S. wages in check. Suddenly the virtuous circle of rising worker incomes leading to greater prosperity was put in reverse gear.

The problem with this new, inverted model is that it rests on rising asset prices and more liberal borrowings. Assets increasingly serve as collateral for borrowing to support consumption. And it isn't simply housing: recall that once upon a time, few people financed the purchase of a car. But this new paradigm doesn't simply rely on debt; it relies on *increasing levels of indebtedness.* Higher and higher levels of borrowings are eventually self-limiting. Nevertheless, the framework that evolved over the last thirty years had the peculiar feature that the authorities increasingly acted as enablers, working to keep asset prices up because a decline was seen as having deleterious economic effects.

The irony is that this perverse outcome, that asset prices could not be permitted to fall much, was the result of Reagan's policies toward trade and regulation (with an emphasis on de-fanging unions). Yet the Reagan administration soon repudiated this stance via currency intervention in the so-called "Plaza Accord." The United States decided to intercede because the dollar and trade deficit had risen to unacceptably high levels, particularly relative to Japan.

In September 1985, the United States reached an agreement with Japan, the UK, France, and West Germany to engage in a coordinated intervention to lower the value of the dollar. The effort was narrowly successful and the dollar continued to fall after the intervention was complete, leading to a decline of the dollar relative to the yen of over 50% from 1985 to 1987. In fact, the markets overshot the levels sought by the United States and its cohorts, leading to another set of interventions, the Louvre Accord, in February 1987, this time to prop up the greenback. However, the G6 nations, despite the firepower committed to this effort, were seen to be pursuing domestic monetary policies inconsistent with the currency measures, and the dollar soon resumed its fall.

Had these interventions worked, the fall in the dollar would have brought back trade to close to a balance, which in turn would have lowered foreign purchases of U.S. assets and likely reduced the U.S. dependence on short-term foreign capital inflows to sustain growth. But contrary to orthodox economic thinking, the trade deficit with Japan persisted, despite the fact that the dollar fell further against the yen than other currencies.[21] From a practical standpoint, the Japanese markets were not open (the Japanese imposed numerous "quality" restrictions that were hard for U.S. companies to satisfy, plus Japanese consumers have a very strong preference for Japanese goods).[22] Japan didn't play by the rules set forth in simple trade models, but policymakers nevertheless defaulted to the model's prescriptions rather than trying to understand the situation at hand.

So the large trade imbalances and resulting large international capital flows persisted. And they were followed in short order by two financial crises: a moderate-sized one in the United States (the savings and loan crisis,[23] along with the less publicized but also painful cratering of leveraged buyout deals, which hit large commercial banks) and the crash in Japan, the result of a counterproductive effort to combat the domestic impact of a fall in exports. The Japanese government lowered interest rates *with the aim of pushing asset prices higher.* From an anonymous Bank of Japan official:

> We intended first to boost the stock and property markets. Supported by this safety net—rising markets—export-oriented industries were supposed to reshape themselves so they could adapt to a domestic-led economy. This step was supposed to bring about an enormous growth of assets over every economic sector. The wealth effect would in turn touch off personal consumption and residential investment, followed by an increase in investment in plant and equipment. In the end, loosened monetary policy would boost real economic growth.[24]

Japanese banks had no notion of cash flow-based lending, and would advance 100% against urban land (meaning central Tokyo, Osaka, and Nagoya). The results were massive real estate and equity markets bubbles (companies often borrowed against real estate to fund *zaitech,* or speculation). The colossal failure of the Japanese experiment, to use rising asset prices to spur consumption, on the assumption that investment and greater growth would follow, was ignored.

Recent research suggests that the two phenomena, high international capital flows and financial crises, are related. Former IMF chief economist Kenneth Rogoff and Carmen Reinhart of the University of Maryland have created a dataset of financial crises going back 800 years. Their conclusions are sobering:

> Serial default on external debt—that is, repeated sovereign default—is the norm throughout nearly every region in the world, including Asia and Europe. . . . Another regularity found in the literature on modern financial crises is that countries experiencing large capital inflows are at high risk of having a debt crisis. Default is likely to be accompanied by a currency crash and a spurt of inflation. The evidence here suggests the same to be true over a much broader sweep of history, with surges in capital inflows often preceding external debt crises at the country, regional, and global level since 1800, if not before.
>
> Also consonant with the modern theory of crises is the striking correlation between freer capital mobility and the incidence of banking crises. . . . Periods of high international capital mobility have repeatedly produced international banking crises, not only famously as they did in the 1990s, but historically.[25]

Let's consider what this implies. First, high levels of international capital movements are at least associated with, and perhaps cause, financial instability. While crises became frequent starting in the late 1980s (Japan's bust was followed by the Mexican crisis in 1995, the Asian crisis in 1997, the Russian default and Long-Term Capital Management implosion in 1998, and the dot-com bubble of 1998–2001), the first major modern episode was the Latin American sovereign debt crisis of the late 1970s and early 1980s. And that, in turn, was not very long after the liberalization of international capital flows that started cautiously in the 1960s and gained steam in the 1970s.

Second, as the intervention to lower the value of the yen shows, international funds flows do not necessarily have a propensity to normalize. There are not strong forces toward equilibrium in these markets. Currencies in particular are known for long periods of misvaluation relative to seemingly fundamental forces, such as health of an economy and trade balances. And even when the yen was forced higher, which by any conventional wisdom should have largely corrected the U.S.-Japan trade imbalance, it persisted.

More recently, the dollar's standing as reserve currency means that letting it fall to the degree required to reduce trade imbalances, particularly with China, could roil financial markets. And the Chinese are not too keen about taking losses on their huge holdings of dollar denominated assets (even though the alternative is buying yet more U.S. assets, which will make the cost of the eventual rebalancing even greater).

In fairness, the idea that high levels of international funds flows produce financial instability is still hotly debated among economists. Yet another approach suggests that a high level of borrowing, which generally goes hand in hand with high capital mobility (the destination country too often winds up having a debt party), can put a modern economy on tilt when debt levels get too high. Physicist Mark Buchanan describes the work of Yale economist John Geanakoplos, and physicists Doyne Farmer and Stephan Thurner:

> In the model, market participants, especially hedge funds, do what they do in real life—seeking profits by aiming for ever higher leverage, borrowing money to amplify the potential gains from their investments. More leverage tends to tie market actors into tight chains of financial interdependence, and the simulations show how this effect can push the market toward instability by making it more likely that trouble in one place—the failure of one investor to cover a position—will spread more easily elsewhere.
>
> That's not really surprising, of course. But the model also shows something that is not at all obvious. The instability doesn't grow in the market gradually, but arrives suddenly. Beyond a certain threshold the virtual market abruptly loses its stability in a "phase transition" akin to the way ice abruptly melts into liquid water. Beyond this point, collective financial meltdown becomes effectively certain. This is the kind of possibility that equilibrium thinking cannot even entertain.[26]

This model highlights a tradeoff ignored (at least until recently) by most economists. All the arguments for deregulation were those of greater efficiency, that less government intervention would lower costs and spur innovation. We'll put aside the question of whether any gains would actually be shared or would simply accrue to the financier class. Regardless, risks to stability never entered into these recommendations. But if we put on our systems engineering hat, stability is always a first order design requirement and efficiency is secondary.

More tightly integrated systems, such as the one produced by trade and capital markets internationalization, are less stable. And as ugly as the idea of capital controls sounds to those trained to believe that more open markets (that is, efficiency) should prevail, the fact is that buffers are precisely the sort of remedy called for to reduce the speed of transmission of shocks to a system. They do reduce efficiency and increase costs. Measures to engineer in stability are a form of insurance. Effective insurance is not free.

But as of the early 1990s, the crises that had taken place—Latin American sovereign debt, the U.S. savings and loans, Japan, and less noticed, smaller crises, such as widespread bank failures in Sweden, Norway, and Finland—were seen as isolated and domestic in origin rather than as part of a larger pattern. So the authorities in the United States merrily continued down the path of implementing policies that, like doping athletes with steroids, produced short-term performance gains at the expense of long-term health.

■ ■ ■ ■ ■

So why, given its sorry history in the Reagan administration, did Clinton Treasury Secretary Robert Rubin endorse a strong dollar policy in 1995?

Follow the money.

Clinton had won the 1992 election with narrow support from business, and Wall Street had been one of his major constituencies.[27] Contrary to his campaign rhetoric, Clinton, almost immediately upon being elected, announced a series of Wall Street-friendly measures, including making deficit reduction a priority and backing a strong dollar, both tonics to the bond market and asset values generally.

However, those overtures to the investing classes proved to be short lived. In 1994, with mid-term elections in the offing and having virtually no accomplishments to tout, the administration decided in February to talk down the dollar. The logic was simple. Japan had continued to be an impossible market to crack, but if the dollar were cheap enough, U.S. imports of Japanese goods would fall so dramatically that the Japanese would be forced to relent.

A broad swathe of American companies would applaud success against Japan. But the New York money crowd was dead set against a sharp fall in the greenback. Protracted currency weakness is anathema to a financial center. Look what happened to Tokyo, once destined to be the dominant hub in the Asian time zone. The end of the bubble era had devastated those aspirations. While New York would never lose out to, say, Toronto, London enjoyed a geographic advantage by its overlap with the Asian and U.S. workdays and might regain its dominant position.

The Clinton policy change caught Wall Street flat-footed. Some firms, badly positioned, took large losses. Compounding their misfortune, some foreign banks reversed their policies of bond-friendly monetary easing, leaving securities firms, which are structurally long bonds, with additional losses. Multinationals were also opposed, seeing currency volatility as a threat.

Congressional Democrats, looking for culprits for the financial upheaval, briefly held hearings on hedge funds. This move further alienated investment bankers. Wall Street donors, almost without exception, halted Democratic National Committee contributions, in some cases even rescinding six-figure pledges.[28] Needless to say, given that the administration had alienated other funding sources, such as tobacco and the oil industry, the mid-term Congressional rout should not have been a surprise. But the Gingrich program did not have popular support, and Clinton assigned high priority to winning over business.

The pressure to reverse the "weaken the greenback" strategy intensified. The Japanese, who had been selling Treasuries to shore up finances at home, threatened retaliatory liquidation. Other Asian central banks were allegedly selling dollar holdings, and OPEC was reported to be considering abandoning its practice of pricing oil in dollars. While some of these threats were overblown or short term in nature, the administration was concerned about the risk of pushing Japan into a death spiral. Even worse, the main goal, of securing support with export-oriented businesses, was not yielding the hoped-for financial rewards.[29]

So the administration made a 180-degree change and salvaged what it could. In late spring 1995, Rubin and other officials started regularly affirming a strong dollar policy. The administration secured a commitment from Japan for better market access, along with an undisclosed deal, acknowledged by both U.S. and Japanese sources, that the Japanese would continue to buy Treasuries. In addition, the Bank of Japan agreed to prevent U.S. bonds being sold by troubled Japanese banks from coming onto the market.[30]

And it turned out there was a bigger constituency for this program than just the moneybags. A strong dollar pressured labor while keeping the Clinton administration's hands clean. Multinationals could buy assets overseas on much better terms. Cheaper imports, particularly commodities, the wage restraints on workers from imports, and the new corporate practice of offshoring, all kept inflation under wraps, another boon for business and investors.

. . . . .

Ambrose Bierce, in *The Devil's Dictionary,* defined a partnership as "When two thieves have their hands plunged so deeply into each other's pockets that they cannot separately plunder a third party." Japan had become our partner.

With the strong dollar policy, the 1980s pattern of substantial international capital flows had become institutionalized. It is important to note that this is not an inherent result of trade. What makes large cross-border investment flows inevitable is large current account deficits or surpluses, not the absolute level of trade. While large capital flows can appear benign, they produce more volatility. Moreover, large flows have the potential to become quickly unbalanced and therefore destabilizing.

One weakness of our current floating currency system, as with the former gold standard, is that there is no penalty for countries that run persistent trade surpluses. In the gold regime, they accumulated larger and larger gold reserves; in our current framework, they accumulate official foreign exchange reserves and private holdings of foreign assets, such as stocks, bonds, and real estate and corporate investments in operations. Thus the surplus country enjoys rising wealth and employment in excess of what its own consumption will support. And many of our trade partners adopted explicit policies of export-led growth. While the strong dollar policy was far from the sole culprit for America's faltering trade position, it certainly did not help.[31]

A second weakness is that making a currency expensive does not necessarily lead to a corresponding shift in trade balances. With Japan, the effort fell short due to the resistance of the Japanese, formally and behaviorally. With certain goods that have no ready substitutes, such as oil, price changes do not lead to large changes in consumption, at least in the short and medium term. Yes, a weaker dollar means America will import less, but substituting domestic production for imports is a structural change that does not happen overnight. The process is protracted, plus some players would need to be convinced that a weaker currency was not transitory before they would invest.

And the third is that "floating" rates can be influenced by central bank interest rate policies. For instance, the Bank of Japan kept dropping its call rate, its overnight interest rate, starting at the end of 1990. Although the relationship is loose, the yen did weaken considerably over the 1990s as interest rates fell, helping Japan have a robust export sector even though its domestic economy was a basket case. Conventional trade-oriented theories of exchange rates say that the currencies of countries running large trade surpluses ought to rise, thus making their exports more costly and reducing their competitiveness. However, these models ignore the role of the financial system. A country like Japan with low interest rates can see its currency become a funding vehicle (recall the discussion of the yen carry trade in chapter 7). Foreigners will gamble on exchange rates, borrowing in the low interest rates and investing at higher interest rates elsewhere. This activity suppresses the price of the funding currency because the speculators must sell the low interest rate currency to buy investments of the country offering higher returns, and the sales of the currency borrowed will keep its price down.[32]

And Japan was soon to have company in the "cheap currency" club, albeit for different reasons.

China pegged its currency at 8.28 renminbi to the dollar in 1994.[33] The initial motivation for setting a fixed rate was to give exporters greater predictability, and this is not a trivial issue. Volatile exchange rates can wreak havoc with planning and profits. Hedging costs money, and even sophisticated players can wind up worse off from trying to protect against exchange rate movements than if they had done nothing.

But as the Chinese economy performed well, China maintained its peg, which increasingly looked to be at an artificially low level (as economies become more successful, their currencies usually rise in value). Like the Japanese before them, China saw trade surpluses with the United States grow and started acquiring U.S. assets. But for many years, this pattern looked benign, since the Chinese surpluses, although sustained, were not large by global standards.[34]

And then the Asian crisis hit. The causes are debated, but external debt has risen sharply in many Asian economies. Many had set interest rates high to attract foreign investors and had currency pegs. Unfortunately they were too successful. The influx of hot money stimulated their economies and produced trade deficits. High domestic interest rates and a fixed exchange rate made borrowing in foreign currencies like the dollar look like a smart move. Thailand in particular went on a debt binge. But that put borrowers at risk of much higher debt-servicing costs if the home currency fell versus the dollar.

Speculators, seeing Thailand's precarious position, started to attack the currency. Thailand wound up depleting its foreign exchange in mounting a defense and was first to let its currency float in July 1997.[35] As the baht plunged, many banks and companies that had borrowed in foreign currencies suddenly saw the debt payments skyrocket, pushing them into insolvency.

Although the Asian countries wanted to organize a bailout, the move was beaten back aggressively by Treasury Secretary Robert Rubin, his deputy secretary, Larry Summers, and Timothy Geithner, then at the IMF but about to assume the role of assistant secretary for international affairs at the Treasury.[36] The IMF provided a rescue package in August, using the same template it had in Mexico in 1995, requiring structural reforms, such as cutting government spending, letting insolvent institutions fail, and raising interest rates. Note that this is almost the polar opposite of the approach advanced economies used to fight the current crisis.[37]

In addition, many of the particulars of Thailand's situation, especially its high domestic savings rate, were very different than the ones operating in Mexico. Some felt that the remedies were in no small measure intended to remake these economies along Western lines.[38] As Marshall Auerback, an investment analyst specializing in the Pacific Rim, observed:

> By killing off the idea of a competing Asian Monetary Fund, Rubin/Summers enabled the IMF to continue in its guise as an ostensibly "neutral" agency, thereby facilitating the implementation of the Treasury's agenda. . . . Of course, the "medicine" the IMF proffered had the ultimate effect of weakening pre-existing financial structures by imposing Western measures of financial restruc-

turing, thereby giving Wall Street a huge stake in the subsequent "reform" agenda introduced: Basel capital adequacy ratios were to be applied. Highly indebted banks and firms were to be closed. Labour laws were to be changed to make it easier to fire workers, facilitating the closures. Regulations on foreign ownership were to be lifted in order to allow foreign banks and firms to buy domestic banks and firms, injecting needed capital and skills. All of which required lots of western style restructuring and "reform," and who better to offer this than America's finest investment bankers?[39]

Independent of the motivation, the results were soon clear. While Thailand would not have had an easy time under any circumstance, the IMF remedies poured gas on a raging fire. The economy went into a deleveraging spiral, similar to what happened in the United States in the Great Depression. As the economy contracted, more and more loans started going bad. Banks responded by cutting back on lending. That meant that even businesses that were sound were suddenly short of funding they needed for routine operations, such as financing inventory purchases. Businesses slashed spending, which steepened the fall in activity in the economy. Even worse, borrowers that had the misfortune to have loans coming due at that time were unable to roll them over as they had expected. They were forced to sell assets in severely depressed markets to pay off the balance. Those liquidations pushed those markets ever lower, and businesses that could not raise enough money to pay off the loans failed, again increasing unemployment and damaging the economy further. Exporters, who, it had been assumed, would make up for the fall in activity (the fall in the baht made them very competitive), were hamstrung by the lack of day-to-day funding. Manufacturing production plunged. Those workers who kept their jobs saw their standard of living fall as inflation spiked.[40]

The baht continued to fall, making the external debt burden worse. The IMF provided more funds in two modifications, relaxed some of the more draconian elements, and the crisis spread. Indonesia and South Korea were particularly hard hit. Many of the affected countries suffered political as well as economic upheaval. During this period, the United States asked China, which was suffering collateral damage, to hold its peg rather than cheapen the renminbi, which would be an expected response. This request, which China accepted, served to reinforce its fixed-rate regime.

The heavy-handed IMF measures were deeply resented in the region and perceived, correctly or not, to have made matters worse. Indeed, in South Korea, the late 1990s dislocation is called "the IMF crisis." Government throughout the region resolved never again to be in the position of having to go to the IMF for help.

So the next best insurance for the now gun-shy Asian countries was keeping their currencies cheap and building up big enough war chests, in terms of foreign exchange reserves, to fend off any attacks from currency speculators. Having undervalued currencies also made their exports attractive, and a strong trade sector would pull them out of the crisis faster.

But cheap currencies and persistent trade surpluses meant some other countries had to have the opposite profile, with an overvalued currency and a persistent trade deficit, a.k.a., overconsumption (or as some prefer, underproduction), that would be funded by borrowing and asset sales. That someone, of course, was the United States.

By 1998, China's trade deficit with the United States was nearly as large as Japan's, with Germany a distant third. The deficits and China's purchases of U.S. assets only continued to mount. China's foreign exchange reserves went from $168 billion in 2000 to $403 billion in 2003 and hit $610 billion by the close of 2004. That led to a flurry of bills in Congress on the Chinese currency policy, some calling for sanctions.[41] Of course, the picture was not as straightforward as the U.S. complaint might suggest. The United States was running a massive Federal deficit, thanks to the Bush tax cuts and Iraq war spending. With a low savings rate, the money had to come from somewhere. Big capital inflows meant a large trade deficit was inevitable.

Nevertheless, China relented and implemented a "dirty float," pegging its official rate a bit over 2% higher and allowing modest movement within a band.[42] But the cautious increase did not change the dynamic. Chinese surpluses and accumulation of foreign assets (necessary to keep the renminbi [RMB] from rising further) only grew, rising to a stunning $2.5 trillion in 2008, consisting of $1.9 trillion in official foreign exchange reserves, the rest in portfolio debt and other items.[43] And not surprisingly, the renminbi still appears too cheap, as the Chinese increased their surplus with the United States in 2008 despite the global slump while those of Japan and other major trading partners had fallen.[44] One study suggested that the RMB, despite a 14% increase in the last year, was still 40% undervalued.[45]

That pattern, minus the dirty float part, held in much of the rest of Asia, with currencies pegged at favorable levels to the greenback. By 2001, capital inflows to the United States had shifted from private investors to "official" sources, meaning central bank purchases of safe securities like Treasuries, to keep their currencies from appreciating.[46] But China and Japan dominated the funds flows, with the Gulf States also important when oil prices were strong.

So as international financial crises continued, the pattern of United States as consumer and borrower of the last resort became more and more entrenched.

. . . . .

Countries that continue to import more than they sell abroad show falling savings rates. In the United States, in the 1980s, the mantra was "twin deficits,"
namely, the U.S. trade deficit and the burgeoning federal deficit. In the 1990s, as
Clinton moved to balance government books but the trade deficit persisted,
household savings started to fall rapidly.

Admittedly, there had been some decay even before then. Personal savings
had fallen from roughly 10% in 1980 and averaged 8% through 1994, then
plummeted to a 1% level from mid-2000 to mid-2007. And even that figure is
flattering. In 2001, the Bureau of Economic Advisers changed its method for accounting for personal savings. Under the old approach, the results for that period would have been –0.6%.[47] By contrast, savings rates in the rest of the world
from 1980 to 2001 were higher, with no sharp mid-1990s decay, save in Canada,
which is closely integrated with the United States. For instance: France averaged
15%; Germany, 12%; Japan, 13%.

The rationalizations were impressive. First was the "wealth effect," that people were saving less because their appreciating stock portfolios and houses were
doing the work for them.[48] While a logical culprit, it ignored the fact that equities were often held in retirement accounts, and thus for many people, equities
were a substitute for corporate pensions, which historically had not shown up
on household balance sheets. And these holdings could not be liquidated prior
without paying taxes and sometimes penalties. Put another way, the distinction
between "investment," which are funds deployed with the hope of multiplying,
and reserves, which are for times of adversity, was confounded. If consumers
invest all of their savings in risky or illiquid assets, they may take losses if they
need to access them on short notice.

Further inspection reveals more holes. If the increase in consumption was
indeed due to a rise in asset values, then the increase in consumption and fall in
savings should have been concentrated in the most affluent households. In fact,
the shift was similar across wealth levels and age groups.[49]

Similarly, home equity was now accessible via borrowing against it, which
also entailed costs. In other words, the public was assuming considerably more
risk.

Another explanation was that labor productivity had risen, and that households expected the gains to continue.[50] By implication, they were spending anticipated increases in earnings before they arrived. Yet as discussed earlier,
workers had stopped participating meaningfully in productivity increases starting in the 1970s. While young workers might assume they would earn more as

they gained experience, and could whittle down their debt, for much of the rest of the population, that idea was quite a stretch.

A third assertion was the idea that financial innovation had given consumers more access to credit, allowing them to spend more freely. This "relaxing liquidity constraints" was code for things like "using credit cards in lieu of savings" and "borrowing before the paycheck arrives." Cut to the chase: this was tantamount to "consumers were borrowing more because they could." And that unflattering theory was given short shrift.[51]

And the debt side of the ledger was just as sobering. The Federal Reserve tracks various measures of personal indebtedness, with an explicit warning that it can't get comprehensive enough information. Nevertheless, it has two proxies: a debt service obligation ratio, which is computation of debt service relative to disposable income, and a broader measure, the financial obligations ratio, which includes commitments like interest on rental property, auto lease payments, homeowners' insurance, and property taxes.[52] Both ratios had increased gradually, with a lot of noise, from 1980 to 1999, and then ramped upward through 2007, with the rise due to an increase in mortgage-related obligations. This was particularly surprising given the fall in long-term interest rates from 2001 onward. If the level of debt had remained the same, the ratio would have fallen.[53]

No matter which story one believed, they all pointed in the same direction: lenders acting in the way Minsky predicted. An unusually long period without a serious recession produced more willingness to take financial gambles.

But hollow justifications of growing consumer borrowing and nonexistent savings continued as the new century progressed. The most remarkable was from Federal Reserve chairman Ben Bernanke in a 2005 speech:

> Some observers have expressed concern about rising levels of household debt. . . . However, concerns about debt growth should be allayed by the fact that household assets (particularly housing wealth) have risen even more quickly than household liabilities. Indeed, the ratio of household net worth to household income has been rising smartly and currently stands at 5.4, well above its long-run average of about 4.8. . . . One caveat for the future is that the recent rapid escalation in house prices . . . is unlikely to continue. . . . If the increases in house prices begin to moderate as expected, the resulting slowdown in household wealth accumulation should lead ultimately to somewhat slower growth in consumer spending.[54]

The flaw in the logic should have been obvious. Indebtedness was rising and incremental savings had been flirting with zero. Debt has to be serviced either out of income, liquidating savings, borrowing against other assets (a self-limiting process), or from the proceeds of asset sales. With real incomes of most Americans stagnant and savings at a low level for a long time, a growing number of consumers were in the position where everything had to work out right for them to make good on their commitments. Unfortunately, luck is no substitute for prudence.

After the unraveling started, the rationalizations of deteriorating personal finances finally came under scrutiny. From a paper published in the *Review* of the Federal Reserve Bank of St. Louis in 2007:

> . . . the recent decline of the personal savings rate to low levels seems to be a real economic phenomenon and may be a cause for concern. After examining several possible explanations for the trend advanced in recent literature, the authors conclude that *none of them provides a compelling explanation* for the steep decline and negative levels of the US personal savings rate.[55] (Emphasis added.)

In other words, the theories advanced at the time were all wet.

·　·　·　·　·

A second major contributor to the growth of leverage and risk taking was the market-friendly posture of Federal Reserve chairman Alan Greenspan, embodied in the so-called Greenspan put. A put is an option that gives an investor the right to sell an instrument at a specified price and is often used as a hedge against losses. Many investors came to believe that the Federal Reserve would intervene in the event of a serious downdraft, similarly reducing their downside exposure.

Greenspan is a contradictory figure. A disciple of neoliberal demigoddess and apostle of rampant individualism Ayn Rand, he was a true believer in the virtues of unregulated markets.

Ironically, the Fed chairman rode roughshod over the dictates of another "free markets" stalwart, the monetary economist Milton Friedman, who had urged central banks simply to set a steady but modest rate for growth in money supply. Indeed, Friedman in his popular writings contended that the Fed had caused the Depression.[56] Hands off on the financial regulatory front, Greenspan was active as far as interest rate interventions were concerned.

But other followers of "free markets" policies would support Greenspan's monetary machinations. Recall that they saw the refusal of workers to accept low enough wages as a factor that made the Great Depression as severe as it was. One way to contain compensation is for the central bank to raise interest rates when inflation starts to build. The logic is that increasing unemployment will moderate pay pressures and also discourage businesses from giving employees pay increases in excess of productivity gains.[57] Ironically, quite a few "free markets" supporters endorse this type of intervention to correct a perceived market failure (labor having undue bargaining power) but reject a raft of others.

Greenspan was also famed for poring over reams of economic data. Wall Street took comfort from his Wizard of Oz act: great and mysterious power, mastery of arcane information, and generally impenetrable pronouncements.

Greenspan's first major act as Fed chairman helped establish his reputation as a friend of financiers. Bankers and economists applauded Greenspan's initial emergency operations during the 1987 crash, only a bit more than two months into his tenure. He and fellow Fed officials judiciously jawboned lenders into continuing to extend credit to market participants.[58] The central bank also lowered the Fed funds rate by 50 basis points.[59]

This operation was an expansion of the central bank's traditional scope. The Federal Reserve's charter makes it responsible for the safety and soundness of the banking system. Subsequent legislation added the duties of promoting growth and price stability. Aiding in the continued operation of financial markets was a new task.

In the wake of the savings and loan crisis, Greenspan again came to the rescue of the financial services industry, dropping rates and producing and maintaining a steep yield curve, meaning a large differential between short-term interest rates and long-term rates. But this action was more in keeping with the Fed's charter. Bank balance sheets had been battered in the savings and loan crisis and the aftermath of the leveraged buyout boom, and many (Citibank in particular, which was rescued by a large investment from Saudi prince Al-Waleed) were undercapitalized. Since banks borrow on a short-term basis and make long-term loans, very low short rates and high long rates meant higher profits, enabling banks to earn their way out of their mess. However, Greenspan had been cautious in making his move. Both Democratic and Republican observers have commented that had Greenspan lowered rates sooner, George Bush might have won the 1992 election.[60]

Greenspan developed an unseemly interest in equity prices, which had never been part of the Fed's job description. Indeed, a May 2000 *Wall Street Journal* story called it an "obsession" that dated to at least 1991.[61] 1994 Federal Open Market Committee records show the chairman pleased at "[breaking] the back of an emerging bubble in equities." December 1996 witnessed his famous "irrational exuberance" remark, widely seen as a comment on stock valuations. Foreign equities swooned overnight, with major indices falling 2% to 4% and the Dow dropping 145 points in its first half hour of trading. Similarly, he voiced skepticism toward the "new era" thinking driving levitating equity prices, in Congressional testimony in February 1997 and July 1998.[62]

Despite seeing signs of frothiness, Greenspan failed to connect other dots. The Fed chairman in the mid- to late 1990s would occasionally remark that imports were helping keep inflation tame, and by extension, he could keep interest rates at their current level without risk of stoking price gains. But this was a flawed view. The price of imports did not reflect the actions of the Fed. A better metric would have been prices excluding imports.[63] A former Federal Reserve economist, Richard Alford, set forth the problem:

> One of the interesting aspects of economic policy in the US is a belief that we exist independent of the rest of the world. . . . most US economists pretend that the rest of the world does not exist, is stable, or that the dollar will quickly adjust so as to maintain US external balances. . . .
>
> If you look at the difference between gross domestic purchases and potential output, by US consumers, businesses, and government—all are above potential output. The only time in recent memory when the difference between these two measures started to narrow was in 2001 when we were in a recession. . . .
>
> The policy goal has been to generate sufficient levels of demand to support full employment. . . . That would be fine if we did not have a net trade sector or at least had a stable net trade sector. But . . . we've had a flood of imports which have depressed prices in tradable goods. Fed Governor Don Kohn . . . said imported deflation knocked 50–100 basis points off measured per annum inflation. At the same time, rising imports have hurt American workers. . . . the underlying problem is not deficient US demand, but a structural external increase in supply (globalization). Given the inability of the dollar to serve as an adjustment mechanism, we are consuming too many imports, but instead of US policymakers addressing this global development, we created a number of unsustainable domestic imbalances to keep employment at politically acceptable levels. Higher levels of debt and asset bubbles have been the result of policy responses to external imbalances.[64]

The nub of the argument is that since the mid-1990s, domestic demand in the United States was in excess of potential output, a claim many economists would find surprising. The most widely used estimates for potential output come from the Congressional Budget Office and for aggregate demand, from the Bureau of Economic Analysis. Those data series, which had seemed reliable for most of the postwar period, indeed showed demand was running below potential output. Based on that, stimulus, such as low interest rates, would be warranted.

But Alford contends that globalization rendered those measures invalid. In the new world of "free markets," the United States has made no effort since the time of the failed Plaza Accord to rein in trade deficits. If we could rely on the trade imbalance correcting itself, we could indeed ignore the export-import sector, which the prevailing approach does. But in these circumstances, another measure of demand, gross domestic purchases, gives a more accurate picture, and it shows that demand ran ahead of potential output by roughly 2% to 6% through 2006.

Consider what this means. The Fed had been overstimulating the domestic economy for a prolonged period, the effects masked by cheap imports and the lack of labor bargaining power.

Greenspan also took comfort from government data that showed that productivity was rising. Improving productivity means the economy can grow at a faster rate without stoking inflation. One rationalization for the willingness of foreigners to lend to and invest in the United States in the later 1990s was ostensibly our better prospects, particularly relative to Europe, where productivity gains seemed wanting.

But Greenspan was using a faulty thermometer. Recent studies have cast doubt on our measures of service industry productivity, which is where the gains occurred, in particular financial services.[65] Another recent study by Dean Baker and David Resnick concluded that U.S. productivity growth from 1995 to 2005 lagged the OECD (Organisation for Economic Co-Operation and Development) average.[66]

Not only was Greenspan's rate target too lax, but he also became ever more willing to come to the rescue of financial markets. Greenspan defenders look to his quick trigger moves, asserting that the Maestro only made small, gradual rate cuts in the wake of the Long-Term Capital Management (LTCM) crisis in 1998, when the impending collapse of the giant hedge fund appeared to threaten the financial system.[67] But other observers contend that the Fed's role in the LTCM rescue, of meeting with LTCM to review its exposures, and convening investment banks (over which it had no meaningful regulatory authority) and large commercial banks to tell them they had a problem they had better address, pronto, was another market-minding activity, outside its traditional purview. Critics argue that had the Fed let LTCM fail, the disruption would have thinned the herd of imprudent risk takers, and made intermediaries far more cautious about lending to unregulated players (the firms the Fed called together were all counterparties to LTCM and had large exposures).

In fact the prevailing economic notions were guaranteed to produce the Greenspan put. The orthodox view was that no one could recognize a bubble in progress; the right approach was to let it burst of its own accord and mop up afterward. But that meant providing liquidity, as in lowering rates, every time something bad happened. So as financial crises became more frequent, so did the Fed's interventions, which served to embolden investors even further.

But Greenspan didn't simply move quickly to prop up troubled markets. He also decided to ignore the famous dictum of another Fed chairman, William

McChesney Martin Jr., that the job of central bankers was to take the punch bowl away just as the party gets going.

Despite Greenspan's initial reservations about ever-rising stock prices, his treatment of stocks and the financial markets generally became more and more asymmetrical. Starting in 1998, Greenspan would telegraph his intention to increase rates well in advance, giving participants ample time to adjust to their depressing effect, while he would make cuts on a surprise basis, which amplified their impact. Traders increasingly believed that the Fed had adopted a policy of protecting them against loss.[68] And that only increased their propensity to take risks.

Proving the classic saying that bull markets are near their ends when the last bears throw in the towel, Greenspan decided, in a reversal of his earlier reservations, that the markets knew best. At the Fed's annual Jackson Hole conference in 1999, he announced his view that the now stratospheric equity valuations were justified by productivity gains. The NASDAQ, perhaps cheered, rose another 50% in the next three months. Inflation hawks in the Fed, such as Laurence Meyer and J. Alfred Broaddus, persuaded Greenspan that rising productivity could stoke inflation because stock prices rose before the fruits of the gains were in the bank, and the anticipatory spending that resulted (remember the famed wealth effect) was stimulative. Greenspan bought the logic and planned in early 2000 to implement a modest set of rate increases, 1.25% over ten months, although he did provide a last jolt of liquidity before that, in anticipation of a Y2K problem that never materialized.

But in a development that would have stunned any previous Fed chairman, the stock market was deemed "too big to fail." As the unwind progressed, the Fed made a surprise 50 basis point cut to shore up asset prices. But the move proved futile, and Greenspan's initial "irrational exuberance" assessment was proven correct. The continuing decline wiped out $8.5 trillion of value from exchange-traded U.S. stocks over the next two years.[69]

∎   ∎   ∎   ∎   ∎

As depicted in the 2000 *Wall Street Journal* story, Greenspan at first considered, then dismissed the idea that the equity market bubble might be related to the 1995 Mexico crisis, the 1997 Asian crisis, and the 1998 Russian default that precipitated the LTCM crisis. Instead, the Maestro looked for explanations within the realm of equities, such as greater stability leading to more robust valuations.

If he and his colleagues been less blinded by the belief system of markets *über alles,* then, instead of poring over the behavior of equities, they might have taken more notice of a bigger, more obvious development that was also more closely related to the Fed's job description, namely, the growth of a large, unregulated parallel banking sector, now popularly known as the shadow banking system. We will return to this topic in the next chapter.

But although components of this system were visible and widely discussed, others were opaque and hard to quantify. (This is similar to the decline in the role of traditional on-balance sheet bank lending in the "originate and distribute" model, in which loans were packaged and structured into different classes of securities to make them more appealing to investors.) So in classic drunk under the street light fashion, the Fed and most economists ignored the effect of a major shift in the financial system.

And that in turn led Greenspan to take the course of action for which he has been most pilloried, namely, dropping the Federal funds rate and holding it at below the rate of inflation for a prolonged period. Negative real interest rates are highly stimulative. Greenspan's justification was that the Federal Reserve needed to combat deflationary forces unleashed by 9/11. If you are a central banker, deflation is an even more dreadful outcome than inflation. When prices fall, the value of debt in real terms rises. Most loans are priced assuming some, perhaps substantial, inflation, which means the future payments will be made in less valuable dollars. When deflation takes hold, the borrower is faced with a commitment that has suddenly become a great deal more costly. He may wind up selling assets, now at lower prices thanks to deflation, and distressed selling on a large scale feeds on itself, producing further downward pressure on prices. Borrowers also try to pay down debt, which slows economic activity. Both the Great Depression and Japan's lost decades were severe and protracted precisely because deflation took hold

Even though the Fed often spends some time gradually easing rates, it rarely holds them at the nadir for more than a quarter or two. Yet the Fed kept its benchmark rate at 1% for a year and at 1.25% for an additional nine months, from November 2002 to August 2004, despite the fact that the dot-com bust recession was widely described as mild and the Bush administration tax cuts led to budget deficits, meaning a fiscal stimulus.[70] Observers also took cheer from a widely cited 2002 speech by Ben Bernanke, in which he described a set of then-novel approaches the Fed could use to combat deflation (many of which he later implemented as Fed chairman in the current crisis) as proof of a "Bernanke credit market put."[71]

This policy was a dramatic departure from the central bank's normal responses, based on an approach called the Taylor rule, named for Stanford economics professor John Taylor. While the Taylor rule did not oppose dropping rates in 2001, it would have called for them to have been increased starting early in 2002, rather than lowered even further and held there for a long time.

Figure 8.3

Federal funds rate, actual and counterfactual (%)

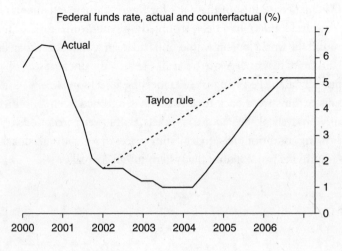

Source: John B. Taylor, 2007

Taylor later felt compelled to write a book, *Getting Off Track* to demonstrate what a blunder the Maestro had made, and argued the housing bubble would not have taken place had his prescription been followed:

Figure 8.4

The Boom-Bust in Housing Starts Compared
with the Counterfactual

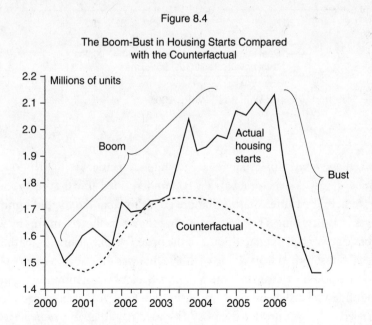

Source: John B. Taylor, 2009

Greenspan ignored warnings while the super low rates were in force. William White, the chief economist of the Bank for International Settlements (a central bank for central banks), had been troubled by synchronized rises in housing prices around the world for some time, and had been telling Greenspan and other central bankers of his concerns, to no avail. He took the unusual step of airing his doubts publicly, at the Fed's August 2003 meeting at Jackson Hole.[72] White argued that the distortions went back to at least 1998, and had been amplified by the "inherently procyclical" behavior of markets, that lower perceptions of risk and easy borrowing conditions lead to levitating prices in a positive feedback loop, in an ever-amplifying process until the system suffers a breakdown.

Figure 8.5

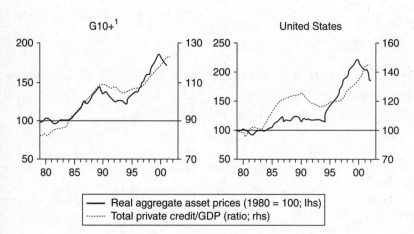

Source: Claudio Borio and William R. White, 2003

Needless to say, Greenspan ignored White's warning.

Indeed, just as structural barriers had undermined efforts to use a cheaper dollar to help the United States sell more goods to Japan, so too did significant changes in U.S. business behavior confound the normal mechanisms by which economic policy had operated. Some of the prized accomplishments of the "free markets" boosters had worked too well. The first was the effort to reduce labor's bargaining power as a way to tame inflation. Second was a movement, spurred by an influential article by Harvard Business School's Michael Jensen in 1993, that called for much greater use of stock-based pay to align top management interests with those of shareholders.

There was a problem with this idea, however. The Jensen approach was intended to solve what is called a principal-agent problem, which is that you may not be able to trust the person you hired to do a good job for you. He may instead serve his own interests first.

But who was in charge of designing these new reward systems? The very same managers who might be out for themselves. The foxes were still in charge of the henhouse, although they concealed their control by having their human resources departments hire executive-friendly compensation consultants. And who approved these pay packages? Directors nominated by the same incumbent management. Can anyone be surprised that they engineered an explosive growth in CEO pay?

Because tax and cosmetic considerations favored equity-linked pay, corporate chieftains became obsessed with pleasing Wall Street. The result was an increased focus on meeting short-term earnings targets at the expense of long-term investment. Starting in 2002, U.S. corporations were running an average net financial surplus of 1.7% of GDP, which contrasts with an average deficit of 1.2% of GDP for the preceding forty years. While firms in aggregate have occasionally run a surplus, J.P. Morgan noted:

> . . . the recent level of saving by corporates is unprecedented. . . . It is important to stress that the present situation is in some sense unnatural. A more normal situation would be for the global corporate sector—in both the G6 and emerging economies—to be borrowing, and for households in the G6 economies to be saving more, ahead of the deterioration in demographics.[73]

Companies were giving more priority to fattening their bottom lines, even if they were actually starving in terms of long-term growth. In all previous postwar economic recoveries, the lion's share of the increase in national income went to labor compensation (meaning increases in hiring, wages, and benefits) rather than corporate profits, according to the National Bureau of Economic Analysis. In the post-2002 upturn, not only was the proportion going to workers far lower than ever before, but it was the first time that the share of GDP growth going to corporate coffers exceeded the labor share.[74]

In other words, despite super low interest rates, despite business friendly deregulation, companies now thought it better to stress containing costs rather than growing. So, loose money tended more and more to fund consumer spending and asset purchases instead. The financial economy was taking precedence over the real economy.

William McChesney Martin's tough-minded program would not be popular with banks. By contrast, Greenspan and his successor Ben Bernanke were acutely sensitive to the banks' needs. They were victims of what Willem Buiter, a London School of Economics professor who has held a number of important policy roles, calls "cognitive regulatory capture."[75] The supposed supervisors had come to see the world through the financial industry's undue sense of self-importance. As a result, they overestimated the relationship between the upheaval in the stock market and deleveraging, which can be deflationary. Remember, as dramatic as the stock market bubble had been, it was not stoked by borrowings. Margin debt at the stock market's peak in 2000 was a mere 2.9% of market capitalization.[76] Yet it appeared the Fed chair was incorrectly drawing an analogy to the collapse of the Japanese bubble, which had featured a large addition to already high levels of lending to real estate and an unprecedented bubble there in commercial and residential real estate, with some of the borrowing against corporate holdings going into the stock market. The damage to Japanese banks indeed proved deflationary, but margin lending was not a significant factor.

By contrast, debt did not play much of a role in the dot-com bubble. Thus while the fall in equity prices would leave investors feeling much poorer, it would not blow back and damage the banking system. Yet Greenspan's actions and Bernanke's remarks, particularly the famed 2002 speech that earned him the moniker "Helicopter Ben" for the idea of throwing cash out of a helicopter to stoke inflation, revealed a Fed in mortal peril of an outcome unwarranted by facts on the ground. And the corollary of the Fed's Wall Street–centric view was they believed the health of the financial sector was the key to the welfare of Main Street.

As a result of Greenspan's and then Bernanke's overly accommodative monetary and regulatory stances, the credit created by the shadow banking system took off.

CHAPTER 9

THE HEART OF DARKNESS

THE SHADOW BANKING SYSTEM SELF-DESTRUCTS

Speculators may do no harm as bubbles on a steady stream of enterprise. But the position is serious when enterprise becomes the bubble on a whirlpool of speculation. When the capital development of a country becomes a by-product of the activities of a casino, the job is likely to be ill-done. The measure of success attained by Wall Street, regarded as an institution of which the proper social purpose is to direct new investment into the most profitable channels in terms of future yield, cannot be claimed as one of the outstanding triumphs of laissez-faire capitalism.

—John Maynard Keynes

Sir Isaac Newton is justly famous for his wide-ranging scientific and mathematical achievements. His tenure at Britain's Royal Mint is less well-known.

Newton's friends and admirers were troubled that the most accomplished scientist of the day was living on a meager academic stipend. One of his supporters, the newly appointed Chancellor of the Exchequer, came up with the inspired idea of appointing Newton to be the Warden of the Mint, a cushy sinecure.

Newton had consulted to the Mint on England's economic woes. Prior to 1661, England's coins were hand produced, making it easy to clip a little of the silver off the edge of a coin and circulate the now lighter coin without attracting attention.

To combat this pilferage, the Mint began producing milled coins, which would make it easier to see tampering. But the clipping of the older coins continued, and by 1695, they were down to 50% of their prescribed weight. The public started to be reluctant to use them as rumors spread that the older coins would be demonetized and thus worth only their much lower value as metal. People bought gold on such a large scale that it reduced the London-Antwerp exchange rate 16% over several months. The government decided to take in all the hammered coins and replace them with milled money.[1]

Newton arrived at a crucial stage, when the Treasury was about to cease accepting older coins for tax payments. But delivery of new coins was well behind schedule, their production in disarray. The shortage of circulating money led to riots, and contemporaries worried that the strife might worsen.[2]

The Mint got more than it bargained for. Newton was an alchemist, and thus an expert in metallurgy. He brought in new equipment, reorganized the fabrication process, and in a mere four months, increased output over sixfold, achieving a European record. He kept meticulous accounts, giving a full report of how millions of pounds of silver moved through the Mint.[3]

Newton pursued counterfeiters with the same vigor. His alchemical research was again an aid, helping him detect fakes. Now Master of the Mint, Newton took to enforcing the rarely invoked punishment for counterfeiting, that of death by hanging and quartering. The physicist conducted his own investigations in London's underworld, ultimately sending an estimated two dozen to the gallows.

·   ·   ·   ·   ·

Coin clipping and counterfeiting are clearly against the law now as in Newton's day. The government still retains control of the creation of currency and historically had significant influence over the creation of loans, through its regulation of capital and reserve requirements for financial institutions.

However, the officialdom does not have the same tight grasp of certain new mechanisms for creating credit. Yet their rapid growth, and then sharp contraction, were driving factors in the crisis. They involved operations and structures that were often not recorded on the balance sheets of banks. As a result, they were not subject to capital requirements and were thus supervised minimally, if at all. These new approaches have sometimes been called "the shadow banking system."

But what do we mean by "shadow banking system"? Let's review the traditional activities of banks. They hold funds in the form of deposits and lend a significant portion of them out.[4] Banks are government-chartered franchises. They submit to the regulatory constraints; in return they receive deposit guarantees (which make it cheaper for them to raise money) and state control over market entry. Preserving bank profitability was (and still is) considered to be desirable, since that led to sounder, better capitalized banks, which in turn produced greater stability.

Regulators supervise banks, which means supervisors inspect banks periodically, require them to make reports, and limit what they do. These enable the authorities to understand not simply the health of individual banks, but also to see activity across the entire banking system.

Bank regulation also allows the authorities to influence the amount of loans that banks provide. For instance, capital adequacy rules limit how much banks can lend against their equity. Modern regulators, following rules stipulated by the Bank for International Settlements (BIS), require banks to hold more capital against loans and credit instruments that are riskier. Thus, banks can make far more in the way of low-risk loans than high-risk ones against the same capital base.

Over the last thirty years, the combination of deregulation, increased competition from securities firms and other nonbanks, and financial innovation put banking earnings under attack. The banks found their best customers of various types cherry-picked by new entrants, and competition between banks became ever more aggressive.

So to preserve profits, they adopted new business models. They decided to take on more risk and use less equity in order to compete, as best they could, with new entrants.[5] That meant moving into banking areas that were largely unregulated—what we have described as the shadow banking system. Initially, this development seemed to be benign. Indeed, banks and other financial companies engaged in these activities for decades with only occasional mishap. But differences in degree can become differences in kind. Financial services firms kept pushing the envelope, using more and more "innovative," which in this case meant more risky, approaches. And some of the most aggressive activities were the ones that showed the most rapid growth.

These changes, accompanied by new types of trading strategies that took hold early in the new millennium, led to vastly more risk taking in these areas, and also greatly increased the demand for the most speculative securitized products.

In traditional banking, the main check on how much credit was extended had been governed by rules, such as reserve and minimum equity requirements.

Now the only bar to extending credit was the ability of members of the system to discipline each other. In the period when these credit products evolved, business cycles were mild. Market participants became more comfortable with the new approaches, and complacency about the dangers grew. Seizing profits took precedence over prudence.

As we will see, this banking under another guise is just as subject to runs and panics as traditional banking. And, again like the old-fashioned sort, shadow banking is what economists call pro-cyclical. That means it expands in good times and contracts in bad, increasing the severity of business cycles and with it, the likelihood of busts following booms.

This largely unregulated financial sector involved three interrelated types of "innovations" that affected credit:

- Securitization (and other off-balance-sheet vehicles)
- Repurchase and reverse repurchase agreements (otherwise known as repos)
- Largely unregulated insurance contracts on debt securities (credit default swaps or CDS)

We will show how in particular, complex debt instruments and credit default swaps fuelled trading strategies that in turn produced an unprecedented level of loans that were underpriced relative to their risk. This was the "wall of liquidity" syndrome at the heart of the global credit mania. These strategies took hold on a large scale starting in 2004 and grew rapidly in 2005 and 2006. They involved tranched products, particularly collateralized debt obligations, that had subprime mortgages as a major building block. The use of credit default swaps enabled bankers to create so-called synthetics which allowed speculators to gamble in much larger volumes than the underlying market of real economy borrowers had permitted. That in turn meant subprime risk was not "contained" but was much larger than the authorities believed. And the firms most heavily exposed, namely European banks, investment banks, and insurers, were under-capitalized and in no position to take the losses that resulted from being on the wrong side of these bets.

•   •   •   •   •

Securitization takes place when an originator, a bank or another type of lender (like an auto company that also provides car loans or leases), sells its loans ("assets," since they generate income) to a special purpose vehicle (SPV). An SPV can be specific to one originator, or can hold assets from many sources. Virtually every type of asset-backed loan, meaning one where the lender can seize a particular piece of property if the borrower defaults, from mortgages to recreational vehicles, motorcycles, and intellectual property, has been securitized. Some types of unsecured consumer loans, such as student loans and credit card receivables, are also grist for this process.

Banks adopted this approach because securitization was less expensive than the traditional process of making loans and retaining them. When banks hold loans, the interest rate needs to be high enough to recoup the cost of equity and FDIC insurance, as well as an allowance for losses.[6] Selling loans to a securitized vehicle can also lead to better accounting treatment.

The cash flows, which are the payments of interest and the eventual repayment of the loan balance, are frequently "structured" to create securities that appeal to different types of investors from a single original pool. They range from AAA instruments with low interest rates through various credit grades to the "equity" layer that can earn high income but is most exposed to losses. Consider a simple example, a pool of 100 mortgages, each with an initial balance of $1. From that, we will create three bonds, A, B, and C, which are "backed" by these 100 mortgages, meaning the mortgages are the only form of security for the bonds. Bond A has a balance of $80, bond B $15, and bond C $5. The rules of the SPV state that as homeowners whose mortgages are in the pool make payments, those payments are used first to pay the balance of bond A, then bond B, then bond C. Even if 20% of the mortgages never pay back a penny, the bond A investors will be made whole (unfortunately we can't say the same for the bond B and C investors, as they receive none of their principal back).

This structuring approach, called "tranching," was adopted by banks because offering products tailored to particular investors' risk appetites enlarged the market for securitized products. It also allowed banks to sell their loans to the SPVs for better prices, in much the same way that butchers sell pigs in parts (for instance, loin, chops, ribs, ham, bacon, knuckles), rather than whole, because they realize more income that way.

Originally, securitization was limited to pools of assets that had explicit or implicit U.S. government guarantees and were perceived as safe, such as mortgages insured by Ginnie Mae, Fannie Mae, and Freddie Mac, that were thus AAA rated. But the market grew considerably as financial firms figured out how to create instruments that were higher credit quality than the underlying loans, through a combination of techniques, such as buying insurance to improve the credit quality and "overcollateralization," which was tantamount to setting a reserve for losses up front, as banks do for loans they keep on their balance sheets. For instance, a pool with a face value of $1,000 might be turned into securities that sold for a total of only $975.

Securitization grew rapidly from the mid-1990s onward. For instance, the total amount of asset-backed securities minus mortgage paper sold in the United States in 1996 was $168 billion, which rose to $1.25 trillion in 2006, the last year before the storm broke.[7] According to Citigroup, banks around the world sold $2 trillion in non-agency (meaning non–Ginnie, Fannie, Freddie) asset-backed securities that year. By contrast, global lending to corporations was roughly $1.5 trillion.[8] Banks also simply sold whole (unsecuritized) loans. In 2006, for every $1.00 of lending, $0.25 was sold.[9]

Some economists were puzzled by both securitizations and the vending of loans, since they knew of no precedents.[10] Moreover, information was lost through this process. Sales and securitization of loans meant banks had no reason to monitor borrowers once they had offloaded loans made to them.[11] A still less recognized problem was the fact that in practice, not all of the tranches of a securitization were equally attractive to the investing public. Deals hinged on the need to find buyers for the less popular tranches. The efforts to deal with this problem were, as we shall see, both highly creative and, in the end, destructive.

A variant on the securitization theme was bank conduits. Banks weren't entirely happy to simply package up loans and sell them. Routine asset sales provided too much profit to the underwriter and not enough to the bank sponsor. So they began looking for new structures to increase their returns.

So conduits were born, quasi-banks, in that they capitalized themselves with short-term liabilities and held long-term, higher-yielding assets. Conduits held specific assets, such as credit card receivables. These conduits were not recorded on banks' balance sheets, even though they had implicit support from the bank sponsor if the assets in the conduit proved to be worth less than the bank claimed when the conduit was created. They were funded primarily with a short-term IOU called asset-backed commercial paper. Asset-backed commercial paper (ABCP) refers to a loan with a specific maturity of up to 270 days, usually 90 to 180 days, that is collateralized by asset-backed securities (that is, if the loan isn't repaid, the creditor can seize the instruments given as collateral).

This structure was a classic "borrow short, lend long" approach. Just like banks themselves, the conduit usually earns more income than its cost of borrowing, but simultaneously runs a funding risk. The conduit needs to replace its maturing ABCP with a new placement, but it may have trouble finding replacement lenders ("rollover risk"). And if the short-term funding markets have become hostile, it is likely that the credit markets overall are stressed.

Assume the value of the assets in the special purpose vehicle collapses or is merely in doubt. The conduit has a funding crisis: commercial paper investors like money market funds will be loath to buy its ABCP, yet the entity still has to pay off the ABCP coming due. Many but not all of them had backup credit lines, so they could borrow from a bank (typically the very same one that sponsored the entity) in case they had a problem paying off the maturing ABCP funding with a new ABCP placement. The tacit assumption was that the parent bank would merely be providing short-term support from the credit lines, that at some not-too-distant point down the road, any conduit that had needed to borrow from the bank sponsor would be able to use ABCP to fund itself again.

The banks' theory as to why they need not record the conduits on their balance sheets was that the conduits were independent entities.[12] Yet contrary to this claim, banks would in fact support some of these supposedly stand-alone vehicles. For instance, one study found that from 1991 to 2001, sponsors intervened in 17 instances on behalf of 89 credit card securitizations.[13] Moreover, as losses on credit card portfolios are reaching unprecedented levels, Citigroup, J.P. Morgan Chase, Bank of America, and American Express have all come to the rescue of off-balance-sheet entities.[14] The banks and their accountants maintained the fiction of an arms' length relationship despite ample evidence to the contrary. Indeed, absent bank support, the conduits could not have been created.

Within the universe of conduits, the dodgiest were SIVs, or structured investment vehicles. They were riskier on just about every axis: lower credit quality of their assets, higher levels of borrowing, and no formal support from their sponsor. But as we will discuss later, when they ran into trouble, investors demanded that their sponsors intervene, so again, the "off-balance-sheet" designation was misleading.

· · · · ·

Repos are another type of collateralized lending that played an important role in the credit crisis.

Repo is short for "sale with agreement to repurchase." In a repo, a party that owns a high-quality bond borrows against it in a pawn shop-like procedure, by selling it to another party with an agreement to buy it back it at a specified future date, including interest. Repos are typically overnight, and funds can thus be readily redeemed if the repo lender decides not to renew the repo.

Repos are thus another way to lend against an asset. The high-quality bond that is sold plays the role of the collateral guaranteeing the loan. The interest paid corresponds to the cost of funding the loan.

Securities firms and banks hold a lot of assets. They also have to settle a tremendous amount of money going in and out on a daily basis. Repos give them an easy way to raise cash or deploy funds on short notice.

A repo can also produce an effect similar to banking, by providing an alternative to making a deposit. Say you are a very big broker-dealer (BBD) and you have some extra cash on hand. BBD is loath to park $100 million for a few days at his friendly bank because the amount is so large that the funds would not be insured. But BBD can "deposit" it with another dealer and get top-quality, highly saleable securities, plus interest. This arrangement serves the same function as a deposit and is more secure.

Borrowers and securities for repo are not treated equally. A lender may require a "haircut" or margin, say lending only $95 against $100 of current market value. That is, he may not lend the full market value of the instrument sold to secure the loan, based on his view of the risk of the borrower and of the odds of unfavorable price changes in the instrument repoed. A small haircut implies that the repo borrower will have correspondingly greater leverage.

Repos have been around for a very long time. But even in the mid-1980s, the repo market consisted solely of Treasury securities, which are safe and highly liquid. Repos only began to become dangerous when, in response to increased demand for paper that could be repoed, more and more dodgy paper became widely accepted as collateral for repos.

Some have argued that the parabolic increase in demand for repos was due in large measure to borrowing by hedge funds.[15] Indeed, Alan Greenspan reportedly used repos as a proxy for the leverage used by hedge funds.[16] Others believe that the greater need for repos resulted from the growth in derivatives. But since hedge funds are also significant derivatives counterparties, the two uses are related.

Brokers and traders often need to post collateral for derivatives as a way of assuring performance on derivatives contracts. Hedge funds must typically put up an amount equal to the current market value of the contract, while large dealers generally have to post collateral only above a threshold level. Contracts may also call for extra collateral to be provided if specified events occur, like a downgrade to their own ratings.[17] (Recall that it was ratings downgrades that led AIG to have to post collateral, which was the proximate cause of its bailout.) Cash is the most important form of collateral.[18] Repos can be used to raise cash. Many counterparties also allow securities eligible for repo to serve as collateral.

Due to the strength of this demand, as early as 2001, there was evidence of a shortage of collateral. The Bank for International Settlements warned that the scarcity was likely to result in "appreciable substitution into collateral having relatively higher issuer and liquidity risk."[19]

That is code for "dealers will probably start accepting lower-quality collateral for repos." And they did, with that collateral including complex securitized products that banks were obligingly creating.

Figure 9.1

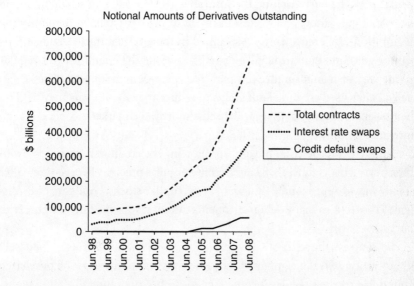

Notional Amounts of Derivatives Outstanding

Source: Bank of International Settlements

As time went on, repos grew much faster than the economy overall. While there are no official figures on the size of the market, repos by primary dealers, the banks and securities firms that can bid for Treasury securities at auctions, rose from roughly $1.8 trillion in 1996 to $7 trillion in 2008. Experts estimate that adding in repos by other financial firms would increase the total to $10 trillion, although that somewhat exaggerates the amount of credit extended through this mechanism, since repos and reverse repos may be double counted.[20] The assets of the traditional regulated deposit-taking U.S. banks are also roughly $10 trillion, and there is also double counting in that total (financial firms lend to each other).

In other words, *this largely unregulated credit market was becoming nearly as important a funding source as traditional banking.*[21] By 2004, it had become the largest market in the world, surpassing the bond, equity, and foreign exchange markets.[22]

· · · · ·

The third major component of the shadow banking system, credit default swaps (CDS), also grew rapidly early in the new millennium and now enjoys a well-deserved notoriety, thanks to the role of CDS in the collapse of American International Group (AIG), the world's largest insurance company.

CDS are economically equivalent to credit insurance and are largely un-regulated.[23] The party writing the insurance (the "protection seller," acting in the role of guarantor) will make a payment to the party buying the policy if a corporation ("reference entity") specified in the CDS contract defaults on its debt or goes into bankruptcy. The party providing the guarantee gets regular payments, just as an insurance company receives premiums on its policies. Originally, banks used credit default swaps to reduce the risk of loans they held on their balances sheets, but as we will discuss shortly, the market morphed into an unregulated casino.

Thus CDS "protection buyers" are shorting the credit risk, poised to profit if the borrower defaults. CDS have become popular precisely because they offer a ready way to approximate shorting a bond (unlike stocks, bonds are often difficult to borrow, so many debt instruments cannot readily be shorted in the cash market).

By contrast, the seller of CDS protection *does* want the borrower to do well. A "protection seller" has many of the same risks and payoffs as if he purchased a bond. He receives regular income (the insurance premiums) just as a bondholder does (the interest payments) and he suffers a loss if the bond defaults. The biggest difference is that the bond buyer buys a security, while a CDS protection seller merely has to post some collateral against the possibility he has to pay out on the contract. Thus CDS allowed investors to take levered bets on bond risks, since the collateral posting requirement is generally much less than the cost of buying the security.

As a result, the bond and credit default swaps markets have become linked via arbitrage. Indeed, the credit default swaps market, which is more liquid than the bond market, often dictates the pricing of new bond issues.

Another important difference between CDS and the credit exposures they "reference" is that, perversely, credit default swap creation is not constrained by activity in the real economy. A company sells bonds if it has a need for funding. By contrast, credit defaults swaps creation is limited only by the need to find two parties to a transaction. Derivatives expert Satyajit Das has noted, "On actively traded names CDS volumes are substantially greater than outstanding debt."[24] For instance, when the demand for collateralized debt obligations began to outstrip supply, credit default swaps were used to create "synthetic" CDOs. This process allowed for risks to be taken on a scale that would be difficult, if not impossible, with traditional instruments

But this "free market" was a quality-free market. Several institutions, most prominently AIG and monoline bond insurers such as MBIA and Ambac, ended up selling CDS protection at a rate that far outstripped their abilities to make good on their guarantees if stress conditions developed. These insurers were massively undercapitalized. As a result, if one of these insurers faced more claims than it could possibly pay out, then scores of institutions that had relied on it for insurance against credit default risks would suddenly *also* find themselves to be undercapitalized. A shock to the system could, and did, set off a death spiral that pulled down other institutions as the failures cascaded.

A second aspect of credit default swaps is that if you own a CDS protection contract, then you are paid off if the underlying bond *defaults*. Suppose that you hold a fire insurance policy on a house you don't own. You'd be delighted if the house were torched by an arsonist; in fact, you might lob a firebomb yourself. Indeed, that sort of behavior cropped up when insurance was first launched in England. As a result, in 1774, England implemented the "British Life Assurance Act" to limit issuance of insurance policies. Only parties who have a legitimate reason to protect against loss (we now call this an "insurable interest") can obtain insurance policies.[25] This concept is now a fundamental tenet of regulated insurance, but was notably absent in the credit default swaps arena.

· · · · ·

All three of these innovations turbo-charged an explosive growth of credit arbitrage strategies by investment banks and hedge funds, which produced the "wall of liquidity" that fueled profligate lending. Greenspan's super-low interest rates post-2001 provided the impetus for these new approaches. Together, these innovations and strategies led to an acceleration in the growth of debt that was not fully recognized by regulators, and to the extent that it was, they saw it as the result of market forces and therefore salutary. And yet, these new activities nevertheless were backstopped by the authorities when hit by a classic bank panic. Understanding the role of credit trading strategies is therefore essential to interpreting what came to pass.

Consider this classic Wall Street joke. On a slow day, some market-makers decide to start trading a can of sardines. Trader A starts the bidding at $1, B quickly bids $2, and several transactions later, E is the proud owner of the tin for $5.

E opens his new purchase and discovers the sardines have gone bad. He goes back to A and says, "You were selling rotten sardines!"

A smiles broadly and says, "Son, those aren't eating sardines. They are trading sardines."

Let's say a large-scale market in trading sardines developed, where the price was $5. But the price of sardines in the real world of eating sardines is only $1. What would happen?

You'd see makers of sardines care only about making trading sardines. They'd ramp up production to satisfy demand at the new miraculously profitable price.

According to orthodox theory, the influx of supply would lead prices to drop from the $5 level.

But in the world of trading sardines, the price is $5 not due to normal supply/demand considerations, but due to dynamics within that market. As long as cheap funding persists, there is virtually unlimited demand for trading sardines at $5. In fact, remember how asset prices and loans interact. If banks are willing to fund a lot of the purchase price of trading sardines at $5, prices could even rise further, since new investors might want to get in on the action. What happens in that scenario?

Anything that can plausibly be called a sardine will go into the can. The can of rotten sardines in the classic story is thus no accident. It is precisely the outcome you expect when manias or other mechanisms that produce sustained price distortions take hold.

Notice how this story is wildly at odds with the prevailing economic theory. First, prices are supposed to be a function of supply and demand. The idea that market participants would want to game prices or would be insensitive to increased supply or falling quality is a direct contradiction to fundamental assumptions such as rationality and perfect knowledge. Recall how Krugman and the vast majority of economists simply refused to look further into burgeoning oil prices and consider mechanisms that might not fit a tidy, simple picture.

That conventional view misses the "trading sardines" versus "eating sardines" dynamic. There is no economic theory of how the financial system interacts with the real economy, save the use of interest rate assumptions as inputs into economic models. The idea that a product could have a very different value in the financial realm (for reasons internal to those markets) than in the real economy is completely ignored. Prices of financial assets are seen as the result of informed decisions. Markets are efficient. Prices are assumed to send valid signals, save some short-term noise. And *there is no place in mainstream theory for prices in financial markets driving and distorting activity in the real economy.* Strangely, this dynamic is well-known empirically. For instance, influxes of speculative "hot money" have repeatedly fueled asset price booms in emerging economies that implode when the speculators exit. But these phenomena sit uncomfortably outside pristine equilibrium theories.

We see a second result vexing to orthodox theory: market outcomes producing socially damaging results. First, if trading sardines go to $5, anyone who really wanted to eat sardines faces much greater costs and much poorer quality. Second, undue resources are devoted to sardine production.

And misallocation of resources is precisely what happened in the credit-glutted United States. Most commentators have focused on the dynamics in the real economy, of seemingly unending rises in housing prices, typical bubble signs of overheated buying, and bad practices, particularly predatory lending. Yet that view misses the impact of the trading-fuelled demand for high yield loans for all sorts, which was particularly acute for risky U.S. mortgages but extended to other credit instruments, such as takeover lending. Cheap funding similarly played a major role in the breakneck pace of mergers and acquisitions, which became more and more frenzied until the onset of the credit contraction, in the summer of 2007. Global mergers for the first six months of 2007 were $2.8 trillion, a remarkable 50% higher than the record level for the same period in 2006.[26] And takeovers for the full year 2006 ran at a stunning seven times the level seen four years prior.[27]

The bubble was in the debt markets, particularly for high-spread, high-risk loans that could be dressed up to look safer than they were. Its effects extended far and wide into the real economy. Credit was the driver, the related asset bubbles mere symptoms.

We will focus on collateralized debt obligations and credit default swaps because they were arguably the most destructive of these new credit products.[28]

We refer here specifically to so-called ABS CDOs, meaning CDOs composed primarily of asset backed securities. These CDOs were based on cash flows from loans (rather than purely from credit default swaps); they have produced catastrophic losses and had clear links to increased lending.[29] When the financial press has discussed CDOs in recent years, it almost always refers to this type unless stated otherwise.

.　.　.　.　.

A key driver of the rapid growth of the CDO market was that demand for AAA securities exceeded supply.[30]

Insurers, pension funds, and banks all had reasons, due to regulatory treatment of their holdings, to buy AAA instruments. They were also popular with foreign investors, particularly foreign central banks, who had to hold ever-growing amounts of dollar assets to fund America's unrelenting trade deficit.

But ever since the Modigliani-Miller theory posited that the value of a company did not depend on its credit ratings, fewer and fewer companies bothered to make the extra effort needed to maintain an AAA. The only native AAA credits were a handful of U.S. and foreign companies and a few sovereign credits.

The elevated level of demand for AAA instruments meant richer prices and skimpier yields than some investors were willing to accept, even when they had institutional imperatives to hold high quality investments. Should they buy AAA paper, and receive lower income due to the keen demand, or buy lower-rated securities that offered more yield, even though they would really rather take less risk (and for investors subject to capital requirements, put up more equity)?

Starting in 2001, conditions fell into place that made premium-yield AAA instruments as well as riskier options seem very attractive, even to those who should have known better. Remember, in finance, if something seems to be too good to be true, it is. The idea that an instrument could pay more interest than other AAA bonds and still legitimately be as safe was questionable from the outset. But a lot of investors had good reason to delude themselves.

When Greenspan dropped the Federal funds rate 1.25%, then 1.0%, the result was a negative real yield, meaning lenders could not charge enough, at least on short-term, safe loans, to compensate for the loss of the purchasing power due to inflation. They had to take more risk, either by lending longer term, or by seeking out riskier borrowers who would pay more interest, just to keep up with the erosion in the value of their money.

Put the dilemma in such simple terms and it was pretty obvious creditors and investors were in a no-win situation. They could go hunting for more income, but only if they were willing to accept higher odds of loss.

A new, large source of AAA instruments that offered a higher yield than, say, Treasuries, would therefore be a prized new choice.

Securitization was one way to create AAA securities out of raw material that was not AAA, such as subprime loans. Assembling together a large number of subprime loans and then subdividing the result into tranches made it seem at least plausible that many of the higher tranches would never be exposed to default risk and so deserved the AAA designation.

But the exposure to subprime was a considerable and underappreciated danger, one grossly underestimated by rating agencies, and hence by most investors. They assumed default rates would not be very high, based on the short history of subprime debt, which did not include a recession.[31] In addition, they were too optimistic about the housing market and believed housing prices would continue to rise. For instance, Robert Rodriguez of First Pacific Advisors recounted a 2007 conference call with the rating agency Fitch about subprime mortgages:

> They were highly confident regarding their models and their ratings. My associate asked several questions. "What are the key drivers of your rating model?" They responded, FICO scores [consumer credit ratings] and home price appreciation (HPA). . . . My associate then asked, "What if HPA was flat for an extended period of time?" They responded that their model would start to break down. He then asked, "What if HPA were to decline 1% to 2% for an extended period of time?" They responded that their models would break down completely.[32]

As we know now, the fall in prices was far worse than 2% for several years running.

. . . . .

In the 2001–2003 period, subprime mortgage bonds seemed like a solution to the yield-hungry investors' problem: the cash flows from the underlying loans could be sliced and diced to produce instruments that fetched an AAA yet offered more interest than Treasuries. The very best of the AAA subprime bonds, the first three of four AAA-rated tranches, were sold to pension funds, insurance companies, and other investors who were keen for relatively high-yield AAA securities.

On the other hand, the very bottom (equity) tranche of a subprime bond could also find buyers. The securitization was structured so that the equity layer would not only pay a high yield, but it would get paid off very quickly, due to the fact that it had a cushion of extra interest available for the equity holder. The short duration and relatively small size of these bonds made them very attractive to a certain class of hedge fund investors. Since they paid off so quickly, these investors could load up on new ones as the ones they already owned paid down. As a result, the equity pieces of subprime bonds also became easy to sell.[33]

But there was little appetite for the AA through BBB layers of a subprime mortgage bond, which accounted for nearly 20% of the total value. There was a cohort of sophisticated investors that were interested. But the small size of this group limited the amount of subprime that could be securitized, and consequently made these investors fairly powerful. Although the theory was, as we have seen, that structured securities would be popular because each tranche would end up finding its niche, the fact that in practice some tranches were harder to sell would have significant repercussions.

CDOs were originally devised as a way to dress up these junior layers and make them palatable to a wider range of investors, just as unwanted piggie bits get ground up with a little bit of the better cuts and a lot of spices and turned into sausage.

Figure 9.2 on page 248 is a simplified version of a typical ABS CDO structure.[34] Going from left to right in the figure, subprime loans first went into a pool. The principal and interest payments were then allotted to various classes of securities, the "subprime mortgage bonds" rated AAA through the "BB/NR" with NR being "not rated" or "equity" layer.

The key difference between these CDOs and other types of structured credit is that they were resecuritizations, made largely out of the unwanted pieces of

Figure 9.2

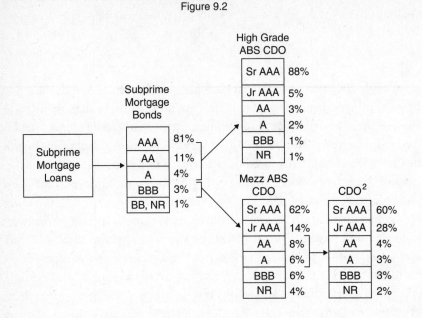

subprime bonds. The CDOs that took the better of the unpopular pieces, the junior AAA, AA, and A layers, were called "high-grade" CDOs. We will focus on the other type, so-called "mezz" ABS CDOs, or simply "mezz" CDOs, which used the BBB or "mezzanine" layer from subprime bond issues. We'll use the mezz CDOs since the synthetic versions mimicked them, although the same general principles apply to the high-grade variant.

Here again, the magic of structured credit alchemy took pools of loans, and turned them into instruments (tranches) that got different credit ratings. As in other structured securities, the bulk of the value of the resulting CDO, meaning the total cash paid to purchase each of the various tranches, was far and away in the AAA-rated tranches, which typically accounted for 75% to 80% of the total proceeds (versus around 90% for the high-grade variant).

The very worst tranche, the ones to take losses first, was the equity tranche, so-called because it was not rated. It usually accounted for 4% to 7% of the value of the deal. Next up were the mezzanine tranches, rated somewhere in the BBBs, the lowest investment grade, and usually 10% of the deal's value.

Finally, until the later stages of the credit mania, the BBB tranches of these CDOs were *again* securities that virtually no one wanted. Often, these unpopular pieces went into later CDOs (the rating agencies tolerated a surprisingly high percentage of pieces from other CDOs in CDOs, up to 30% in a so-called high-grade CDO and 10% in a mezz CDO). In other cases these pieces were attractive to rather exotic investors. But the fact that there was always a problem placing some pieces of the otherwise sought-after CDOs meant that CDOs, in some respects, resembled a Ponzi scheme.

To recap: in these second generation pools, the riskier cash flows from the original subprime bonds were again allocated to various tranches, many of which were then rated AAA. In other words, these CDOs *took the worst risk exposures from weak mortgages and used financial technology to create new instruments of which anywhere from 75% to 90% was designated AAA.*

By contrast, the similar sounding collateralized loan obligation (CLO) simply took a large pool of takeover loans and tranched the payments on them. There was no second round, no resecuritization. Thus even though CLOs started with a riskier type of loan, the end result was in most cases less fraught than CDOs.

ABS CDOs were the financial equivalent of turning pigs' ears into silk purses, and in the end, they worked about as well. How could anyone at the time have convinced himself that these junior exposures to low credit quality instruments could produce AAA-rated paper? The problem is that procedures that made some sense on first generation securitizations were dangerously misleading here.

It's easy to blame rising real estate prices and ratings agencies, but the real roots lie again in flawed economic models.

Recall the discussion of correlation risk from chapter 3. The theory, developed by Harry Markowitz and William Sharpe, was that investors could create an optimal portfolio that suited their appetite for risk. But to do that, they needed to find investments whose prices moved differently, and they needed to have precise information about how these prices would move in relationship to each other ("covary") *in the future.* In other words, this was a clever idea that would seem to have little practical application, except that a whole industry of faux science was constructed on this flawed foundation.

The way this approach was applied to structuring collateralized debt obligations was particularly dubious. The ratings agencies, the monoline insurers, and many investors looked at the risk of default using correlation models. But correlation is a concept in financial economics used to estimate overall portfolio risk based on price movements of the instruments in that portfolio in relationship to each other. If the price of one holding increases 5% in a day, another could change in a whole range of ways: up even more, up but not as much, no change, or down a lot or a little.

But if one loan defaults, the next will either default or not default. Only simple binary outcomes are possible. Thus using Markowitz/Sharpe-type models to analyze defaults was fundamentally wrongheaded.

Now it is possible that even an inappropriate correlation model could have been brute forced to this task, just as the handle of a screwdriver can be an effective hammer. But the users of these tools made a second error: their correlation models showed that the diversification of resecuritization, of going from a single subprime bond to a new vehicle composed largely of risky bits of subprime bonds, reduced risk in a meaningful way. But that was bogus.

The typical pool backing a subprime mortgage-backed bond would have had typically 4,000 to 5,000 mortgages. So the pool in theory was already diversified, although it could have some concentrated exposures, for instance, by geography (were the loans only in few states?). But the flaw was in thinking that there was much diversity in these pools to begin with. By contrast, when this same approach was applied to corporate loans, there was bona fide lowering of overall default exposure, since, say, a chemical company faced different business challenges and had different management than a telecom.[35]

But with so many mortgages in a single mortgage bond, it would resemble what in stock investing would be called an index with a tilt, for instance, an equity market proxy with an overweighting of a particular sector considered desirable, such as technology or high dividend stocks. So the resecuritization would not reduce the underlying risk save by eliminating any skewing and moving the exposure closer to a subprime index. The only other risk reduction would be due to the fact that a portion of a CDO would need to consist of lower-risk assets, which could be better quality mortgages (although some, like Alt-As, in fact proved to be no improvement) or completely different types of loans, like equipment leases.

Thus the risk reduction of going from a subprime bond tranche to a CDO based on subprime bond tranches was in fact very minor. The market reaction to the original subprime deal should have been a tipoff. Remember, pretty much no one wanted those BBB to AA bits. That means possible buyers thought the default risk was high, and they weren't getting paid enough to take it.

So those very same pieces were put into these subprime CDOs. And remember, the "mezz" variety of this type of CDO took the BBB pieces. *That slice gets wiped out if losses on the underlying pool of loans reaches 8% to 12%.*[36] The models optimistically treated that outcome as impossible across a whole bunch of subprime bond deals. Yet a Moody's report as of September 2009 shows "pipeline" losses of 22% and expected losses of 25.3% across all the 2005 to 2008 subprime mortgage pools underlying the bonds they track.[37]

Thus, unless the CDO manager did a spectacular job of selecting bonds, the investors in ABS CDOs took massive, often total, losses. For instance, a Bloomberg run shows 1,590 ABSCDO tranches that originally had an "investment grade" rating from Standard & Poors, meaning BBB or higher.[38] As of this writing, only 29 are still investment grade. And remember, 75% to 90% of the original value of these deals was in AAA-rated tranches.

. . . . .

During the late nineties, investors naively came to believe that double digit stock market returns were normal. While many portfolio managers had assumed unrealistic future returns, those with long time horizons, like life insurance companies and pension funds, were in a particularly acute bind, since many had fallen below their targets. As a result, they were under considerable pressure to boost returns. And because their funds simultaneously were expected to invest primarily in safe assets, the return needed on the rest was particularly high. In the low interest rate environment of 2001 and after, the problems became even worse.

As it happened, investors managed to convince themselves there was a way to convert the lead of an unfavorable environment into gold: hedge funds. The equity bear market of 2000–2002 and a dearth of obvious investment ideas suddenly bestowed hedge funds with the aura not merely of respectability, but also of sophistication. They were no longer speculative, unregulated cowboys, too racy for clean-living fiduciaries. Hedge funds were the place to be. The success of pioneering institutional investors such as Yale's endowment enticed others to follow. Fund consultants, gatekeepers to many pension funds and endowments, started treating them as a separate asset class. In their alchemical system, the magic designation "asset class" means that the investors who pay the consultants' fees must put some money in every asset class, otherwise, horrors, they might miss being on the efficient investment frontier.[39]

Hedge funds, now bearing the *Good Housekeeping* seal of approval from the fund consultants, saw a large influx of new money. Estimates of hedge fund industry size vary, since its members are not required to report to anyone other than their investors and many are secretive. But experts agree the funds showed enviable growth in the wake of the dot-com bust. For instance, Morningstar, which includes mainly large hedge funds in its database, shows a compound annual growth rate of nearly 20% in assets managed from 2002 to 2007.[40]

Why such robust growth? Investors expect to see at least low double digit returns on a net basis to justify the fat fees and confirm the supposed superior skill of the hedgie. To deliver that minus the fund's fees (typically 2% annually, plus 20% of the profits) and recoup transaction costs, and sometimes an additional layer of fees from a fund of funds manager, hedge funds need to make a gross return of over 20%.

To meet that level, a fund manager would need to be unusually skilled and/or take a great deal of risk, often in the form of leverage. Or like Bernie Madoff, he could simply lie about his results.

Hedge funds are expected to adhere to a particular style, such as "event driven" (speculating on the outcome of takeovers), "market neutral" (meaning they offset long and short positions so as not to be exposed to the direction of equity markets), or "global macro" (making bets in favor of or against international markets, such as German bonds of Brazilian equities; George Soros's raid on the pound was a global macro play).

Strategies that focused on debt instruments became the hot new area. It sounded fresh and sophisticated, always a siren song to investors. The newly fashionable style of structured credit strategies accounted (by some estimations) for roughly 28% of the total funds deployed in this period—over $400 billion after allowing for the use of borrowings.[41] And these hedge funds were far from the only paricipants. Investment banks and European banks were significant, probably larger in aggregate, and some hedge funds with broad mandates, such as global macro, were also active players.

Most engaged in a *levered spread play in illiquid assets.* That is a fancy way of saying:

- The hedge funds and investment banks bought assets that produced income, in this case, tranches of various structured credit transactions.
- They hedged some of the risks of those investments, and still had income left over.
- They borrowed a ton to improve returns or invested in instruments that behaved as if the hedge fund had borrowed a great deal (small changes in the performance of the underlying assets would produce very large swings in the value of the chosen instrument).
- Because the instruments used for these strategies didn't trade much, their prices were not volatile, which made them look less risky to investors than they were.

The traders were therefore making extremely leveraged bets using credit-based assets. As we will see, this was tantamount to the riskiest sort of banking.

In fact, the net effect of the resecuritization using these bottom layers was *leverage on leverage.* It has the effect of adding another layer of borrowing to an investment that was already geared. Let us say you are an investor in a fund, and for every dollar you invest, the fund borrows four. That means your one dollar of investment backs five dollars of assets. But if you borrowed half of the money you put in, the effective leverage is even higher thanks to the fact that the supposed equity was not real equity, but itself was partly borrowed. In reality, only one dollar of risk capital supports ten dollars of investment. The use of these bottom tranches, the ones that were equity-like even if they were not called "equity," to create new deals that had their own equity and near-equity slice, produced a similar result, but with much greater ultimate leverage.

· · · · ·

The willingness in capital markets to hold large volumes of AAA-rated structured credit instruments, no matter how complex, was not the sole reason for the so-called "infinite bid" for this product in the later stages of the lending boom.

In June 2005, the International Swaps and Derivatives Association (ISDA), an industry association for over-the-counter derivatives dealers, created the protocol that allowed credit default swaps to be written on asset-backed instruments, such as the subprime mortgage bond tranches that went into CDOs. In 2006, a company called Markit launched a credit default swaps index that referenced a basket of twenty subprime mortgage issues, with different prices for each tranche. That provided another way to hedge, since dealers and investors could buy and sell protection on particular tranches of the index.

Credit default swaps on asset backed securities suddenly created a whole new range of possibilities. Yes, CDOs had often used insurance even before the ISDA change, but it was provided by insurers with AAA ratings, like AIG and the so-called monolines such as MBIA and Ambac. They stuck to providing credit enhancement for the top tranches, often to provide a guarantee that reduced capital requirements for large financial firms, as we discussed in chapter 7.

Now new players could also provide protection, enlarging the universe of possible suppliers of credit and lowering the price of borrowing. Moreover, it was now possible to buy guarantees on the risky tranches. The new credit default swaps on lower-rated securities opened up exciting possibilities for hedge funds and the proprietary trading desks of investment banks, hedge fund-like units that speculated with the house's money. Now they could go short mortgage bond tranches, meaning they would profit if their prices fell. They could also use CDS to construct trades that mimicked being short the rated tranches of an ABS CDO, such as the super senior or the BBB layer.

Meanwhile, the appetite for CDOs was insatiable in 2005 and 2006. In those years, demand was so overheated that *Financial Times* editor Gillian Tett noted,

The big, dirty secret of the securitization world was that there was such a fre-
netic appetite for more and more subprime loans to package into CDOs that
the supply of mortgage loans had started lagging behind demand.[42]

Using the new market in CDS on lower tranches, packagers (usually major
capital markets firms) found a way to cope with the dearth of supply of raw material of CDOs. They created and sold so-called synthetic collateralized debt obligations in impressive volumes.

Synthetic CDOs used the premiums from guarantees on (technically, "referencing") subprime mortgage bonds to provide cash flow to investors. Since a
lot of players wanted to hedge the risk of holding these bonds, there was no constraint on creating these deals. Synthetic asset-backed CDO issuance was in close
to a one-to-one ratio with cash CDOs, with CDOs backed by loans at $490 bil-
lion and those consisting solely of credit default swaps at $450 billion. Those
levels were both double the 2005 volumes.[43] Many of the CDOs issued were also
hybrids, containing both ordinary cash bonds (subprime bonds) and synthetic
bonds (from guarantees on subprime bonds).

But why were investors so keen, one might even say desperate, to buy such
complicated, opaque assets? We come back to our trading sardines. Market participants convinced themselves that that had largely eliminated default risk and
could focus on mere pricing differentials between different types of instruments.
It didn't matter what was in that $5 can, if you had a cheap hedge against the risk
that it was rotten.

And some hedge funds played a very direct role in teeing up new deals, and
as a result, greatly increased demand for loans. Put simply, in the later stages,
hedge funds and investment banks were not only big buyers, but also big creators
of trading sardines. And trading sardines is exactly what they were. Indeed, some
of the strategies made no sense unless the tins' contents were certain to be bad.

· · · · ·

In the early years of the explosive growth of collateralized debt obligations which
were manufactured heavily from residential mortgages, the end buyers of the
AAA tranches of CDOs were typically pension funds and insurance companies,
hungry for AAA paper that offered higher-than-normal yields. Even with strong
demand for the AAA tranches, the growth of the product had historically been
constrained by the need to find someone to take the nasty lower layers. While the
"mezz" or BBB slice was often finessed by rolling it into a new deal, investors in
the top tranches did want to see that someone was on the hook for the losses.
The CDO manager, who identified and vetted the instruments that went into the

deal, was expected to take at least some of the equity tranche; hedge funds were the usual suspects for the balance.[44]

But in late 2005, those patterns all started to change. Demand from historical cash (i.e., "real money") AAA buyers started to soften. CDOs looked to become victims of their own success. As the product became more popular, high demand led to higher prices, which meant lower yield, when higher income than other AAA instruments had been their raison d'être. And as the structures became riskier and riskier, some traditional buyers started to cool on the product.

But in its place, even stronger demand rose as the trading sardines market took over. The major investment banks and European banks showed an uncharacteristic willingness to eat their own cooking, at least as far as the AAA tranches were concerned, thanks to bogus accounting that *allowed traders to be paid bonuses on profits not yet earned.*

The "negative basis trade" that we saw in chapter 7 was the grist for this strategy. The simplest version of the negative basis trade occurred when the packager of a deal (meaning the investment bank that would in the normal course of events merely underwrite the deal) kept some of one of the AAA tranches of a collateralized debt obligation and hedged it with a credit default swap.[45] The treatment, for internal reporting and bonus purposes, was the equivalent to accelerating the future earnings from the bond, less the cost of the AAA insurance and funding costs.

We know how this movie ended. Many of those AAA-rated CDO tranches are now toxic waste, and the AAA guarantors of this paper, like AIG and the so-called monoline insurers, MBIA and Ambac, are no longer rated AAA. The whole procedure was a sham. As the Bank for International Settlements blandly noted, "Substantial losses were subsequently incurred."[46]

· · · · ·

But it gets better. So far the story is that there was insatiable demand for manufactured high yield AAA instruments because a bunch of people got high on their ability to game their firms' bonus systems. This behavior was increasingly aided and abetted by hedge funds and proprietary trading desks at investment banks that pursued credit-based strategies that, due to less frequent price fluctuations, looked less risky than they really were. This sort of reckless abandon is a sure sign the end of a cycle is nigh.

All of this additional trading had the rather nasty side effect of creating considerable demand for the worst subprime paper, the higher yielding, meaning the dreckier, the better.

Hedge funds and banks following similar strategies would engage in what they called "credit arbitrage" or a "correlation trade." The name "correlation trade" comes from the fact that the traders were looking for misvaluations of the correlation risk implicit in the pricing of the various tranches. Whatever the merits of this rather arcane idea, the strategy often wound up looking like a simple interest rate spread play.

As you went up the tranches of a CDO, the yield dropped. The equity tranche would pay a higher coupon, at least until defaults started to hit, than the next higher tranche, BBB, and so on. And the cost of buying protection was even lower than the coupon on any tranche. That meant for any layer in the CDO parfait, you could buy it ("go long"), and use the income to buy CDS protection against a higher-rated slice ("go short").[47] That way, you would be betting that the higher-rated tranche would fall in price while still showing a profit on a current basis—known in the industry as a "long-short trade."

For instance, an investment bank could buy the BBB tranche, and buy CDS protection in order to go short against the next higher slice in the same deal, the single A layer.

Let's see how this strategy plays out under different scenarios. Suppose the economy hums along, housing prices keep rising and subprime borrowers keep paying or refinancing their loans. As long as enough pay so that the BBB slice of the CDO is undamaged, then you receive the full coupon on it, while paying a bit less for your CDS on the next higher layer. So you make money.

Suppose, on the other hand, that the housing market crashes and all of the underlying mezzanine subprime bonds become worthless. Then you lose your coupon on the BBB, but your CDS protection against the A tranche pays off. You again make money.

The way you lose money with this strategy is if *only* the equity and BBB tranches become damaged but the A and all higher tranches remain intact. Since as we have discussed, *all* of the tranches in a mezz CDO referenced some of the worst risk exposures from subprime mortgages, it seemed entirely reasonable that the BBB and A tranches in the resulting CDO would be *very* unlikely to behave differently from each other.

This credit arbitrage strategy[48] was therefore a good one for traders who thought that subprime was going to end badly, but didn't know when, and so didn't want to go broke shorting subprime in the meantime. The strategy also produced increased appetite for the lower layers of CDOs, which naturally made it considerably easier to create new CDOs.

Let's consider what that means:

- This type of investing created demand for subprime and other dodgy mortgages, like option ARMs (adjustable-rate mortgages). They were now prized not because investors wanted to own them but simply because their high yields made them great vehicles for trading strategies or bonus boosting.
- The demand for these risky mortgages was so great that not enough could be created, hence the extensive use of synthetics. But all that demand for the income from credit default swaps (which was equivalent to providing insurance on the risk of default) lowered what it cost to buy this protection. That via arbitrage lowered the interest required of subprime borrowers even more. The derivatives and the related trading strategies were making the product even cheaper. The tail was wagging the dog.

Like other transactions involving illiquid assets, these transactions were "marked to model." The CDO tranches involved in these strategies were not subject to the noise of daily market price moves. As mentioned earlier, that made them more attractive to the fund of funds and fund consultant gatekeepers. Remember, lower variability of the monthly prices makes a fund look better to investors, since modern finance defines volatility as a type of risk. Illiquidity, which should have been seen as a risk, was instead viewed favorably.[49]

. . . . .

Let's consider an even more exciting variant. The really smart guys were the ones who realized how deranged this all was, and *used the bottom tranches to fund a short subprime bet.* They weren't simply trying to match exposures in a crude fashion, but were using the high payout of the lower tranches as a cheap way to finance and considerably lower the cost of a wager against the subprime market.

Recall that the ability to issue CDOs depended on being able to place the slices that took the first losses: the pesky mezz and equity tranches, often referred to as nuclear waste. Since there was so much demand for the AAA tranches that they were overpriced, it should follow that the lower tranches, particularly the equity piece, were cheap and therefore attractive. But even so, the equity tranche was exotic and normally only a limited number of buyers was receptive.

Since the equity tranche was the scarce part of the CDO equation, anyone who funded it became the sponsor of a deal.[50] An investment bank might round up a CDO manager, which was often just a guy or two with a Bloomberg terminal, to handle the assemblage of assets for the CDO and assist in marketing it.[51] The investment bank would provide the warehouse funding until the CDO was launched (for free, a sign of how lucrative they thought the business was) and would structure and sell it. The hedgie at a minimum had veto rights over the assets put in the CDO and could even say what bonds and loans it wanted in the deal. We set forth how this process worked, plus the ultimate consequences to the participants, in appendix II.

One hedge fund, Magnetar, went into the business of creating subprime CDOs on an unheard-of scale. The fund is named for a neutron star with a powerful magnetic field that emits gamma rays and other forms of toxic radiation. Magnetar named the deals they sponsored after constellations (for instance, Orion, Cetus, Sagittarius).[52]

What exactly did Magnetar do? They created a ton of product through their Constellation program, although you would have to know the industry to get the joke. Magnetar's name appears nowhere on the offering documents, nor do they have an official legal relationship to the deals.

Magnetar supplied the funds for the equity tranche of each deal they sponsored. They also went short many of the rated tranches in the same deals.[53]

Understand how this arrangement works. Magnetar owns the equity layer, which throws out a lot of cash for perhaps a year or two and then starts to decay quickly. They bet against the better slices, short *the very same deals they created,* via the credit default swaps that were the dominant constituent of these CDOs.[54] The difference between this strategy and the ones described above is that the correlation trade-type investors were roughly matching their exposures. Magnetar used the rich cash distribution of the equity layer to fund a much bigger short bet against BBB rated subprime bond tranches than their long equity position.

Remember, the equity layer suffers defaults first, and only when it is exhausted do the mezz and higher layers start seeing cash flow shortfalls. That means Magnetar's strategy makes no sense if the equity layer performs well: in that case Magnetar and other funds that went this route would have bought a lot of insurance (via credit default swaps) for no good reason, and only earned a meager positive spread or even have shown modest losses.[55] It looks even worse if the equity layer defaults while the mezz and better rated tranches continue to pay out. *It only works if the deal is so bad that the equity, plus the higher layers, are all toast.*

Magnetar would not make its target returns on the equity tranche alone. *The deals had to fail for them to succeed.* It was common for funds like Magnetar to let a trading desk know what parameters it wanted, and the traders would in turn line up suitable investments with the CDO manager. Magnetar influenced the transaction by mandating a certain equity return, which meant the

CDO would have to hold the "spreadiest" (i.e., riskiest) crap. As the *Wall Street Journal* put it, "Magnetar swooped in on securities that it believed could become troubled but were paying big returns."[56] And Magnetar appears to have succeeded in achieving the highest profit result, namely, teeing up deals that went bust. As an employee of a firm that packaged some of Magnetar's deals explains:

> At their peak, Magnetar was *THE* driver of RMBS [residential mortgage backed security] CDO issuance. The size of their "Constellation" program was the most amazing thing I've seen in my entire career. . . .
>
> Magnetar's idea was that CDOs were destined for long term failure—that the leverage on leverage based on cr*p assets made the BBB tranches long-term zeros. And, they realized that while most other hedge funds were content shorting the BBB tranches from subprime RMBS, shorting BBB tranches from RMBS CDOs was a much more slam dunk of a trade. The commentary is right . . . without someone willing to fund the equity of a CDO there was no way to get one done. So, Magnetar made the logical leap . . . they'd fund the equity necessary to create the structures and then short a multiple of the bonds their equity money had allowed to be created.
>
> The gravy was that the equity was typically good for one or two VERY HEFTY cashflow distributions—i.e., these structures went terrifically bad, but it usually took a little while from a timing perspective for that to happen. So, their carry cost of the shorts was offset by the one or two equity payments. After that, their upfront costs were covered and they would own the 100 point options for free.
>
> Magnetar made A TON of money . . . I'd expect every bit as much as Paulson [a hedge fund manager who earned $15 billion shorting subprime mortgages in 2007].[57]

If credit defaults swaps were regulated, this would be insurance fraud on a massive scale. But since the industry has fought tooth and nail to keep CDS free of any pesky restrictions, what Magnetar did was completely legal. Magnetar was in fact doing what it was supposed to do, namely looking out only for its investors.

Anyone involved in these transactions probably understood the implicit logic, even if no one acknowledged it. But there is a remarkable absence of anyone who could be pinned with liability. Magnetar officially had no legal relationship to these deals. The investment bank packager/structurer was off the hook as long as he made reasonable disclosure (and remember, the standards are much lower here than for instruments that fall in the SEC's purview). The rating agencies get off scot-free, thanks to their First Amendment exemption (discussed in chapter 6).[58] The lawyers involved in the deal are responsible only to their clients, meaning the structurer/packager, and cannot be sued by unhappy investors. The only party on whom liability could be pinned is the CDO manager, who does have a fiduciary responsibility to all investors, not just the sponsor. But the fact that the party who in theory had the most to lose, Magnetar, approved their investments, would seem to exculpate the CDO manager.

Now let us look at what the Constellation program meant for the subprime market as a whole. The *Wall Street Journal* reported its total program at $30 billion, but industry participants contend the amount was higher.[59] A member of one of the firms that packaged Magnetar's deals remarks:

> You cannot over-estimate all the places Magnetar touched. That Lehman was involved doesn't surprise me. If you told me of a major broker/dealer who had an active CDO underwriting group that *DIDN'T* work with Magnetar . . . that would surprise me. At their peak, they were the 8000 pound gorilla. Spreads on BBB/BBB-subprime RMBS [residential mortgage backed securities] would breathe out past where their arb made sense and they'd line up eight more deals. Rinse and repeat. The credits didn't matter nor really did the managers they contracted. To them it was pure structured arb. When the math of spread vs. structure vs. offer for BBB CDO protection lined up, they would reload the trade.[60]

Industry sources believe that *Magnetar drove the demand for at least 35%, perhaps as much as 60%, of the subprime bonds issued in 2006.* And Magnetar had imitators, including the proprietary trading desks at the major dealers; thus, its strategy is arguably the most important influence on subprime bond issuance in 2006–2007.

But how does the math work? Remember, these deals are resecuritizations. And notice how the dynamic has flipped. Before, CDOs had been created as a way to make the lower-rated bits of structured credits more palatable to investors. But that logic was increasingly turned on its head. Suddenly, CDOs were popular, and the mezz variety was in particularly hot demand. And Magnetar was creating mezz CDOs.

But the BBB layer is a very small constituent of the original subprime bond deal, only 3%. Let's make some simple (and actually, conservative) assumptions.

What most commentators have missed, but the industry understood full well, was the massive leverage involved. Even though Magnetar provided only the equity layer, a mere 5%, perhaps even less, doing so made the "higher" 95% of the CDO possible. We will use $30 billion for the size of their program. It extended from mid-2006 to mid-2007, but the bulk of the subprime mortgages referenced in the deals were probably 2006 vintage. This seems particularly likely given that in 2007, investment banks that were long subprime inventory were desperately unloading it into CDOs, and many of those bonds were 2006 issues.[61]

So to make the calculation simple, we'll assume 20% was comparatively benign stuff and exclude it from this computation. That is consistent with Lazard

Asset Management's finding that by the second half of 2006, over 80% of the assets of mezzanine CDOs were subprime, up from a mere 60% in the first half of 2005.[62] We are assuming that 80% of the remaining assets in the CDO was synthetic, which means only 20% of the subprime component was actual BBB tranches of subprime bonds.

Further assume that 80% of the subprime component of these CDOs was 2006 vintage BBB subprime tranches. You get:

($30 billion × 80% × 80% × 20%) / 3% = $128 billion

Although this is just a back of the envelope calculation, $128 billion is 28% of the total of $448 billion in subprime mortgage backed securities issued in 2006.[63] This calculation assumes that 20% of the BBB subprime tranches were from 2007, so you have an additional $32 billion of subprime demand generated that was excluded from the estimate of 2006 subprime mortgage demand.

We have ignored the fact that, of the 20% of supposed semi-decent non-subprime stuff circulating in the second half of 2006, as much as half, or 10% of the total, could be and often was lower rated tranches of mezz CDOs. Including that would intensify the impact of Magnetar's deals. When you allow for the concentrated effect of BBB CDOs in the remaining 20% non-subprime, plus the fact that the program size was probably higher than the $30 billion reported in the *Wall Street Journal,* it is entirely plausible that Magnetar deals account for 35% of 2006 subprime issuance, or more.

How can that possibly be? It was leverage, spectacular leverage. If you look at the non-synthetic component, *every dollar in mezz ABS CDO equity that funded cash bonds created $533 dollars of subprime demand.*[64]

Is it any wonder than anyone in the United States who had a pulse could get a mortgage?

And we've only discussed the cash bond component. Remember, 80% of the deals are assumed to be synthetics, meaning they consisted of credit default swaps against ("referencing") particular subprime bonds. The total synthetic component in this example was $30 billion × 80% × 80%, or $19.2 billion notional amount of credit default swaps on BBB tranches.

That may not sound as sexy until you work through the implications. This $19.2 billion is in addition to existing subprime bond exposures. The resulting losses never would have occurred without the use of credit default swaps. On top of that, anything that happened with those BBB tranches was hugely geared. The synthetic component created demand for subprime loans by a less direct mechanism, by compressing credit spreads. That is a fancy way of saying they lowered interest rates.

Credit default swap spreads and cash bond spreads are linked via arbitrage. If credit default swap spreads tighten, that is tantamount to having the price of the credit default insurance drop. The protection writers (guarantors) receive less, and the protection buyers pay less. When that happens, spreads on the related bonds drop, which lowers the cost of borrowing.

Now, price is supposed to be a function of supply and demand. We have two parties, a protection buyer and a protection seller. At first blush, it is not obvious why having a lot of new credit default swaps on subprime, thanks to the synthetics in Magnetar's deals, would compress spreads and hence lower subprime borrowing costs.

The trick? The use of the CDO brought new protection sellers to the table.

Historically, the CDS protection writers on CDOs were AIG and the monolines, who provided guarantees only on AAA tranches. The CDS protection buyers were hedgers or shorts. Even though the new ISDA protocol had opened up shorting on the lower-rated subprime and other mortgage bond tranches, that market was not very deep.

Many players were interested in being short the lower rated subprime bond tranches, but they were not willing to pay very much. They saw it as a dangerous wager to pay a lot to be short subprime debt. Even if these speculators felt they were certain to be right in the long term, the cost of funding the bet could erode the profits considerably if it took a while for the market to crumble. But if there was a way to coax—or more accurately, hoodwink—more guarantors into the market at favorable prices, that would not only increase market depth at current pricing but could even squeeze spreads even tighter.

When a CDO consists largely or entirely of synthetic assets, the investors in the CDO are effectively protection sellers, or guarantors. So if the investors bought synthetic, or largely synthetic, CDOs instead of CDOs that contained bonds, that was tantamount to additional supply on the protection seller side. And we had new entrants, all of whom convinced themselves that they were not at risk in acting as guarantors. The correlation traders who speculated with the lower-rated tranches matched their exposures. The AAA investors, increasingly investment banks and European banks, were either hedging their positions with insurance companies, primarily the so-called monolines, or convincing themselves that the inventory piling up on their balance sheet was just a temporary problem and would soon be sold. Their participation tightened credit default swap spreads, and then, by arbitrage, subprime bond spreads as well, finally lowering rates for subprime borrowers.

Thus the much celebrated subprime shorts were one of the primary causes of the financial crisis. Their use of credit default swaps greatly inflated the level of subprime exposures, and the eventual losses, well above what they would have been otherwise. And the parties on the other side of this trade were in large measure the capital markets players, such as investment banks and European banks, who held AAA CDO inventory, and insurers of various sorts. These institutions were all highly levered and therefore fragile. All suffered or will suffer terminal losses; the survivors owe their existence to massive taxpayer bailouts, central bank subsidies, and regulatory forbearance.

·   ·   ·   ·   ·

Now it is impossible to know the exact impact of increased CDO creation due to subprime shorts, but there is every reason to think it was considerable. Incremental demand in an overheated market will have a disproportionate impact, and the housing market was already looking frothy in 2005, as commemorated by a June 2005 article in *The Economist*.[65] Mortgage industry graybeard Lew Ranieri, who effectively created the mortgage-backed securities industry at Salomon Brothers in the 1980s, dates the toxic phase of subprimes to roughly the third quarter of 2005 through early 2007, and points to a sudden shift in demand and attitude toward the riskiest assets.[66] That coincides almost exactly with when ISDA made credit default swaps on asset-backed securities and exposures like CDO tranches possible, in June 2005, after allowing for the lag required for the new hunger to result in more mortgage creation.

And while we have focused on CDOs and subprime, the salient characteristic of the runup to the credit crisis was the spectacular underpricing of risk. Very risky bonds and loans showed abnormally low interest rates. The ABS CDOs weren't the only place heavily synthetic structures were in use.

Commentators who have looked at the role of structured credit have concluded, contrary to popular perception, that it was the credit mania that drove asset bubbles in housing, commercial real estate, and corporate takeovers. As former Goldman Sachs managing director Nomi Prins wrote:

> Wall Street pushed lenders. Lenders pushed borrowers. That's how it worked. Don't let anyone tell you otherwise. If you can borrow at 1 percent and lend it out at 6 or 8 or 13 percent, you can make money. Even the squirrels in my backyard can make money at that play.[67]

·   ·   ·   ·   ·

In early 2007, the ABX started flashing warnings. These subprime indexes started falling, along with other instruments and companies exposed to subprime. But the rest of the credit market remained unimpaired, at least for the moment.

That changed in August 2007, the first acute phase of the credit crisis. Spreads in the interbank markets, the bulwark of banking liquidity, jumped (rising spreads mean higher risk perception; lenders demand more interest). Asset-backed instruments having nothing to do with subprime, like commercial paper (short-term debt, typically 90 to 180 days) backed by credit card receivables, saw buyers evaporate.

Remember our discussion of bank conduits earlier in this chapter. The riskiest type, the structured investment vehicles or SIVs, often contained subprime debt, along with other sorts of loans. Suddenly no one wanted to have anything to do with vehicles tainted with subprime exposures. But these conduits were mini-banks, dependent on short-term funding, so investor distaste meant they could no longer replace maturing IOUs (in this case, commercial paper) with new borrowings.

If these off-balance-sheet vehicles had lived up to their name, the unraveling might have played out differently. One would have expected these entities to have liquidated or negotiated with investors on a case-by-case basis.[68] But investors in SIV paper demanded that their bank sponsors stand behind them. And that put a big question mark over Citigroup, which had been very active in SIVs. Suddenly, no one was certain where the daisy chain of exposures led. The subprime crisis had morphed into a classic bank panic.

The next run occurred in the new nonbank credit market, repos. If SIVs liquidated (and some did), then a lot of asset-backed paper might be dumped on the market, producing fire-sale prices.

Before the crisis, repo haircuts had been near zero. Figure 9.3 shows what happened to the repo haircut on an index composed of nine types of bonds, primarily structured debt:[69]

Another tabulation, in Figure 9.4, shows that the haircuts on AAA tranches of asset-backed CDOs, which in April 2007 had been a mere 2% to 4%, sky-rocketed to 95% by August 2008, before the Lehman crisis. That effectively means no one would lend against this paper.

What happened? Assume you are a bank or a big broker-dealer. Half of your funding comes from repos, or out of a $100 balance sheet, $50. If you are a traditional bank, you might have $10 of equity. But in this modern world of fancy finance, you are likely to have a balance sheet more like that of a broker-dealer, with less equity, say $3 or $4.

If your repo haircut on that $50 rises by 20%, you are suddenly $10 short. Your friendly pawnbroker will now only lend $40 against collateral that recently provided you with $50. To get that missing $10, you either need to increase the

Figure 9.3

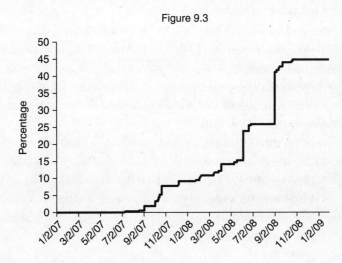

Source: Gary B. Gorton and Andrew Metrick, 2009

Figure 9.4

Typical haircut or initial margin

In percent

	April 2007	August 2008
US Treasuries	0.25	3
Investment grade bonds	0–3	8–12
High-yield bonds	10–15	25–40
Investment grade corporate CDS	1	5
Senior leveraged loans	10–12	15–20
Mezzanine leveraged loans	18–25	35+
ABS CDOS		
AAA	2–4	95[1]
AA	4–7	95[1]
A	8–15	95[1]
BBB	10–20	95[1]
Equity	50	100[1]
AAA CLO	4	10–20
Prime MBS	2–4	10–20
ABS	3–5	50–60

ABS = asset-backed security; CDO = collateralized debt obligation; CDS = credit default swap; CLO = collateralized loan obligation; MBS = mortgage-backed security; RMBS = residential mortgaged-backed security. Theoretical haircuts as CDOs are no longer accepted as collateral.

Source: IMF

right hand side of the balance sheet by selling common stock to raise new funds, or shrink the left side by liquidating assets. Investors, even the rich Middle Eastern sorts, were cool on making investments in financial firms as of late 2007, so the only course of action was asset sales. But the larger haircut suggested the value of assets was already in doubt, and selling them (or others) would push prices down even more. The impaired value of collateral would not only be validated, it would get worse. And you as bank or broker-dealer are now insolvent, which is finance-speak for bankrupt.[70]

When large numbers of repo borrowers suddenly had their access to the repo ATM restricted, and they still needed the dough, their only option was to sell something to make up the shortfall, which in this case could be just about anything. That scramble for cash transmitted stress from the structured credit market, where the increase in repo haircuts was large, to all sorts of unexpected places. One widely observed phenomenon during the month after the Lehman bankruptcy was sudden downdrafts in markets that should not have been affected much by the upheaval, like gold. It was obviously a large sale by someone under stress, presumably a hedge fund.

Remarkably, the authorities only partially understood what was happening. The Fed made a series of cuts to its benchmark borrowing rate, the Federal funds rate, and also to its discount rate (effectively, an emergency lending facility). The Fed thus saw this as a liquidity crisis, believing that the panic was an overreaction and the underlying assets were still good quality. If the Fed made it cheap to borrow, so the logic went, banks could fill that $10 hole until cooler heads prevailed.

But this was not a liquidity crisis, it was a solvency crisis. It wasn't that lenders to banks and various holders of fancy financial paper were now irrationally panicked; they understood that they had been irrational, profligate lenders. They knew this was going to end badly; the open questions were who was most exposed and how badly. And the problem was bigger than the banking system that the Fed and central bankers could readily reach.

Increasingly desperate measures confirmed that this meltdown was no mere liquidity crisis. The Fed and Treasury launched an alphabet soup of facilities that, after the initial Term Auction Facility, were aimed not at banks, but at trying to prop up the impaired nonbank players and particular markets under stress: commercial paper, asset-backed securities of all sorts, even the better grades of the now-toxic dreck that the hedge funds so eagerly bought (as long as a bank, not a hedge fund, was the owner).

Late in the game, in 2009, the Fed made an effort to intervene in the repo market, realizing only then that it was not only a major factor in the crisis but also rife with conflicts of interest.[71] For convenience, lenders and borrowers do not deal with each other directly but go through a clearing bank that among other things values the collateral and advances funds while transactions are being booked.[72] The biggest of the clearing banks are J.P. Morgan and Bank of New York. It is the clearing banks that decide what haircuts to apply, and that means a clearing bank can damage a rival when it is wobbly.

And that may have happened with Lehman. The bank's largest creditors sued its clearing bank, J.P. Morgan, alleging it struck the fatal blow to the ailing investment bank by withholding $17 billion of cash and securities the Friday before it collapsed.[73]

The Fed's plan to address the problem by creating a central utility appears designed to deal with that problem. But it also has a second effect: it makes it much easier for the Fed to backstop the repo market, and that is likely the real goal of this plan.

■ ■ ■ ■ ■

Now let's take this one step further: where did the lending boom come from, exactly? As you may recall from the last chapter, the Fed and Treasury would have us believe that the "savings glut," a.k.a., the Chinese, was the culprit. And the Chinese, along with other central banks in trade surplus countries, did play a role in this drama, through their continued appetite for AAA securities, along with others predisposed toward AAA paper (recall that starting in 2001, foreign central banks became the major actors in buying U.S. Treasury and agency paper).

The average global savings rate over the last 24 years has been 23%. It rose in 2004 to 24.9%. and fell to 23% the following year.[74] It seems a bit of a stretch to call a one-year blip a "global savings glut," but that view has a following. Similarly, if you look at the level of global savings and try deduce from it the level of worldwide securities issuance in 2006, the two are difficult to reconcile, again suggesting that the explanation does not lie in the level of savings per se, but in changes within securities markets.[75]

At the same time, other data do lend support to the notion that the shadow banking system was the main culprit in the meltdown. Bank lending has contracted far less than its murky twin. Although global corporate lending did fall from its peak of $2 trillion in 2007 to $1.5 trillion in 2008, that level was on par with 2006. Between the second and third quarter of 2008, U.S. bank credit increased 1%, and between the third and fourth quarter, banking industry consultants Oliver Wyman estimated that it contracted by 0.5%.[76]

By contrast, while $1.8 trillion of asset-backed bonds were issued in 2006, only $200 billion were floated in 2008, and issuance through mid-2009 was "minimal."[77] Similarly, Credit Suisse pegs the contraction in "shadow money" in private debt securities since 2007 at $3.6 trillion, or 38%, due primarily to the substantial increase in repo haircuts, plus a dearth of new issues and a fall in prices.[78]

*   *   *   *   *

It is easy to be overwhelmed by the vast panorama of financial instruments and strategies that have grown up (and blown up), in recent years. But the complexity of these transactions and securities is all part of a relentless trend: toward greater and greater leverage, and greater opacity.

The dirty secret of the credit crisis is that the relentless pursuit of "innovation" meant there was virtually no equity, no cushion for losses anywhere behind the massive creation of risky debt. Arcane, illiquid securities were rated super-duper AAA and, with their true risks misunderstood and masked, required only minuscule reserves. Their illiquidity and complexity also meant their accounting value could be finessed. The same instruments, their intricacies overlooked, would soon become raw material for more leverage as they became accepted as collateral for further borrowing, whether via commercial paper or repos.

But even then, the bankers still needed real assets, real borrowers. Investment bankers screamed at mortgage lenders to find them more product, and still, it was not enough.

But credit default swaps solved this problem. Once a CDS on low-grade subprime was sufficiently liquid, synthetic borrowers could stand in the place of subprime borrowers, paying when the borrowers paid and winning a reward when real borrowers could pay no longer. The buyers of CDS were synthetic borrowers that made synthetic CDOs possible. With CDS, supply was no longer bound by earthly constraints on the number of subprime borrowers, but could ascend skyward, as long as there were short sellers willing to be synthetic borrowers and insurers who, tempted by fees, would volunteer to be synthetic lenders, standing atop their own edifice of risks, oblivious to its precariousness.

Institution after institution was bled dry. Yet economists and central bankers applauded the wondrous innovations, seeing increased liquidity and more efficient loan intermedation, ignoring the unhealthy condition of the industry.

The firms that had been silently drained of capital and tied together in shadowy counterparty links teetered, fell, and looked certain to perish. There was one last capital reserve to tap, U.S. taxpayers, to revive the financial system and make the innovators whole. Widespread anger turned into sullen resignation as the public realized its opposition to the looting was futile.

The authorities now claim they will find ways to solve the problems of opacity, leverage, and moral hazard.

But opacity, leverage, and moral hazard are not accidental byproducts of otherwise salutary innovations; they are the direct intent of the innovations. No one at the major capital markets firms was celebrated for creating markets to connect borrowers and savers transparently and with low risk. After all, efficient markets produce minimal profits. They were instead rewarded for making sure no one, the regulators, the press, the community at large, could see and understand what they were doing.

Magnetar and its imitators made unbelievable profits by finding a nexus of spectacular leverage, eager demand, and camouflaged risks. Whether you like the results or not, their novel use of an arcane instrument was exceptionally clever. If the world had been spared their cunning, the insanity of 2006–2007 would have been less extreme and the unwinding milder. But the hedge funds were not the only ones who fed this strategy; the other institutions who carried out the same correlation trade strategy and European bank staff padding their pockets with negative basis trades are just as culpable.

Viewing the underlying problem as one of bubbles misses the true dynamic. When borrowed funds pump up asset values, the unwind damages financial intermediaries, and that has far more serious repercussions than the loss of paper wealth alone. Leverage offers a strategic point at which regulators can intervene. Supervisors can tackle debt levels surgically by barring certain types of instruments and practices. But this effort can take place only if authorities do not cede control of the financial system to the inmates. Unfortunately, to a large degree, that has already happened.

CHAPTER 10

PLUS ÇA CHANGE, PLUS C'EST LA MÊME CHOSE

Blaming individuals is no substitute for acknowledging the failure of a system.
—Mervyn King, Governor of the Bank of England

In early February 2009, newly installed Treasury Secretary Timothy Geithner set forth his plan, if you could call it that, for dealing with the financial crisis. The initial release was widely derided for its sketchiness.[1] But even that preliminary version clearly showed that the incoming Obama team was every bit as much of a hostage to the financial services industry as the Bush administration had been. In hindsight, this should have been no surprise, given the large contributions Wall Street made to the Obama campaign,[2] the close connections that Geithner and head of the National Economic Council Larry Summers had to major financial players, and their role in designing policies that played a direct role in the crisis.

One of Geithner's four initiatives was "stress tests" to assess the risks that banks carried on their books. Those deemed to need more capital would receive

funds on an interim basis until they could raise money privately.[3] What was notable about this choice was the refusal to have bank bondholders (who had chosen to provide these firms with risk capital) take losses via restructurings (say,
forced conversions of their debt into equity), which would have made many of
the floundering big players sound. Instead, the most straightforward (albeit
painful and tricky to implement[4]) solution was dismissed in favor of making
the taxpayer the bagholder for financial service industry excesses.

Putting banks into receivership, and reprivatizing them down the road, is
actually a well-established practice, but the FDIC can usually find takers for their
assets and deposits on a short timetable, so these interventions do not raise complex procedural or political issues. Even though history shows this approach is
the fastest path out of a financial crisis, it was clearly off the table as far as large
financial players were concerned.[5] Instead, another of the four measures, the so-
called public private investment partnerships (PPIP), billed as a way to remove
toxic assets from bank balance sheets, was clearly a back-door subsidy.[6]

Another move taken during this period was the relaxation of "fair value"
accounting rules. That gave the banks considerable latitude in valuing supposedly illiquid securities, in effect enabling them to not mark them down.[7] The
big problem here was the bogus "illiquidity" claim, oft repeated in the media as
gospel. It wasn't that the vast majority of the toxic assets weren't trading; investors like hedge fund manager John Paulson said there was "plenty of liquidity," even in "opaque areas."[8] The real impediment was that banks were carrying
these positions at prices well above the bid in the marketplace. Claiming "illiquidity" was a pretext for banks to maintain fictitious valuations and thus avoid
recognizing losses.

The effect of this change was that it represented a form of what is called
regulatory forbearance, which is a fancy way of saying the regulators give waivers
for known problems on the assumption that now is not the time to impose
tough requirements. Holding the banks to their normal capital requirements,
which the now-phony accounting finessed, allowed them to pretend they were
in better shape than they really were, and thus raise less equity.

But this sort of move was the polar opposite of what history had shown to
be the best approach. An IMF study of 124 banking crises concluded:

> Existing empirical research has shown that providing assistance to banks and
> their borrowers can be counterproductive, resulting in increased losses to
> banks, which often abuse forbearance to take unproductive risks at govern-
> ment expense. The typical result of forbearance is a deeper hole in the net
> worth of banks, crippling tax burdens to finance bank bailouts, and even more
> severe credit supply contraction and economic decline than would have oc-
> curred in the absence of forbearance.[9]

As the stress tests moved forward, it quickly became clear that they were an exercise in form over substance. Ben Bernanke had remarked that the fall in bank stock prices was "detached from real US economic fundamentals."[10] No one had a problem with a "detachment" from sanity when lenders were on a risk bender, charging way too little for the possible downside, with the result that asset prices, ranging from houses to commercial property to corporate takeovers (which helped boost equity markets) were inflated as a result. Recall that in the late 1990s Greenspan had gone from worrying about "irrational exuberance" to becoming a stock market tout.

The new theory of irrational despondence had the convenient effect of denying that problems were real and deep-seated and instead shifted the blame away from the authorities onto pesky, foolish investors. Hmm, what happened to the idea that markets ever and always knew best?

In fact, it was obvious that the aim of policy was to restore status quo ante rather than clean up the rotting foundations of the financial system. A Treasury announcement stated that the vast majority of banks had enough capital to be "considered well capitalized, the uncertain economic environment has eroded confidence in the amount and quality of capital held by some."[11] This confirmed that the official view was that the problem was merely one of perception, and that even the supposed problem children were fine. In other words, the results were determined before the stress test exercise was even underway.

It should come as no surprise that the exams were roundly and deservedly derided by anyone who knew much of anything about banks and was not in on the con job. Bill Black, a former senior bank regulator, put it bluntly: "There are no real stress tests going on."[12] The "adverse" scenario that determined how much dough the banks might need if things turned out badly was far from dire enough. Mainstream economists increasingly came to the view that the downside case looked like a middle-of-the-road forecast.[13] The process also made insufficient allowance for the just-starting avalanche in commercial real estate.[14]

Not only was there not enough stress in these "stress tests," they were not much of a test either. The normal practice in a regulatory exam is for the supervisor to sample loan files. The authorities made no review of these documents. In the past, it has taken well over a hundred examiners months to go over a single loan portfolio of a large bank. But here, roughly 200 examiners were allotted to 19 banks, a mere ten examiners on average across a broad range of businesses.[15] Moreover, the authorities punted on evaluating the exposures most likely to cause havoc if the economy weakened further, meaning the trading books of the big capital markets players, Citigroup, Bank of America (the reluctant new owner of Merrill), J.P. Morgan, Morgan Stanley, and Goldman.[16] They were simply asked to run scenarios using their own risk models, the same ones that had performed so dismally and were the very reason they were in this fix!

It is rarely a good sign when comics provide more pithy and insightful commentary than the pundits. The American comedy show *Saturday Night Live* gave the best synopsis. Its Timothy Geithner poseur made a mock address to the nation:

> Earlier this week, I reported to you the results of the so-called stress tests my department ran on the nation's 19 largest banks. This was an effort to determine each bank's fiscal soundness. . . . Tonight, I would like to reveal to you, the American people, the results to part 2 of the stress tests, the written exam taken by all 19 banks' CEOs. . . . Initially, my department had planned to give each bank a numerical grade of one to 100, 100 being a perfect score. But then we decided that might unfairly stigmatize banks who scored low on the test because they followed reckless lending practices or were otherwise not good at banking. So we changed to a simple pass/fail system.
>
> However, on reflection, a few of us felt that system was too rigid, so we changed it once again, to pass/pass*. This seemed less judgmental and more inclusive. Eventually, at the banks' suggestion, we dropped the asterisk and went with a pass/pass system. Tonight, I am proud to say that after the written tests were examined, every one of the 19 banks scored a "pass." Congratulations, banks![17]

The process was a sham, and as the tests proceeded, the news leaks made it painfully obvious.[18] First, the bank negotiated down the amount of additional equity they needed to raise. Citigroup's shortfall was lowered from $35 billion to $5 billion, Bank of America's from over $50 billion to $33.9 billion, and Wells Fargo's from $17.9 to $13.9 billion. The reductions at other banks were lower on an absolute basis but larger in percentage terms.[19] Shortly thereafter, the *Financial Times* reported another major concession. Originally, the capital shortfall was to be met by private fundraising in the next six months, a time frame established at the outset; otherwise the Treasury would satisfy the shortfall (with strings attached). But the banks were told privately they didn't have to comply, it would be fine if they came up with less money.[20]

The dishonesty is stunning. In his initial remarks about the financial rescue operation to the Senate Banking Committee, Geithner stressed the need for an open process:

> It all begins with transparency. We propose to establish a new framework of oversight and governance of all aspects of our Financial Stability Plan. The American people will be able to see where their tax dollars are going and the return on their government's investment. They will be able to see whether the

conditions placed on banks and institutions are being met and enforced. They will be able to see whether boards of directors are being responsible with taxpayer dollars and how they're compensating their executives. And they will be able to see how these actions are impacting the overall flow of lending and the cost of borrowing.[21]

In reality, the official pronouncements about the stress test results and process weren't honest and complete. The real deal, as the waiver on fundraising reveals, was an unwritten understanding between the Treasury and the banks, versus the phony version presented to the public. If the public couldn't even rely upon the headline number in the tests (the amount of money they were supposed to raise), was there any other aspect they could trust? How many other winks and nods were there between the Treasury and banks that weren't leaked to the press?

In fact, obfuscation, distortion, and Orwellian double-speak have been the hallmark of the Obama administration's response to the financial crisis. Bush and his Treasury Secretary Henry Paulson tried to kick the can of the escalating crisis down the road to the incoming team, but conditions decayed too quickly for that to remain a viable strategy. They quickly embarked on a series of ad hoc, frequently inconsistent emergency measures, culminating in the heinous $700 billion Troubled Asset Relief Program (TARP), which gave the Treasury secretary more spending power than the annual budget for the Pentagon and explicitly put him beyond the reach of law.

Team Obama did that one better by putting up a more polished facade and the semblance of more order, while continuing large-scale handouts to the banking industry, with transparency and accountability notably absent. For instance, Geithner promised that taxpayers "will be able to see how these actions are impacting the overall flow of lending and the cost of borrowing." Yet five months later, the special inspector general for the TARP program, Neil Barofsky, reported on a survey his office conducted on how the moneys received under the program were used and called on the Treasury Department to gather more information.[22] Rather than getting a "Yeah, we're working on that," the request to the Treasury instead elicited a "We don't think that's worth doing" response, a direct contradiction of the commitment made to Congress.[23]

Moreover, the Treasury has used the FDIC and Federal Reserve as off-balance-sheet funding vehicles, circumventing the Constitutional requirement for Congressional approval of disbursements, in this case, for further funding for bank backstops. For instance, Congress authorized an increase in the FDIC's borrowing limit from $30 billion to $500 billion to provide enough wherewithal to contend with a large bank failure. However, the Obama administration was deemed likely to deploy the added firepower to an improper, indeed, possibly illegal, use: to support one of the two Public-Private Investment Partnership programs.[24] Similarly, of the $134 billion actually provided to AIG (of $180 billion on offer), $92.5 billion came from the Fed, $43.5 billion in the form of borrowings on a line of credit, and $49 billion via Fed purchases of AIG toxic assets that were then placed in . . . special purpose vehicles! The Fed, a latecomer to the shadow banking party, had proven to be a quick study.

Willem Buiter, a former member of the Bank of England's Monetary Policy Committee and advisor to central banks, took a dim view of these proceedings:

> The financial shenanigans used by the Fed (in cahoots with the US Treasury) to limit accountability for these capital losses [on the Bear and AIG bailouts] are quite unacceptable in a democratic society. Clearly, the US authorities are using the financial engineering tricks and legal constructions whose abuse by the private financial sector led to our current predicament, to engage in Congressional- and tax payer accountability avoidance/evasion. To watch the regulators engage in regulatory arbitrage is astonishing.[25]

The regulators had gone far beyond the well-established tendency of minders to become too sympathetic to the wants and needs of their charges, a reverse Stockholm syndrome called regulatory capture. As mentioned earlier, Buiter deemed the financial industry version *cognitive regulatory capture,* in which the authorities were so deeply indoctrinated that they had come to see the world through the eyes of the large financial players. Buiter had had the nerve to tell that to the members of the Fed at its Jackson Hole conference in August 2008, less than a year before the stress test charade unfolded: "The Fed listens to Wall Street and believes what it hears. . . . This . . . partial and often highly distorted perception of reality is unhealthy and dangerous."[26] Needless to say, his comments were not well received.[27]

But by 2009, the alignment of the interests of the supposed supervisors and their subjects had become even more complete. The continued life support operation for the financial services industry managed to finesse a far more fundamental issue: as of early 2009, *the government support to the banking industry was so extensive that from an economic standpoint, it owned most of the top players.*[28] Remember, the large capital markets firms were effectively bust as of October–November 2008. But for taxpayer munificence, they would all be dead.

The front-door equity infusions via the TARP were only the tip of the iceberg. The total funds committed to various rescue operations exceeded $8.5 trillion by the end of 2008, and the commitments only kept growing.[29] The Treasury and Fed had also done a massive backdoor rescue through AIG, by bizarrely paying out in full on credit default swap contracts being unwound in late 2008 and honoring the commitments of its securities lending operation.[30] AIG was de facto bankrupt; the standard procedure in bankruptcy is to pay creditors only to the extent that the assets in the business permit it.[31] In AIG's case, that would certainly have meant only a partial payment. Handling these agreements as if AIG were healthy was thus another hidden subsidy. The government instead should have reduced the payout to reflect the true current value of the positions. If the powers that be felt it necessary to provide more funds to prevent damage to the financial firms on the other side of these deals, it should have received equity as compensation for any additional amount.

Instead, the no-questions-asked AIG unwinds continued in January and February of 2009. One market-maker on the receiving end said, "We have never done as big or as profitable trades—ever."[32] New money, some of it clearly an overpayment, effectively went from the Fed and Treasury to firms like Goldman ($12.9 billion), Société Générale ($11.9 billion), and Deutsche Bank ($11.8 billion) with no strings attached.[33]

Similarly, in March 2009, the Fed announced it would increase the size of its balance sheet by as much as a bit over trillion dollars through new or increased purchases of mortgage bonds, Agency bonds (meaning Fannie, Freddie, and Ginnie), and long-dated Treasuries. These purchases would raise prices of the bonds, thus lowering interest rates, a boon to the banks and borrowers.[34] In July 2009, the Special Inspector General for the TARP released a report cataloguing the support extended:[35]

Figure 10.1

INCREMENTAL FINANCIAL SYSTEM SUPPORT, BY FEDERAL AGENCY SINCE 2007 ($ TRILLIONS)			
	Current Balance	Maximum Balance as of 6/30/2009	Total Potential Support Related to Crisis
Federal Reserve	$1.4	$3.1	$6.8
FDIC	0.3	0.3	2.3
Treasury — TARP (including Federal Reserve, FDIC components)	0.6	0.6	3.0
Treasury — Non-TARP	0.3	0.3	4.4
Other: FHFA, NCUA, GNMA, FHA, VA	0.3	0.3	7.2
Total	**$3.0**	**$4.7**	**$23.7**

Source: Office of the Special Inspector General of the Troubled Assets Relief Program.

Commentators focused on, then dismissed, the $23.7 trillion total, since the amount actually deployed, via loans, equity infusions, and guarantees, was considerably less (and some have used other approaches to compute the amount on offer and have come up with lower figures. One September 2009 tally, for instance, comes to a $11.6 trillion result[36]).

But that argument misses the true significance of the $23.7 trillion figure. That was the amount that could have been deployed in this crisis. Even if the authority for some of these facilities is expiring, it would take little effort to revive them. A massive safety net has been created for the financial services industry. And the amount currently in use, $3 trillion, is hardly small change. Moreover, of that amount, only $477 billion, or 16% of the funds deployed, went to programs arguably targeting individuals, a stark reminder of whose interests are really being served by these rescues.[37]

Despite the de facto ownership and extensive welfare program, the United States treated the financiers with kid gloves. By contrast, countries like Norway, Finland, and Sweden, whose responses to their early 1990s banking crises are widely touted as models, cut their underwater banks no slack. All three countries sacked the management and boards of failed institutions and installed replacements. They did not micromanage, but instead set strict targets for restructuring the balance sheets, cutting costs, and improving risk controls. They also took steps to improve supervision and regulation.[38] Similarly, General Motors and Chrysler were both required to produce extensive plans describing how they would mend their ways, and the CEO of GM was ousted. By contrast, the financial services industry, which has received vastly greater subsidies, has had virtually no demands made of it.

Instead, we have institutionalized a dangerous arrangement, that of *socialized losses and privatized gains*, a "heads I win, tails you lose" setup, a looter's wet dream. This welfare for the financier class is far more pernicious than the ordinary sort of dole. There all you have at risk is the money you hand out through formal programs. You know what the maximum damage might be. But here, the unrepentant banksters can carry on as before, take outsized risks, and pay themselves richly until they blow themselves up again. There is no mechanism to claw back their inappropriately won gains, probably the best method, save criminal sanctions, to discourage them from going back to their destructive practices (more accurately, destructive to everyone else but them).[39]

We've hit the point where handouts are going to financiers without providing any benefit to the supposed objects of the exercise, namely, bank balance sheets. When the PPIP program to offload toxic loans finally did its first transaction, in September 2009, the results appear to be the worst of all possible worlds: the Obama administration pressing forward with an initiative rife with internal contradictions in order to preserve the illusion that the government was tacking the banking mess. Not only are subsidies even worse than the skeptics had predicted, they are not even going to banks, the supposed object of this exercise.

The PPIP was designed to give investors incentives to buy dud assets from banks, with the clear hope that the prices realized would be well above market levels, hence reducing the losses banks already had on their books but had not realized. But the first transaction was done not with a viable bank, but with one that failed months ago and was in the hands of the FDIC![40] As economics commentator James Kwak explains:

> The only possible justification for these subsidies is that they are necessary to restore health to the banking system, by taking toxic assets off the balance sheets of banks. But these toxic assets are already the property of the U.S. government. This means that the government owns 100% of the upside and 100% of the downside on those assets.
>
> Or at least it did until last week. Then it gave half the upside to an investment fund—"Residential Credit Solutions of Fort Worth, a three-year-old company founded by Dennis Stowe, a veteran of the subprime mortgage industry"—and kept all of the downside to itself. What could they possibly have been thinking?[41]

The financial firms on the government tab continued, indeed even increased their risk taking when the successful Nordic model would dictate cutting it considerably. For instance, Goldman's financial statements show that it increased its wagers while on life support. The firm's Value at Risk (VaR) rose on both a gross and net basis[42] in the first and second quarters of 2009 compared with the same periods in each of the preceding two years. The increase was so large that even given the doubts about VaR, the change almost certainly meant greater risk taking.[43] Net VaR, probably the more important measure, was 33% higher in the second quarter 2009 versus the same period in 2008.[44] In fact, more risk taking is precisely what you'd expect with a de facto government guarantee.

Similarly, Wells Fargo lowered its rate of reserving for loan losses in the first quarter of 2009, when other banks were increasing their reserves. Loan loss reserves are a haircut taken in anticipation of future losses; a bank which is underreserved will show higher earnings now and take bigger lumps later. Another surprise was that Wells and Wachovia separately had charged off bad loans totaling $6.1 billion in the fourth quarter of 2008 (in layperson-speak, a charge-off is when a bank deems a loan to be beyond redemption). By all accounts, the first quarter of 2009 was even worse, yet the next quarter, when Wells owned Wachovia, the merged bank took only $3.3 billion of charge-offs.[45]

An extreme example of banks carrying on recklessly is Citigroup and its Phibro commodities trading unit. Let's start with the obvious: commodities trading is not a financial activity that the government should be backstopping. There are already active commodities exchanges that serve the useful social function of helping producers and manufacturers hedge against price changes. The Phibro unit is not an important or even an ancillary part of the crucial credit infrastructure that the authorities rushed to save. And Citigroup is already heavily dependent on government support, with the Treasury soon to be a 34% owner.[46]

But it gets even better. The Phibro operation, headed by Andrew Hall, is a proprietary trading business, which means it was gambling with your and my money. And Hall had a deal that would make most hedge fund managers green with envy. The typical hedge fund pays its own overhead, has to deal with pesky investors and fund consultants, and, for its trouble, gets a 2% annual fee and 20% of the profits. Hall and his buddies had Citi fronting their infrastructure costs, and they keep "below 30%" of the profits.[47] While the exact amount has not yet come to light, it seems likely that "below 30%" is well north of 20%. But even that does not recap the full extent of the bennies he enjoyed through the bank. For any levered trading operation, the cost of funding (i.e., how much and how cheaply you can borrow) affects profit. Hall's cost of funding through Citi is lower than if he decamped, started a hedge fund, and had to finance himself, an additional subsidy to his venture.

Hall made over $100 million personally in 2008 and was fighting to keep his pay deal in place at Citi for 2009. Although his unit has been a major contributor to profits in good years, he has, not surprisingly, also lost significant amounts.[48]

Citi needs to get out of the "too big to fail" category; Hall's unit is a stand-alone operation. It would be an ideal candidate for disposal. The counterargument, that Citi "needs" it for the earnings to pay back the TARP, makes no sense. The point of the TARP is to preserve the safety of the *critical* elements of the banking system, not shareholder profits. Funding activities like this (and that includes proprietary trading at other banks) is an abuse of the taxpayer. If Citi minus Phibro is not very profitable, it is high time that sorry fact is exposed and addressed. As of this writing, Hall has agreed to modify his contract and Citigroup has said it intends to restructure Phibro. Nevertheless, the hue and cry it took to achieve that (probable) result is telling.[49]

Through-the-looking-glass thinking has become pervasive. Instead of firmly reining in the banks, the Treasury instead was uncomfortable with and inconsistent about exercising authority, reacting to charged but largely superficial issues like pay and the use of private jets. While the symbolism, that the bankers have a deep-seated sense of entitlement, does point to more fundamental issues (very badly aligned incentives), the regulators merely flailed about, floating a few proposals that engendered blood-curdling howls from the industry. The Treasury promptly backed down and life continued more or less as before for the financiers.

In fact, the media have fallen in firmly with financial industry cheerleading, applauding banks "paying back" TARP money and acting as if they now should be treated as free of all constraints, despite the massive subsidies to the industry still in place. That's misleading, since the ease of satisfying the TARP terms was the result of yet another unrecognized subsidy, namely, the gross under-pricing of the TARP funding. As derivatives expert turned venture capitalist Roger Ehrenberg noted,

> Goldman . . . stood with the rest of Wall Street as a firm with longer-dated, less liquid assets funded with extremely short-dated liabilities. . . . [CEO] Lloyd Blankfein smartly paid the full $1.1 billion requested. He looked like a hero for doing so, a true US patriot repaying the US Government in full for its lifeline, thanking the US taxpayer in the process. $1.1 billion . . . $1.1 billion . . . Hmm . . . something doesn't seem right. You know why it doesn't seem right? **BECAUSE THE US TREASURY MIS-PRICED THE FREAKING OPTION.**
>
> There is not a Wall Street derivatives trader on the planet that would have done the US Government deal on an arms-length basis. Nothing remotely close. Goldman's equity could have done a digital, dis-continuous move to-wards zero if it couldn't finance its balance sheet overnight. Remember Bear Stearns? Lehman Brothers? These things happened. Goldman, though clearly a stronger institution, was facing a crisis of confidence that pervaded the mar-ket. Lenders weren't discriminating back in November 2008. . . . So what is the cost of an option to insure a $1 trillion balance sheet and hundreds of billions in off-balance sheet liabilities teetering on the brink? Let's just say that it is a tad north of $1.1 billion in premium.[50] (Emphasis in original.)

Artful misdirection has come from the very top. President Obama, in a speech on financial reform on the anniversary of Lehman's collapse, tried to paint the government salvage operations as a good deal for the public, pointing to the fact that the government had earned 17% on the TARP funds repaid to date.[51] Not only, per Ehrenberg, was that return inadequate given the risks assumed, but more important, it gave the misleading impression that this result was represen-tative of the results that would be achieved for all TARP equity injections. In fact, this was cherry-picking, pure and simple. The strongest banks have paid their money back. Holding them up as an example is no different than an investor touting the performance of stocks he just sold at a profit, while neglecting to mention the declines in other investments he still owns.[52] Third-party efforts to estimate TARP results overall have come up with significant losses.[53]

. . . . .

While some efforts for reform are underway, the odds are high that they will be symbolic and, to the extent they fail to take on more fundamental issues, ineffectual. That outcome is likely due to the failure or, more accurately, unwillingness to look at root causes of the crisis and address them. Efforts have instead been directed at ameliorating symptoms.

For instance, during the acute phases of the credit crisis, central banks pumped money into the interbank markets because that was where the stress was appearing. They only partially perceived that the implosion of the shadow banking system was leading anyone who had access to bank credit to use it to fill the greatly reduced access to other funding options. The authorities did see and take some measures to try to prop up other short-term funding markets, like the asset-backed commercial paper market (via guaranteeing money market funds and, in the United States, later creating a facility to support the issuance of asset-backed commercial paper). But the efforts to address the upstream causes, the securitization process, the repo market, and credit default swaps, have been slow in coming and halfhearted.

To illustrate: in theory, one of the easiest pieces of the equation to address should be the rating agencies. There are only three right now that matter, they are not powerful political players, and their performance has been so abject that it should be relatively easy to bring them to heel. Yet the difficulty in doing so shows that the rating agencies are effective lobbyists; they do so indirectly, through the standards setters, like the SEC and the Bank for International Settlements.

One powerful remedy would be to limit the rating agencies' First Amendment exemption from lawsuits. As incredible as it may seem, rating agencies have successfully contested litigation over their ratings by claiming their grades are mere journalistic opinions, despite the central role given to ratings in many types of regulations, including bank capital adequacy and Federal Reserve collateralized lending facilities. That view is finally being challenged, not as a result of a legislative change, but by a judge's decision to allow a lawsuit to proceed. Her logic? That the ratings, in this case, on notes backed by subprime debt, served a small audience of potential investors, and thus were not "matters of public concern."[54]

Greater liability would force the ratings agencies to charge more for their opinions. That in combination with efforts at the SEC to encourage the formation of new nationally recognized statistical ratings organizations, as the ratings agencies are awkwardly called, would lead to more new entrants. These measures, in combination with prohibitions against going to multiple firms to get the best grade and the separation of the giving of advice on structuring from actual ratings, would go a long way toward remedying the problem.

But the SEC proposals fall far short of that. Yes, they are already encouraging new entrants and have increased oversight of the agencies. They have also proposed implementing restrictions on ratings shopping and more disclosure of methodologies and results.[55] However, there is less here than meets the eye. Read between the lines, and the main remedy is tougher SEC oversight and enforcement. It isn't hard to see that that is unlikely to be forthcoming. As we discussed earlier, the SEC cannot bring criminal charges on its own, and the Department of Justice has seldom gone after complex financial cases. They demand too many resources relative to their headline value. And Congress, which has many members who have big finance as heavy campaign contributors, kept the SEC starved of enforcement staff. Accordingly, the SEC chairman, Mary Schapiro, has floated the idea of having the agency self-fund as other U.S. financial regulators do, since the fees it collects are larger and more certain than Congressional approvals.[56] Even now the SEC is overburdened.[57] After the furor over the crisis dies down, it isn't hard to imagine that the SEC budget will come under pressure again.

Similarly, the proposal to create a consumer protection agency for financial products is both a helpful but nevertheless inadequate measure. Retail investors and users of credit products now are often presented with products that are complex by design, with hidden traps and snares that the provider sincerely hopes the user will fall into. This is predatory behavior and correctly needs to be curbed. The industry has proven remarkably unwilling to restrain itself, and the frequency and magnitude of the abuses has finally elicited pushback.

But consumers are far from the only victims of overly complicated "gotcha" financial products. As we saw in chapter 7, the circle of chumps who buy tricky financial products that they don't understand goes well beyond retail investors. They include municipalities, and often endowments, pensions funds, and insurance companies. But as we pointed out, they don't complain much, since they often have a great deal to lose in revealing their own cluelessness.

The institutional buyers of complex products in many ways are in a worse position than consumers. Disclosure there is actually pretty extensive, but in teeny print and in terminology beyond the understanding of many ordinary citizens. By contrast, with complex derivatives, the description of product features is far less than what securities laws call for. As we saw in chapter 6, the formulas that describe the derivative product are frequently impenetrable to the buyers, which serves the same objective of the barely readable typeface in credit card agreements, namely, making it hard for the user to understand the real deal.

A quick fix would be to regulate derivatives like securities. That still gets into the SEC enforcement issues we discussed above, but it would greatly improve disclosure and give burned users better grounds for private lawsuits. It would also be beneficial to make the sellers of these products responsible for verbal misrepresentations of the risks.

But these illustrations raise a broader issue: why is there such reluctance to undertake needed fundamental reform, given the damage to the global economy wrought by the financiers?

Let's review four theories, some of which we have touched on earlier:

- **Cognitive regulatory capture,** meaning the regulators have adopted the industry world view, which makes them reluctant to act.
- **Extortion,** meaning that the financial services industry controls infrastructure that is essential to capitalism, and cannot be displaced except at very high cost. Think of what happened to the civilization at Ur when the king shut down the overly powerful lenders.
- **State capture,** meaning the financial services industry now has the status of oligarchs in third world countries, having used its economic clout to buy so much political influence that they largely dictate policy regarding its interests.
- **Paradigm breakdown,** meaning key elements of the current system are no longer viable, but that is a possibility that no one is prepared to face, since the old system seemed to work well for a protracted period. Thus the authorities reflexively put duct tape on the machinery rather than hazard a teardown.

All these factors play a role in the hesitance to impose tough reforms, but the most intractable and least recognized is the last, the difficulty of seeing that the failings of the current system are deeply rooted and not amenable to simple remedies. Any resolution of the major problems facing the financial system would take a good deal of time, care, and persistent effort, and would simultaneously be highly politicized. That makes it very likely that the financial services industry will derail or blunt reform efforts. That in turn means the current paradigm will be patched up and restored to service only to fail again. This pattern will replay until the breakdown is beyond repair.

Cognitive regulatory capture. To underscore Willem Buiter's charge, U.S. regulators, particularly the Fed, see the world through Wall Street's eyes. A major exception is the FDIC, which is oriented toward banking examination, a police function, but it lacks the expertise in capital markets businesses to play a useful role in devising policy.

The alignment of perception results from the fact that the financial services industry is the channel for market intelligence. Yes, the Federal Reserve has trading desks of its own at the Federal Reserve Bank of New York. But they operate only in the money and foreign exchange markets, which are deep and liquid, and where information services like Bloomberg terminals give a good window on current conditions. Thus the Fed's information about what is happening in the financial system beyond these areas comes of necessity from the financiers themselves, meaning the institutions the Fed regulates or the industry members that sit on its boards and advisory groups. The Fed is a cloistered organization and does not appear to get much input from other sources.[58] No wonder the Fed and other regulators share the financial establishment's view on many matters; they literally *are* the eyes through which they see some markets.

But the perceptual bias extends to areas where it would not be hard to get other readings. For instance, in May 2007, when worries about subprime mortgages were rising, staff in the Federal Reserve's Banking Supervision and Regulation division appeared unwilling to recognize predatory lending as a contributing factor, and seemed confident that the markets had worked well.[59]

Extortion. In the cognitive regulatory capture scenario, the authorities have drunk Wall Street's Kool-Aid. They genuinely believe that what is best for the financier class is best for the economy, and by extension, society. With extortion, the authorities might actually recognize the industry needs to be curbed, but are daunted by the task. And the fear of doing much leaves the perpetrators effectively in charge.

Over the last few chapters, we have discussed the recent evolution of capital markets, in particular the declining importance of traditional bank lending in comparison to "market based credit," as Timothy Geithner called it. In this model, banks and other originators source loans, which are then packaged into instruments and sold to investors.

The provision of credit is essential to any economy beyond the barter stage, and has become particularly important to advanced economies. As the scope of banking activities has increased, so too have the supports, from the creation of the Federal Reserve System to Great Depression safety nets like deposit guarantees and Federal Home Loan banks. Other countries that had long-standing and effective regulatory regimes have also adopted the backstopping model, albeit as a crisis response. For instance, the Bank of England had broad discretionary powers, and contained bank failures through ad-hoc intervention. That system had worked well. The last bank run prior to Northern Rock in 2007 was Overend Gurney in 1866. But long-standing success led to legislative complacency. Certain rules were not brought up to date when the Bank of England's role was changed as the result of the implementation of the "tripartite system" in 1997, which divided responsibility for the oversight of the financial system among the Bank of England, the Treasury, and the newly created Financial Services Authority. The failure to define roles clearly has come under attack, with the House of Lords issuing a particularly critical report.[60]

For a host of reasons, the capital markets have evolved into a highly concentrated format, with a comparatively small number of firms controlling infrastructure deemed essential to the functioning of commerce. Many factors favor high concentration: network effects, the scale of operations needed to compete effectively (operations in major financial centers, product scope, and related technology investments), and the difficulty for those outside the industry to acquire the needed know-how. That means that even if the powers that be try to make capital markets players smaller and more numerous, the cost and information advantages of being bigger means that the industry will tend to re-evolve back to fewer, larger players.

Thus the tendency for a relatively small number of capital markets firms to become dominant is an inherent feature of the system. Having a policy mix that favored "market based credit" when lending is essential to modern commerce made "too big to fail" firms inevitable.

For instance, the Bank of England, in its April 2007 Financial Stability report, highlighted the increasing systemic importance of what it called large complex financial institutions as a source of vulnerability. And the danger resulted not simply from their size but also from "their pivotal position in most markets."[61]

To put the problem more simply: it is hard to discipline someone who has a knife at your throat.

To be honest, there is not much evidence of recognition of this fundamental conundrum among top U.S. regulators. They are either cautious while trying to wrap their actions in bolder-sounding rhetoric to appease the public, or are pushing hard on narrow issues (for instance, the FDIC's Sheila Bair in her efforts to get management changes at Citigroup and force a restructuring). But lower-level staff members may be more eager to take action yet are intimidated by the complexity of the task.

State capture. Former IMF Chief Economist Simon Johnson has argued forcefully that the United States is effectively in the hands of financial oligarchs, a banana republic in denial. A common emerging economy road to ruin is that a successful cadre of businessmen becomes more and more powerful. Emboldened, they make bigger gambles, recognizing that they can likely fob off any bad outcomes onto the government.[62] And in the end they do just that, borrowing too much money and leaving bankruptcies in their wake.

Johnson argues that America hews to the pattern he has seen up close at the IMF: the elites that drove the economy off the cliff will make or break any reform programs. At least some of them need to be willing to take losses so that an effective restructuring can move forward.

, Johnson points to a major difference between traditional power mongering and the version practiced by Wall Street. Even though the financial services industry is one of the largest political donors, before the crisis it rarely had to exercise power in an overt way. It had gone one step further than Buiter's cognitive regulatory capture. "Free markets" enjoyed a broad and deep following. Many economists and policy makers tacitly accepted that stewards of the machinery purported to allocate capital to its best use deserved to be at the apex of the capitalist system.

The strongest proof of Johnson's thesis comes not in the number of former Goldman employees that occupy positions of influence, but in how the financial crisis and massive, widely resented bailouts have done nothing to curb the clout of the banking and securities industry lobbies. The evidence of their undiminished power comes in their continued successes even after the crisis was advanced, both the struggles that came to light, such as the stress test farce, and the ones won behind the scenes.

A key victory for banks was stymieing legislation to allow judges to modify residential mortgages in bankruptcy cases. This isn't as big a change as one might imagine; judges already have that authority in commercial bankruptcies, and for other types of loans (yachts, for instance) in consumer bankruptcies. Moreover, the authority granted is not open-ended. The key concept is that a secured loan is backstopped by the value of the property. The judge is permitted to lower the principal amount of the loan to the current market value of the security. For residential mortgages, this would have helped cut the Gordian knot of impediments to loan modifications. The bill was defeated in the Senate, with twelve Democrats voting against it.[63] The banking lobby also succeeded in stopping legislation to impose ceilings on credit card interest rates.[64]

But the most telling indicator is how little real reform was embodied in the proposals put forward by the Obama administration in June 2009. Banks deemed too big to fail are merely monitored, not required to downsize or restrain their risk taking. Systemic oversight was to be placed in the hands of the Federal Reserve, the most bank friendly of all the major regulators, rather than a newly created, independent body that might be less forgiving.[65] Rating agencies still are to be paid by the company seeking the rating, an inherent conflict of interest. There are also no measures to increase the liability of financial firm executives and key employees, criminalize activities, beef up enforcement, or require banks to move to longer-term incentive schemes with clawbacks for traders and managers who deliver losses.[66] Measures like the creation of a pay oversight czar for companies who still have TARP funding are certain to do little more than collect a few scalps, if that. Focusing only on current TARP recipients, rather than the much larger network of beneficiaries of taxpayer largesse, and then only on the highest paid employees, is, by design, a sop to the public rather than a genuine effort to force change.

Team Obama put forward another round of more aggressive reform ideas prior to the G20 meetings at the end of September 2009, as this book was going to press. EU leaders have been particularly critical of the banking industry (easy for them, one might say, now that London and New York are dominant financial centers). Was this a serious change of posture, or as a cynic might note, merely an effort to get in front of a mob and call it a parade?

Measures that were announced early due to their obvious political appeal, meaning high appeasement value relative to real cost and inconvenience to the banksters, like the creation of a new consumer protection agency, are further along in the legislative process and have already been watered down substantially. A key proposal, to require banks to offer plain vanilla products, such as simple mortgages and low fee, low interest credit cards, was excised. This provision would have enshrined a notion remarkably absent from most reform talk: that banks enjoy substantial state support precisely because they serve a crucial role in modern economies. They are utilities and should be treated as such, subject to far-ranging and intrusive oversight, with circumscribed activities and explicit service requirements.

But that stance is a direct contradiction of the finance *über alles* model. Stripped-down banking products would undermine sales of the more complicated, higher margin types. Can't have any threats to industry profits, now can we? And even the weakened version of this bill will probably be cut back even further. As *The New York Times* noted, "The legislation still faces major hurdles in Congress, where bankers hold considerable political sway."[67]

The handwriting is already on the wall for how some reform proposals will be neutered. One promising-sounding one is settling credit default swaps transactions through a central clearing house. On the surface, this idea is appealing. Having a central hub allows for consistent levels of collateral to be posted against these trades, reducing the odds of an AIG-style blow-up whenever a guarantor was found to be unable to meet its obligations. We explain shortly why this idea is fatally flawed, begging the question of why Timothy Geithner pushed it in the first place.

Needless to say, industry lobbyists are chipping away at the proposal, pointing out basic impediments like "Not all standardized contracts can be cleared."[68]

But what about initiatives that appear consistent with what we have called for, such as a plan under development at the Federal Reserve to curb bank risk taking by policing compensation procedures, for instance by prohibiting multi-year bonus guarantees and clawing back unwarranted pay?[69] Again, it is not clear how much enthusiasm the Fed has for this idea; it appears designed to put the

United States, rather than the obstreperous French, in control of the international debate on this issue.[70]

Again and again, half-hearted measures are diluted even further. The financial services industry had a proud history of using its own version of FUD, which for high-tech companies is "fear, uncertainty, and doubt," but for Wall Street lobbyists translates into "fear, uncertainty, and delay." Reform measures over the last twenty years have been blunted or blocked. Only one of the two major proposals recommended by the Brady Commission after the 1987 crash was implemented. The furor over derivatives losses in the 1994–1995 period produced a series of hearings, finger wagging, and various proposals to Do Something. The industry successfully fought a rearguard action, then took the tack that a lull in scandals meant everything was fine and no action needed to be taken. And the inmates are running the asylum. Attentive readers may recall that industry lobbyist Mark Brickell co-opted SEC chairman Arthur Levitt, who worked fist and glove with him to beat back derivatives regulation in 1994 and 1995 and to win credit default swaps a permanent exemption from regulation in 2000.[71]

And inertia has prevailed yet again. Recall that in the last two G20 summits (November 2008 and April 2009) the assembled world leaders accepted the idea that imposing reforms while the financial system was wobbly was too risky. Now that conditions appear to have stabilized, the G20 is on to other issues.[72]

Paradigm breakdown. One of the troubling features of the discussion of the crisis has been the recognition of the role of so-called global imbalances as a factor in the debt binge in the United States and other advanced economies, and the widespread attitude of resignation toward that problem. The tacit assumption is that the United States cannot act unilaterally. The United States first took a posture of benign neglect, but the current administration is taking a slightly different tack. The focus of the G20 discussions has shifted from banking reform to the nebulous notion of creating a framework for addressing global imbalances. Ironically, the financial crisis has led to miraculous progress. The U.S. trade deficit has fallen sharply because scarce credit has strangled consumption and trade financing.[73] But exhortations to meet medium term goals, far enough away that no one will be held accountable for failing to meet them, is simply another way to kick the can down the road.

Similarly, the policy of the authorities in the United States has been explicitly to try to shore up asset values, out of the belief that we discussed earlier, that the markets are simply wrong about the need for housing prices and other financial assets to correct. Yet numerous analyses have found that residential real estate prices in many markets, including the United States, the UK, Ireland, Spain, Australia, the Baltics, and much of Eastern Europe, rose to levels well out of line with historical relationships to income and rentals. There was also pervasive underpricing of credit risk, as noted in the Bank of England's April 2007 stability report.

Yet the strategy of the powers that be has been to try to restore status quo ante. Albert Einstein defined insanity as "doing the same thing over and over again and expecting different results." It is one thing to try to patch up what you have on an emergency basis due to the need to respond quickly, and quite another to regard that as a viable long-term solution.

The situation we are in now echoes that of the Great Depression. Although scholars still debate its causes eighty years later, a persuasive view comes from MIT economics professor Peter Temin. Temin, in his *Lessons from the Great Depression,* first sets forth the prevailing explanations and explains why each falls short. He argues that the culprit was the impact of World War I on the gold standard.

Recall that starting roughly in the 1870s, major European economies increasingly adopted the gold standard, and a long period of prosperity resulted.[74] The regime was suspended in the UK and the major European powers during the war. Afterward, they moved to restore it, sometimes at considerable cost (England, for instance, suffered a nasty downturn in the early 1920s). But the aftereffects of the war meant the Edwardian period framework was unworkable. The deflationary forces they set in motion could have been countered by countercyclical measures after the Great Crash. But that was impossible with the gold standard. Indeed, as Temin notes, "Holding the industrial economies to the gold-standard last was about the worst thing that could have been done."[75]

Now readers may have trouble with that comparison, particularly since the conventional wisdom is that our policy responses have been so much better than those of the early 1930s. But the key point here is that *the institutional framework locked the major actors into a particular set of responses.* They were not able to see other paths out because they conflicted with an architecture and a set of beliefs that had comported themselves well for a very long time. It's hard to think outside a system you grew up with. And remember, the gold standard did not break down overnight; the process took more than a decade.

Let's use a different metaphor to illustrate the problem. Say a biotech firm creates a wonder crop, the most amazing creation in the history of agriculture. It yields far more calories per acre than anything else, is nutritionally extremely complete, and can be planted and harvested with far less machinery and equipment than any other plant. It is tasty and can be prepared in a wide variety of ways. It is sweet too, so it can be used in place of sugar and high fructose corn syrup at lower cost. We'll call this XCrop.

XCrop is added as a new element in the food pyramid and endorsed by nutritionists and public health officials all over the globe. It turns out that XCrop also is an aphrodisiac and a stimulant (hmm, wonder how they engineered that in) and between enhanced libido and more abundant food supplies, the world population rises at a faster rate.

Sales of XCrop boom, displacing traditional agriculture. A large amount of farmland is turned over from growing other types of produce to XCrop. XCrop is so efficient that agricultural land is taken out of production and turned to other uses, such as housing, malls, and parks. While some old-fashioned farms still exist, they are on a much smaller scale and a lot of the providers of equipment to traditional farms have gone out of business.

Twenty years into the widespread use of XCrop, doctors discover that diabetes and some peculiar new hormonal ailments are growing at an explosive rate. It turns out they are highly correlated with the level of XCrop consumption in an individual's diet. Long-term consumption of high levels of XCrop interferes with the pituitary gland, which controls almost all the other endocrine glands in the body and the pancreas.

The public faces a health crisis and no way back. It would be very difficult and costly to put the repurposed farmland back into production. Some of the types of equipment needed for old-fashioned farming are no longer made. And with the population so much larger than before, you'd need even more farmland than before. The world population has become dependent on the calories produced by XCrop, so going off it quickly means starvation for some. But staying on it is toxic too. And expecting users simply to restrain themselves will likely prove difficult. The aphrodisiac and stimulant effects of XCrop make it addictive.

Advanced economies have become hooked on debt technology, which, like XCrop, is habit forming and hard to wean oneself off of due to its lower cost and the fact that other approaches have fallen into partial disuse (for instance, use of FICO-based credit scoring has displaced evaluations that include an assessment of the borrower's character and knowledge of the community, such as stability of his employer). In fact, the current debt technology results in information loss, via disincentives to do a thorough job of borrower due diligence (why bother if you are reselling the paper?) and monitoring of the credit over the life of the loan. And the proposed fixes are not workable. The Obama proposal, that the originator retain 5% of the deal and take correspondingly lower fees, is not high enough to change behavior. And a level that would be high enough to make the originator feel the impact of a bad decision would undercut the cost efficiencies that made securitization popular in the first place. You'd have better decisions, but less lending, and higher interest rates. That's ultimately a desirable outcome, but as in the XCrop situation, no one seems prepared to accept that *a move to healthier practices will result in much more costly and less read-*

ily available debt. The authorities want to believe they can somehow have their cake and eat it too.

A second set of difficult institutional problems results from the internationalization of capital markets. Effective regulation of global capital markets players requires a consistent regime of rules and enforcement across geographies. This approach is unlikely to succeed in the absence of the establishment of powerful international bodies devoted to that task. That in turn represents a major threat to national sovereignty. International "harmonization," the current compromise, is a step forward but is likely to prove inadequate.

Financial firms are masters of regulatory arbitrage, and as their wealth and influence have grown, they are also showing considerable skill at manipulating political processes. A point of leverage has been to play competing financial centers against each other. For instance, one impetus for the strong dollar policy was the desire to bolster New York's standing as a financial center. Similarly, the UK, to compete with U.S. deregulation, implemented some rules that were even more accommodating than the ones stateside, a regulatory race to the bottom. For instance, in Lehman's final days, the firm transferred $8 billion from its UK broker-dealer subsidiary to provide funding to the parent company in the United States. It appears Lehman raided UK client accounts, something prohibited under U.S. law. If the broker-dealer does not go bankrupt, its customers should come out more or less whole. Even though Lehman collapsed, its U.S. broker-dealer subsidiary did not. Neither did Drexel's in that firm's implosion.[76]

But the Lehman example illustrates a broader point: that the pressures on legislators and regulators to grant waivers, to assure the "competitiveness" of their respective financial centers, lead to a pressure to lower standards. Thus even if effective new regimes were to be implemented, the banking classes are certain to set them against one another.

． ． ． ． ．

It would be better if I were wrong, but the assessment above suggests that we will not get effective reforms until the financial system is so badly damaged that the influence of financiers weakens considerably. Even then, that is unlikely to happen in the absence of in-depth post-mortems, with the process public enough to expose bad practices and maintain pressure on politicians.

The complexity of financial products makes that less likely. In the Great Depression, Ferdinand Pecora, the fourth in a series of chief counsels to the Senate Banking Committee inquiry into the causes of the 1929 crash, pushed the chicanery into the limelight. More than two years of hearings elicited a great deal of damaging testimony from money chieftains. Both the substance of the abuses uncovered and the outrage over them helped secure the passage of effective and durable securities laws that put the markets on a much sounder footing and restored them to their proper role of handmaiden to commerce, not its master.

But in the United States, key policy positions are held by people like Larry Summers, Timothy Geithner, and Ben Bernanke, who helped design the policies that drove the financial system off the cliff. When a CEO presides over a disaster, he is usually fired. The reason isn't simply that he has been incompetent; even if he were generally able but made a horrid error in judgment, he would have a great deal of difficulty in undoing his own work. While ego often plays a role, an equally powerful impediment is the inability to recognize and correct for one's own blind spots.

For instance, despite the volumes of ink spilled on the crisis, there has been perilous little discussion of leverage on leverage vehicles like CDOs, which as discussed earlier, made the system vastly more precarious by allowing more and more debt to be piled on top of teeny slices of equity. Regulators and the press have chosen not to go there because they are hard to investigate, both from a practical and technical standpoint. There are comparatively few people directly involved; the data on the market and industry practices are fragmented and incomplete, making it hard to get independent information; the products are also arcane and difficult to understand. This sort of activity should be one of the top priorities for reform, yet has any regulator bothered to make serious inquiries? Instead, they are all engaging in drunk under the street light behavior, looking at where they can readily see rather than where the biggest problems lie. Rather than making a diagnosis and using it to determine the best course of action, they are instead treating symptoms.

The failure to do any sort of sustained investigation into crisis causes, be it Pecora style, or the more disciplined process of the Brady Commission, formed in the wake of the 1987 crash, suggests that the authorities do not want to know how widespread the rot is. That in turn points to two further possibilities. One is that an effective investigation would show that quite a few powerful people were culpable. A second is that exposing the full extent of problems would call many fundamental operations of the financial system into question, confirming that the current paradigm is no longer viable. That revelation, even if true, is politically unacceptable.

The path we are on now is simply to provide larger and more extensive backstops to the financial system. This, like the mushrooming indebtedness that created this mess, is self-limiting. At some point, the obligations become so large that borrowers and guarantors cannot make good on their promises and default.

We have not built enough checks into the process to assure that the banking classes will not go out and create the same train wrecks again on a grander scale. In fact, as things stand now, they are almost guaranteed to do precisely that. First, they know if they err again, they will be rescued. The precedent is a powerful signal to take even bigger bets than before. Second, the TARP is only the tip of the iceberg of an extensive web of support and de facto subsidies to the financial system. The notion that all they "owe" is paying back the TARP is spurious. (And to add insult to injury, the Congressional Oversight Panel has charged that the warrants were bought out at unduly low prices.[77])

To produce desirable outcomes, economic theory posits that buyers and sellers should bear the full costs of their actions. That is the reason we have regulations against pollution; policy makers recognize that the consequences of environmental damage are not reflected in the polluter's expenses. The result is their goods are effectively underpriced relative to the full toll exerted on society, so other remedies are put in place.

The massive subsidies to the financial system mean that all participants, not simply the capital markets players at the heart of the machine, but also those who use its underpriced products, benefit from government support. That was once considered acceptable, since the industry was managed so that the executives and employees involved did not benefit unduly from this process. Minus the rents the members of the industry extracted for themselves, which in days of yore were not egregious, the various forms of support could be seen as delivering broad social benefits via lowering the cost of capital to businesses and consumers, which would presumably promote overall growth.

But those assumptions no longer hold. The subsidies, both explicit and implicit, have grown, and cheap credit is now XCrop, a seemingly salutary creation that is now consumed at toxic levels. One sign of the imbalance is the financialization of industrial companies. Over one-third of General Electric's pretax earnings come from businesses like consumer lending. Financial services make a large contribution to the bottom line at a wide range of companies, including Ford, General Motors, John Deere, Caterpillar, Pitney Bowes, Sony, and Honda.[78] And that's before allowing for the fact that many large companies treat their treasury operations as a profit center.

The industry is not only getting far greater support than before, but has also gotten a free pass for the pain it has inflicted on innocent bystanders. Yet unlike polluters, such as the makers of dioxins or asbestos producers, none of the perpetrators has been fined for the damage done or forced to clean it up. Instead, in a remarkable display of brazenness, members of the industry complain how they need to be paid at exorbitant levels for all the profits they claim to have created individually. They are pathologically unable to see that the very large capital flows, like a richly stocked stream of fish, are not a natural occurrence, but the result of policies, many designed to favor the financier class, ranging from restricted entry (broker-dealers, primary dealers, depositaries) to tax policy (favored treatment of capital gains, performance fees for hedge funds and private equity firms, tax deductibility of mortgage interest payments) to broader economic policies (priority given in trade negotiations to opening capital markets, importance given to containing inflation, the Greenspan and Bernanke "puts") to the burgeoning financial welfare programs (the Fed's hodgepodge of special facilities, the rescue of AIG, FDIC guarantees of bank-issued debt).

As former Columbia Business School professor Amar Bhidé noted:

> In fact, one of the sorriest consequences of our financial system is the toll exacted on the legitimacy of providing great rewards for great contributions. Finance certainly contributes to prosperity, but the vast wealth secured in recent years by a small number of financiers does not map into a commensurate increase in created or financed new industries or turned around failing companies. Rather they have used subsidized borrowing to leverage the returns of questionable schemes, secure in the knowledge that if things go wrong the authorities will step in, trying to shore up asset prices or prop up failing counterparties.[79]

And remember, it isn't just the people at the banks proper who gain. Where would hedge funds be if Goldman and Morgan Stanley, both big lenders and support service providers to that industry via their prime brokerage operations, had been allowed to go bust? Where would private equity funds be without the cheap debt that the wide range of subsidies helps provide? Even merger and acquisition professionals, who by virtue of being in a fee business rather than using capital have a better claim than most for deserving to eat what they kill, also gain from low cost funding. Far more deals get done, and at higher prices, when credit is plentiful. And that subsidized funding is not manna from heaven, but the result of government policies friendly to their interests.

Some banking systems have gotten too big for their government minders to back them up credibly. Iceland, which ballooned its debt to an imposing near 900% of GDP (versus the comparatively tame 375% of GDP for the United States), managed the impressive feat of bankrupting its central bank. The Netherlands, although not at obvious risk, has a financial sector larger than its government can realistically guarantee.[80] Ditto Switzerland and Germany. Some commentators see the UK as vulnerable, with its banks' balance sheets in aggregate constituting 450% of GDP.[81] In fact, according to Willem Buiter and Anne Siebert, a country is vulnerable if it is comparatively small, has a large financial sector with significant foreign currency exposures, a currency that is not the reserve currency, and limited government borrowing capacity.[82]

Now that list would seem to exempt the United States. And ironically, that fact, as well as ideology, may explain America's comparative complacency in cleaning up its banking mess. By contrast, Mervyn King, the governor of the Bank of England, has said that banks "too big to fail" are too big, and called for the problem to be addressed through some combination of limiting bank activities, putting much greater capital requirements in place, and implementing a system to put large and complex financial players into bankruptcy.[83] While the United States is discussing putting a regime in place for very large institutions, so-called "Tier One financial holding companies," the details have been scant, and there has been a notable absence of tough statements like King's.

Some have argued that even the United States is at risk in the not-too-distant future of suffering a loss in faith of dollar assets, even Treasuries.[84] Even if the United States can continue to use its reserve currency standing to the benefit of bank miscreants, it is likely to run into political obstacles to further support for the banking system. Indeed, the Fed and FDIC sleights of hand seem intended to disguise the true extent of support. Remarkably, despite the considerable anger over the rescue of AIG, the media has not taken much interest in the fact that the U.S. insurer has provided $300 billion in credit default swaps to European banks to permit them to circumvent regulatory capital requirements. The European markets understood this well; their bank stocks tumbled when the giant U.S. insurer appeared to be on the verge of collapse. The U.S. bailout was in part a rescue of the European banking system.[85]

Similarly, one of the reasons for handling Citigroup with kid gloves isn't merely its size, but also its foreign exposures. Citi has roughly $500 billion in foreign deposits out of a total balance sheet of a tad under $2 trillion.[86] While some may be guaranteed through the national regimes under which those banks operate, presumably a lot are not. If the United States were to provide any assurances to these depositors, it would lead to outrage (why weren't the uninsured depositors of, say, IndyMac made whole?). But a run on Citi would be devastating, and could also lead to the withdrawal of deposits from the branches of other banks operating outside their home countries.

Although some observers allege that Lehman was permitted to fail for nefarious reasons, at the time it seemed obvious that some failing institution had to die to illustrate that the administration was willing to draw the line somewhere. The bailout antipathy was considerable, and Lehman was seen to be dispensable. Although the United States is now operating on an official "No More Lehmans" policy, a rescue that operated significantly to the benefit of non-U.S. parties could produce a large backlash and might impede future salvage operations.

Thus even if the United States thinks it has installed extensive safety nets under the banking system, it may find that political or practical obstacles prevent them from operating as planned.

．　．　．　．　．

Even though I am dubious that the United States will enact effective and durable financial system reforms any time soon, I would be delighted to be proven wrong, and offer a short set of suggestions. Any prescriptions assume that the supposed representatives of the public manage to free themselves of the corruption of influence by the financial lobby. Should they fail, the looting will continue, as will corrosion of the notion that the United States and other economies with powerful banking interests are indeed nations of laws. History shows that making a mockery of democratic processes, if not halted soon enough, leads to bad outcomes, such as violence, authoritarianism, and the rise of demagogues.

The reason for offering comparatively few proposals is that it is easy to dissipate energy and political capital on remedies that generate good headlines yet merely serve to rearrange the deck chairs on the Titanic. For example the various plans to encourage more mortgage modifications under the Bush and Obama administrations fall into this category. We were not alone in correctly predicting these initiatives would have little impact. Anything short of direct measures to cut the Gordian knot of servicer and mortgage securitization impediments, such as allowing judges to write down mortgage principal in bankruptcy, was bound to fail. Thus we provide only a short list of items we deem to be high priority.

Any effective reform plan needs to tackle these issues frontally:

Real reform will reduce the availability and increase the cost of credit and will probably lower liquidity. Effective insurance is not free. The financial service industry's first line of attack will be that new rules will make borrowing more expensive. But that is where we are now with our Potemkin reforms. The high profits that Wall Street firms are reporting are due in part to wider bid-asked spreads, a sign of lower liquidity. Aside from the areas where the government is trying to lower borrowing costs and is having some success, such as mortgages, credit is costly and scarce. For example, 2009 Federal Reserve surveys of bank executives show a rising proportion tightening standards for credit card and other consumer loans.[87]

That argument needs to be turned on its head. What got the global economy in this mess in the first place was underpriced debt. Cheap loans are not a right, nor are they necessarily a boon, and their low cost is in no small measure due to government intervention. Similarly, abundant liquidity appears to

operate more to the benefit of speculators than real economy users by facilitating and perhaps encouraging frequent trading. In 1985 the average holding
period of a New York Stock Exchange stock was twenty-two months. By 2004,
it had fallen to eleven months and is now approximately seven months.[88] Can
those who own shares for that short a time be deemed to be investors?

**Reducing the "connectedness" of the financial system must be an explicit
goal.** The world of funding and hedging markets has become "tightly coupled,"
which is an undesirable trait from a systems design standpoint. It means that
processes move from one step to the next with no ability to interrupt the se-
quence. Another bad aspect of tightly coupled systems is that measures that
are intended to reduce risk, but that fail to change the way the system functions, often make matters worse. For instance, in early 2008, Congress raised the
ceiling on so-called conforming mortgages with the intent that Fannie Mae
and Freddie Mac would help unfreeze the mortgage markets. The result? Investors were spooked by the idea that the two government sponsored agencies,
which had formerly been for the most part limiting their activities to high-
quality mortgages, were being pressured to take on much more risk. Prices on
so-called agency paper fell, producing losses to holders, ultimately bringing
down Bear and a clutch of hedge funds. And the mortgage markets remained
frozen.[89]

This line of thinking is a direct reversal of recent policy, which regarded
high transaction volumes and low trading prices as a plus.

**Improving capital buffers of regulated institutions, without restricting
leverage-on-leverage vehicles and mechanisms, would be unproductive.** As we
illustrated, a great deal of gearing was generated outside the banking system
through collateralized debt obligations and credit default swaps. Although some
of these gates will presumably be closed now that the horse has left the barn and
is in the next county, regulators need to be attentive and proactive in anticipat-
ing where and how new "innovations" might achieve the same end.

Punishments need to be tough. Banking and securities laws need to reinstitute much tougher sanctions for misdeeds, including jail time. The biblical
injunction "To whom much is given, much is expected" is not part of the financial services canon. Members of the industry will thus need to be held to
that standard by other means.

In terms of specific remedies:

Shrink the credit default swaps market as much as humanly possible.
Credit default swaps, an important example of casino operations masquerading
as "innovation," need to be curbed. CDS are fee-generating machines for the financial services industry. They have almost no legitimate uses, and even those
come at considerable cost. The volume of CDS alone, at more than four times

the outstanding amount of bonds, is not consistent with risk transfer, and says a great deal of the activity is mere betting.[90] The superintendent of insurance for New York State, Eric Dinallo, estimated that 80% of the CDS outstanding in 2008 were speculative.[91]

Even the supposed plusses of credit default swaps are in fact no boon. Widespread use of credit default swaps has led to a generalized loss of credit screening and monitoring. This is a system-wide loss of information crucial to making sound credit decisions that cannot be compensated for by other means. The party in the best position to assess whether a borrower will make good on his commitments is the person making the original loan. A lender can obtain information not available by other means, such as investigating company records, assessing the caliber of management, and visiting operations. In the old-fashioned world of banking, they would also monitor the borrower.

The industry's defenses of credit default swaps do not tally with the facts. One argument is that they provide greater liquidity to bondholders than if they traded the underlying security. That is simply incorrect, since a CDS is not an exact offset for the actual bond, which the investor still owns. Moreover, relying on credit default swaps, as opposed to selling a bond, introduces another element of risk, counterparty exposure. Similarly, mergers and restructurings often leave the supposedly guaranteed party less than fully covered.[92]

If a bondholder wants out of a particular instrument, he can simply sell it. Even in the stone ages of the early 1980s, bondholders did want to adjust their exposures, by trading. Investors did not perceive liquidity of corporate bonds to be a problem. Conversations with market participants confirm that idea that bondholders were suffering due to lack of liquidity in the much more advanced markets of a decade and a half later is a canard.

Even more important, credit default swaps have resulted in tangible, large-scale damage beyond the poster child, AIG. As we demonstrated in chapter 9, credit default swaps were integral to a trading strategy that created strong demand for the very worst subprime mortgages, making what might have been a problem into a disaster. That scheme would be a clear case of fraud if CDS were correctly treated as insurance, but is perfectly kosher in the Wild West of unregulated markets.

Similarly, due to the unreliable behavior of correlation models that influence the pricing of some CDS, some big companies that wanted to sell bonds to raise new funds had to pay prices far higher than was warranted by their credit quality at various points in 2008.[93] As discussed earlier, credit default swaps also drain rather than add liquidity to markets under stress.

Finally, credit default swaps require bagholders, or parties willing to absorb risk. Real-world insurers make an art form of writing policies to cover those who in most cases do not need it, cleverly crafting terms so as to limit their exposure, and in some cases, fighting to delay or block claims. By contrast, in the funhouse-mirror world of credit default swaps, the risk takers for the most part have been chumps, either irresponsible actors like AIG's Financial Products Group, or hapless buyers like the fire brigades in Australia who had no idea what they were really being sold. Even if these sales to the functional equivalent of widows and orphans were legal under local securities laws, they were fraudulent in intent.

So why not ban new credit default swaps and let the existing exposures roll off over time? As much as I would prefer that, any cutoff could lead to highly dysfunctional behavior to scramble to get deals done before the drop dead date. Moreover, it would be difficult for both users and intermediaries with large credit default swaps exposures to manage their existing positions if the product were banned, which could lead to dislocations. It is probably the lesser evil to make credit default swaps more costly and less attractive to reduce their use, and consider going into runoff mode once the market shrinks further.

As much as putting them on exchanges sounds like an attractive option, it is not a sound idea, nor is its less ambitious cousin of creating a clearinghouse. In theory, putting credit default swaps on an exchange or in a clearinghouse would decrease the interconnections in the financial system by forcing those who write protection to put up sufficient margin, a sort of down payment on their loss exposure, to assure they can make good on their promise to pay. That is the procedure in options exchanges. Exchange failures are less frequent than financial crises. In theory, if an exchange were to collapse, the damage would not propagate to the rest of the financial system. However, the options and equity exchanges in fact were on the brink of failure in the 1987 crash, a not-well-known fact, and the failure of one exchange would have led to much greater damage. They were saved only by a margin of three minutes when Tom Theobald, then the head of Continental Illinois, gave a waiver on $400 million that the Chicago Mercantile Exchange, where S&P 500 futures traded, owed the bank, due to a customer's failure to pay. Without that, the Merc would not have opened and would likely have failed.[94] The New York Stock Exchange was also at risk of not opening, and its chairman John Phelan feared if it did close, it would never open again.[95] Had the Merc collapsed, the odds of a knock-on NYSE failure were high.

But an exchange or clearinghouse that cannot be adequately capitalized is no benefit; in fact, it may be worse than the status quo because it creates a concentrated point of failure, just as AIG did. A CDS exchange or clearinghouse is certain to have insufficient margin posted against its contracts.

The problem with credit default swaps is they are not derivatives in the normal sense. They are not priced in relationship to an underlying instrument or benchmark; there is no way to look at history to make crude estimates of risk or ways to use related markets to hedge.[96] That makes it difficult to determine how much initial margin is appropriate.

Credit default swaps "jump to default," meaning the spreads widen massively when an event such as a bankruptcy means that a payout on a CDS agreement is imminent. As a result, the guarantor must put up a much bigger performance bond in the form of more collateral. Allowing for the possibility of those large increases means a much larger initial deposit. But an initial commitment that substantial would be well out of line with what traders would be willing to pay. Inevitably, the argument will be that the allegedly large initial margin requirements would kill the product, and the exchange/clearinghouse would proceed, with the house holding too little in the way of financial buffers. In addition, traders expect to be able to reduce their collateral by offsetting open positions, which would further reduce the margin they post with the exchange; shortcomings in the current methodologies make that a questionable procedure.[97]

That in turn means the exchange or clearinghouse would be vulnerable to liquidity problems of its own. Regulators would probably be unwilling to recognize that they had simply created another "too big to fail" institution and thus could also lose the resolve to shrink the market.

Moreover credit default swaps influence, via arbitrage, the cost of bond issuance. Putting CDS on an exchange thus would not, in and of itself, do much to reduce cross-market connections.

The discussion above assumes all credit default swaps would go through an exchange or clearinghouse. But that notion appears to be a fig leaf. Current proposals allow for an enormous "out," that of having "customized" CDS continue to be offered through the existing mechanisms. This loophole would allow the industry to carry on much as before, with the justification (sadly accurate) that the volume in any one "standardized" CDS would be too low for it to be suitable to be listed on an exchange.

An insurance, or proctology, model is a better route for containing risk. Anyone who was a protection seller would have to submit to being regulated as a credit default swaps guarantor. That would mean having to meet standards for capital adequacy and liquidity in the operation making the promise to pay. It also allows for more points of failure, since the regulator could put limits on exposures to individual risks, so that any particular or likely-to-be-related defaults would not be concentrated in a single counterparty. It would also end the practice of using hapless quasi-retail investors like town councils in exotic locales as dumping grounds for camouflaged exposures.

Most important, this model would allow for the implementation of a longstanding concept from insurance, that of insurable interest, which allows parties to protect themselves against risk only to the extent that they have a bona fide reason. Aside from the Magnetar case, there have been other instances of questionable practices, namely, of bondholders pushing companies into default to collect on their (probably much larger) CDS position when a workout would have been more productive from a real economy perspective.[98]

The nuisance of being regulated in this fashion would serve to reduce the size of the market.

Limit guarantees to crucial, socially important banking and capital markets activities. While "too big to fail" is a legitimate concern, the fixation on that problem results in treating symptoms rather than root causes. Authorities (on an emergency basis) have been forced to put supports under large complex financial institutions, which are involved both in providing crucial credit functions as well as businesses that do not merit public support. As Martin Wolf, the respected economics editor of the *Financial Times,* put it, "They are expensive wards of the state and must be treated as such."[99] If large banks and capital markets firms are not commercial businesses that can be permitted to fail, they must be regulated as utilities.

We recommend a modified return to a Glass-Steagall regime, but with an addition we consider essential: now that capital markets players enjoy explicit state support, formerly lightly regulated investment banking activities need to have strict limits and intrusive oversight. This system would have distinct regulatory regimes for depositaries and investment banks, with no credit cross-subsidization permitted (i.e., the depositary could not make loans or use deposits to fund the investment bank; each entity, if it were under a parent organization, would have to meet its equity requirements separately; no financial supports across entities permitted). While in theory there might be advantages to being a financial supermarket from a marketing perspective, any products sold offered by one entity and sold by another (say a fund managed by the investment bank sold to the customers of the depositary) would be on the same terms for accounting and compensation purposes as if marketed by a third party.

- **Depositaries** would be limited to making traditional loans and using plain vanilla hedges. Banks are restricted to activities that bank examiners can understand. They can participate in the credit default swaps market through regulated CDS insurance subsidiaries. They could also engage in pure fee businesses such as acting as trustees and custodians.
- **Investment banks** can engage in money and capital markets operations, such as underwriting and distributing equities and bonds, and market-making. They too can participate in the credit default swaps

market through regulated CDS insurance subsidiaries. They would also be permitted to engage in pure fee businesses, such as mergers and acquisitions and asset management, provided that the asset manager does not rely on financing provided directly or indirectly by the investment bank (that is, no private equity funds where the bank lends to the fund). The investment bank can also engage in simple interest rate and currency swaps. It can serve as a broker of exchange-traded derivatives but not use its balance sheet for anything other than simple swaps, underwritings, and market-making in the product categories in which it is an underwriter.[100] Proprietary trading and the trading and sale of other OTC derivatives would be prohibited. Failure to place an underwritten deal would be deemed an impermissible loan and subject to fines

It is not crucial to reinstitute Glass-Steagall, since the depositary would be firewalled from any other financial activities. However, from a regulatory standpoint, there might be merit in reinstituting the split, partly because the industries have such different competitive dynamics. The economics of capital markets businesses strongly favor bigger firms over time, while traditional banking is cost competitive on a very small scale; the idea that bigger banks are natively more profitable is a canard pushed by bank CEOs to justify consolidation, since the pay of top bank executives is highly correlated with size of institution.

Other financial firms can to do as they please. However, they cannot secure credit from the firms inside the regulatory *cordon sanitaire* except in the form of counterparty exposures (short-term funding against collateral, with those activities subject to regulatory oversight to assure that only high quality, liquid instruments were used for these loans, with sufficiently high haircuts). Lending to hedge funds, save against specific positions on conservative terms, would be barred, as would warehouse facilities and bridge loans.

This approach of ring-fencing the socially productive financing functions and restricting credit extension to more speculative investors would reduce the size of bank balance sheets. The supposed talent in risky trading businesses in "too big to fail" banks would presumably decamp and join existing boutiques or set up new ventures. However, anyone involved in strategies that depended on cheap funding might not find an exit as easy as they had imagined. Presumably, new private sources of risk capital, such as specialized lenders, or funds raised for the purpose of providing credit to riskier financial players, would partially fill the gap, but at higher cost and with lower-sized facilities than under the old regime.

We believe this approach is in the long run more effective than simply trying to come up with a mechanism for putting "too big to fail" institutions into bankruptcy. The unpleasant fact is some firms, like Citigroup, have exposures so wide-ranging and complex that the idea that they could be wound down in an orderly fashion is sheer fantasy. Prohibition of risky activities and strict regulation of core functions will reduce the size of these firms and make them less failure prone.

Tighten other regulations to close gaps and extend liability to responsible parties. Derivatives are often used to evade regulation, and have become a fruitful ground for predatory behavior, since disclosure standards are far lower than for securities. Derivatives should be regulated under the regime of the instrument they most resemble. As we discussed, credit default swaps are really insurance in another guise, and are best regulated in an insurance framework.

More broadly, regulators need to move from rule-based notions to principles-based practices, a.k.a., "if it walks like a duck and quacks like a duck, it's probably a duck." One of the reasons financial firms have been so successful at regulatory arbitrage is that the authorities have taken a hands-off, procedural posture, which had the effect of allowing industry incumbents to exploit loopholes. A low tolerance policy toward creativity designed to evade standards would go much further than trying to craft airtight regulations.

Legislators also need to restore secondary liability. Attentive readers may recall that a Supreme Court decision in 1994 disallowed suits against advisors like accountants and lawyers for aiding and abetting frauds. In other words, a plaintiff could only file a claim against the party that had fleeced him; he could not seek recourse against those who had made the fraud possible, say, accounting firms that prepared misleading financial statements. That 1994 decision flew in the face of sixty years of court decisions, practices in criminal law (the guy who drives the car for a bank robber is an accessory), and common sense. Reinstituting secondary liability would make it more difficult to engage in shoddy practices.

Toughen enforcement and penalties. Heretofore, the main consideration in fraud and dubious practices was the cost and odds of getting caught versus the rewards of the scheme. Even though CSFB brokers' IPO kickbacks could have been subject to criminal charges, prosecutors have chosen not to pursue that route.[101] Part of that is due to the resources required to prosecute financial frauds; it also stems from the fact that, as with Enron, firms can weave their way through complex rules and devise transactions that are economically destructive, yet pass the accounting and legal smell tests. Thus any new legislation needs to incorporate broader tests of economic substance to serve as a check against too-clever-by-half deal structuring.

In addition, regulators need far larger enforcement budgets. Given the multi-trillion dollar tab of the bailouts, a few hundred million on tougher and more sophisticated oversight is a cheap investment. The authorities need to adopt a much more bloody-minded attitude. No more Greenspanian "let a thousand flowers bloom." If they don't understand what one of their charges is proposing to do, they should not allow it.

Regulators should also invest in creating focused teams with deep expertise on complicated products. The industry will scoff and claim that mere public servants cannot possibly match the "talent" level of the industry. But consider: Federal judges are all highly seasoned and skilled, yet choose to serve for far less than they could earn in the private sector. Similarly, the Department of State has a cadre of very able career staff. Contrary to financial services industry PR, capable individuals do drop out mid-career for a host of personal reasons. An elite enforcement team would only need to attract a few experienced individuals to make a great difference in the effectiveness of oversight.

■   ■   ■   ■   ■

Readers may have noticed that I offer no remedies for the economics discipline, even though the disasters visited on us were all the result of its prescriptions. If criticism from within the profession has fallen on deaf ears, and its members for the most part choose to defend their clearly broken models and dubious methodologies, yet another salvo, particularly from a mere outsider, is certain to be rejected with prejudice.

But the profession has chosen to grasp the reins of power. If it will not assume the duty of care that goes with that role, then it falls upon the rest of us, the consumers of its advice, to hold it to a much higher standard. Doctors, who have more science to back their interventions than economists do, have a code of professional ethics and are subject to liability. Yet with greater legitimate authority and responsibility, they now submit, albeit often begrudgingly, to pesky patient questions based on Internet research. And sometimes those annoying patients are right, even if it means finding an open-minded practitioner to pursue their hunches.

Unfortunately, not unlike what has transpired in the financial services industry, the measures taken by the economic profession since the 1950s have done more to benefit the incumbents than the society in which they operate. The "mathing up" of the discipline has created a barrier to entry that puts many of its workings beyond the scrutiny of the broader population that has to live with the consequences of its advice. And to make matters worse, some economists seem particularly zealous about protecting the value of their union card, and retort with superficial responses that do not engage the issues raised, while often simultaneously disparaging the source as not qualified to opine on such demanding matters.

The economy is far too important to all of us to leave to experts, particularly when their recommendations often have little in the way of empirical foundations. Both experts and charlatans rely on intimidation, such as the use of arcane (even if useful) terminology and a dismissive attitude to deter reasonable queries. We all need to get in the habit of demanding support, not sound bites or sixth-grade level opinion pieces, but reasoned and complete explanations of why economists believe what they believe. That was the reason for adopting mathematical exposition in the first place, to make the logic and evidence behind their reasoning explicit and transparent. It's time they adopt that standard for communication with the public.

AFTERWORD

Find out just what any people will quietly submit to and you have the exact measure of the injustice and wrong which will be imposed on them.

—Frederick Douglass

In his last speech in office, President Dwight Eisenhower warned Americans not of an external enemy but a more insidious threat:

> This conjunction of an immense military establishment and a large arms industry is new in the American experience. The total influence—economic, political, even spiritual—is felt in every city, every State house, every office of the Federal government . . . The potential for the disastrous rise of misplaced power exists and will persist.[1]

Eisenhower described how private interests that present themselves as vital to public safety can subvert democracy. While arms merchants can claim to be essential to national security, the major financial players are, by contrast, a menace to society. Andrew Haldane, the Executive Director for Financial Stability at the Bank of England, concluded that it was impossible for the financial services industry to pay for the damage it wrought in the global debacle. The lowest plausible estimate of the total costs that he could come up with, amortized over twenty years, still resulted in a first year's bill that exceeded the total market capitalization of the biggest banks.[2] That means that any intervention to reduce the harm they do is warranted.

In the aftermath of the meltdown, the case for bold action was sound. The history of financial crises showed that the least costly approach is to resolve mortally wounded organizations, install new management, set strict guidelines, and separate out bad loans and investments in order to restructure and sell them. Shuttering sick banks is hardly a radical idea; the FDIC does it on a routine basis. So the difference here did not lie in the nature of the exercise, but its operational complexity.

In early 2009, the banking industry was on the ropes. This juncture was a crucial window of opportunity. Widespread, vocal opposition to the TARP demonstrated that a once-complacent populace had been roused. Reform, if proposed with energy and confidence, wasn't a risk; indeed, it was just what voters wanted.

But incoming president Obama failed to act. Rather than bring vested banking interests to heel, his team instead chose to reconstitute, as much as possible, the very same industry whose reckless pursuit of profit had thrown the world economy off the cliff. There would be no "Nixon goes to China" moment from the architects of the policies that created the crisis, namely Treasury Secretary Timothy Geithner, Federal Reserve Chairman Ben Bernanke, and Director of the National Economic Council Larry Summers.

Obama's repudiation of his campaign promise of change locked his administration into a course of action. He would have no choice other than working fist in glove with the banksters, supporting and amplifying their own, well established, public relations campaigns.

Thus Obama's incentives have been to come up with "solutions" that paper over problems, avoid meaningful conflict with the industry, minimize complaints, and restore the old practice of using leverage and investment gains to cover up stagnation in worker incomes. Potemkin reforms dovetail with the financial service industry's goal of forestalling measures that interfere with its looting. The only difficulty has been how to fool the now-impoverished public into thinking Mussolini-style corporatism represented progress.

One technique has been inadequate postmortems. The Financial Crisis Inquiry Commission, deliberately hamstrung by an unrealistic time schedule, skimpy funding, weak leadership, and a cumbersome process for issuing subpoenas, exceeded expectations by issuing a readable report that simply validated conventional wisdom. The Federal Reserve fought efforts to have it disclose information about its emergency lending programs, delaying its release till after U.S. reform legislation was passed, thus depriving its drafters of critical input. As a result, competing theories of what caused the meltdown led to dissent and watered-down remedies.

Another tactic has been to depict inadequate reform measures as serious and effective. The financial system is now tightly coupled, which means that dislocations in one sector propagate across the network, crippling seemingly unrelated products and participants. The solution is structural change: reducing the size and interconnectedness of the major actors.

The Dodd Frank bill, by contrast, simply inconveniences the industry at the margin. Described as a "promise to write a bill later," it used a host of studies and rulemaking processes to dump the process on complicit regulators.[3] Its Volcker rule, meant to end state-backstopped proprietary trading, merely limits the size of principal investments and allows for position-taking on dealer desks, with the degree of oversight still uncertain.

Efforts to tame risk in derivative markets by moving them onto clearinghouses are bogged down in technical debates, with Geithner pushing to exempt foreign exchange entirely. The widely-touted resolution authority is another sham, since a U.S.-based regime cannot override bankruptcy laws in foreign jurisdictions. It is also ill equipped to handle the practical difficulties of winding down large derivatives books. A more bloody-minded effort in the UK by the Bank of England and the Financial Services Authority to split banks along retail/wholesale lines was watered down by aggressive industry lobbying.

The failure of the U.S. reforms is so obvious that Geithner didn't attempt to defend them in a meeting I attended. Instead, he argued that Basel III rules compensate by requiring financial firms to hold more capital. But Basel III preserves the risk weighting system that banks gamed, with the resulting lower reserves leading directly to their near-death experiences.[4] Other critics highlight additional shortcomings: an unduly attenuated phase-in, failure to harmonize accounting, and neglect of pretty much all of the shadow banking system.[5]

Nevertheless, the jockeying produced one instructive case study. Citigroup sold Phibro unit to Occidental Petroleum. Oxy paid only liquidation value, meaning no premium for the earning potential of its head trader Andrew Hall's supposed money machine. Why? His returns were heavily dependent on high leverage, cheap funding, and market intelligence from other trading desks. These concentrated capital and information flows do not come about naturally, but result from industry-favoring policies. His example illustrates that the claim that highly profitable traders are worth their exorbitant pay is often a fiction.

Predictably, the lack of meaningful penalties and restrictions means looting continues unimpeded. Wall Street's 2009 and 2010 bonuses beat 2007's banner year, while the real economy is mired in flagging activity and high unemployment.

That brings us to a final outcome of this debacle. A radical campaign to reshape popular opinion recognized the seductive appeal of the phrase "free markets." Powerful business interests, largely captive regulators and officials, and a lapdog media took up this amorphous, malleable idea and made it a Trojan horse for a three-decades-long campaign to tear down the rules that constrained the finance sector. The result has been a massive transfer of wealth, with its centerpiece the greatest theft from the public purse in history. This campaign has been far too consistent and calculated to brand it with the traditional label, "spin." This manipulation of public perception can only be called *propaganda*. Only when we, the public, are able to call the underlying realities by their proper names—*extortion, capture, looting, propaganda*—can we begin to root them out.

WHY NEOCLASSICAL ECONOMISTS
USE A ROBINSON CRUSOE ECONOMY
TO REPRESENT THE DEMAND FUNCTION

To illustrate the manifest incoherence of neoclassical economics, we give a simplified exposition of how the neoclassical demand function fails as a "scientific" theory when extended from a single consumer to multiple consumers. We examine the attempted repair, which employs the construct of a single consumer whose tastes do not change with income or over time ("static"), as a proxy for the society-wide demand function. The attempted repair fails as well.[1]

. . . . .

To make things easy, economists start with a single consumer and two goods, say bread and eggs. Remember the marginal utility concept. Even though more is better, in most cases an additional bit more is less valuable. Going from one egg to two eggs is more fulfilling than from nine eggs to ten.[2]

In our system, more income is always better, since you can have more of both bread and eggs. So in chart 1, each line illustrates how a consumer would trade off eggs versus bread at a particular income level based on his preferences. They are utility curves, or indifference curves, since at each point on the same curve, the consumer has the same utility, or is equally satisfied at any point on his personal utility curve. In other words, a particular consumer might regard himself as equally well off if he had eight eggs and one roll of bread as he would with six rolls of bread and two eggs.

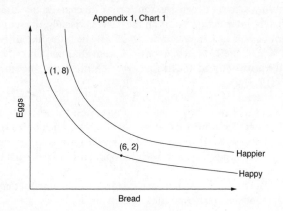

Appendix 1, Chart 1

Each line represents a different income level. Further out ("Happier" versus "Happy") is also better, since that represents higher income. Note how the shape stays the same. The consumer is assumed to like bread and eggs in the same ratio no matter how rich he becomes. Thus our prototypical consumer, who was as satisfied with eight eggs and one roll of bread as he was with six rolls of bread and two eggs, is assumed, at a higher level of income, to be as happy with eighty eggs and ten rolls of bread as with sixty rolls of bread and twenty eggs (in other words, no allowance is made for the fact that richer consumers who can afford lots of eggs might develop a weakness for egg-intensive undertakings like soufflés and change their bread/eggs trade-off).

The next trick is to draw a "budget line." Let's say the consumer's income is $3,000. If eggs cost $1 each and bread costs $3, the most bread he can buy is 1,000 rolls and the maximum amount of eggs is 3,000 eggs.

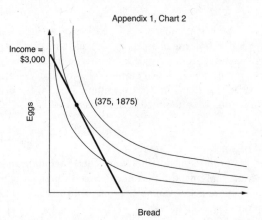

Appendix 1, Chart 2

Voila! Where the budget line meets the furthest away indifference curve (meaning one it only touches tangentially) is where the consumer is best off, based on his preferences and income. Remember, the fact that that is the furthest "away" indifference curve that his budget line can reach means it represents his highest personal welfare.

And if prices change, the slope of the line changes, and the optimal mix of goods shifts. If eggs remain at $1 and bread falls to $2, a rational consumer will eat more bread than when bread was more expensive. You can see on chart 3a that the change in prices leads to a different intersection point on the curves (visually, the set point of the maximum amount of eggs he can consume, which is where the line intersects with the Y axis, in this case stays the same, while the maximum amount of bread he can buy varies. The cheaper the price of bread, the further away the intersection point of the budget line with the x-axis).

So far this seems pretty obvious. And the combination of the utility curves and changing prices also proves one of the economist's best friends, the downward sloping demand curve. Chart 3b shows that when you plot how much bread the consumer will buy at various prices, derived from chart 3a, you get a downward sloping line. As you see, if we keep the price of eggs fixed and keep dropping the price of bread, the more bread the consumer will buy.

Now this all looks consistent, but we need to stop and point out that even at this very simple level the model is starting to break internally.

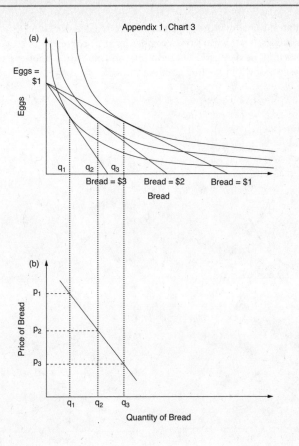

Appendix 1, Chart 3

Look again at chart 3a. It assumes the consumer has an income of $3,000, and then looks at the impact on his consumption if the price changes (in this toy economy, consumers only spend, there is no savings). But consumers are also producers. Another part of the assumption set is that changes in prices affect consumer incomes. Thus it would be incorrect to assume that a change in prices would leave the consumer with the same $3,000 income. Except in the very specific exception that his exposure to the eggs versus bread-producing parts of the economy was exactly proportional to that particular change in relative prices, his income will go up or down.

Visually, on chart 3a, that is represented by the fact that the budget line intersects the y-axis at one point and pivots from it as bread prices change. In reality, the second budget line would start higher or lower on that axis to reflect whether the consumer gained or lost from the change in bread prices.

We've introduced the problem of changing incomes at this juncture (which, as we stress, is part of the overall model), as opposed to having it incorrectly finessed, as it is in the textbook version. But let us revert to the original story.

So let's assume higher and lower budgets but keep the eggs and bread trade-off the same. The resulting line of how consumption changes as someone gets richer or poorer is called an Engels curve.[3]

Note here that the shape of the Engels curve depends on how much the consumer likes bread versus eggs. That wasn't true for the demand curve (you can go back and play with it yourself). The demand curve for any consumer with stable preference will always slope downward, while the Engels curve can take any shape.

Appendix 1, Chart 4

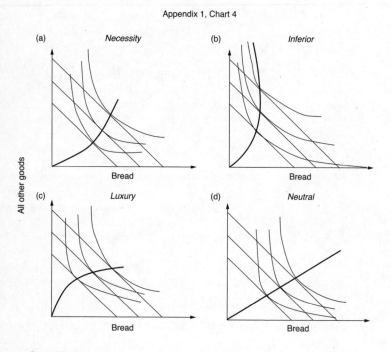

Source: Steve Keen, 2002

Notice how in some cases the Engels curve will move closer to the X axis as the consumer gets richer, while in other cases, it moves further away. That reflects how the consumer regards the commodity in question. For instance, in 4a, the item is a necessity. He does buy more, but at a much reduced rate, as he gets richer. How many rolls of bread can one person use, after all? Contrast that with 4c, luxury products, where as he gets richer, he buys proportionally more. The other two cases are inferior goods, where as the consumer gets richer, he buys less because he switches to something better (think butter versus margarine), and the last picture is "neutral" goods that he continues to consume in the same ratio to income.

Now a market is not one individual; Robinson Crusoe does not make for much of an economy. *Yet when we go beyond a single individual, the model breaks down.* The assertion of the neoclassical adherents that more open markets provide better outcomes is unproven even on a theoretical level.

To prove that unchecked individual activity automagically produced the greatest collective good, as Jeremy Bentham and his followers believed, they needed to paint a picture similar to the one of the individual consumer: that society, based on its collective preferences, can achieve a mix of outputs that is optimal. The optimality is "proven" by the fact in the simple bread and eggs example above that you could find a single point where the budget line met the "furthest away" indifference curve. If you moved away from that point, you are worse off.

To go from an individual to a society in turn requires constructing demand curves and preference curves, meaning Engels curves for society as a whole, and seeing how the two interact. And since society is no more than a collection of individuals, you need to be able to achieve it via summing up individual preferences.

Understand further: if you can't establish this in a simple two-goods economy, you certainly can't prove it in a more complicated setting.[4]

Problem number one: the social demand curve does not slope downward in a nice linear fashion (remember from chapter 2 that nonlinear phenomena are terribly vexing for economists). In fact, it can have kinks, or even be flat or upward sloping in sections. Despite the seeming universality of the downward sloping demand curve in models presented to laypeople and undergraduate economics students, neoclassical economists are quite familiar with the fact that it isn't that tidy even in theory. The Sonnenschien-Mantel-Debreu theorem shows that while the demand curve is generally downward sloping, its irregularities mean it can intersect other lines in multiple places.

Problem number two: as we highlighted earlier, changes in price curves change incomes. In our simple example, we had treated the budget line, eggs versus bread, as separate from earnings. But prices also determine income, so changes in egg prices versus bread prices will affect the relative position of egg producers versus bakers.

Now recall that when an individual got wealthier, he was assumed to have the same relative desire for bread and eggs; the curves were nested. But if you assume consumers with different curves, and then factor in the impact of changing prices, you will get aggregate utility curves that intersect (the math is more complicated, but conceptually, the person with the higher income has more weight in the computation, which influences the curve shape).

Chart 5 on page 314 shows that when you draw different budget lines (how much eggs and bread you can buy at different price mixes and total income of the society), you will get one intersection point with one mix versus the other.

The solid lines are one set of prices and resulting indifference curves; the dashed lines are a second set of prices and curves. And notice there we have permitted the incorrect simplification that the budget line stays anchored on the y-axis, but that should move, too.

When you have nested curves, as in our single-person example, you can prove that you can find a single point on the curve furthest away. That point is optimal, since it represents the highest attainable level of welfare for that level of spending power with those prices.

But when you go to multiple curves that intersect each other, you cannot prove which price mix and resulting set of outcomes is better. In fact, the smooth curves shown in the picture to illustrate the point are a simplification to illustrate the problem. A social utility curve for multiple consumers is far more jagged, as the picture illustrates.

Even if you assume straight aggregate demand lines (which as we discussed above aren't a valid assumption either) you can have multiple intersections. And per above, the utility curves intersect, which means in the messier combo (multiple jagged utility lines that intersect, jagged demand curves) you not only have multiple equilibria, but they are on different indifference curves, none of which is clearly "better" (as in consistently further away). Thus the elaboration of the system merely shows that there are

Appendix 1, Chart 5

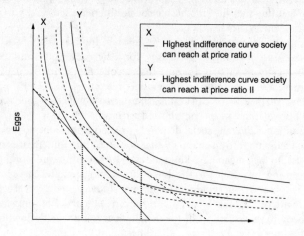

Source: Steve Keen, 2002

Appendix 1, Chart 6

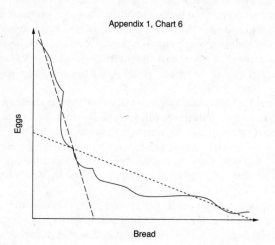

Source: Steve Keen, 2002

multiple possible outcomes, with *no way of knowing if any is "best" as far as collective welfare is concerned.*

This may seem trivial, but it is very damaging to the theory. The claim that an idealized neoclassical system produces greater social welfare is unproven as soon as you have multiple consumers, meaning even the most trivial economy! How can you meaningfully speak of exchange, trade, and price formation in a Robinson Crusoe economy? Does he trade eggs and bread with himself just for fun?

In fact, that is pretty much what economists assume to salvage the theory. To make this toy economy "prove" the desired result (the sum of individual choices produces optimal social results) you need to neuter the concept of individuality. The theories say one of two sets of conditions has to apply. The first set was rejected because it requires having fixed income distributions (no one gets richer or poorer when prices change relative to each other), which is unpalatable (open markets are supposed to produce winners and losers, after all). The more acceptable set of restrictions that produces the desired output is to have Engels curves with a constant slope (meaning a straight line, no multitude of shapes, as we saw earlier) and they all have the same slope (which means they have to be parallel).

But consider one other issue. Go back to the original Engels curves (chart 4). Notice how they all start from where the x- and y-axes intersect? They have to. The least a consumer can consume is zero of either good. As he gets more income, he moves away from that (0,0) point.

So if the Engels curves for all consumers have to be parallel (have the same slope) AND they have to go through the (0,0) point, there is only one Engels curve. *All consumers must have the same taste.*

So how do the theorists rationalize this fix to the model? They use a "representative agent," one person with static tastes who serves as a proxy for all. The assumptions needed to produce these results sound even worse than the oft-cited horrors of Communist central planning: everyone consumes the same goods, rationed in the same proportion for both the rich and the poor. Gee, at least in the old Soviet Union, those at the top of the food chain got perks, like dachas and drivers.

What does that mean in practice? We glossed over it earlier, but remember the utility curves for a single consumer, how they were all nested? As income rises, tastes are assumed to remain the same. That is clearly absurd. Poor people spend everything they have on necessities, like food, fuel, and shelter. Wealthier people will spend more in absolute amounts on the basics (they eat fancier meals and have bigger houses), but the basics will be much less as a proportion of income (they buy luxuries, such as theater tickets and yachts, which are not in the struggling individual's buying mix). But in the world of microeconomics, people spend their income in the same proportion on various items no matter how much money they have (the term of art is that consumers have homothetic preferences).

Similarly, tastes are assumed to remain constant over one's life. A consumer that lives on beer, Coke, and Chinese food in college isn't permitted to move on to scotch, lattes, and sushi. That means it explicitly disallows innovative new products to become popular. The success of iPods, for instance, means consumers have to buy less of the established goods to switch to the new products. But no, that sort of thing isn't permitted in the model. In other words, the sort of innovation and progress that is one of the oft-cited advantages of capitalism conflicts sorely with this model.

APPENDIX II
HOW TO SHORT SUBPRIME IN LARGE QUANTITIES

Time and place: Sometime in 2006, somewhere in the United States.

Cast of characters: Hedgie: A certain hedge fund manager who has decided to go short in subprime in as large a volume as possible. His scheme will involve several other characters:

Manager: A CDO manager, a guy with a Bloomberg terminal.

Dealer: A large broker-dealer who will structure the CDO.

Monoline: A bond insurer.[1]

WHAT IS RUNNING THROUGH HEDGIE'S MIND?

Hedgie knows that BBB subprime residential mortgage-backed securities are largely toxic sludge. Credit default swaps against BBB RMBS are traded on the ABX index and on single names in the over-the-counter market, but volume is so thin that if he took a big short position, it would show up quickly and distinctly and blow spreads out incredibly wide.

Fortunately, the CDS market is used to handling supply and demand stemming from the regular issuance of CDOs. If Hedgie can find a way to melt into the crowd of longs and shorts associated with CDOs, then Hedgie will be able to take an attractively large short position and everything will work out smoothly.

STEP BY STEP:

1. Hedgie goes to dealer and says, "I'm axed[i] to buy $50 million of mezz[ii] ABS CDO equity, I just need to achieve a return of 20% on the equity and get good treatment if I want to hedge myself by buying CDS on the underlying BBB resi[iii] bonds."

2. Dealer winks back at Hedgie and pretends he believes that Hedgie is serious about "hedging" his CDO investment, even though both of them understand that Hedgie's interest lies in having the CDO crater.

3. Hedgie would prefer to have the deal be a hybrid, 20% cash and 80% synthetic assets, and with 35% cash and 65% synthetic liabilities.[2]

---

[i]I want
[ii]mezzanine
[iii]residential

4. The equity is 5% of the total liabilities, so $50 million equity means $1 billion in the whole CDO. The cash portion of the assets is 20%, so $200 million is largely BBB subprime RMBS, mostly purchased from the Dealer's RMBS new issue pipeline. The synthetic portion is 80%—the remaining $800 million of risk in the CDO will be premiums paid to the CDO on CDS referencing various BBB RMBS bonds. The Dealer will intermediate that trade, the other side, or protection buyers, being hedge funds, other dealers, etc. who are insuring themselves against the BBB RMBS reference obligations. The CDS will be against different[3] names than those appearing in the 20% of cash bonds.

CDO Liability Structure[iv] (Dollars in millions)

Class A1 Super Senior VFN[4]	$650.0	65.00%
Class A2 Jr AAA Cash	112.5	11.25
Class B AA Cash	85.0	8.50
Class C A Cash	52.5	5.25
Class D BBB Cash	50.0	5.00
Equity Cash	50.0	5.00
Total	$1000.0	100.00%

CDO Asset Structure (Dollars in millions)

Cash RMBS	$200.0	20.00%
Cash Account (to reserve against CDS)	150.0	15.00
Net unfunded CDS	650.0	65.00
Total	$1000.0	100.00%

5. Dealer finds Manager, who is proud of his ability to pick RMBS bonds cleverly and analyze their credit risk. Manager will get paid ten basis points of the outstanding CDO notional for his contribution, plus an incentive fee if the deal performs well.[5]
6. Manager selects the subprime bonds that will go into the deal, both the ones that go directly into the cash portion and the ones referenced by the CDS in the synthetic portion.
7. Hedgie, having put up the equity, gets veto power over the bonds in the CDS.[6]
8. Dealer lets clients know that a new CDO is coming out and they'll have the opportunity to buy $800 million total worth of CDS protection against the names in the synthetic part of the CDO.[7]
9. At a certain time, say Friday at 1 P.M., the bidding process is complete and the highest bid for protection (in terms of basis points) on the notional of each name winds up with the CDS protection against that name. Hedgie has been simultaneously trying to buy $200 million[8] of CDS protection against some of the same names, with his bids camouflaging their way in among the excess of supply of CDS protection offered by the issuance of this CDO.[9] If necessary, on Friday at

---

[iv]Cash flows are paid sequentially down, which basically means that losses eat through the structure from the bottom up.

1 P.M., Hedgie, being a favored customer of Dealer, can get a "last look" at the bids for CDS protection and come over the top of current bidders.

10. Dealer has now committed to sell CDS protection against $800 million of assorted BBB trash.[10] At the moment this is exclusively the Dealer's risk, so Dealer needs to get rid of this risk as quickly as possible.

11. That means coming up with investors in the CDO.[11]

12. Dealer spends a few weeks marketing the cash CDO paper, from the junior AAA down to the BBB, globally. As everyone knows, bankers have too much of a sense of propriety to woo clients with cocaine and hookers, but sales tactics are aggressive. These investors collectively put up $350 million of cash for their portion, including the $50 million of equity that was pre-placed with Hedgie.

13. Dealer also needs some Monoline to take on the $650 million super-senior AAA risk by writing CDS protection against that portion of the CDO.

14. Monoline is seduced by the whopping twelve basis points of spread on the super senior notes,[12] so it signs up for the job.[13]

15. The deal closes: Dealer buys $800 million of CDS on the BBB RMBS from the CDO,[14] so he is now flat risk.[15] Dealer takes down all the CDO paper, transferring the $350 million of cash CDO paper to the customers and Hedgie, and buying $650 million of CDS from Monoline against the Class A1 Super Senior. The junior investors in the CDO will take losses first if write-downs on the cash bonds or credit events on the CDS occur.

16. Hedgie is now the proud owner of $50 million of equity paying 20% (until losses on the underlying BBB RMBS occur), as well as $200 million of CDS against the CDO. Hedgie paid 180 basis points on the CDS, so for an upfront cost of 5% of the CDO, the net annual carry of Hedgie's position is

$$(5\% \times \$1BB \times 20\%) - (\$200MM \times 180bps) = \$10MM - \$3.6MM = \$6.4MM$$

That means that Hedgie's annual carry for this short position is positive 427 bps.[16]

WHAT HAPPENS LATER, AFTER THE MELTDOWN?

1. Hedgie's position pays 427 basis points for a while, while the equity is intact. The subprime bonds were originated in 2006 and 2007, so it doesn't matter what Manager bought, they're all bad and will soon be worth zero.

2. Spreads on CDS explode and Hedgie cashes out his CDS that were once priced at 180 basis points at 10,000.

3. The junior investors in the CDO didn't get out in time and lose everything.

4. Even though the super senior AAA tranches are losing value fast, Monoline's insurance contracts are highly customized and don't require Monoline to post collateral.[17]

5. But Monoline still has to take huge mark to market losses on its balance sheet. The shareholders of Monoline dump its stock. Death spiral ensues.

6. The CDO will now be expecting Dealer to fund the A1 Super Senior VFN note as the CDO needs cash to settle all the bad CDS that it wrote, and it has already burned through the 35% that was put up by junior investors. That means that CDO will now expect Dealer to fund the A1 Super Senior VFN note. Dealer had hedged his exposure to the trust's AAA by buying CDS from the CDO, who had bought CDS from Monoline. But Mololine is using the fine print of its contract to avoid putting up collateral. Dealer desperately tries to buy CDS protection against a Monoline downgrade or default.

7. Spreads blow out on Monoline's corporate CDS, further contributing to Mono-line's death spiral.

8. The auditors of Dealer tell him to write down his hedge with Monoline on the CDO's AAA. Dealer takes huge mark to market loss. Death spiral ensues.

9. The U.S. Treasury decides that Dealer is systemically important and puts him on life support.

10. Subprime borrowers blow up. CDO blows up. Monoline blows up. Shadow bank-ing system implodes. International capital markets lock solid. U.S. public debt balloons. Greenspan spots flaw in "free markets" ideology.

11. Hedgie buys a Pacific island and a yacht and sails off into the sunset.

NOTES

INTRODUCTION

1. John Maynard Keynes, *Essays in Persuasion* (London: MacMillan, 1931), 383.

CHAPTER 1

1. Gerard Baker, "Welcome to the 'Great Moderation,'" *TimesOnline*, January 19, 2007, http://www .timesonline.co.uk/tol/comment/columnists/article1294376.ece.
2. Robert J. Shiller, "Challenging the Crowd in Whispers, Not Shouts," *The New York Times*, November 1, 2008, http://www.nytimes.com/2008/11/02/business/02view.html.
3. Ibid.
4. Raghuram G. Rajan, "Has financial development made the world riskier?," Proceedings, Federal Reserve Bank of Kansas City, August 2005, 313–369.
5. Justin Lahart, "Mr. Rajan Was Unpopular (But Prescient) at Greenspan Party," *Wall Street Journal*, January 2, 2009, http://online.wsj.com/article/SB123086154114948151.html; and Justin Lahart, "Ignoring the Oracles: You Are With the Free Markets, or Against Them," Real Time Economics [blog], January 1, 2009, http://blogs.wsj.com/economics/2009/01/01/ignoring-the-oracles/.
6. Gillian Tett, "Structured finance explosion may sap power from bankers," *Financial Times*, January 12, 2007, http://www.ft.com/cms/s/9eacd2b8-a1e1–11db–8bc1–0000779e2340.html.
7. Gillian Tett, "The unease bubbling in today's brave new financial world," *Financial Times*, January 19, 2007, http://www.ft.com/cms/s/0/92f7ee6a-a765–11db–83e4–0000779e2340.html.
8. Gillian Tett, "Fed official warns that collateralised debt investors do not understand risks," April 13, 2005, *Financial Times*, http://www.ft.com/cms/s/0/bbb5eaf0-abb8–11d9–893c–00000e2511c8.html.
9. Gillian Tett, "Clouds sighted off CDO asset pool," *Financial Times*, April 18, 2005, http://www .ft.com/cms/s/1/457d7ab8-b03d–11d9-ab98–00000e2511c8.html.
10. Ibid.
11. Ibid.
12. Martin Wolf, "Equities look overvalued, but where is the turning point?," *Financial Times*, March 6, 2007, http://www.ft.com/cms/s/2f0dbc36-cc13–11db-a661–000b5df10621.html.
13. Krishna Guha, "Little evidence of subprime spillover," *Financial Times*, March 28, 2007, http:// www.ft.com/cms/s/88eecfe4-dcc9–11db-a21d–000b5df10621.html.
14. Timothy Geithner, "Credit Markets Innovations and Their Implications," speech, 2007 Credit Markets Symposium hosted by the Federal Reserve Bank of Richmond, Charlotte, N.C., March 23, 2007, available at http://www.newyorkfed.org/newsevents/speeches/2007/gei070323.html.
15. *Bank Credit Analyst*, quoted in Irving Fisher, "Out of Keynes's shadow," *The Economist*, February 12, 2009, http://www.economist.com/businessfinance/displayStory.cfm?story_id=13104022.
16. Ben S. Bernanke, "The Economic Outlook," testimony before the Joint Economic Committee, U.S. Congress, Washington, D.C., May 5, 2009, available at http://www.federalreserve.gov/news events/testimony/bernanke20090505a.htm.
17. Tim Duy, "When Does Faith in Financial Engineering Wane?," Tim Duy's Fed Watch [blog], March 1, 2009, http://economistsview.typepad.com/timduy/2009/03/when-does-faith-in-financial-engineering-wane.html.

18.   Izabella Kaminska, "The dollar shortage problem, evaluated," FT Alphaville [blog], August 5, 2009, http://ftalphaville.ft.com/blog/2009/08/05/65406/the-dollar-shortage-problem-evaluated/.

19.   As discussed in chapter 10, the Office of the Special Inspector General of the Troubled Assets Relief Program comes up with the even larger tally of $23.7 trillion; Mark Pittman and Bob Ivry, "Financial Rescue Nears GDP as Pledges Top $12.8 Trillion," Bloomberg.com, March 31, 2009, http://www.bloomberg.com/apps/news?pid=20601087&sid=armOzfkwtCA4&refer=home.

20.   Timothy R. Homan, "Job Losses in U.S. Slow as Unemployment Climbs to 26-Year High," Bloomberg.com, September 5, 2009, http://www.bloomberg.com/apps/news?pid=newsarchive&sid=aVmZJLQoKv2g.

21.   Martin Crutsinger, "Fed Reports Record Fall In Household Net Worth," Huffington Post [blog], March 12, 2009, http://www.huffingtonpost.com/2009/03/12/fed-reports-record-fall-i_n_174352.html.

22.   Ambrose Evans-Pritchard, "Only a united front at the London G20 can save the world from ruin," *Telegraph,* March 28, 2009, http://www.telegraph.co.uk/finance/comment/ambroseevans_pritchard/5067491/Only-a-united-front-at-the-London-G20-can-save-the-world-from-ruin.html.

23.   "IMF Note on Global Economic Policies and Prospects," March 19, 2009, executive summary and full text available at http://www.imf.org/external/np/g20/031909a.htm.

24.   Stanley White, "Japan exports dip, stimulus effect may be waning," Reuters, August 26, 2009, http://www.reuters.com/article/ousiv/idUSTRE57P15720090826.

25.   Carmen M. Reinhart and Kenneth S. Rogoff, "Is the 2007 US Sub-Prime Financial Crisis so Different? An International Historical Comparison," *American Economic Review,* American Economic Association, vol. 98(2), 339–44, May 2008, http://www.nber.org/papers/w13761.pdf; and Carmen M. Reinhart and Kenneth S. Rogoff, "The Aftermath of Financial Crises," December 19, 2008, paper presented at the American Economics Association, http://www.economics.harvard.edu/faculty/rogoff/files/Aftermath.pdf.

26.   String theory is a notable exception, but that has caused consternation both within and outside the discipline of physics.

27.   Simon Kuznets, "National Income, 1929–1932," 1934, 73rd Cong., 2d ses., 124, 7. Note that the "Nobel" prize winners referred to throughout are recipients of the Sveriges Riksbank Prize in Economic Sciences in Memory of Alfred Nobel. This award was not one of the ones set forth in the will of Alfred Nobel, but these honorees participate in the same ceremony at which the traditional Nobel prizes are bestowed.

28.   Sean Butler, "Measurement Matters," GPI Atlantic, June 5, 2004, http://www.gpiatlantic.org/clippings/mc_gpi01.htm.

29.   Robert F. Kennedy address, University of Kansas, Lawrence, Kansas, March 18, 1968.

30.   Michael Prowse and Amity Shlaes, "Is Inequality Good for You?," *Financial Times Weekend,* December 7–8, 2002.

31.   James Banks, Michael Marmot, Zoe Oldfield, and James P. Smith, "Disease and Disadvantage in the United States and in England," *The Journal of the American Medical Association* 295, no. 17 (May 3, 2006): 2037–2045, http://jama.ama-assn.org/cgi/content/full/295/17/2037; and Mauricio Avendano, Maria Glymour, James Banks, and Johan P. Mackenbach, "Health Disadvantage in US Adults Aged 50 to 74 Years: A Comparison of the Health of Rich and Poor Americans With That of Europeans," *American Journal of Public Health* 99, no. 3 (March 2009): 540–548.

32.   Commission on the Measurement of Economic Performance and Social Progress—Draft Summary, June 2, 2009, http://www.stiglitz-sen-fitoussi.fr/documents/draft_summary.pdf.

33.   Dani Rodrik, "The Globalization Numbers Game," Dani Rodrik's blog, May 7, 2007, http://rodrik.typepad.com/dani_rodriks_weblog/2007/05/the_globalizati.html.

34.   Saijel Kishen, "Scholes's Platinum Grove Fund Halts Withdrawals After Losses," November 6, 2008, Bloomberg.com, http://www.bloomberg.com/apps/news?sid=aWQVwbD5Hfxw&pid=20601087.

35.   "Former Merrill CEO Thain resigns from BofA," MSNBC, January 23, 2009, http://www.msnbc.msn.com/id/28793175/.

36.   "We See Opportunity," Goldman Sachs 2007 Annual Report, 86, available at http://www2.goldmansachs.com/our-firm/investors/financials/archived/annual-reports/attachments/entire-2007-annual-report.pdf.

37.   Alex Berenson, "A Year Later, Little Change on Wall St.," *The New York Times*, September 11, 2009, http://www.nytimes.com/2009/09/12/business/12change.html.

38.   William Buiter, "If it's broke, fix it–but how?," William Buiter's Maverecon [blog], April 18, 2008, http://blogs.ft.com/maverecon/2008/04/if-its-broke-fix-it-but-how/.

39.   Simon Johnson, "The Quiet Coup," *The Atlantic*, May 2009, http://www.theatlantic.com/doc/200905/imf-advice.

CHAPTER 2

1.   While often attributed to Yogi Berra, some suggest that this quotation should be attributed to the little-known computer scientist Jan L. A. van de Snepscheut or the virtually unknown Chuck Reid.

2.   Grant Smith, "Oil $200 Options Rise 10-Fold in Bet on Higher Crude," *Bloomberg*, January 7, 2008, http://www.bloomberg.com/apps/news?pid=20601087&sid=aERkSvnAUV_U&refer=home.

3.   Edmund Conway, "George Soros: Rocketing Oil Price Is a Bubble," *Telegraph*, May 26, 2008, http://www.telegraph.co.uk/finance/newsbysector/banksandfinance/2790539/George-Soros-rocketing-oil-price-is-a-bubble.html; and Mack Frankfurter, "The Mysterious Case of the Commodity Conundrum, Securitization of Commodities, and Systemic Concerns (Part 3)," *The Market Oracle*, April 30, 2008, http://www.marketoracle.co.uk/Article4526.html.

4.   Daniel Dicker, "One Way to Tame Speculation in Oil Futures," *The Street.com*, June 27, 2008, http://www.thestreet.com/p/_search/rmoney/oil/10423562.html.

5.   Steven Mufson, "Oil Prices Defy Easy Calculation," *Washington Post*, April 11, 2008, http://www.washingtonpost.com/wp-dyn/content/article/2008/04/10/AR2008041003778.html.

6.   Michael Patterson and Elizabeth Stanton, "Oil Rally Topped Dot-Com Craze in Speculators' Mania," *Bloomberg*, June 13, 2008, http://www.bloomberg.com/apps/news?pid=20601087&sid=a9wRqtCtGjZY&refer=home.

7.   Phil Izzo, "Bubble Isn't Big Factor in Inflation," *Wall Street Journal*, May 2, 2008, http://online.wsj.com/article/SB121026120931177437.html.

8.   Paul Krugman, "The Oil Nonbubble," *The New York Times*, May 12, 2008, http://www.nytimes.com/2008/05/12/opinion/12krugman.html; _____, "Fuels on the Hill," *The New York Times*, June 27, 2008, http://www.nytimes.com/2008/06/27/opinion/27krugman.html; and _____, "Speculative Nonsense, Once Again," Conscience of a Liberal [blog], June 23, 2008, http://krugman.blogs.nytimes.com/2008/06/23/speculative-nonsense-once-again/.

9.   Caroline Baum, "World Is 'Drowning in Oil' (Again) After Drought," *Bloomberg*, October 28, 2008, http://www.bloomberg.com/apps/news?pid=newsarchive&sid=aZ_wEtBdohjM.

10.   Ianthe Jeanne Dugan and Alistair MacDonald, "Traders Blamed for Oil Spike," *Wall Street Journal*, July 28, 2009, http://online.wsj.com/article/SB124874574251485689.html.

11.   Prepared Testimony of Philip K. Verleger Jr. to the Permanent Subcommittee on Investigation of the U.S. Senate Committee on Homeland Security and Governmental Affairs and the Subcommittee on Energy of the U.S. Senate Committee on Energy and Natural Resources, December 11, 2007, http://www.petersoninstitute.org/publications/papers/verleger1207.pdf.

12.   Futures prices at expiration are supposed to converge with spot prices when the futures contract expires and, therefore, theoretically there should be no difference.

13.   Robert Mabro, *Dow Jones Newswires*, quoted in Randall Dodd and Jason Hoody, "Learning Our Lessons: A Short History of Market Manipulation and the Public Interest," Financial Policy Forum, April 2, 2002, http://www.financialpolicy.org/DSCSPB3.htm.

14.   Bassam Fattouh, "OPEC Pricing Power: The Need for a New Perspective," Oxford Institute for Energy Studies, WPM 31, March 2007, http://www.oxfordenergy.org/pdfs/WPM31.pdf.

15.   Thomas Ferguson, *Golden Rule: The Investment Theory of Party Competition and the Logic of Money-Driven Political Systems* (Chicago: University of Chicago Press, 1995), 150–157.

16.   One can argue that this happy result falls short of conclusive proof. The United States had roughly 50% of world GDP when the war ended and was in a unique position, both in its role in helping to rebuild war-torn countries and through its ability to shape postwar institutions and arrangements.

17.   John Maynard Keynes, *The General Theory of Employment, Interest and Money* (London: MacMillan, 1936), v–vi.

18.   John R. Hicks, "IS-LM: An Explanation," *Journal of Post-Keynesian Economics* 3 (1980–1981): 139.

19. Robert Skidelsky, *John Maynard Keynes: The Economist as Saviour, 1920–1937* (Philadelphia: Trans-Atlantic Publications, 1994), 512.

20. "Paul A. Samuelson: The Sveriges Riksbank Prize in Economic Sciences in Memory of Alfred Nobel 1970: Biography," Nobelprize.org, http://nobelprize.org/nobel_prizes/economics/laureates/1970/samuelson-bio.html.

21. F. A. Hayek, *The Collected Works of F.A. Hayek,* vol. 4, *The Fortunes of Liberalism: Essays on Austrian Economics and the Ideal of Freedom,* ed. Peter G. Klein (Chicago: University of Chicago Press, 1992), [0]p. 5.

22. Arjo Klamer, *Conversations with Economists: New Classical Economists and Opponents Speak Out on the Current Controversy in Macroeconomics* (Totowa, N.J.: Rowman & Allanheld, 1984), 49.

23. Paul Davidson, *The Keynes Solution: The Path to Global Economic Prosperity* (New York: Palgrave Macmillan, 2009), 170, quotes Samuelson: "I asked myself: why do I refuse a paradigm that enables me to understand the Roosevelt upturn form 1933 to 1937? . . . I was content to assume there was enough rigidity in relative wages and prices to make the Keynesian alternative to Walras operative."

24. There were efforts, both by the Hoover administration and business, in the early 1930s, to preserve wage levels. Although most economists now believe they worsened the Depression, they are not a sufficient explanation for why it happened.

25. Paul Davidson, *The Keynes Solution: The Path to Global Economic Prosperity* (New York: Palgrave Macmillan, 2009), 170.

26. David Colander and Harry Landreth, "Political Influence on the Textbook Keynesian Revolution: God, Man, and Laurie [*sic*] Tarshis at Yale," 3, http://community.middlebury.edu/~colander/articles/Political%20Influence%20on%20the%20Textbook%20Keynesian%20Revolution.pdf.

27. Ibid.

28. Davidson, 168.

29. Ibid.

30. Donald M. McCloskey, "Other Things Equal: The A-Prime/C-Prime Theorem," *Eastern Economic Journal* 19, no. 2 (Spring 1993): 235, available at http://deirdremccloskey.org/docs/pdf/Article_287.pdf.

31. Duncan K. Foley, "An Interview with Wassily Leontief," *Macroeconomic Dynamics* 2 (1998): 128.

32. Randy Albelda, Christopher Gunn, and William Waller, *Alternatives to Economic Orthodoxy: A Reader in Political Economy* (Armonk, N.Y.: M.E. Sharpe, 1987), 24; and T. Morgan, "Theory versus empiricism in academic economics: update and comparison," *Journal of Economic Perspectives* 2, no. 1 (1988): 159–164.

33. Foley, 128.

34. "Ergodicity" in fact has a very particular meaning, far narrower that the approximation we use here. Samuelson was invoking it for its implications for statistical analysis, that you could use past data to predict the future. Moreover, his assertion that "rigor" necessitates assuming ergodicity is putting the cart before the horse. Only certain types of physical phenomena in fact are ergodic, and the hard sciences do not attempt to force phenomena into an ergodic template.

35. Greg Davidson and Paul Davidson, *Economics for a Civilized Society,* rev. ed. (Armonk, N.Y.: M.E. Sharpe, 1996), 65.

36. Davidson, 37.

37. William Nack, "The Breaking Point," *Sports Illustrated,* November 1, 1993, http://sportsillustrated.cnn.com/vault/article/magazine/MAG1137939/1/index.htm.

38. Joe Drape, "Derby Nears, but Safety Rules Don't," *The New York Times,* March 23, 2009, http://www.nytimes.com/2009/03/24/sports/othersports/24derby.html.

39. Paul A. Samuelson, "What Classical and Neoclassical Monetary Theory Really Was," *Canadian Journal of Economics* 1 (1968): 11–12; reprinted in R. W. Clower, ed., *Monetary Theory* (Hammondsworth, Middlesex: Penguin, 1969).

40. Notice in this proof that initial conditions mattered and were an explicit part of the problem to be solved.

41. The sensitivity to initial conditions makes this a nonergodic problem. Given that what would seem to be a not-all-that-hard problem was in fact a showstopper because it was nonergodic, one has to again question Samuelson's assertion that "science" is ergodic. It is more accurate to say that real science includes both solvable and unsolvable problems, as does mathematics.

42.   The proof also establishes that the solution is Pareto optimal.

43.   Milton Friedman, "The Methodology of Positive Economics," in *Essays in Positive Economics* (Chicago: University of Chicago Press, 1953), reprinted in Daniel M. Hausman, ed, *The Philosophy of Economics: An Anthology* (New York: Cambridge University Press, 1994), 187–188,

44.   Donald N. McCloskey, *The Rhetoric of Economics*, 2d ed. (Madison, WI: University of Wisconsin Press, 1985), 57–60.

45.   David Card and Alan B. Krueger, "Minimum Wages and Employment: A Case Study of the Fast-Food Industry in New Jersey and Pennsylvania," *American Economic Review* 84, no. 4 (September 1994): 772–793.

46.   Reed Garfield, "Raising the Minimum Wage: The Illusion of Compassion," Report for the Joint Economic Committee, Congress of the United States, April 1996, available at http://www.house .gov/jec/cost-gov/regs/minimum/illusion.htm.

47.   To make the math manageable, economists use only the least random form of randomness in their models, a considerable limitation.

48.   DSGE models are perfectly capable of describing very complex dynamics in response to a shock.

49.   While options do not lock the user into a price, options are much more costly than futures, with longer-dated options far more expensive than shorter-term ones. There are clearly better and worse ways to try to hedge risk, but the fundamental problem is that any hedging strategy entails some assumptions as to what the future might hold and how to best protect against it. Recognizing a risk late may make any hedging strategy too costly to be productive.

50.   Satyajit Das, "OTC Derivative Regulation Proposals—Neat, Plausible and Wrong!" Satyajit Das's Blog: Fear & Loathing in Financial Products, July 17, 2009, http://www.wilmott.com/blogs/ satyajitdas/index.cfm/2009/7/17/OTC-Derivative-Regulation-Proposals—Neat-Plausible-and-Wrong.

51.   Richard Lipsey and Kelvin Lancaster, "The General Theory of Second Best," *The Review of Economic Studies* 24, no. 1 (1956–1957): 11–32.

52.   We are using the term "optimum" but note the optimum is a Pareto optimum, meaning no one can be made better off in material terms without making someone else worse off. Note that that includes situations that most people would not consider optimal in any broader sense, such as one person having all the wealth in the world while everyone else starves.

53.   There is ample evidence that emerging economies do better to erect barriers around infant industries until they have developed sufficiently to compete in international markets.

54.   In fairness, development economists have done a fair bit of real-world study to ascertain what policy mixes seem to work best. However, many fundamental issues, like how active a role government should play, are hotly debated within that community.

55.   Mark Blaug, "Disturbing Currents in Modern Economics," *Challenge* 41, no. 3 (1998a): 13–17.

56.   E. Roy Weintraub, *How Economics Became a Mathematical Science* (Durham, N.C.: Duke University Press, 2007), 261–262.

57.   Paul Neurath, *From Malthus to the Club of Rome and Back: Problems of Limits to Growth, Population Control, and Migrations* (Armonk, N.Y.: M.E. Sharpe, 1994), 63.

58.   Ibid., 64.

59.   Haynes Bonner Johnson, *Sleepwalking through History: America in the Reagan Years* (New York: Norton, 1991; reprint edition with new foreword and afterword, 2003), 129. Citations are to the 2003 edition.

60.   Publishing a paper that manages to reconcile aspects of these theories is not the same as integrating them into a well-elaborated paradigm. We'll discuss in chapter 5 how other attempts to explain behavior that makes no sense in the neoclassical paradigm, like gift giving, have the effect of stripping the theories of predictive power.

61.   George A. Akerlof, "The Market for 'Lemons': Quality Uncertainty and the Market Mechanism," *Quarterly Journal of Economics* 84, no. 3 (1970): 488–500.

62.   Barry Eichengreen, "The Last Temptation of Risk," *The National Interest*, April 30, 2009, http:// www.nationalinterest.org/Article.aspx?id=21274.

63.   Dani Rodrik, "Blame Economists, Not Economics," *Guatemala Times*, March 11, 2009, http://www .guatemala-times.com/opinion/syndicated/roads-to-prosperity/887-blame-the-economists-not-economics.html.

64. Peter Dorman, "Economics Was OK, It Was Only the Economists who Failed (Disputed)," EconoSpeak [blog], May 10, 2009, http://econospeak.blogspot.com/2009/05/economics-was-ok-it-was-only-economists.html.

65. While some models appear to incorporate these considerations, they do so only in narrow contexts and neuter or ignore them elsewhere. In other words, a paper will deal with a single phenomenon that is vexing to neoclassical economics and keep the rest of the assumptions intact. To illustrate: some agency models include a cost of effort that managers incorporate into their maximization problem, accommodating laziness to some degree. Models of agency costs do let agents maximize subject to the temptation to cheat and be lazy. But this falls right into Dorman's critique: when economists are focusing on agency cost, they incorporate the other conventional assumptions about firm behavior wholesale. But models that focus on anything other than agency cost will fail to include slothful, greedy managers. This style of paper, which shows that newfangled economic theories can still happily cohabit with neoclassical economics, provided you do it one issue at a time and don't require it to be incorporated into the model, has become an important genre. Yet as Dorman describes, the corpse marches on in the negative space of all the piecemeal attempts to kill it.

66. Study cited in Stanford University, "Economists Discuss Relevance of Their Profession," press release, February 11, 1997, Stanford University, http://news.stanford.edu/pr/97/970212state ofeco.html.

67. Ibid.

68. Foley, 121, 128.

69. William Easterly, "Empirics of Strategic Interdependence: The Case of the Racial Tipping Point," National Bureau of Economic Research Working Paper Series, Working Paper 15069, June 2009, available at http://www.nyu.edu/fas/institute/dri/Easterly/File/NBER_empirics_strategic.pdf.

70. Henry Kaufman, "Our Risky New Financial Markets," Wall Street Journal, August 15, 2007, http://online.wsj.com/article/SB118714343807498116.html.

71. Heilbroner, in his *Behind the Veil of Economics: Essays in the Worldly Philosophy* (New York: Norton, 1989), defined economics as "the process by which society marshals and coordinates the activities required for its provisioning," and noted that "the economy" was a distinct part of a larger "society" (14). Studies of the sort mentioned by Leonhardt serve to blur those distinctions.

72. Quoted in Stanford University press release, "Economists discuss relevance of their profession."

73. Jon Elster, "Excessive Ambitions," in his *Capitalism and Society* (forthcoming, September 2009), 26 of author draft.

74. William Easterly, "Maybe we should put rats in charge of foreign aid," Aid Watch [blog], May 7, 2009, http://blogs.nyu.edu/fas/dri/aidwatch/2009/05/maybe_we_should_put_rats_in_ch.html.

75. Alan Gerber and Neil Malhotra, "Can Political Science Literatures Be Believed? A Study of Publication Bias in the *APSR* and the *AJPS*," Washington University in St. Louis (paper available at http://polmeth.wustl.edu/retrieve.php?id=640), quoted in Kevin Drum, "Lies, Damn Lies, and . . . . ," Political Animal by Steve Benen [blog], September 20, 2006, http://www.washington monthly.com/archives/individual/2006_09/009531.php.

76. Jon Elster, "Excessive Ambitions," in *Capitalism and Society* (forthcoming, September 2009), 19 of author draft.

77. Daniel Ellsberg, *Secrets: A Memoir of Vietnam and the Pentagon Papers* (New York: Viking Penguin, 2002[0]), 237–238.

78. Ibid., 348.

79. Susan Webber, "The Incredible Shrinking Corporation," *Across the Board* (November/December 2005): 53, available at http://www.auroraadvisors.com/articles/Shrinking.pdf.

80. William Buiter, "More on robbing the US tax payer and debauching the FDIC and the Fed," William Buiter's Maverecon [blog], March 26, 2009, http://blogs.ft.com/maverecon/2009/03/more-on-robbing-the-us-tax-payer-and-debauching-the-fdic-and-the-fed/.

CHAPTER 3

1. Peter Thal Larsen, "Goldman pays the price of being big," *Financial Times*, August 13, 2007, http://www.ft.com/cms/s/0/d2121cb6–49cb–11dc–9ffe–0000779fd2ac.html.

2. Ibid.

3. Paul De Grauwe, Leonardo Iania, and Pablo Rovira Kaltwasser, "How Abnormal Was the Stock Market in October 2008?" *Eurointelligence,* November 11, 2008, http://www.eurointelligence .com/article.581+M5f21b8d26a3.0.html.

4. John Dizard, "Switching boats in midstream to ride out credit storm," *Financial Times,* August 14, 2007, http://www.ft.com/cms/s/0/0739ecac–49fe–11dc–9ffe–0000779fd2ac.html.

5. Benoit Mandelbrot and Richard L. Hudson, *The (Mis)behavior of Markets: A Fractal View of Risk, Ruin, and Reward* (New York: Basic Books, 2006), 44–45.

6. Pearson's work cited in Jaume Masoliver, Miquel Montero, Josep Perelló, and George H. Weiss, "The Continuous Time Random Walk Formalism in Financial Markets," *Journal of Economic Behavior and Organization* 61, no. 4 (December 2006): 577–598.

7. While Samuelson believed that financial markets were "micro efficient," meaning it was hard to beat the market via securities selection, he thought they were "macro inefficient," meaning the market as a whole could be mispriced and it would be possible to act on that observation, whether from a profit or policy standpoint.

8. Donald MacKenzie, *An Engine, Not a Camera: How Financial Models Shape Markets* (Cambridge, Mass.: MIT Press, 2008), 46.

9. Mandelbrot and Hudson, 66.

10. MacKenzie, 50–51.

11. MacKenzie, 51–52.

12. "Derivatives Strategy Hall of Fame 1997," *Derivatives Strategy,* March 1997, http://www .derivativesstrategy.com/magazine/archive/1997/0397fea1.asp.

13. There are also higher order derivatives that affect option pricing, but they generally come into play when hedging trading books or trying to find profit opportunities to exploit.

14. Remember that an investor does not have to exercise the option to profit. If the value of an option has increased due to favorable price movements, the investor can simply sell it.

15. MacKenzie, 160.

16. Nassim Nicholas Taleb, *The Black Swan: The Impact of the Highly Improbable* (New York: Random House, 2007), 297.

17. MacKenzie, 5.

18. Ibid., 39, 71.

19. Ibid., 70.

20. J. Poterba and L. Summers, "Mean reversion in stock returns: evidence and implications," *Journal of Financial Economics* 22 (1988): 27–60.

21. L. H. Summers, "On Economics and Finance," *Journal of Finance* 40, no. 3 (July 1985): 633–635.

22. MacKenzie, 141–142.

23. Ross, 322.

24. Bernstein, xix–xx. This is an exaggeration. Option theory has not pervaded land sales, New York's jewelry district, an active trading market with a form of repos, nor the art market, to name a few of many exceptions.

25. There are some obvious flaws with this division of responsibility. First, asset allocations are based on correlation models, which, as we will discuss, are flawed. Second, allocation changes tend to be on an arbitrary timetable, usually driven by organizational timetables. The third flaw is that the investment manager is closer to opportunities in the markets he covers and is probably better able than the fund manager to decide whether it is preferable to be fully invested in his sector or to have a high cash allocation.

26. MacKenzie, 254.

27. ADP, Exxon Mobil, Johnson & Johnson, and Microsoft.

28. MacKenzie, 106–107.

29. Ibid., 108.

30. Ibid., 112–113.

31. Paul Samuelson, "Efficient Portfolio Selection for Pareto-Lévy Investments," *Journal of Financial and Quantitative Analysis* 2, 107–122; Robert Blattberg and Thomas Sargent, 1971, "Regression With Non-Gaussian Stable Disturbances: Some Sampling Results," *Econometrica,* 39 (1967): 501–510.

32. MacKenzie, 113.

33. Paul Cootner, ed., *The Random Character of Stock Market Prices* (Cambridge, Mass.: MIT Press, 1964), 337.

34. MacKenzie, 115.

35. William Sharpe, quoted in Steve Keen, *Debunking Economics: The Naked Emperor of the Social Sciences* (Australia: Pluto Press, 2002), 233.

36. Eugene Fama and Kenneth French, "The Cross-Section of Expected Stock Returns," *Journal of Finance* 47 (June 1992): 427–465.

37. Peter L. Bernstein, *Capital Ideas Evolving* (New York: John Wiley & Sons, 2007), 94.

38. Ibid., 100–103.

39. Roger Lowenstein, *When Genius Failed: The Rise and Fall of Long-Term Capital Management* (New York: Random House, 2001), 28, 31.

40. Satyajit Das, "The More Things Change. . . . Amaranth," Satyajit Das's Blog: Fear & Loathing in Financial Products, January 26, 2007, http://www.wilmott.com/blogs/satyajitdas/index.cfm/2007/1/26/Fear-and-Loathing-in-Derivatives—The-More-Things-ChangeAmaranth.

41. MacKenzie, 138.

42. Lowenstein, 196.

43. President's Working Group on Financial Markets, "Hedge Funds, Leverage, and the Lessons of Long-Term Capital Management," report, April 1999, 12.

44. There is some dispute over LTCM's risk management failures. Roger Lowenstein contends that the causes were multiple short vol bets plus sheer punting, where LTCM took point-of-view positions in markets in which it had no information advantage. Donald MacKenzie argues that the LTCM principals were prudent, using VaR based on five years of data (!) plus running stress tests on more extreme events. But those were single-market calamities, not the multi-market storm of 1998.

45. Saijel Kishan, "Scholes's Platinum Grove Fund Halts Withdrawals After Losses," *Bloomberg*, November 6, 2008, http://www.bloomberg.com/apps/news?sid=aWQVwbD5Hfxw&pid=20601087.

46. Bess Levin, "Layoffs Watch: Platinum Grove," Dealbreaker [blog], November 11, 2008, http://www.dealbreaker.com/2008/11/layoffs-watch-platinum-grove.php.

47. Katherine Burton and Saijel Kishan, "Meriwether Said to Shut JWM Hedge Fund After Losses," *Bloomberg*, July 8, 2009, http://www.bloomberg.com/apps/news?pid=newsarchive&sid=aN2lwUiCKGMM.

48. Satyajit Das, "The More Things Change. . . . Amaranth," Satyajit Das's Blog: Fear & Loathing in Financial Products, January 26, 2007, http://www.wilmott.com/blogs/satyajitdas/index.cfm/2007/1/26/Fear-and-Loathing-in-Derivatives—The-More-Things-ChangeAmaranth.

49. David X. Li, "On default correlation: A copula function approach," *Journal of Fixed Income* 9 (2000): 43–54.

50. Felix Salmon, "Recipe for Disaster: The Formula That Killed Wall Street," *Wired*, February 23, 2009, http://www.wired.com/techbiz/it/magazine/17–03/wp_quant?currentPage=all.

51. Barry Ritholtz, "Misunderstanding Prediction Market Failures," The Big Picture [blog], February 14, 2007, http://bigpicture.typepad.com/comments/2007/02/misunderstandin.html.

52. Felix Salmon, "Recipe for Disaster: The Formula That Killed Wall Street," *Wired*, February 23, 2009, http://www.wired.com/techbiz/it/magazine/17–03/wp_quant?currentPage=all.

53. Ibid.

54. Ibid.

55. Abigail Moses, Hamish Risk, and Neil Unmack, "Credit Swaps Thwart Fed's Ease as Debt Costs Surge," *Bloomberg*, March 6, 2008, http://www.bloomberg.com/apps/news?pid=20601109&sid=aB8RuoKZoKRM&refer=home.

56. Ibid.

57. Geraud Charpin, "View of the day: Credit markets," *Financial Times*, April 30, 2008, http://www.ft.com/cms/s/0/370d9b26–16be–11dd-bbfc–0000779fd2ac.html.

58. GARCH, which is Generalized Auto Regressive Conditional Heteroscedasticity. It is an econometric model that is used to forecast volatility of the returns on stock price. It uses past variances to estimate current variances, and hence suffers from "the past may not be a good proxy for the future" shortcomings endemic within financial economics.

59. Nassim Nicholas Taleb, "The Fourth Quadrant: A Map of the Limits of Statistics," Technical Appendix, *Edge*, September 15, 2008, http://www.edge.org/3rd_culture/taleb08/taleb08_index.html.

60.   Investors can use leverage to create portfolios superior to ones on the efficient investment frontier.

61.   Lucas Ayres, B. de C. Barros, and Alexandre Di Miceli Da Silveira, "Overconfidence, Managerial Optimism and the Determinants of Capital Structure," Working Paper, February 2007, available at http://ssrn.com/abstract=953273.

62.   Mark Simon, Susan M. Houghton, and Karl Aquino, "Cognitive Biases, Risk Perception, and Venture Formation: How Individuals Decide to Start Companies," *Journal of Business Venturing* 15, no. 2 (March 2000): 113–134.

63.   Lowenstein, 176–177.

CHAPTER 4

1.   Donald MacKenzie and Yuval Millo, "Constructing a Market, Performing Theory: The Historical Sociology of a Financial Derivatives Exchange," *American Journal of Sociology* 109 (2003): 110–115.

2.   Jeremy Bentham, *An Introduction to the Principles of Morals and Legislation*, ed. J.H. Burns and H.L.A. Hart (1970; reprint, London: Methuen, 1982), 12.

3.   Bentham took the term from Hume, but defined it not in terms of external impact but subjective outcomes.

4.   Critics charge this theory has been roundly disproven, as shown by how slowly the economy reacts to new information. For instance, if rational expectations were valid, the U.S. economy would have shown much more rapid disinflation after the Volcker-administered money supply tightening, not the gradual disinflation that resulted.

5.   Keynes did not originate this observation; it dates back to at least Bernard Mandeville's "Fable of the Bees" in 1705.

6.   Wayne Shafer and Hugo Sonnenschein, "Market Demand and Excess Demand Functions," in *Handbook of Mathematical Economics, ed.* Kenneth J. Arrow and Michael D. Intriligator, v. 3, (North-Holland, Amsterdam, 1993), 672.

7.   Christopher D. Carroll, "Requiem for the Representative Consumer? Aggregate Implications of Microeconomic Consumption Behavior," *American Economic Review* 90, no. 2 (May 2000): 110–115.

8.   Other fundamental criticisms come from C. E. Ferguson and Geoffrey Colin Harcourt. The underlying debate was the "Cambridge capital controversy" of the 1960s, which pitted Sraffa and the University of Cambridge's Joan Robinson, against American economists like Paul Samuelson and Robert Solow on the question of whether "capital" can possibly exist as something separate in the economy. If it can't, then its value cannot determine profits, which in turn means marginal rates of return have no meaning. The result is the neoclassical model works only under constant returns to scale, which is clearly not the case. You can do general equilibrium models provided there is no "capital"—just a mess of different goods with all kinds of rates of returns.

9.   Economists may argue that their notion of "reason" is less stringent than the layperson's concept and extends only to maximization of subjective expected utility. But "maximizing subjective expected utility" means knowing your own personal utility function and your own probability distribution (as in what you assess the odds of various future events to be). But evidence against this argument goes back to experiments by decisions theorists in the 1950s and 1960s, such as Maurice Ailias in 1953 and Daniel Ellsberg in 1961, of normative preferences trumping reality. Put it another way, people are not good enough at math, nor do they tend to employ it enough in routine decisions for them to maximize expected subjective utility. And of course, behavioral economists, starting with David Kahneman and Amos Twersky, widely considered the fathers of behavioral economics, showed irrationality via the impact of framing.

10.   Herbert Alexander Simon, *The Sciences of the Artificial*, 3d ed. (Cambridge, Mass.: MIT Press, 1996), 81.

11.   Ibid., 61.

12.   Herbert A. Simon, "From Substantive to Procedural Rationality" (1976). In *Method and Appraisal in Economics*, edited by Spiro J. Latsis (New York: Cambridge University Press, 1980), 135.

13.   Frank Knight, *Risk, Uncertainty and Profit* (1921; reprint, Chicago: University of Chicago Press, 1971), 19–20.

14.   Corry Azzi and Ronald Ehrenberg, "Household Allocation of Time and Church Attendance," *Journal of Political Economy* 83, no. 1 (1975): 28.

15. John P. Laitner, "Bequests, Golden-age Capital Accumulation and Government Debt," *Economica,* 46, no. 84 (1979): 403.

16. K.E. Boulding, "Review of collard, altruism and economy: A study in non-selfish economics," *Journal of Political Economy* 87, no. 6 (1979): 1383.

17. Schefrin, 3.

18. Amartya Sen, "Rational Fools," *Philosophy and Public Affairs* 6 (1977): 331–332.

19. Study by Robert Feldman cited in David Livingstone Smith, "Natural-Born Liars," *Scientific American,* June 2005, http://www.scientificamerican.com/article.cfm?id=natural-born-liars.

20. Theodore Gray, "For that Healthy Glow, Drink Radiation!," *Popular Science,* August 17, 2004, http://www.popsci.com/scitech/article/2004–08/healthy-glow-drink-radiation.

21. Robin Marris and Dennis C. Mueller, "The Corporation, Competition, and the Invisible Hand," *Journal of Economic Literature* 18, no. 1 (1980): 32.

22. Amitai Etzioni, *Moral Dimension: Toward a New Economics* (New York: Free Press, 1988), 137.

23. William Kornhauser, *The Politics of Mass Society* (1959; reprint, New Brunswick, N.J.: Transaction Publishers, 2008).

24. George J. Stigler, "Competition," in *International Encyclopedia of Social Sciences,* ed. William A. Darity (New York: Macmillan, 1968, 3), 181.

25. Adam Smith considered education an essential public good.

26. An oft-discussed halfway house is John M. Clark's "workable competition," first published in 1940, and influential in the Eisenhower administration, as embodied in the "pretending to be neutral but really not" 1955 *Report of the Attorney General's National Committee to Study Anti-Trust Laws.* The report echoed Clark's position that less-than-perfect competition was "workable" if it was preferable to the next best option (ahem, how do you prove that? Can we go visit an economy in a parallel universe?), if its market power was not "excessive" (a subjective judgment), and if it produced more benefit than harm. The problem is that this theory, invoked to support an antitrust policy that was friendlier to large corporate interests, rested on research by Clark dating back to 1923 that found that trade associations that "exchanged information" managed to avoid "ruinous competition." The problem is that you can't have it both ways in the neoclassical paradigm. If you allow for sellers to avoid "ruinous competition" you have allowed for coordination, which, while it may be perfectly legal, clearly does shift power back to producers. Trying to permit sellers to blunt competition effectively acknowledges the unacknowledged problem above: that the world of perfect competition, a mainstay of many economic models, is a disastrously unappetizing setting for businesses, and they will take whatever steps they can to move away from that position.

27. Richard Lipsey and Kelvin Lancaster, "The General Theory of Second Best," *The Review of Economic Studies* 24, no. 1 (1956–1957): 11.

CHAPTER 5

1. Luigi Zingales, "Capitalism After the Crisis," *National Affairs,* no. 1 (fall 2009), http://www.nationalaffairs.com/publications/detail/capitalism-after-the-crisis.

2. Daniel B. Klein and Charlotta Stern, "Is There a Free-Market Economist in the House? The Policy Views of American Economic Association Members," *American Journal of Economics and Sociology* 66, no. 2 (April 2007): 314–315.

3. Ben Goldacre, "Funding and Findings: The Impact Factor," *Guardian,* February 14, 2009, http://www.guardian.co.uk/commentisfree/2009/feb/14/bad-science-medical-research.

4. Klein and Stern, "Is There a Free-Market Economist in the House? The Policy Views of American Economic Association Members," 315.

5. Ibid., 328–329.

6. Robert L. Heilbroner, *Behind the Veil of Economics: Essays in the Worldly Philosophy* (New York: Norton, 1989), 72.

7. Ferguson, 1995, 35.

8. "The Pragmatic Professor," *Time,* March 3, 1961, http://www.time.com/time/magazine/article/0,9171,897654–1,00.html.

9. "The Day of the Bear," *Time,* June 8, 1962, http://www.time.com/time/magazine/article/0,9171,896282,00.html.

10. It is worth noting that the social programs were more widely accepted in the past than they are portrayed in retrospect. Friedman himself advocated a negative income tax, which Richard Nixon backed but was unable to get enacted into law, as more efficient than welfare.

11. Davidson, 2009, 176.

12. Ibid.

13. H. Scott Gordon, "The Economic Theory of a Common-Property Resource: The Fishery," *Journal of Political Economy*, 62 (1954): 124–142.

14. Michael Lewis, "Wall Street on the Tundra," *Vanity Fair*, April 2009, http://www.vanityfair.com/politics/features/2009/04/iceland200904.

15. Amar Bhidé, "Efficient Markets, Deficient Government," *Harvard Business Review* (November– December 1994): 129; online version available at http://hbr.harvardbusiness.org/1994/11/efficient-markets-deficient-governance/ar/1.

16. Most Americans choose to forget the enormous boost the U.S. pharmaceutical industry gets from the research funded by the National Institutes of Health (NIH), or the priority given in trade negotiations to opening capital markets, an opportunity promptly exploited by leading U.S. players.

17. It goes without saying that Japan has not been as astute in devising policies for its financial sector.

18. Keynesians argue that monetary policy is ineffective in a depression, while monetarists believe that steady growth in the money supply will prevent depressions from happening.

19. Paul Volcker (chairman of the Fed from 1979 to 1987) used money supply targets in his efforts to beat back inflation in the early 1980s. This was a radical experiment, since the monetary authority had previously pegged interest rates. The central bank under Volcker instead focused primarily on M1, which is designed to measure funds that are easy to spend, and includes currency in circulation and checking account deposits.

     Central banks for the most part had not tried this approach before because how much money supply increases or decreases affect the economy also depends on the velocity of money (crudely, how quickly do people spend money once they have it) and that is not stable. But the central bank had political reasons for trying this approach too, since a change signaled tough-mindedness to investors. However, Volcker found it hard to meet his targets, and a difficult situation was made worse by the growth of new products that by today's standards are simple, like the interest-paying "negotiated order of withdrawal" account, a new type of bank deposit. NOW accounts, which paid interest but also allowed limited check writing, did not fit neatly into the traditional categories like M1 versus the next broader measure, M2, which include M1 plus "close substitutes" like savings deposits. By 1982, the relationship between M1 and key economic variables like inflation and growth had broken down completely.

20. "The Intellectual Provocateur," *Time*, December 19, 1969, http://www.time.com/time/magazine/article/0,9171,941753,00.html; Friedman did believe government should provide some public goods.

21. Felipe Moreno, "Silent Revolution: An Early Export from Pinochet's Chile," *GCG Georgetown University* 2, no. 2 (2008): 92.

22. Milton Friedman, "Free Markets and the Generals," *Newsweek*, January 25, 1982, 59.

23. Greg Palast, "Tinker Bell, Pinochet and The Fairy Tale Miracle of Chile," 2006, http://www.gregpalast.com/tinker-bell-pinochet-and-the-fairy-tale-miracle-of-chile–2/.

24. Moreno, 93.

25. Allende also suffered opposition from the Left when he wavered on his reforms.

26. Ibid., 94.

27. Sources vary remarkably on the true economic performance during this period. Some accounts claim 30% GDP growth from 1975 to 1979, others assert a 13% fall. The World Bank shows a nearly 15% decline in 1975, followed by 4.1% growth in 1976, 8.6% growth in 1977, 7.5% growth in 1978, and 8.7% growth in 1979. There is also disagreement on the depth of the 1982–1983 depression.

28. Michel Duquette, "The Chilean Economic Miracle Revisited," *Journal of Socio-Economics* 27, no. 3 (1998): 299–321.

29. Palast.

30. George A. Akerlof and Paul M. Romer, "Looting: The Economic Underworld of Bankruptcy for Profit," Brookings Papers on Economic Activity 24, Brookings Institute, Washington, D.C., 1993 18–23.

31. Duquette.

32. Moreno, 94.

33. Duquette.

34. Palast.

35. Joseph Stiglitz, interview, *Commanding Heights: The Battle for the World Economy* (PBS), undated, transcript available at http://www.pbs.org/wgbh/commandingheights/shared/minitextlo/int _josephstiglitz.html.

36. Ibid.

37. Social programs have grown since the 1990s. Chile's former finance minister attributes 40% of poverty reduction to these efforts.

38. Moreno, 94.

39. Galeano quoted in Stephanie Rosenfeld, "The Myth of the Chilean Miracle," *Multinational Monitor,* August 9, 1998, http://www.multinationalmonitor.org/hyper/issues/1994/08/mm0894_12 .html.

40. Franklin Foer, "Russia's Sick Economy," *Slate,* June 7, 1998, http://www.slate.com/id/1097/.

41. Joseph E. Stiglitz, "Whither Reform: Ten Years of the Transition," (keynote address, World Bank Annual Bank Conference on Development Economics, Washington, D.C., April 28 30, 1999) 1, available at http://siteresources.worldbank.org/INTABCDEWASHINGTON1999/Resources/ stiglitz.pdf

42. Bernard Black, Reinier Kraakman, and Anna Tarassova, "Russian Privatization and Corporate Governance: What Went Wrong?," *Stanford Law Review* 52 (2000): 1731–1808.

43. David McClintick, "How Harvard Lost Russia," *Institutional Investor Magazine,* Americas and International Editions, January 24, 2006, available at http://jboy.chaosnet.org/misc/docs/articles/ shleifer.pdf.

44. Joseph E. Stiglitz, "Whither Reform: Ten Years of the Transition," (keynote address, World Bank Annual Bank Conference on Development Economics, Washington, D.C., April 28 30, 1999) 3, available at http://siteresources.worldbank.org/INTABCDEWASHINGTON1999/Resources/ stiglitz.pdf

45. Bernard S. Black, Renier H. Kraakman, and Anna Tarassova, 2000, "Russian Privatization and Corporate Governance: What Went Wrong?" *Stanford Law Review,* 52: 1731, available at http:// ssrn.com/abstract=181348 or doi:10.2139/ssrn.181348

46. The move to demonize the New Deal and unions is ironic. Contrary to revisionist history, Roosevelt had considerable business support from a "multinational power block," a coalition of internationally oriented commercial banks, investment banks, and capital intensive industries, in their day the innovative, internationally oriented enterprises using advanced management practices. These groups all had reason to prefer more social welfare and better union rights as the price of social stability (1934 saw widespread labor strife and a near breakdown of the conservative craft union the American Federation of Labor, because of the fear that it would be supplanted by Communist-leaning elements). More stability made for a better climate for investment. The capital-intensive firms, for which labor was a not-overly-large component of total production costs and which had a need for ready access to the financial markets, saw that tradeoff as favorable to them.

    Similarly, the Glass-Steagall Act, which separated commercial and investment banking, is now popularly depicted as a victory of the little guy over big finance. In fact, it was promoted by the Rockefeller interests, and the smaller investment banks allied to break the dominant position of the House of Morgan (which was forced to split into the bank J.P. Morgan and the investment bank Morgan Stanley). See Ferguson, 1995, 117 and 148–149.

47. David Brock, *The Republican Noise Machine: Right Wing Media and How it Corrupts America* (New York: Three Rivers Press, 2004), 40.

48. Ibid., 42.

49. John S. Saloma III, *Ominous Politics: The New Conservative Labyrinth* (New York: Farrar, Strauss and Giroux, 1984), 66–67.

50. Ibid., 8, 15–16.

51. Ibid., 22.

52. David Dickson and David Noble, "By Force of Reason: The Politics of Science and Technology Policy," in *The Hidden Election: Politics and Economics in the 1980 Presidential Campaign,* ed. Thomas Ferguson and Joel Rogers (New York: Pantheon, 1981), p. 261.

53. Ibid., 270.
54. Ibid., 272.
55. Ibid., 274.
56. Note this theme came in concert with a push to restrict the rights of labor and reduce government services. Yet if deregulation were to produce the gains in productivity that the proponents said it would, query why labor and services would have to suffer.
57. Steve Teles, *The Rise of the Conservative Legal Movement: The Battle for Control Over the Law* (Princeton, N.J.: Princeton University Press, 2008), 103.
58. Dickson and Noble, 270.
59. Teles, 107.
60. "Judges Get a Crash Course in Economics," *Fortune Magazine*, May 21, 1979.
61. Saloma, 76.
62. Teles, 216–217.
63. Ibid., 217–218.

CHAPTER 6

1. Technically, the issue was not simply one of models as most people think of them, which is that they are static tools and people plug numbers into them. In those days, to price a complex derivative meant you had to know how you would hedge the risk, and that was not trivial. My client O'Connor would find it could take as much as week to figure out how to price a complex derivative, and in some cases, BT could not even come up with a price. However, it is not clear the trades that resulted in these losses were all that daunting; they were simply beyond the skill level of the clients.
2. Frank Partnoy, *Infectious Greed: How Deceit and Risk Corrupted the Financial Markets* (New York: Macmillan, 2003), 50–51.
3. Parnoy, 2003, 53.
4. Kelley Holland and Linda Himelstein, "The Bankers Trust Tapes," *Business Week,* October 16, 1995, http://www.businessweek.com/1995/42/b34461.htm.
5. Timothy L. O'Brien, "The Deep Slush at Bankers Trust," *The New York Times,* May 30, 1999, http://www.nytimes.com/1999/05/30/business/the-deep-slush-at-bankers-trust.html?scp=1&sq=he%20Deep%20Slush%20at%20Bankers%20Trust&st=cse.
6. John Maynard Keynes, *The General Theory of Employment, Interest and Money* (London: MacMillan, 1936), 176.
7. Partnoy, 1999, 82.
8. Ibid., 188.
9. Ibid., 1999, 185–186.
10. Ibid., 194.
11. Ibid., 78–79.
12. Ibid., 179.
13. Nomi Prins, *It Takes a Pillage: Behind the Bailouts, Bonuses, and Backroom Deals from Washington to Wall Street* (Hoboken, N.J.: John Wiley & Sons, 2009), 118.
14. Eric J. Weiner, *What Goes Up: The Uncensored History of Modern Wall Street as Told by the Bankers, Brokers, CEOs, and Scoundrels Who Made It Happen* (New York: Little, Brown, and Company, 2005), 110.
15. Many commercial banks clearly issued bonds and stocks as part of their capital structure, while most savings and loans then were mutuals.
16. Myron Kandel, "Cannibals at Work," *The New York Times,* May 10, 1987, http://www.nytimes.com/1987/05/10/books/cannibals-at-work.html.
17. If you don't think this happens, I have a bridge I'd like to sell you. I have clients who will no longer work with investment banks unless absolutely necessary because they were burned by having divisions put in play.
18. Ron Chernow, *The House of Morgan: An American Banking Dynasty and the Rise of Modern Finance* (New York: Grove Press, 1990; reprint edition with new preface, 2001), p. 625.
19. John O. Matthews, *Struggle and Survival on Wall Street: The Economics of Competition among Securities Firms* (New York: Oxford University Press, 1994), p. 12.

20. The author consulted to the U.S. operations of some large European banks during this period.

21. "Further Discussion of Capital Markets Options—Sumitomo Bank Limited." McKinsey & Company, October 3, 1985 (private report prepared for a client). This is significant because in those days block trades were generally traded upstairs, meaning the NYSE member would effectively buy at market and quickly redistribute to other buyers. The order would still be reported on the exchange.

22. Michael Hayes, "The Vanishing Partnership," *RegisteredRep,* January 1, 2000, http://registeredrep .com/mag/finance_vanishing_partnership/.

23. Lazard Frères also remained private, but it was an M&A boutique with only a very small capital markets business and hence not subject to capital pressures. Goldman accepted outside investors, most notably Sumitomo Bank in 1986, but as special limited partners, thus preserving its partnership structure.

24. Michael Keeley, "Deposit Insurance, Risk, and Market Power in Banking," *American Economic Review* 80, no. 5 (1990), 1183–1200.

25. Partnoy, 2003, 18–19.

26. Alan Greenspan, "Government Regulation and Derivative Contracts" (speech, Financial Markets Conference of the Federal Reserve Bank of Atlanta, Coral Gables, Fla., February 21, 1997), available at http://www.federalreserve.gov/BoardDocs/Speeches/1997/19970221.htm.

27. Frank Easterbrook and Daniel Fischel, *The Economic Structure of Corporate Law* (Cambridge, MA: Harvard University Press, 1991), 285.

28. Robert Prentice, "The Case of the Irrational Accountant: A Behavioral Insight into Securities Fraud Litigation," *Northwestern University Law Review* 5, no. 1 (2000): 136.

29. Brandon Becker and Jennifer Yoon, "Derivative Financial Losses," *Journal of Corporation Law* 21 (1995): 215, 219–239.

30. Partnoy, 2003, 69–70.

31. Satyajit Das, *Traders, Guns & Money: Knowns and Unknowns in the Dazzling World of Derivatives* (Harlow, UK: Financial Times Prentice Hall, 2006), 11. Note Das indicates that some of the details of his accounts have been modified to protect client confidentiality, but he has confirmed that the general practice illustrated by his example was far from uncommon.

32. Partnoy, 1999, 90–91.

33. Partnoy, 1999, 253.

34. Manuel Roig-Franzia, "Credit Crisis Cassandra," *Washington Post,* May 26, 2009, http://www .washingtonpost.com/wp-dyn/content/article/2009/05/25/AR2009052502108.html.

35. Partnoy 2003, 142–143.

36. "Ex-Trader Cleared of All Charges," *The New York Times,* June 9, 2000, http://www.nytimes.com/ 2000/06/09/business/ex-trader-cleared-of-charges.html; and "Ex-Trader Cleared of Charges," *Wall Street Journal,* June 12, 2000, A26.

37. *Central Bank of Denver v. First Interstate of Denver,* 511 U.S. 164 (1994).

38. Partnoy, 2003, 172.

39. Peter Goodman, "Taking a Hard Look at a Greenspan Legacy," *The New York Times,* October 8, 2008, http://www.nytimes.com/2008/10/09/business/economy/09greenspan.html.

40. The economic substance of CDS is identical to insurance, and those who write the protection in most cases are required to post collateral, just as "Names" in the insurance house Lloyd's of London did.

41. Peter S. Goodman, "Taking a hard look at a Greenspan legacy," *The New York Times,* October 8, 2008, http://www.nytimes.com/2008/10/09/business/worldbusiness/09iht–09greenspan.16804 435.html?pagewanted=1&%2359;brooksley%20born&%2334&%2359&_r=1&sq&st=cse&%23 59;%20rubin&scp=3

42. Partnoy, 2003, 295.

43. Joseph R. Mason and Josh Rosner, "Where Did the Risk Go? How Misapplied Bond Ratings Cause Mortgage Backed Securities and Collateralized Debt Obligation Market Disruptions," May 3, 2007, pp. 11–12, http://ssrn.com/abstract=1027475.

44. Ibid., 19–20.

45. Daniel Gros and Stefano Micossi, "The Beginning of the End Game . . . ," VoxEU [blog], September 20, 2008, http://www.voxeu.org/index.php?q=node/1669.

46.   "Eye on the Bailout: AIG," *ProPublica,* undated, http://bailout.propublica.org/entities/8-aig. Note that the $180 billion is the total size of the commitments, not total expenditures.

47.   Kathy Swan, reporter, "Local Councils Hit by Subprime," *Inside Business,* Australian Broadcasting Corporation (ABC), transcript available at http://www.abc.net.au/insidebusiness/content/2007/s2164831.htm.

48.   Gwladys Fouché, "Sub-prime Chill Reaches the Arctic," *Guardian,* June 30, 2008, http://www.guardian.co.uk/business/2008/jun/30/subprimecrisis.creditcrunch.

49.   Achim Dübel, interview, "Germany's Subprime Crisis: Interview With Achim Dübel," The Institutional Risk Analyst [blog], May 27, 2009, text available at http://us1.institutionalrisk analytics.com/pub/IRAstory.asp?tag=362.

50.   Joe Mysak, "Largest U.S. Municipal Bankruptcy Looms in Alabama," *Bloomberg,* April 11, 2008, http://www.bloomberg.com/apps/news?pid=20601039&sid=ahSJgzIBbboA&refer=home.

51.   Alan Katz, Lorenzo Totaro, and Elisa Martinuzzi, "'Impossible to Understand' Swap Burns 290-Person Italian Hamlet," *Bloomberg,* June 18, 2009, http://www.bloomberg.com/apps/news ?pid=20601109&sid=a04MS8q.QQTM.

52.   Mark Whitehouse and Serena Ng, "Insurance Deals Spread Pain of U.S. Defaults World-Wide," *Wall Street Journal,* December 23, 2008, http://online.wsj.com/article/SB122999335538628723.html.

53.   Tyler Durden, "The Kenosha School District Is All About Riskless Subprime Synthetic CDOs," Zero Hedge [blog], June 15, 2009, http://www.zerohedge.com/content/kenosha-school-district-all-about-riskless-subprime-synthetic-cdos.

54.   Charles Duhigg and Carter Dougherty, "From Midwest to M.T.A., Pain From Global Gamble," *The New York Times,* November 1, 2008, http://www.nytimes.com/2008/11/02/business/02global .html.

55.   One has to marvel at the stupidity of the lender. There was more than one set of chumps in this deal.

56.   Das, 237.

57.   Serena Ng and Carrick Mollenkamp, "Pioneer Helped Merrill Move Into CDOs," *Wall Street Journal,* October 25, 2007, http://online.wsj.com/article/SB119326927053270580.html.

58.   Jody Shenn, "Bank CDO Losses May Reach $77 Billion, JPMorgan Says," *Bloomberg,* November 27, 2007, http://www.bloomberg.com/apps/news?pid=20601087&sid=aKx.Gintu5so&refer =home.

59.   Bradley Keoun, "Merrill Sells $8.55 Billion of Stock, Unloads CDOs," *Bloomberg,* July 29, 2008, http://www.bloomberg.com/apps/news?pid=20601087&refer=home&sid=a6IfH7HIhBmg.

60.   Securities Industry and Financial Markets Association, "Global CDO Market Issuance Data," report, undated, p. 1, available at http://www.sifma.org/research/pdf/CDO_Data2008-Q4.pdf. One source of unending frustration is that market size estimates for opaque markets like CDOs vary considerably.

61.   Per a CDO trader who asked to be remain anonymous, in an e-mail message dated September 21, 2009.

CHAPTER 7

1.   Securities and Exchange Commission, "In the Matter of ORLANDO JOSEPH JETT," Broker-Dealer Proceeding, March 5, 2004, http://www.sec.gov/litigation/opinions/33–8395.htm.

2.   Partnoy, 2003, 177.

3.   Sylvia Nasar, "Jett's Supervisor at Kidder Breaks Silence," *The New York Times,* July 26, 1994, http://www.nytimes.com/1994/07/26/business/jett-s-supervisor-at-kidder-breaks-silence.html?page wanted=all.

4.   Partnoy, 2003, 177.

5.   Securities and Exchange Commission, "In the Matter of ORLANDO JOSEPH JETT."

6.   Sylvia Nasar, "Jett's Supervisor at Kidder Breaks Silence."

7.   Those were the amounts reported at the time; the SEC later found that Jett showed profits of $264 million when his losses were $75 million.

8.   Partnoy, 2003, 182.

9.   Leah Nathans Spiro, "Now It's Joseph Jett's Turn," Review of Joseph Jett, *Black and White on Wall Street* (New York: Morrow, 1999), in *BusinessWeek,* May 10, 1999, http://www.businessweek.com/1999/99_19/b3628042.htm.

10. Peter Truell, "Jett, Ex-Kidder Trader, Must Repay Millions," *The New York Times*, July 22, 1998, http://www.nytimes.com/1998/07/22/business/jett-ex-kidder-trader-must-repay-millions.html.

11. Obviously, top management may have understood and been complicit, but it appears in most cases that they drank their own Kool-Aid.

12. Scheherazade Daneshkhu, "Kerviel Case Raises Difference between Virtual and Fake Trades," *Financial Times*, June 10, 2008, http://www.ft.com/cms/s/0/05f86082-3713-11dd-bc1c-0000779fd2 ac.html.

13. Timothy Geithner, "Credit Market Innovations and Their Implications," (speech, 2007 Credit Markets Symposium hosted by the Federal Reserve Bank of Richmond, Charlotte, N.C., March 23, 2007), available at http://www.newyorkfed.org/newsevents/speeches/2007/gei070323.html.

14. Remember, big risk management mistakes lead to government intervention. So the banks are ultimately gambling with taxpayer money.

15. Alan Greenspan, "Banking in the Global Marketplace" (speech, Federation of Bankers Associations of Japan, Tokyo, Japan, November 18, 1996), available at http://www.federalreserve.gov/BoardDocs/Speeches/1996/19961118.htm.

16. George A. Akerlof and Paul M Romer, "Looting: The Economic Underworld of Bankruptcy for Profit," Brookings Papers on Economic Activity 24, Brookings Institute, Washington, D.C., 1993, pp. 2–3.

17. William K. Black, *The Best Way to Rob a Bank Is to Own One: How Corporate Executives and Politicians Looted the S&L Industry* (Austin, Tex.: University of Texas Press 2005), xv.

18. William Black, "Reexamining the Law-and-Economics Theory of Corporate Governance," *Challenge* 46, no. 2 (2003), 22–23.

19. Recall from chapter 5 that the law and economics movement sought to have neoclassical economics colonize legal theory and practice.

20. For instance, Akerlof, then president of the American Economics Association, gave an address at its 2008 annual meeting that was deemed even by some sympathetic to it as radical. What was his shocking idea? That economics consider human behavior.

21. Partnoy, 2003, 297–298.

22. Even though a $350 million restatement for two years of activity sounds like a big number, GE's 1993 pretax earnings in 1993 were $6.6 billion.

23. "The Cost of Bear's Crisis to Its Employees," DealBook [blog], March 16, 2008, http://dealbook.blogs.nytimes.com/2008/03/16/the-cost-of-bears-crisis-to-its-employees/.

24. Heidi N. Moore, "Lehman Employees and the Wall Street Compensation Model," Deal Journal [blog], September 12, 2008, http://blogs.wsj.com/deals/2008/09/12/lehman-employees-and-the-wall-street-compensation-model/.

25. "Enron Employees Ride Stock to Bottom," *CNN.com/Law Center*, January 14, 2002, http://archives.cnn.com/2002/LAW/01/14/enron.employees/.

26. Jennifer Hughes, "In Death Do We Part," *Financial Times*, July 8, 2009, http://www.ft.com/cms/s/0/1f09ef42-6bf0-11de-9320-00144feabdc0.html.

27. "To a degree" because past practice has shown that emergency action and safety nets will be extended to firms outside the formal backstopping regime, like Long-Term Capital Management, Fannie Mae and Freddie Mac, and AIG.

28. Kidder's decision to have Jett learn a market he had never traded before was unusual, but STRIPS were considered less demanding than commercial mortgage obligations, Jett's previous area of experience.

29. "Further Discussion of Capital Markets Options—Sumitomo Bank Limited," McKinsey & Company, October 3, 1985 (private report prepared for a client). Merrill Lynch had McKinsey do an extensive competitor study on Salomon, down to the layout of its trading floor.

30. Satyajit Das, *Traders, Guns & Money: Knowns and Unknowns in the Dazzling World of Derivatives* (Harlow, UK: Financial Times Prentice Hall, 2006), 184; and Roger Lowenstein, *When Genius Failed: The Rise and Fall of Long-Term Capital Management* (New York: Random House, 2001), 8.

31. Unlike stocks, where the customer pays a commission, a market maker will give a bid, or offered price. While some large accounts will deal directly with traders, many are handled by salesmen, who are expected to earn their keep by adding their own markup onto the dealer's price based on

their knowledge of the customer. Box seats at sporting events are an invaluable aid to institutional salesmen.

32. Lowenstein, 2001, 4.

33. Ibid., 11.

34. Michael Lewis, "What Wall Street's CEOs Don't Know Can Kill You," *Bloomberg*, March 26, 2008, http://www.bloomberg.com/apps/news?pid=20601039&sid=aSE8yLAyALNQ&refer=columnist_lewis.

35. Partnoy, 2003, 86.

36. Michael Lewis, "The End of Wall Street's Boom," *Portfolio*, November 11, 2008, http://www.portfolio.com/news-markets/national-news/portfolio/2008/11/11/The-End-of-Wall-Streets-Boom. Note Gutfreund's pay was left in the dust by Michael Milken's earnings, which were $500 million in his peak year. But that came to light later in the decade. Many believed he could not have earned that much legitimately.

37. Partnoy, 2003, 85.

38. Ibid.

39. Michael Lewis, "The Man Who Crashed the World," *Vanity Fair*, August 2009, http://www.vanityfair.com/politics/features/2009/08/aig200908?currentPage=1.

40. "French Find New Hero In Rogue Trader," *Javno*, January 28, 2008, http://www.javno.com/en-economy/french-find-new-hero-in-rogue-trader_118587.

41. Partnoy, 2003, 86.

42. Robert J. McCartney, "Salomon's Mines: What Makes These Traders Tick?," *The Record*, September 29, 1991.

43. Partnoy, 2003, 98–99.

44. Ibid., 100.

45. Ibid., 101.

46. Ibid.

47. Ibid., 107.

48. Just because this was a rough-and-ready industry norm does not mean it was achieved with any precision.

49. Susan Pulliam and Randall Smith, "CSFB's Defense: We Didn't Break IPO Rules," *Wall Street Journal*, June 12, 2001.

50. Tom Cahill, "CSFB's Mack Targets Goldman, Morgan Stanley: Mission Possible?," *Bloomberg*, January 17, 2002.

51. T. N. Dupuy. *Understanding War: The History and Theory of Combat* (New York: Paragon House Publishers, 1987), 109.

52. Some firms did have some success in combating the departure problem, via having a large amount of annual bonus in restricted stock, as Lehman did. Lehman staff of any meaningful seniority were unhireable because the cost of buying out their restricted stock would generally be prohibitive. But while it may have prevented business-dampening defections, practices like this did not help contain compensation. The firms that used stock as a handcuff aspired to pay at least competitively.

53. Steve Fishman, "Burning Down His House," *New York Magazine*, November 30, 2008, http://nymag.com/news/business/52603/.

54. Of the major capital markets players, Deutsche Bank, Société Générale, Credit Suisse, and Paribas have not needed explicit bailouts, but they all had capital support via AIG credit default swaps, which were backstopped by the U.S. government. All have taken very large trading losses, and since the financial crisis took hold first in the United States, they benefited from the Fed's and ECB's emergency measures before the trouble hit Europe full bore. Absent the massive liquidity injections by central banks, these banks are almost certain to have perished. Moreover, most analysts have criticized Barclay's refusal to accept bailout funds as putting management prerogatives over what is best for the business and the financial system.

55. Those who suggest that Goldman is an exception forget its $30 billion CDS exposure to AIG, a major risk management screwup, and the fact that it sought and received a costly $5 billion capital injection from Warren Buffett. The firm was on the ropes with the rest of the industry.

56. Joe Nocera, "Risk Mismanagement," *The New York Times*, January 2, 2009, http://www.nytimes.com/2009/01/04/magazine/04risk-t.html?pagewanted=all.

57. Firms also look at VaR and other risk measures over longer periods, but the problem there is that they have fewer data points to work with, making "fixes" for the tail range even more dubious.
58. Gillian Tett, *Fool's Gold* (New York: Free Press, 2009), 34.
59. "The Role of Valuation and Leverage in Procyclicality," CGFS Papers 34, Committee on the Global Financial System, Bank for International Settlements, April 2009, 10, available at http://www.bis.org/publ/cgfs34.pdf.
60. Nassim Nicholas Taleb, "The Fourth Quadrant: A Map of the Limits of Statistics," *Edge*, September 15, 2008, http://www.edge.org/3rd_culture/taleb08/taleb08_index.html.
61. Ibid.
62. Leo Lewis, "The Kimono Traders," *The Times*, August 3, 2007, http://women.timesonline.co.uk/tol/life_and_style/women/article2187250.ece.
63. Wanfeng Zhou, "Carry Trade Unwinding Roils Currency Markets," *MarketWatch*, February 27, 2007, http://www.marketwatch.com/story/carry-trade-unwinding-roils-currency-markets.
64. "Shorting the Subprime Market," Whiskey and Gunpowder [blog], January 25, 2008, http://whiskeyandgunpowder.com/shorting-the-subprime-market/.
65. Portfolio insurance was a hedging strategy marketed by a number of money managers, the most famous being Leland, O'Brien, and Rubinstein. It required selling index futures in a computer-driven process to limit losses when stock prices dropped. But as users learned in the 1987 crash, the automated selling fed on itself. As futures prices fell, investors in equities (the cash market) retreated to the sidelines. And in retrospect, the belief that the insurance would work led investors prior to the crash to take more risk, for instance, by holding lower cash balances than they would have otherwise.
66. Aline van Duyn and Nicole Bullock, "Bad New on Lehman CDS," *Financial Times*, October 11, 2008, http://www.ft.com/cms/s/0/25137702–972d–11dd–8cc4–000077b07658.html.
67. Due to varying definitions of what "subprime" is, I have seen wide variations in market size estimates, $500 billion (Stratfor citing Reuters) to $2 trillion (Center for Responsible Lending). Most estimates cluster around $1.1-$1.2 trillion.
68. "In the Fog of Volatility, the Notional Becomes Payable," Institutional Risk Analyst [blog], October 27, 2008, http://us1.institutionalriskanalytics.com/pub/IRAstory.asp?tag=319.
69. Because the big auto companies had been downgraded again and again over a period of years, the disruptive effects were blunted. The biggest danger to the markets is a swift decline in a firm with a lot of debt outstanding.
70. As the United States learned in Iraq, having a solid estimate of the personnel needed to prosecute an operation successfully is crucial. That is why letting officers operate freely within a "commit level" is an illusory check. If an officer engages the enemy using a large force within his commit level, but that initiative proves to be insufficient for success, more troops may wind up being deployed (at that point, the cost of exit may look higher than that of further engagement). Via such incremental decisions (at the time called "escalation"), the United States got more deeply mired in Vietnam.
71. Richard Kline, comment on "Why Big Capital Markets Players are Unmanageable," Naked Capitalism [blog], comment posted July 9, 2009, http://www.nakedcapitalism.com/2009/07/why-big-capital-markets-players-are.html.
72. Richard Bookstaber, "Conversations with the Trading Desk," Richard Bookstaber blog, December 2, 2007, http://rick.bookstaber.com/2007/12/conversations-with-trading-desk.html.
73. That of course assumes the trader would have exited the position well, which is a self-serving but seldom questioned assessment.
74. Bookstaber, "Conversations with the Trading Desk."
75. "The Role of Valuation and Leverage in Procyclicality," CGFS Papers 34, Committee on the Global Financial System, Bank for International Settlements, April 2009, p. 5, available at http://www.bis.org/publ/cgfs34.pdf.
76. Susanne Craig and Deborah Solomon, "Bank Bonus Tab: $33 Billion," *Wall Street Journal*, July 31, 2009, http://online.wsj.com/article/SB124896891815094085.html#mod=testMod
77. David Trone and Ivy De Dianous, "3Q08 Preview: Hedges Work, Loss Narrows, No New Raise," Fox-Pitt Kelton Cochran Caronia Waller, August 15, 2008; Michael Hecht, Scott Buck, and Thang To, "Meeting with Mgmt; Lowering Numbers on De-Leveraging and Risk Exposure Reduction plus Choppy Environment; Maintain Neutral," Bank Of America, August 14, 2008; Jeff

Harte and Devin Ryan, "Waiting for September and Reducing Estimates: LEH," Sandler, O'Neill and Partners, August 22, 2008; Brad Hintz, Michael Werner, and Vincent M. Currotto, "LEH: Analyzing the Firm's Shrinking Options . . ." Bernstein Research, September 8, 2008; Guy Moszkowski, M. Patrick Davitt, "Cutting Forecasts on Asset-Sale Scramble, Capital Raising," Merrill Lynch, September 8, 2008; Michael Hecht, Scott Buck, and Thang To, "Lots of Talk, Not Enough Action; Reduce Ests. & Target; Reiterate Neutral," Bank Of America, September 11, 2008; William F. Tanona, Betsy Miller, and Neil C. Sanyal, "Uncertainty remains; removing from Americas Buy List," Goldman Sachs, September 11, 2008; Mike Mayo and Matt Fischer, "Downgrade from Buy to Hold on rating agency reports," Deutsche Bank, September 11, 2008; Meredith Whitney, Kaimon Chung and Joseph Mack, "LEH Likely Forced Into Liquidation," Oppenheimer, September 14, 2008; Lauren Smith and Joel Jeffrey, "LEH: The 'Unthinkable' Happened—LEH Is Gone, Nowhere to Turn . . . Event—," Keefe, Bruyette, & Woods, September 15, 2008; James Mitchell and John Grassano, "Rating Agency Risk Too High," The Buckingham Research Group, September 11, 2008.

78. "Special Bailout Edition," BloggingHeads TV, October 1, 2008, http://bloggingheads.tv/diavlogs/14850

79. Lehman Brothers Holdings, Inc., "Form 10-Q For the quarterly period ended May 31, 2008."

80. Yves Smith, "So Where, Exactly, Did Lehman's $130 Billion Go?" Naked Capitalism [blog], July 10, 2009, http://www.nakedcapitalism.com/2009/07/so-where-exactly-did-lehmans–130.html.

81. David Einhorn, "Accounting Ingenuity" (speech, Ira W. Sohn Investment Research Conference, May 21, 2008), p. 6, available at http://www.scribd.com/doc/13940022/Accounting-Ingenuity-David-Einhorn-Speech-at-the-Ira-W-Sohn-Investment-Research-Conference-May–21–2008.

82. Yves Smith, "So How Did Lehman Deliver? A Not-Very-Pretty Possibility," Naked Capitalism [blog], June 17, 2008, http://www.nakedcapitalism.com/2008/06/so-how-did-lehman-delever-not-very.html.

83. Jonathan Weil, "Lehman's Hedge-Fund Deals Leave Public in Dark," *Bloomberg*, July 3, 2008, http://www.bloomberg.com/apps/news?pid=20601110&sid=aYbKSTZ5ZYpM.

84. Quoted in Susan Pulliam, Randall Smith, and Michael Siconolfi, "U.S. Investors Face An Age of Murky Pricing," *Wall Street Journal*, October 12, 2007, http://online.wsj.com/article/SB119214581308956665.html?mod=hpp_us_whats_news.

85. Susan Pulliam, Randall Smith, and Michael Siconolfi, "U.S. Investors Face An Age of Murky Pricing."

86. Serena Ng, "As LBO Debt Plunges, Wall Street Clients Miss the Mark," Deal Journal [blog], September 13, 2007, http://blogs.wsj.com/deals/2007/09/13/as-lbo-debt-plunges-wall-street-clients-miss-the-mark/.

87. Susan Pulliam, Randall Smith, and Michael Siconolfi, "U.S. Investors Face An Age of Murky Pricing."

88. Ibid.

89. Yves Smith, "Bear Death Watch: Why It Failed," Naked Capitalism [blog], March 14, 2008, http://www.nakedcapitalism.com/2008/03/bear-death-watch-why-it-failed.html.

90. Greg Farrell, "BofA Linked to Merrill Writedowns," *Financial Times,* March 19, 2009, http://www.ft.com/cms/s/0/9a8dfa20–14d7–11de–8cd1–0000779fd2ac.html.

91. Comments on "Merrill Writedowns: The Plot Thickens," Naked Capitalism [blog], comments posted March 20, 2009, http://www.nakedcapitalism.com/2009/03/merrill-writedowns-plot-thickens.html.

92. Jonathan Weil, "Wells Fargo Gorges on Mark-to-Make-Believe Gains," *Bloomberg,* August 22, 2007, http://www.bloomberg.com/apps/news?pid=conewsstory&refer=conews&tkr=WFC:US&sid=aY8m0nta94GA#.

93. Ibid.

94. Jennifer Hughes, "Auditors Get Set for Tough Talks with Clients," *Financial Times,* November 5, 2007, http://www.ft.com/cms/s/0/f15af834–8bd6–11dc-af4d–0000779fd2ac.html.

95. John Glover, "Banks Face $100 Billion of Writedowns on Level 3 Rule," *Bloomberg,* November 7, 2007, http://www.bloomberg.com/apps/news?pid=20601087&sid=a5qWBy1C9plo.

96. Peter Eavis, "Wall Street Playing with More Funny Money," *Fortune,* November 12, 2007, http://money.cnn.com/2007/11/12/magazines/fortune/eavis_level3.fortune/index.htm.

97. "Sample Letter Sent to Public Companies on MD&A Disclosure Regarding the Application of SFAS 157 (Fair Value Measurements)," U.S. Securities and Exchange Commission, Division of Corporation Finance, March 2008, http://www.sec.gov/divisions/corpfin/guidance/fair-

valueltr0308.htm; and Floyd Norris, "If Market Prices Are Too Low, Ignore Them," Notions on High and Low Finance [blog], March 28, 2008, http://norris.blogs.nytimes.com/2008/03/28/if-market-prices-are-too-low-ignore-them/.

98. Jennifer Yousfi, "Rising Tide of Level 3 Assets a 'Disaster Waiting to Happen,'" *Money Morning,* April 21, 2008, http://www.moneymorning.com/2008/04/21/rising-tide-of-level-3-assets-a-disaster-waiting-to-happen/.

99. Aline van Duyn and Francesco Guerrera, "Financial Groups' Problem Assets Hit $610bn," *Financial Times,* December 10, 2009, http://www.ft.com/cms/s/0/0627def0-c6f8–11dd–97a5–0000 77b07658.html.

100. U.S. banks managed to dodge this bullet simply because the Federal Reserve had not yet implemented Basel II, the updated Bank of International Settlements rules that determine how much capital banks must hold. Basel II has very detailed risk weighting provisions that were devised before these new instruments were created. For instance, the initial synthetic collateralized debt obligations transaction, J.P. Morgan's BISTRO, became known as "Bank of International Settlements Total Rip Off" due to the very favorable treatment given AAA tranches under Basel II rules (see Tett, 2009, p. 64). While the U.S. regulators observed many of the principles embodied in Basel II, they did not implement quite a few of the particular rules. The net result was that European banks could be far more leveraged than their U.S. counterparts.

101. This illustration comes from a UBS employee, and others familiar with market practice have confirmed its broad outlines. The Swiss National Bank required UBS to make extensive public disclosure of the losses it incurred in collateralized debt obligations and other structured products.

102. Tett, 2009, 138

103. The bond amortizes, so average life is more relevant for this purpose than final maturity.

104. How much relief was provided by an AAA hedge of an AAA position varied by firm.

105. Every institution that allowed for AAA hedges of AAA positions to free up capital reportedly saw large volumes of "negative basis trades." Sources differ on whether the practice was universal or merely widespread. There is consensus that it was extensive and probably universal at European banks. The most knowledgeable sources contend it was pervasive at U.S. banks and investment banks, although less favorable regulatory treatment plus higher funding costs would have reduced the number of situations where the trade was attractive.

106. Per an employee of a large European bank who has asked to remain anonymous, personal e-mail communication with author, July 20, 2009.

107. UBS, "Shareholder Report on UBS's Write-Downs," April 18, 2008, 13, available at http://www.ubs.com/1/ShowMedia/investors/agm?contentId=140333&name=080418ShareholderReport.pdf.

108. Susan Pullman, Serena Ng, and Randall Smith, "Merrill Upped Ante as Boom In Mortgage Bonds Fizzled," *Wall Street Journal,* April 16, 2008, http://online.wsj.com/article/SB1208307308446 18031.html.

109. This notorious "liquidity put" occurred in Citigroup CDOs that had issued short-term debt. If the CDO was unable to borrow via selling commercial paper, a short-term IOU, the bank was obligated to buy commercial paper from the CDO.

110. Carol Loomis, "Robert Rubin on the Job He Never Wanted," *Fortune,* November 28, 2007, http://money.cnn.com/2007/11/09/news/newsmakers/merrill_rubin.fortune/index.htm?postversion =2007111119.

CHAPTER 8

1. Karl Moore and David Lewis, *The Origins of Globalization* (New York: Routledge, 2009), 48.

2. Ibid., 51.

3. William N. Goetzmann, *Financing Civilization,* http://viking.som.yale.edu/will/finciv/chapter1 .htm.

4. "The Beginnings of Globalization," *Globe and Mail,* April 8, 2009, quoted in http://www.mcgill .ca/channels/spotlight/item/?item_id=105999.

5. Goetzmann.

6. Moore and Lewis, 52.

7. Even though the Japanese stock market also boomed and collapsed along roughly the same timetable as the Japanese real estate mania, lending against real estate was the main culprit in

both bubbles, as companies borrowed against their land and used the proceeds for various forms of *zaitech* (speculation), including stock market speculation. Margin lending was not a major factor in the stock market bubble.

8.   Contrary to the Western view, the Japanese ascribed virtually all the value of real estate to land. In the 1980s, they did not use any cash flow–based approaches for valuing real estate.

9.   Jennifer McNulty, "New Book by UCSC Economist Examines Japan's 'Bubble Economy,'" *Currents,* October 13, 1997, http://www.ucsc.edu/oncampus/currents/97–10–13/hutchison.htm.

10. Rob Parenteau, "Reality Intrusion," Naked Capitalism [blog], July 7, 2009, http://www.naked-capitalism.com/2009/07/reality-intrusion.html.

11. This level is a big increase over historical norms. In the 1960s, conventional wisdom among banks was that they should not lend more than 50% of deposits. FDIC data show that the loan to deposit ratio was 51% in 1960. It rose to 85% by 1985. Banks in the old days would put the reserves for deposits in ready-saleable investments like Treasuries.

12. Christopher Condon, "Reserve Primary Money Fund Falls Below $1 a Share," *Bloomberg,* September 16, 2008, http://www.bloomberg.com/apps/news?pid=20601087&sid=a5O2y1go1GRU.

13. C-Span, Washington Journal, February 6, 2009.

14. Hyman P. Minsky, "The Financial Instability Hypothesis," Working Paper No 74, May 1992, 7–8.

15. Gunduz Caginalp, Kevin McCabe, and David Porter, "The Foundations of Experimental Economics and Applications to Behavioral Finance: The Contributions of Nobel Laureate Vernon Smith," *Journal of Behavioral Finance* 4, no. 1 (2003): 4.

16. Wolfgang Münchau, "Recession Is Not the Worst Possible Outcome," *Financial Times,* July 6, 2008, http://us.ft.com/ftgateway/superpage.ft?news_id=fto070620081307228551.

17. China's currency, the renminbi (RMB), was overvalued in the 1980s and early 1990s despite devaluations since 1985. Inflation outpaced the reductions in official rate, leaving the real cost of exports higher. The RMB was devalued twice in 1992, and a new system, including a peg, was implemented in 1994.

18. Thorsten Beck, Berrak Buyukkarabacak, Felix Rioja, and Neven Valev, "Who Gets the Credit? And Does It Matter? Household vs. Firm Lending across Countries," VoxEU [blog], July 9, 2009, http://www.VoxEU.org/index.php?q=node/3753.

19. "Savings versus Liquidity," *Economist,* August 11, 2005, http://www.economist.com/finance/displaystory.cfm?story_id=E1_QNSQRJG; and "The Global Saving Glut: Rest in Peace? Mirage? Bete noir?," Econbrowser [blog], June 22, 2009, http://www.econbrowser.com/archives/2009/06/the_global_savi.html.

20. Thomas Palley, "The Debt Delusion," Thomas Palley: Economics for Democratic and Open Societies [blog], February 26, 2008, http://www.thomaspalley.com/?p=99.

21. The Federal Reserve tried tightening to support the dollar in the spring and summer of 1978 and even launched a dollar defense package in November 1978. The Treasury in January 1978 had announced that it was using the Exchange Stabilization Fund (think of it as a special facility that allows the Treasury to intervene to boost or weaken the dollar without a direct impact on domestic money supply) and was willing to draw on its reserves at the IMF to bolster the dollar. The Reagan administration, by contrast, took the position that the markets knew best until the 1985 Plaza Accord intervention.

22. The U.S. trade deficit finally responded to the currency weakness in December 1987, falling 44%.

23. The savings and loan (S&L) crisis was largely the result of deregulation and eviscerated supervision. Fraud was the main cause, not honest but misguided investments. See William Black, *The Best Way to Rob a Bank is to Own One: How Corporate Executives and Politicians Looted the S&L Industry* (Austin, TX: University of Texas Press, 2005).

24. Quoted in Tomohiko Taniguchi, *Japan's Banks and the "Bubble Economy" of the Late 1980s* (Princeton, N.J.: Center of International Studies, Program on U.S.-Japan Relations, Princeton University, 1993), quoted in Michael Pettis, "China's Savings Problem and the Consumption Constraint," China Financial Markets [blog], June 20, 2009, http://mpettis.com/2009/06/china's-savings-problem-and-the-consumption-constraint/.

25. Carmen Reinhart and Kenneth Rogoff, "This Time It's Different: A Panoramic View of Eight Centuries of Financial Crises," NBER Working Papers 13882 (National Bureau of Economic Research, Washington, D.C.), 2008; working paper discussed in Carmen Reinhart, "Eight Hun-

dred Years of Financial Folly," VoxEU [blog], April 19, 2008, http://www.voxeu.org/index.php?q =node/1067.

26. Mark Buchanan, "This Economy Does Not Compute," *The New York Times*, October 1, 2008, http://www.nytimes.com/2008/10/01/opinion/01buchanan.html.

27. Thomas Ferguson, "Blowing Smoke: Impeachment, the Clinton Presidency, and the Political Economy," in *The State of Democracy in America*, ed. William J. Crotty (Washington, D.C.: Georgetown University Press, 2001), 205.

28. Ibid., 210.

29. Ibid., 212–214.

30. Ibid., 214–215.

31. The existence of persistent trade surpluses need not be a feature of floating rate systems; the weakness is not the system itself, but the lack of global political will to avoid manipulating rates to obtain a trade advantage.

32. Alan Ahearne, Joseph Gagnon, Jane Haltmaier, Steve Kamin, Christopher Erceg, Jon Faust, Luca Guerrieri, Carter Hemphill, Linda Kole, Jennifer Roush, John Rogers, Nathan Sheets, and Jonathan Wright, "Preventing Deflation: Lessons from Japan's Experience in the 1990s," International Finance Discussion Papers 729, Board of Governors of the Federal Reserve System, June 2002, 55, 62, available at http://www.federalreserve.gov/pubs/ifdp/2002/729/ifdp729.pdf.

33. The Chinese currency had been overvalued in the 1980s and early 1990s and had been devalued twice in 1992. The level chosen in 1994 corresponded to the swap rate, which was considered a good proxy of its fair value.

34. Alicia Garcia Herrero and Tuuli Koivu, "Can the Chinese Trade Surplus Be Reduced with Exchange Rate Policy: Consequences for Asia," paper published by the Centre de Recherche en Developpement Economique et Finance Internationale, January 2007, 3, available at http://www .defi-univ.org/IMG/pdf/Garcia-Herrero-Koivu.pdf.

35. William C. Hunter, George G. Kaufman, and Thomas H. Krueger, eds., *The Asian Financial Crisis: Origins, Implications, and Solutions* (New York: Springer, 1999), 194.

36. Ed Harrison, "Guest Post: Asia Breaks Free from Geithner and Summers," Naked Capitalism [blog], May 6, 2009, http://www.nakedcapitalism.com/2009/05/guest-post-asia-breaks-free-from .html.

37. Some would argue that the United States and other developed economies learned from the policy errors of the Asian crisis.

38. Richard Halloran, "China's Decisive Role in the Asian Financial Crisis," *Global Beat Issue Brief* 24, January 27, 1998.

39. Marshall Auerback quoted in Ed Harrison, "Guest Post: Asia Breaks Free from Geithner and Summers," Naked Capitalism [blog], May 6, 2009, http://www.nakedcapitalism.com/2009/05/guest-post-asia-breaks-free-from.html.

40. Hunter, Kaufman, and Krueger, 195–196.

41. "China's Currency: A Summary of the Economic Issues," Congressional Research Service Report for Congress RS21625, last updated June 2009, pp. 1, 2, available at http://opencrs.com/ document/RS21625/. [AU: Is this correct?]

42. Peter Goodman, "China Ends Fixed-Rate Currency," *Washington Post*, July 22, 2005, http://www .washingtonpost.com/wp-dyn/content/article/2005/07/21/AR2005072100351.html.

43. Brad Setser, "The (Almost) $2.5 Trillionaire . . .," Follow the Money [blog], May 24, 2009, http:// blogs.cfr.org/setser/2009/05/24/the-almost–25-trillionaire/.

44. "U.S. International Trade: Trends and Forecasts," Congressional Research Service Report for Congress RL33577, last updated May 2009, available at http://opencrs.com/document/RL33577/; and Daniel Workman, "US Global Trade Debt by Country: 2007 American Deficit Statistics for Top Import & Export Partners," *Suite101*, February 1, 2008, http://import-export.suite101.com/ article.cfm/us_global_trade_debt_by_country.

45. William R. Cline and John Williamson, "Equilibrium exchange rates," VoxEU [blog], June 18, 2009, http://www.voxeu.org/index.php?q=node/3666.

46. "Changing Causes of the U.S. Trade Deficit," Congressional Research Service Report for Congress RL21951, last updated May 2008, available at http://opencrs.com/document/RS21951/2005– 04–22/.

47. "What's Behind the Low U.S. Personal Saving Rate?," *FRBSF Economic Letter* 2002–09 (March 29, 2002), available at http://www.frbsf.org/publications/economics/letter/2002/el2002–09.pdf.

48. Karen E. Dynan and Dean M. Maki, "Does Stock Market Wealth Matter for Consumption?" Finance and Economics Discussion Series 2001–23, Board of Governors of the Federal Reserve System, 2001, http://www.federalreserve.gov/pubs/feds/2001 (accessed March 2002); and Dean M. Maki and Michael G. Polumbo, "Disentangling the Wealth Effect: A Cohort Analysis of Household Saving in the 1990s," Finance and Economics Discussion Series 2001–21, Board of Governors of the Federal Reserve System, 2001, http://www.federalreserve.gov/pubs/feds/2001.

49. Jonathan Parker, "Spendthrift in America?: On Two Decades of Decline in the U.S. Saving Rate," NBER Working Papers 7238, National Bureau of Economic Research, Washington, D.C., 1999.

50. "What's Behind the Low U.S. Personal Saving Rate?"

51. Ibid.

52. "Household Debt Service and Financial Obligations Ratios," Federal Reserve Board, June 29, 2009, available at http://www.federalreserve.gov/releases/housedebt/.

53. Ibid.

54. Ben Bernanke, "The Economic Outlook," testimony before the Joint Economic Committee, U.S. Congress, Washington, D.C., May 5, 2009, available at http://www.federalreserve.gov/newsevents/testimony/bernanke20090505a.htm.

55. Massimo Guidolin and Elizabeth A. La Jeunesse, "The Decline in the Personal Savings Rate: Is it Real and Is it a Puzzle?," *Review,* Federal Reserve Bank of St. Louis, November/December 2007, 491.

56. Despite the impressive detail of the influential *A Monetary History of the United States,* Friedman and his coauthor Anna Schwartz fail to prove their case, that the Fed could have prevented the Great Depression (note in later, nonacademic writings, Friedman asserted that the Fed had caused the Depression). Indeed, the charge that the Fed was responsible for the contraction of the money supply in 1930 is inaccurate. The monetary base, which the Fed controls, did increase, but the money supply fell nevertheless due to a collapse in transaction volumes (the "pushing on a string" syndrome).

57. Even though alert readers may recall that Samuelson also saw wage stickiness as a contributor to the Depression (Paul Davidson, *The Keynes Solution: The Practical Path to Global Economic Prosperity* [New York: Palgrave MacMillan, 2009], 76.), he and his fellow Keynesians do not see further pressure on workers to accept lower wages as a viable solution. Their position is that demand becomes deficient, and, therefore, the remedy is to address the resulting problem directly.

58. Bob Woodward, "Crash of October 1987 Challenged Fed Chief," *Washington Post,* November 13, 2000, http://www.washingtonpost.com/ac2/wp-dyn/A1742–2000Nov11?language=printer.

59. John Tamny, "In 2008, Shades Of October 1987," *Forbes,* July 2, 2008, http://www.forbes.com/2008/07/01/fed-bernanke-greenspan-oped-cx_jt_0702dollar.html.

60. Per Ferguson, 2001.

61. Jake Schlesinger, "How Alan Greenspan Finally Came to Terms with the Market," *Wall Street Journal,* May 8, 2000, quoted in "The Federal Reserve and the Stock Market: A View from 2000," Brad DeLong's website [blog], October 5, 2005, http://www.j-bradford-delong.net/movable_type/2005–3_archives/001469.html.

62. Marshall Auerback, "A Surprise Fed Rate Cut Entrenches The Notion Of A 'Greenspan Put,'" Prudent Bear, April 23, 2001. (This is an Internet article, no longer available online, archived by the author.)

63. Even then, that is less than ideal, since substitution of more expensive domestic products with cheaper imports will also have a price-dampening effect on home-country goods, but it is at least a better approximation.

64. Richard Alford, interview, "Fed Risk: Interview with Richard Alford," The Institutional Risk Analyst [blog], May 27, 2008, text available at http://us1.institutionalriskanalytics.com/pub/IRAstory.asp?tag=283. This is not a widely held view, but Alford is not alone. Axel Leijonhufvud and Tim Duy are in the same camp.

65. Paul Krugman, "Reconsidering a Miracle," Conscience of a Liberal [blog], April 16, 2009, http://krugman.blogs.nytimes.com/2009/04/16/reconsidering-a-miracle/.

66. Center for Economic and Policy Research, "U.S. Productivity Growth Still Trails Europe," press release, June 12, 2007, CEPR, http://www.cepr.net/index.php/press-releases/press-releases/us-

productivity-growth-still-trails-europe/; the paper is "'Usable Productivity' Growth in the U.S.: An International Comparison, 1980–2005," Report of the Center for Economic and Policy Research, June 2007, available at http://www.cepr.net/index.php/publications/reports/qusable-pro-ductivityq-growth-in-the-us-an-international-comparison–1980–2005/.

67. Donald L. Luskin, "The Greenspan Myth," *Wall Street Journal,* September 13, 2007, http://on-line.wsj.com/article/SB118964506628925912.html.

68. Auerback, "A Surprise Fed Rate Cut Entrenches The Notion Of A 'Greenspan Put.'"

69. Joseph Stiglitz, *The Roaring Nineties: A New History of the World's Most Prosperous Decade* (New York: Norton, 2004), 6.

70. Federal Reserve Bank of New York, "Historical Changes of the Target Federal Funds and Discount Rates," Federal Reserve Bank of New York, last updated December 22, 2008, http://www.newyorkfed.org/markets/statistics/dlyrates/fedrate.html.

71. Henry Maxey, "Cracking the Credit Market Code," Ruffer LLP, April 2007, 18. This is a privately circulated paper.

72. Beat Balzli and Michaela Schiessl, "Global Banking Economist Warned of Coming Crisis," *Der Spiegel,* July 8, 2009, http://www.spiegel.de/international/business/0,1518,635051,00.html.

73. Susan Webber, "The Incredible Shrinking Corporation," *Across the Board,* November/December 2005, 53, available at http://www.auroraadvisors.com/articles/Shrinking.pdf.

74. Ibid., 52–53.

75. Willem Buiter, "Lessons from the North Atlantic Financial Crisis," Willem Buiter's Maverecon [blog], May 28 2008, http://blogs.ft.com/maverecon/2008/05/lessons-from-the-north-atlantic-financial-crisis/.

76. Eben Esterhuizen, "Are Margin Loans a Major Cause for Concern?," Seeking Alpha [blog], January 18, 2008, http://seekingalpha.com/article/60627-are-margin-loans-a-major-cause-for-concern.

CHAPTER 9

1. Richard Kleer, "The 1696 Recoinage," *The Literary Encyclopedia,* October 14, 2003, http://www.litencyc.com/php/stopics.php?rec=true&UID=1304.

2. Manuela Hoelterhoff, "Newton Hangs Forger, Invents Banking, Loses Millions in Bubble," *Bloomberg,* July 23, 2009, http://www.bloomberg.com/apps/news?pid=newsarchive&sid=a8aXs xUg4tdw.

3. Ibid.

4. The post-Keynesians argue, vociferously and with data to support their views, that loans come first, deposits come later. But for our purposes, the fact that there is liquidity risk (banks put out money in loans, which are illiquid, funded to a significant degree by deposits, which depositors expect to be able to claim in full at any time) is more germane than the "which comes first" question.

5. Michael Keeley, "Deposit Insurance, Risk, and Market Power in Banking," *American Economic Review* 80, no. 5 (1990): 1183–1200.

6. These factors were driving securitizaton as of the mid-1980s; when the author was at McKinsey back then, the firm had some widely used charts that showed how significant the costs of FDIC insurance and bank capital for on-balance sheet lending were relative to the cost of securitization. The fact that the rating agencies over time allowed higher effective leverage (as shown in greater permissiveness in required credit enhancement) became important in the later phases of the growth of securitization.

7. Gary Gorton, "Slapped in the Face by the Invisible Hand: Banking and the Panic of 2007," paper prepared for the Federal Reserve Bank of Atlanta's 2009 Financial Markets Conference: Financial Innovation and Crisis, May 11–13, 2009, 25.

8. Gillian Tett, "Finger of blame points to shadow banking's implosion," *Financial Times,* April 23 2009, http://www.ft.com/cms/s/0/36b8e90c–3033–11de–88e3–00144feabdc0.html.

9. Gorton, "Slapped in the Face by the Invisible Hand," 26.

10. Actually, loans were sold in Ur, but everyone presumably knew or could find out about everyone else, so there may have been no information loss.

11. Gorton, "Slapped in the Face by the Invisible Hand," 27.

12. Specifically, they said conduits should be accorded the accounting treatment of SFAS 140, "Accounting for Transfers and Servicing of Financial Assets and Extinguishments of Liabilities" (SFAS

140). But were the conduits independent entities? SFAS 140 paragraph 9c states, "The transferor does not maintain effective control over the transferred assets through either (1) an agreement that both entitles and obligates the transferor to repurchase or redeem them before maturity."

13. Joseph R. Mason, Eric James Higgins, and Adi Mordel, "Asset Sales, Recourse, and Investor Reactions to Initial Securitizations: Evidence Why Off-balance Sheet Accounting Treatment Does Not Remove On-balance Sheet Financial Risk," May 22, 2009, available at SSRN: http://ssrn.com/abstract=1107074.

14. Saskia Scholtes and Francesco Guerrera, "Banks rush to rescue of credit card trusts," *Financial Times,* June 24. 2009, http://www.ft.com/cms/s/0/a600eed0–60f9–11de-aa12–00144feabdc0.html.

15. A lot of hedge funds are funded with total return swaps, which are actually repo agreements where not just the cash flows, but changes in the value of the instruments exchanged flow through to the hedge fund. The hedge fund gets all the income and ups and downs, but it doesn't own the securities; the broker-dealer keeps the securities on its book, and the whole arrangement is funded through huge repo agreements. Hedge funds were able to use agreements like these in order to achieve impressive amounts of leverage. For instance, suppose that a AAA CDO paid a 20 basis points coupon (over LIBOR). The costs of funding a repo on the CDO were typically only 2 basis points over LIBOR, while the haircut was 5%, so 20:1 leverage. Therefore the hedge fund could take nearly all of the 20 basis points spread (because the funding costs were so low) and then leverage them at 20:1, resulting in spreads larger than 350 basis points for the repoed CDO.

16. Henry Maxey, "Cracking the Credit Market Code," Ruffer LLP, April 2007, 18. This is a privately circulated paper.

17. Ibid., 11.

18. International Swaps and Derivatives Association, "ISDA Margin Survey 2008," 2008.

19. "Collateral in Wholesale Financial Markets: Recent Trends, Risk Management and Market Dynamic," 2.

20. Gorton, "Slapped in the Face by the Invisible Hand," 29–30.

21. Repos are obviously included on bank balance sheets, and thus subject to capital requirements, but are treated very favorably.

22. Henry C. K. Liu, September 29, 2005, 2http://henryckliu.com/page15.html.

23. Insurers' activities in credit default swaps were not as unsupervised as many commentators have portrayed them to be. For AIG and the monolines, the creation of CDS-writing subs required express regulatory authority, frequently from several layers of regulators. The CDS "financial products" subsidiary was reviewed and approved first by the New York insurance department, and some of them have said restrictions were imposed on what could be written from the entity. Similarly, AIG and some of its peers operated their financial products units out of the UK, where the FSA reviewed and regulated them. Among the things considered by the regulators: collateral posting requirements, products insured, and ratings of the products insured.

24. Satyajit Das, "The Credit Default Swap ('CDS') Market—Will It Unravel?" Satyajit Das's Blog, May 30, 2008, http://www.wilmott.com/blogs/satyajitdas/index.cfm/2008/5/30/The-Credit-Default-Swap-CDS-Market—Will-It-Unravel.

25. V. Prashanth, "Necessity of Insurable Interest in Insurance Contracts," Corporate Law Cases, *All India Reporter,* Nagpur, India (August 1, 2008), http://ssrn.com/abstract=1302372.

26. Lina Saigol and James Politi, "M&A deals soar despite credit concerns," *Financial Times,* June 28, 2007, http://www.ft.com/cms/s/0/67e4ddc2–25a6–11dc-b338–000b5df10621.html.

27. Tett, 148.

28. Many industry participants depict CLOs as a type of CDO, and go to some lengths to refer to CDOs as "ABS CDOs" for the CDOs that were built from bonds, as opposed to the sort that used credit default swaps. As we have mentioned, however, CDOs are resecuritizations, and thus are intrinsically far more complex and leveraged than CLOs. Despite whatever other similarities they might have, this difference is so fundamental that it seems misleading to lump the two together (given that CLOs actually have more in common with a simple structured securitization than a CDO). Our use is also similar to that of the financial media, who also tend to use "CDO" to refer to ABS CDOs as opposed to CLOs. Where this all starts to get muddy is when discussing synthetic products, meaning ones based on credit default swaps rather than loans. There, it is common for a synthetic CLO to be called a "synthetic CDO." But that term is also used for a synthetic CDO

made largely from credit default swaps that reference mortgages. We hope knowledgeable readers will forgive our finesse here, which we thought would make the discussion more accessible to generalists.

29. While cash and synthetic products were interchangeable for most investors, the mechanisms by which they affected the underlying loan markets were different. In the interest of not inducing the dreaded My Eyes Glaze Over syndrome in generalist readers, we are sticking largely with the more accessible product.

30. This may seem to contradict the statement that some loan pools would use overcollateralization, meaning they set the value of the securities trust for less than the face value of the loans. But in this case, the face value would be lower than market value if they were simply sold to a third party. In the example in the text above, if all the pieces of a structured vehicle together were priced at $975, the value of the whole loan was almost certainly lower, say $970.

31. There had been a market for subprime mortgages in the 1990s (which showed considerable losses by the end of the decade), but those mortgages were mainly on manufactured housing, and thus not comparable to the post-2000 subprime market.

32. Robert L. Rodriguez, "Absence of Fear," (speech, CFA Society of Chicago), June 28, 2007), available at http://www.fpafunds.com/news_070703_absense_of_fear.asp.

33. This structure was often called a NIMlet, in memory of an earlier NIM (net interest margin bond) structure that had been used by thinly capitalized mortgage issuers. In 1998, the original NIMs failed, due to weak structural features, and the market cooled way down. The new NIM or NIMlet had enough excess interest that was available before losses started accruing that it got paid off very quickly. As is unsurprising, the NIMs were pretty binary bonds—either they worked and you got your money back fast, or losses came in higher than you expected and you got nothing back at all.

34. There was a great range for structures for CDOs, but a very high percentage of the deal would inevitably be rated AAA.

35. Keep in mind that while it is true that diversification can reduce risk, as we have discussed, the approaches used in financial economics to quantify risk reduction are not sound.

36. Attentive readers may notice the difference between the percentages in Figure 9.2 and the percentages shown here. The illustrative CDO chart shows the par amount of each tranche, that is, the amount the structurer expected the various investors to pay for each slice. However, these deals had loss cushions for the rated tranches above and beyond that provided by the equity investor. First, all subprime RMBS have overcollateralization, which was tantamount to recognizing some losses up front. Second, they had "excess spread," meaning the interest paid out to all the rated bondholders was less than the interest paid, at least if the mortgages performed, on the underlying loan pool.

37. Amita Shrivastava, Deepika Kothari, Karandeep Bains, Trevor Harris, Cecilia Lam, Joseph Rocco, William Fricke, Debash Chatterjee, Sally Acevedo, Brian Harris, and Celia Chen, "Moody's Resi Landscape," Moody's Investors Services, September 17, 2009, 16. Pipeline losses consist of losses incurred to date plus expected losses based on current serious delinquencies. Ratings agencies can forecast pipeline losses with a high degree of certainty.

38. Excel spreadsheet prepared by Olivier Daviron, via personal e-mail communication to author, September 28, 2009.

39. Those of you who were awake during chapter 3 will remember that blob ("rough circle") that Harry Markowitz drew. If you are A students, you might also recall that being on the perimeter of that blob was a very good thing. The fancy term for that is now "efficient investment frontier" or similar client-intimidating mumbo-jumbo. But since thinking about that too hard might lead to embarrassing questions, particularly since Markowitz and Sharpe have moved on from that idea, fund consultants like to claim the hedge funds can produce "alpha," which is a fancy way of saying they can beat the market. Since so few funds actually do that, the funds and their minders have moved on to new finesses, like claiming the funds produce "synthetic beta" when anyone who understands what that really means also recognizes you can produce that far more cheaply than the fat fees hedge funds charge. But the fund consultants have little incentive to lift that veil.

40. "2007 DATABOOK: Hedge Funds," *Pensions & Investments* 35, no. 26 (December 24, 2007): 38–40, http://search.ebscohost.com/login.aspx?direct=true&db=buh&AN=28157481&site=ehost-live.

41. Maxey, "Cracking the Credit Market Code." These strategies involved a high amount of borrowing, so the share of "funds invested," as in assets under management multiplied by the leverage used in that strategy, is much greater than normal style comparisons, which are based on AUM (assets under management, meaning before borrowing), would indicate.

42. Tett, 124–125.

43. Bank of England, "Financial Stability Report," 21 (April 2007), vol. 16, available at http://www .bankofengland.co.uk/publications/fsr/2007/fsrfull0704.pdf.

44. New accounting treatment post Sarbanes Oxley for SPVs meant some parties that might otherwise be logical targets for the equity were ruled out because they might be required to consolidate the entire deal. The general takers of the equity were the CDO managers and hedge funds. Until late 2006, most investors wanted to see that the manager had skin in the game and therefore expected the manager to hold at least some meaningful portion. This investor requirement started to break down in 2006. Bank-sponsored CDO managers and other standalone managers of ABS CDOs and CLOs would sell off some or all of the equity during that time. The sudden demand for the equity layer is indirect confirmation that others were copying the Magnetar strategy.

45. These deals were not underwritten in the traditional sense (as in for public offerings) but since many banks did warehouse the instruments that went into a CDO, the use of the term would not be misleading.

46. "The Role of Valuation and Leverage in Procyclicality," CGFS Papers 34, Committee on the Global Financial System, Bank for International Settlements, April 2009, 12, available at http://www .bis.org/publ/cgfs34.pdf.

47. This was generally done not by shorting the CDO tranche directly, but tranches of the underlying bonds that would be considered to be good proxies, or an ABX sub-index.

48. Another version was the so-called correlation trade. A trader could describe this strategy succinctly as follows: the position was delta neutral, but it would pay off handsomely if correlation went to 1 (e.g., due to the fact that the market was mispricing correlation by having such massive spread differentials between AAA super senior and mezzanine/equity tranches).

49. The illusion that lack of price movement due to illiquidity was tantamount to stability not only distorted how investors and consultant evaluated hedge fund performance, but also affected how dealers looked at their counterparty exposures. Dealers were willing to repo rated ABS CDO paper for hedge funds at very cheap levels due to "stable prices." A CDO trader who asked to remain anonymous reported (via comments on a draft of this chapter on September 3, 2009) that "Bear Stearns Asset Management was getting only a 2% haircut against its AAA and AA ABS CDO paper before they blew up. With that kind of haircut it was really the dealers who got stuck with losses once the fund vaporized."

50. The CDO manager would usually be required to retain 20% of the equity tranche, but that was generally in lieu of receiving fees.

51. The manager didn't even collect and disburse the payments, the trustee did that. All the manager did was paper the trade, which tricked investors into thinking the deal was "arms length" from the underwriter. Usually managers were ex-bankers themselves, looking to cash in on the 10 basis points (0.10%) senior management fee on billions of assets under management with little or no staff.

52. Serena Ng and Carrick Mollenkamp, "A Fund Behind Astronomical Losses," *Wall Street Journal,* January 14, 2008, http://online.wsj.com/article/SB120027155742887331.html.

53. Comment on chapter draft by CDO trader who asked to remain anonymous, September 3, 2009.

54. Ng and Mollenkamp, "A Fund Behind Astronomical Losses."

55. Whether they showed a profit or not ("had positive or negative carry") would depend on how large a short bet they put on relative to their long position. But they could go short in a significant way on the income initially thrown off by an equity tranche.

56. Ibid.

57. Per an employee of a large European bank who has asked to remain anonymous, personal e-mail communication with author, July 20, 2009; on the John Paulson hedge fund profits of $15 billion for shorting subprime, see Gregory Zuckerman, *The Greatest Trade Ever: The Behind-the-Scenes Story of How John Paulson Defied Wall Street and Made Financial History* (New York: Broadway Books, 2009), 2. Magnetar, a $9 billion hedge fund, was reported in the Ng and Mollenkamp story to have earned 25%, which is not Paulson-level results unless their subprime gains were offset by

losses, and one source has said that was the case. Our purpose in analyzing Magnetar's assumed structure was to assess the consequences for the fund's counterparties and the market as a whole, not to estimate how much Magnetar earned. Using the assumptions in appendix II, that Magnetar was net short $150 million subprime for every $1 billion of CDOs created, a $30 billion program, would have given them a total short position of $4.5 billion. However, hedge fund manager John Paulson (who relied mainly on more costly ABX shorts) also launched $5 billion of pure synthetic CDOs, a different structure than Magnetar used, and he bought ALL the CDS protection in those deals (see Zuckerman, 179–182). Had Magnetar done the same with the structure we assumed, their total short position on a $30 billion program would be $22.5 billion, which is a comparable scale to Paulson's position (at one point he held CDS against $25 billion of subprime RMBS). Ironically, to the extent that Magnetar did not buy all the CDS created by its ABS CDOs (as Paulson did for his smaller, pure synthetic program), other subprime shorts like Paulson were the beneficiaries. Any CDS created by these new CDOs that were surplus to the sponsor's needs had the effect of lowering the cost of going short for others who were shorting subprime.

58. As this book goes to press, a precedent on a lawsuit may erode this exemption as far as complex instruments are concerned. We discuss this case briefly in chapter 10.
59. Per Thomas Adams, former managing director at Ambac and FGIC, personal e-mail communication with author, September 17, 2009, and comment on chapter draft by a CDO trader who asked to remain anonymous, September 3, 2009.
60. Per an employee of a large European bank who has asked to remain anonymous, personal e-mail communication with author, July 20, 2009. Keep in mind that while the equity tranche threw off very rich payments, investors did not get substantially all of their money back in only two payment periods. If they were lucky, they might get their principal back in one and one half to two years.
61. Per Thomas Adams, personal e-mail communication with author, September 22, 2009.
62. Ronald Temple, "Clarifying the US Mortgage Crisis: Context and Consequences," Lazard Investment Research, December 2006, 6, http://www.lazardnet.com/lam/us/tpd/pdfs/Inv_Research_Mortgage_Crisis.pdf.
63. Tanta, "Subprime 2000–2006," Calculated Risk: Finance and Economics [blog], October 9, 2007, http://www.calculatedriskblog.com/2007/10/subprime–2000–2006.html.
64. [1/(3% x 5%)] x 80%. Some readers may quibble that this analysis differs from the usual construction of leverage, in which the very bottom-most layer drives the deal. The bottom-most tranche was the driver for CDOs, and we focused on the equity tranche there. However, as we have mentioned, for the subprime mortgage security, there was ample demand for the equity layer of a subprime mortgage security, so it was not a limiting factor in creating those deals. Recall that subprime equity tranches could always find buyers. Mortgage companies were happy to keep equity until about 2002, when a structure called the net interest margin bond, a pool of interest backed by the excess interest (interest paid to the equity holder after overcollateralization was reached and losses were covered), was introduced. Due to the short duration of net interest margin bonds, they appealed to some hedge funds, who would buy new ones as the older ones paid down. Thanks to this structure, the equity in subprime bonds became very liquid. So it was placing the BBB to AA tranches, particularly the BBB, that constrained the sale of subprime RMBS.
65. "The global housing boom," *The Economist,* June 16, 2005, http://www.economist.com/business/displaystory.cfm?story_id=E1_QDSJDNS.
66. Tanta, "Ranieri on the MBS Market: It's Broke," Calculated Risk: Finance & Economics [blog], April 28, 2007, http://www.calculatedriskblog.com/2007/04/ranieri-on-mbs-market-its-broke.html.
67. Nomi Prins, *Other People's Money: The Corporate Mugging of America* (New York: New Press, 2004), 7.
68. This is how it played out in the Canadian asset–backed commercial paper market. Investors were told they could either force the liquidation of the conduits and lose most of their investment, or convert their short-term commercial paper into term notes that would match the maturity of the assets in the vehicle. None of the Canadian dealers took back their conduits.
69. Gary B. Gorton and Andrew Metrick, "Securitized Banking and the Run on Repo," Yale ICF Working Paper No. 09–14, July 29, 2009, http://ssrn.com/abstract=1440752. Note the chart is Figure 4, 39; the table which sets forth the index composition is Table I, Panel D, 47.
70. Gorton, "Slapped in the Face by the Invisible Hand," 33–34.

71. A regulator who has asked to remain anonymous said that the Fed had been concerned for quite some time about the repo market. Money market funds would lend several hundred billions of dollars to broker-dealers via repos, taking collateral ranging from Treasuries to mortgage-backed securities to paper that was even more exotic. The fear was that this had become a very important yet unreliable source of funding for the broker-dealers. A major firm could become insolvent overnight if enough repo funding was withdrawn, as happened with Bear Stearns (via e-mail to the author, September 8, 2009).

72. Henny Sender and Michael Mackenzie, "Fed plans repo markets revamp," *Financial Times*, June 21, 2009, http://www.ft.com/cms/s/0/d1c74b5c–5e99–11de–91ad–00144feabdc0.html?ftcamp=rss.

73. Iain Dey and Danny Fortson, "JP Morgan 'brought down' Lehman Brothers," *Times Online*, October 5, 2008, http://business.timesonline.co.uk/tol/business/industry_sectors/banking_and _finance/article4882281.ece.

74. "Integrity vs. Intelligence," Vox Populi [blog], June 30, 2009, http://voxday.blogspot.com/ 2009/06/integrity-vs-intelligence.html.

75. Maxey, "Cracking the Credit Market Code," 18–19.

76. Note that the seemingly static loan volumes mask a more complicated dynamic. Some firms that lost access to so-called market-based credit did have backup bank credit lines, and most of these assuredly used them. Thus the flat loan volume is likely a combination of some lending shifting out of the shadow banking system back to conventional banks, together with a contraction in other types of bank loans.

77. Tett, "Finger of blame points to shadow banking's implosion."

78. Tyler Durden, "Chasing the Shadow of Money," Zero Hedge [blog], May 17, 2009, http://zero-hedge.blogspot.com/2009/05/chasing-shadow-of-money.html.

CHAPTER 10

1. Yves Smith, "Geithner Plan Smackdown Wrap," Naked Capitalism [blog], February 10, 2009, http://www.nakedcapitalism.com/2009/02/geithner-plan-smackdown-wrap.html.

2. Thomas Ferguson, "Financial Regulation? Don't Get Your Hopes Up," TPMCafé [blog], April 17, 2008, http://tpmcafe.talkingpointsmemo.com/2008/04/17/financial_regulation_dont_get/.

3. "Geithner's Opening Statement to Senate Banking Committee," available at Real Time Economics [blog], February 10, 2009, http://blogs.wsj.com/economics/2009/02/10/geithners-opening-statement-to-senate-banking-committee/.

4. Aaron Task, "Part II: U.S. Too 'Politically Frightened' to Admit Truth About Banks, FT's Wolf Says," *TechTicker*, February 9, 2009, http://finance.yahoo.com/tech-ticker/article/172116/Part-II-U.S.-Too-%22Politically-Frightened%22-to-Admit-Truth-About-Banks-FT's-Wolf-Says;_ylt=Ak ocv0eYXCCcLFgI.Ou6MgG7YWsA?tickers=XLF,SKF,FAZ,C,BAC,JPM,WFC; and Martin Wolf, "Big Risks for the Insurer of Last Resort," *Financial Times*, March 5, 2009, http://www.ft.com/ cms/s/0/825cf2ea–09b9–11de-add8–0000779fd2ac.html.

5. Smith, "Geithner Plan Smackdown Wrap."

6. Yves Smith, "Now It's Official: Public Private Partnership to Overpay for Toxic Bank Assets," Naked Capitalism [blog], March 16, 2009, http://www.nakedcapitalism.com/2009/03/now-its-official-public-private.html.

7. John Carney, "Mark To Market Reform Approved By Accounting Board," Clusterstock [blog], April 2, 2009, http://www.businessinsider.com/mark-to-market-reform-approved-by-accounting-board–2009–4.

8. Paul Kedrosky, "John Paulson's Year-End Letter," Infectious Greed [blog], January 30, 2009, http://paul.kedrosky.com/archives/2009/01/30/john_paulsons_y.html.

9. Luc Laeven and Fabian Valencia, "Systemic Banking Crises: A New Database," IMF Working Paper, November 2008, 4, http://www.imf.org/external/pubs/ft/wp/2008/wp08224.pdf.

10. "Bernanke Says Stock Market Ignoring Fundamentals," *Reuters*, February 25, 2009, http://www .financialpost.com/story.html?id=1328498.

11. Rebecca Christie and Robert Schmidt, "U.S. Sets a Six-Month Deadline for New Bank Capital," *Bloomberg*, February 25, 2009, http://www.bloomberg.com/apps/news?pid=20601087&sid=az64z r5U0X.E&refer=home.

12. Yves Smith, "William Black: 'There Are No Real Stress Tests Going On,'" Naked Capitalism [blog], February 17, 2009, http://www.nakedcapitalism.com/2009/02/william-black-there-are-no-real-stress.html.

13. Yves Smith, "Bank Stress Tests Now Officially a Garbage In, Garbage Out Exercise," Naked Capitalism [blog], April 18, 2009, http://www.nakedcapitalism.com/2009/04/bank-stress-tests-now-officially.html.

14. Yves Smith, "Details on Banks' Victory Over Treasury in Stress Tests Emerge," Naked Capitalism [blog], May 9, 2009, http://www.nakedcapitalism.com/2009/05/details-on-banks-victory-over-treasury.html.

15. Yves Smith, "Bank Stress Testing: Less Than Meets the Eye," Naked Capitalism [blog], February 12, 2009, http://www.nakedcapitalism.com/2009/02/bank-stress-testing-less-than-meets-eye .html; and Smith, "Bank Stress Tests Now Officially a Garbage In, Garbage Out Exercise."

16. Daniel Wagner, "Fed Tests Harder on Regional Banks," *Associated Press,* April 21, 2009, http://www.sddt.com/News/article.cfm?SourceCode=20090421fad.

17. "Geithner Cold Open," *Saturday Night Live,* original airdate May 10, 2009, available at http://www.nbc.com/Saturday_Night_Live/video/clips/geithner-cold-open/1099562/.

18. One has to wonder who was tipping off the press. The banks did not gain from showing how supine the Treasury was; it seems reasonable to surmise it was government employees unhappy with the process.

19. Of these reductions, some of the ones at Citigroup do appear defensible, since they had some pending sales of businesses that had been signed but had not yet closed. However, there is widespread agreement that the assumptions on future profits, which was an important source for strengthening the banks' capital bases, were too optimistic.

20. Francesco Guerrera, Saskia Scholtes, and Krishna Guha, "US banks claim line softened on $74bn," *Financial Times,* May 8, 2009, http://www.ft.com/cms/s/0/963b0ad2–3be0–11de-acbc–00144fe abdc0.html.

21. "Geithner's Opening Statement to Senate Banking Committee," available at Real Time Economics [blog].

22. Rebecca Christie, "TARP Inspector Urges Treasury to Track Banks' Aid More Closely," *Bloomberg,* July 19, 2009, http://www.bloomberg.com/apps/news?pid=20601087&sid=aFDeDo5TkPMs.

23. Silla Brush, "TARP Watchdog Says Treasury Lacking Bank Data," *The Hill,* July 18, 2009, http://thehill.com/homenews/administration/50799-tarp-watchdog-says-treasury-lacking-bank-data. While money is clearly fungible, Barofsky found banks were able to say how they were using the money. Perhaps more important, why did Geithner promise to keep track of the efficacy of expenditures if he had no intention of doing so?

24. Willem Buiter, "More On Robbing the US Tax Payer and Debauching the FDIC and the Fed," Williem Buiter's Maverecon [blog], March 26, 2009, http://blogs.ft.com/maverecon/2009/03/more-on-robbing-the-us-tax-payer-and-debauching-the-fdic-and-the-fed/. The only reason that that did not come to pass on a large scale was that the program in question, the Legacy Loans program, was so badly thought out that it never got off the ground in a meaningful fashion.

25. Ibid.

26. John Fraher and Scott Lanman, "Ex-BOE Official Slams Fed, Sparking Hottest Jackson Hole Debate," *Bloomberg,* August 24, 2008, http://www.bloomberg.com/apps/news?pid=20601087&sid =ayUAEYi51WG0&refer=home.

27. Fraher and Lanman, "Ex-BOE Official Slams Fed, Sparking Hottest Jackson Hole Debate," *Bloomberg,* August 24, 2008, http://www.bloomberg.com/apps/news?pid=20601087&sid=ayUAE Yi51WG0&refer=home . In case readers think I am being unfair in mentioning the Fed and the stress tests in the same sentence, the guilt by association is richly deserved. The Fed and Treasury have been working hand in glove throughout the crisis. Moreover, the Fed, in Congressional testimony, indicated it intends to adopt and build on the superficial stress test procedures.

28. John Kay, "How the Competent Bankers Can Be Assisted," *Financial Times,* March 3, 2009, http://www.ft.com/cms/s/0/5da077fe–082b–11de–8a33–0000779fd2ac.html.

29. Alexis Leondis, "Tallying Trillions in Bailout, Bankruptcy: Commentary," *Bloomberg,* December 31, 2008, http://www.bloomberg.com/apps/news?pid=newsarchive&sid=aYwo1tZqGFgA.

30. Sudeep Reddy and Michael R. Crittenden, "Fed's Kohn Concedes Risk in AIG Rescue," *Wall Street Journal,* March 6, 2009, http://online.wsj.com/article/SB123629999083146775.html.

31. The treatment of AIG is another peculiar example of how Americans' distaste for anything that looks like nationalization can to lead to policy remedies that are much worse. AIG was technically

79.9% owned by the government, the excuse for not assuming full control being the same as used with the Fannie and Freddie conservatorships: that full ownership would require AIG's debts to be consolidated with other government debt. Ahem, if the Fed found out a way to treat acquired AIG assets as off-balance sheet, I am sure Hank Paulson could have figured out a way had he put his mind to it. And irrespective of whether the ownership was 79.9% or full, the U.S. government gave AIG far more latitude than a private owner of that magnitude would have.

32. Tyler Durden, "Guest Post: The Banks Were Profitable In January And February Thanks To . . . AIG," Naked Capitalism [blog], March 29, 2009, http://www.nakedcapitalism.com/2009/03/guest-post-banks-were-profitable-in.html.

33. Julie MacIntosh and Alan Beattie, "AIG publishes counterparty list," Financial Times, March 15, 2009, http://www.ft.com/cms/s/0/a62fbd5a–11b7–11de–87b1–0000779fd2ac.html?ftcamp=rss.

34. Yves Smith, "On the Fed's 'Shock and Awe,'" Naked Capitalism [blog], March 19, 2009, http://www.nakedcapitalism.com/2009/03/on-feds-shock-and-awe.html.

35. Office of the Special Inspector General for the Troubled Asset Relief Program, "Quarterly Report to Congress," July 21, 2009, Chart 3.5, http://www.sigtarp.gov/reports/congress/2009/July2009_Quarterly_Report_to_Congress.pdf.

36. Barry Ritholtz, "Bailout Costs to Date," The Big Picture [blog], September 25, 2009, http://www.ritholtz.com/blog/2009/09/bailout-costs-to-date/.

37. Ibid. Of the $3.025 trillion currently deployed, the programs that in part or in their entirety benefit individuals directly are: Bush stimulus package ($168 billion), Obama stimulus package ($303 billion), Cash for Clunkers ($2.88 billion) and the HUD programs ($3.25 billion).

38. Knut Sandal, "The Nordic Banking Crises in the Early 1990s—Resolution Methods and Fiscal Costs," in The Norwegian Banking Crisis, edited by Thorvald G. Moe, Jon A. Solheim, and Bent Vale, Original Papers 33 (Oslo: Norges Bank, 2004), p. 94, available at http://www.norges-bank.no/upload/import/publikasjoner/skriftserie/33/hele_heftet.pdf. Regulatory reforms fell short in Sweden; its banks are now involved in sure-to-end-badly misadventures in the Baltics.

39. As this book goes to press, the Federal Reserve has been reported to be considering clawbacks. However, given its extraordinarily industry-friendly posture, and a recent barrage of threats by Congress to subject its activities ex monetary policy-setting to far more scrutiny, this appears to be more of an effort to try to cultivate its image as a tough-minded regulator and defend its turf than an authority it plans to wield seriously.

40. Edmund Andrews, "F.D.I.C. Sells Failed Bank's Troubled Mortgages to Private Investor," The New York Times, September 16, 2009, http://www.nytimes.com/2009/09/17/business/17loans.html?_r=1.

41. James Kwak, "Just Baffling," The Baseline Scenario [blog], September 24, 2009, http://baselinescenario.com/2009/09/24/just-baffling/.

42. Gross VaR would take the loss estimate for each business and add them up; net allows for the fact that some risks partially offset each other.

43. Satyajit Das, "No Ponzi Game Can Ever Be Allowed to Stop," DNA India, August 8. 2009, http://www.dnaindia.com/money/interview_no-ponzi-game-can-ever-be-allowed-to-stop_1280538.

44. John Kemp, "Goldman, Liquidity and VAR," Reuters Blogs, July 16, 2009, http://blogs.reuters.com/commentaries/2009/07/16/goldman-liquidity-and-var/.

45. Paul Jackson. "A Game of Credit Cost Smoke and Mirrors at Wells Fargo?," Housing Wire, April 9, 2009, http://www.housingwire.com/2009/04/09/credit-cost-smoke-at-mirrors-at-wells-fargo/.

46. Michael Siconolfi and Ann Davis, "Citi in $100 Million Pay Clash," Wall Street Journal, July 26, 2009, http://online.wsj.com/article/SB124848894204180877.html#mod=testMod.

47. Ibid.

48. "Citi Trader, Who Made $100 Million Last Year, Insists on Keeping His Deal in Place," Naked Capitalism [blog], July 25, 2009, comment of 2:48 P.M., July 25, 2009, http://www.nakedcapitalism.com/2009/07/citi-trader-who-made–100-million-last.html.

49. Bradley Keoun, "Pandit to Revamp Phibro, Says $100 Million Too Much," Bloomberg, September 18, 2009, http://www.bloomberg.com/apps/news?pid=newsarchive&sid=aLZVm1JMcXcM.

50. Roger Ehrenberg, "Fixing Wall Street? The Feds Blew It," Information Arbitrage [blog], August 2, 2009, http://www.informationarbitrage.com/2009/08/fixing-wall-street-the-feds-blew-it.html.

51. "Text of Obama's Speech on Financial Reform," The New York Times, September 14, 2009, http://www.nytimes.com/2009/09/15/business/15obamatext.html.

52. Jonathan Weil, "Too-Big Banks Can Take Comfort in Obama's Math: Jonathan Weil," *Bloomberg*, September 15, 2009, http://www.bloomberg.com/apps/news?pid=20601039&sid=aDi3gjYfB0h0.

53. "Taxpayer Losses Decrease after Ten of the Nation's Leading Banks Pay Back TARP Funds Ethisphere TARP Index Still Down $148.2 Billion Overall as of June 19," Ethisphere, June 22, 2009, http://ethisphere.com/ethisphere-tarp-index-report/.

54. Jonathan Stempel, "Rating agencies lose free-speech claim," *Reuters*, September 3, 2009, http://www.reuters.com/article/companyNews/idUKTRE58256420090903.

55. Austin Kilgore, "SEC Chair Seeks Transparency of Credit-Rating Agencies," *Housing Wire*, July 14, 2009, http://www.housingwire.com/2009/07/14/sec-chair-seeks-transparency-of-credit-rating-agencies/.

56. Joanna Chung, Brooke Masters, and Francesco Guerrera, "SEC chief in call for funding shake-up," *Financial Times*, August 5, 2009, http://www.ft.com/cms/s/0/4bcd5bd6–81f8–11de–9c5e–00144feabdc0.html.

57. Ibid.

58. Note it would take some effort to obtain this input, since knowledge of over-the-counter markets is by nature limited to the dealers, their customers, and professionals hired by them. Nevertheless, there are also independent experts who could offer a check on the guaranteed-to-be-positive view the financial industry will present of its wares and operations.

59. Yves Smith, "Disturbing Conversation with Fed Official on Subprimes," Naked Capitalism [blog], May 8, 2007, http://www.nakedcapitalism.com/2007/05/disturbing-conversation-with-fed.html.

60. "The tripartite system 'was responsible for the crisis'" *Politics.co.uk*, June 2, 2009. http://www.politics.co.uk/news/economy-and-finance/the-tripartite-system-was-responsible-for-the-crisis—$1300239.htm

61. Bank of England, "Financial Stability Report," issue no. 21 (April 2007), p. 7, available at http://www.bankofengland.co.uk/publications/fsr/2007/fsrfull0704.pdf.

62. Simon Johnson, "The Quiet Coup," *The Atlantic*, May 2009, http://www.theatlantic.com/doc/200905/imf-advice.

63. Yves Smith, "Bankruptcy Cramdown Defeated: Banksters Again Prevail Over Real Economy," Naked Capitalism [blog], April 30, 2009, http://www.nakedcapitalism.com/2009/04/bankruptcy-cramdown-defeated-banksters.html.

64. Carl Hulse, "Senate Rejects Limit on Credit-Card Interest Rates," The Caucus [blog], March 13, 2009, http://thecaucus.blogs.nytimes.com/2009/05/13/senate-rejects-limit-on-credit-card-interest-rates/.

65. Even the Office of the Comptroller of the Currency took a tougher line on subprime lending than the Fed did.

66. Robert L. Borosage, "Gut Check Time on Shackling Wall Street," Huffington Post [blog], June 23, 2009, http://www.huffingtonpost.com/robert-l-borosage/gut-check-time-on-shackli_b_219870.html.

67. Steve Labaton, "White House Pares Its Financial Reform Plan," *The New York Times*, September 23, 2009, http://www.nytimes.com/2009/09/24/business/24regulate.html?_r=1&ref=business

68. Patrick Temple-West, "Clearing Derivatives at Issue," *The Bond Buyer*, September 18, 2009, http://www.bondbuyer.com/article.html?id=20090917PBPAT08G.

69. Damian Paletta an Jon Helsenrath, "Bankers Face Sweeping Curbs on Pay," *Wall Street Journal*, September 18, 2009, http://online.wsj.com/article/SB125324292666522101.html.

70. Thorald Barker, "Fed Abandons Its Reserve on Banker Pay," *Wall Street Journal*, September 21, 2009, http://online.wsj.com/article/SB125330954120723935.html.

71. Frank Partnoy, *Infectious Greed: How Deceit and Risk Corrupted the Financial Markets* (New York: Macmillan, 2003), 142–143, 185.

72. Simon Johnson, "G10 Thinking: 'In the Medium Run, We Are All Retired,'" The Baseline Scenario [blog], September 22, 2009, http://baselinescenario.com/2009/09/22/g20-thinking-in-the-medium-run-we-are-all-retired/.

73. Menzie Chinn, "The G20 and Rebalancing," Econbrowser [blog], September 24, 2009, http://www.econbrowser.com/archives/2009/09/the_g20_and_reb.html.

74. The absence of major wars didn't hurt either.

75. Peter Temin, *Lessons from the Great Depression* (Cambridge, Mass.: MIT Press, 1989), 33–34.

76. John Hempton, "The 1934 Securities Act and All That," Bronte Capital [blog], October 14, 2008, http://brontecapital.blogspot.com/2008/10/1934-securities-exchange-act-and-all.html.

77. Robert D. Orol, "Banks Buying Back TARP Warrants at a Discount, Panel Says," *MarketWatch,* July 10, 2009, http://www.marketwatch.com/story/banks-buying-back-tarp-warrants-at-discount-panel?siteid=bnbh.

78. Satyajit Das, "Mark-to-Make Believe—Accounting Practices and the Credit Crisis," unpublished article, 7.

79. Amar Bhidé, "In Praise of Primitive Finance," *The Economists' Voice* 6, no. 3, article 8 (2009): 4–5, http://www.bepress.com/cgi/viewcontent.cgi?context=http%3A%2F%2Fwww.bepress.com%2Fev&article=1534&date=&mt=MTI0OTI3NjIxNw%3D%3D&access_ok_form=Continue.

80. Willem Buiter, "Save Banking, Not the Bankers or the Banks; the Case of ING," Willem Buiter's Maverecon [blog], February 13, 2009, http://blogs.ft.com/maverecon/2009/02/save-banking-not-the-bankers-or-the-banks-the-case-of-ing/.

81. Willem Buiter, "How Likely Is a Sterling Crisis or: Is London Really Reykjavik-on-Thames?," Willem Buiter's Maverecon [blog], November 13, 2008, http://blogs.ft.com/maverecon/2008/11/how-likely-is-a-sterling-crisis-or-is-london-really-reykjavik-on-thames/.

82. Ibid.

83. Jill Treanor, "King Calls for Banks to Be 'Cut Down to Size,'" *Guardian,* June 17, 2009, http://www.guardian.co.uk/business/2009/jun/17/king-in-bank-reform-call.

84. Willem Buiter, "Can the US Afford a Keynesian Stimulus?" Willem Buiter's Maverecon [blog], January 5, 2009, http://blogs.ft.com/maverecon/2009/01/can-the-us-economy-afford-a-keynesian-stimulus/.

85. Paul Kedrosky, "How the U.S. Saved the European Banking System," Infectious Greed [blog], September 30, 2008, http://paul.kedrosky.com/archives/2008/09/30/how_the_us_save.html.

86. Yves Smith, "Citi and Federal Government in New Non-Rescue Rescue Talks," Naked Capitalism [blog], March 10, 2009, http://www.nakedcapitalism.com/2009/03/citi-and-federal-government-in-new-non.html.

87. Jeff Bater, "Consumer Credit Fell Again in May," *Wall Street Journal,* July 8, 2009, http://online.wsj.com/article/SB124708075158413361.html?mod=googlenews_wsj.

88. Vaughn S. Armstrong and Norman D. Gardiner, "Individual Investors, Electronic Trading, and Turnover," paper presented at the Allied Academies International Conference, Maui, Hawaii, October 13–16, 2004, 1, available at http://www.alliedacademies.org/Public/Proceedings/Proceedings15/pase-3-2-maui04.pdf ; Interview of Russell Napier, "Napier Expects U.S. Recession on Asian 'Credit Boom': Video," *Bloomberg,* September 23, 2009, http://www.bloomberg.com/apps/news?pid=newsarchive&sid=aBBdFq4_cIBM.

89. Yves Smith, "How the Prisoner's Dilemma and Unintended Consequences are Accelerating the Credit Crisis," Naked Capitalism [blog], March 17, 2008, http://www.nakedcapitalism.com/2008/03/how-prisoners-dilemma-and-unintended.html.

90. Satyajit Das, "OTC Derivatives Regulation Proposals—Neat, Plausible, and Wrong!" Satyajit Das's Blog: Fear & Loathing in Financial Products, July 17, 2009, http://www.wilmott.com/blogs/satyajitdas/index.cfm/2009/7/17/OTC-Derivative-Regulation-Proposals—Neat-Plausible-and-Wrong.

91. "Following the A.I.G. Money," *The New York Times,* March 14, 2009, http://www.nytimes.com/2009/03/15/opinion/15sun1.html?_r=1.

92. Satyajit Das, "Credit Crash?" Wilmot [blog], February 2007 attachment, 7, http://www.wilmott.com/blogs/satyajitdas/enclosures/creditcrash-sdas(feb2007).pdf.

93. Abigail Moses, Hamish Risk, and Neil Unmack, "Credit Swaps Thwart Fed's Ease as Debt Costs Surge," *Bloomberg,* March 6, 2008, http://www.bloomberg.com/apps/news?pid=20601109&sid=aB8RuoKZoKRM&refer=home; and Geraud Charpin, "View of the Day: Credit Markets," *Financial Times,* April 30, 2008, http://www.ft.com/cms/s/0/370d9b26–16be–11dd-bbfc–000779fd2ac.html.

94. Donald MacKenzie, *An Engine, Not a Camera: How Financial Models Shape Markets* (Cambridge, Mass.: MIT Press, 2008), 3.

95. MacKenzie, 189.

96. We have pooh-poohed the widespread use of Gaussian distributions to estimate risk. Instead, the Chicago options exchanges base margin requirements on Lévy-stable distributions, which are a much better proxy.

97. Satyajit Das, "OTC Derivatives Regulation Proposals—Neat, Plausible, and Wrong!"
98. Gillian Tett, "Insight: Kazakh Bank Falls Foul of CDS," *Financial Times*, April 30, 2009, http://www.ft.com/cms/s/0/fa0428ee–35a7–11de-a997–00144feabdc0.html.
99. Martin Wolf, "Big Risks for Insurer of the Last Resort," *Financial Times*, March 5, 2009, http://www.ft.com/cms/s/0/825cf2ea–09b9–11de-add8–0000779fd2ac.html.
100. Obviously, market-making inevitably involves short-term position taking, but regulators can monitor the size and nature of overnight positions to ascertain whether the trading operations have strayed into proprietary trading.
101. Partnoy, 2003, 281.

AFTERWORD

1. Dwight David Eisenhower, Farewell Address to the Nation, January 17, 1961.
2. Andrew G Haldane, "The $100 Billion Question," (comments, Institute of Regulation & Risk, Hong Kong, March 30, 2010), http://www.bis.org/review/r100406d.pdf.
3. David Dayen, "Geithner Poised to Gut New Derivatives Rules with Foreign Exchange Swaps Exemption," Firedoglake [blog], March 21, 2011, http://news.firedoglake.com/2011/03/21/geithner-poised-to-gut-new-derivatives-rules-with-foreign-exchange-swaps-exemption/.
4. London Banker, "More on the lunacy of the Basel Accords," London Banker [blog], December 18, 2010, http://londonbanker.blogspot.com/2010/12/more-on-lunacy-of-basle-accords.html.
5. Richard Smith, "More Evidence of Undercapitalization/Insolvency of Major Banks," Naked Capitalism [blog], January 21, 2011, http://www.nakedcapitalism.com/2011/01/more-evidence-of-undercapitalizationinsolvency-of-major-banks.html?utm_source=feedburner&utm_medium=feed&utm_campaign=Feed%3A+NakedCapitalism+%28naked+capitalism%29.

APPENDIX I

1. This section is derived from Steve Keen, *Debunking Economics: The Naked Emperor of the Social Sciences* (Australia: Pluto Press, 2002), chapter 2, "The Calculus of Hedonism." Keen presents additional supporting materials at his website www.debunkingeconomics.com.
2. Note how already one can think of exceptions, that a consumer might not want eggs at all unless he had, say, three so he could make an omelet.
3. Note we have skipped some elements of the construct, such as the "utility hill" and "revealed preferences."
4. Recall we dispatched the Arrow-Debreu theorem, which endeavors to do just that using extremely restrictive assumptions, in chapter 2. Note as the discussion progresses that further theories build on the unsatisfactory "fix" to the problem described here, not a path that comes out of Arrow-Debreu.

APPENDIX II

1. Some deals were also funded by AIG or by a large bank. The large bank would typically prefer to be hedged, but it's possible that some banks invested in CDOs without being hedged.
2. Hedgie needs the deal to be partly synthetic so that there will be CDS involved to allow him to take his short position. The cash/synthetic ratio in assets has to do with the supply of BBB RMBS bonds. The cash/synthetic ratio in liabilities, on the other hand, has to do with wanting a monoline to sign up for the super senior piece, which is important to Dealer, since he wants to be "off risk." A monoline would only be interested if the super senior was rated super AAA, and the ratings agencies wouldn't give it that high of a rating unless the ratio was 35% or higher. In addition, some monolines were not willing to insure a deal that was purely synthetic on the asset side, so if Hedgie wanted to launch multiple CDOs, he would find much more monoline capacity for a structure that included some cash RMBS, and 20% is roughly the minimum acceptable level.
3. Because it was believed that the consequent diversification of subprime exposure would measurably improve the quality of the CDO.
4. VFN stands for "Variable Funding Note." The note is initially unfunded, but the CDO can draw upon it if it runs out of cash to settle its CDS.
5. Ironically, given the purpose of this CDO.
6. Which under the circumstances Hedgie will probably use to make sure that there are no dangerously high quality names in the CDO, such as loans 2004 vintage from when lending standards had not decayed so seriously.

4. Recall we dispatched the Arrow-Debreu theorem, which endeavors to do just that using extremely restrictive assumptions, in chapter 2. Note as the discussion progresses that further theories build on the unsatisfactory "fix" to the problem described here, not a path that comes out of Arrow-Debreu.

APPENDIX II

1. Some deals were also funded by AIG or by a large bank. The large bank would typically prefer to be hedged, but it's possible that some banks invested in CDOs without being hedged.

2. Hedgie needs the deal to be partly synthetic so that there will be CDS involved to allow him to take his short position. The cash/synthetic ratio in assets has to do with the supply of BBB RMBS bonds. The cash/synthetic ratio in liabilities, on the other hand, has to do with wanting a monoline to sign up for the super senior piece, which is important to Dealer, since he wants to be "off risk." A monoline would only be interested if the super senior was rated super AAA, and the ratings agencies wouldn't give it that high of a rating unless the ratio was 35% or higher. In addition, some monolines were not willing to insure a deal that was purely synthetic on the asset side, so if Hedgie wanted to launch multiple CDOs, he would find much more monoline capacity for a structure that included some cash RMBS, and 20% is roughly the minimum acceptable level.

3. Because it was believed that the consequent diversification of subprime exposure would measurably improve the quality of the CDO.

4. VFN stands for "Variable Funding Note." The note is initially unfunded, but the CDO can draw upon it if it runs out of cash to settle its CDS.

5. Ironically, given the purpose of this CDO.

6. Which under the circumstances Hedgie will probably use to make sure that there are no dangerously high quality names in the CDO, such as loans 2004 vintage from when lending standards had not decayed so seriously.

7. So that the synthetic CDS protection that will be bought by the CDO later will have a counterparty.

8. Hedgie would make more in the long run by trying to buy close to the full $800 million worth of additional supply of CDS against BBB RMBS. But that would make Hedgie have a substantial carry on his short, and Hedgie doesn't know when the credit bubble is going to pop and doesn't want to be constrained in the number of deals he can do in the meantime.

9. Basically a form of front-running.

10. The sale of CDS does not take place until the CDO closes. But these commitments are taken seriously – even though Dealer might prefer to walk away in some cases, doing so will break the CDO and be a big hit to Dealer's reputation. There could even be legal repercussions.

11. The bank is taking the risk here of ending up as the counterparty to the CDS if the CDO deal fails, and so typically tries to sell the CDS protection close to the time when the deal closes.

12. From a feature article from the May 2004 issue of *Credit* magazine: "Those super senior buyers and sellers of credit protection are attracted by the security of the investment, which is often referred to as a 'quasi-quadruple-A' or triple-A-plus tranche, and is therefore, presumably a more solid credit than the US government or the World Bank, which of course is not possible. Nevertheless, it is broadly accepted that the risk embedded in the super-senior tranche of a synthetic [CDO] referencing a pool of investment-grade assets is remote in the extreme."

13. Monoline is on risk for claims payments once the underlying defaults burn through the 35% cash provided by the junior investors.

14. Which he was long in via the "CDO warehouse."

15. Things can change, though . . .

16. If the pool of BBB RMBS bonds are 100% correlated, which is Hedgie's central trading thesis (and it wasn't wrong), then Hedgie's net notional position is -$200MM + $50MM = -$150MM notional. So Hedgie's annual carry for this short is $6.4MM/$150MM = 427 bps.

17. All of the monoline bond insurers had these sorts of contracts, but AIG was different and had to post collateral immediately upon a credit event.